The Thinking Reed

The Thinking Reed

Intellectuals and the Soviet State
1917 to the Present

BORIS KAGARLITSKY

Translated by Brian Pearce

VERSO
London · New York

First published by Verso 1988
This revised paperback edition published by Verso 1989
© 1988 Verso
All rights reserved

Verso
UK: 6 Meard Street, London W1V 3HR
USA: 29 West 35th Street, New York NY, 10001-2291

Verso is the imprint of New Left Books

British Library Cataloguing in Publication Data

Kagarlitsky, Boris, *1958–*
   The thinking reed : intellectuals and the Soviet
   state from 1917 to the present.
   1. Soviet Union. Intellectual life, 1917–
   I. Title
   947.084

   ISBN 0-86091-961-7

Library of Congress Cataloging-in-Publication Data

Kagarlitsky, Boris, 1958–
   The thinking reed: intellectuals and the Soviet state, 1917 to
  the present / Boris Kagarlitsky: translated by Brian Pearce. —
  Rev. ed.
      p.   cm.
   Translated from Russian
   Bibliography: p.
   Includes index.
   ISBN 0-86091-961-7
   1. Soviet Union—Intellectual life—1917–   2. Soviet Union—
  Politics and government—1917–   3. Soviet Union—Politics and
  government—1985–   I. Title.
  DK266.4.K34   1989
  947.084—dc20

Typeset by Leaper & Gard Ltd, Bristol, England
Printed in Finland by Werner Söderström Oy

Contents

Publisher's Note

Part One of this book, 'The Thinking Reed', was completed in 1982 and subsequently circulated in *samizdat*. It is published here for the first time. Part Two includes two articles written by Boris Kagarlitsky in 1987, and an interview with him by Robin Blackburn.

We would like to thank the editors of *New Left Review* for permission to publish 'The Intellectuals and the Changes', which originally appeared in NLR 164, July–August 1987. We also wish to thank the editor of the *Times Literary Supplement* for permission to reprint the article by Boris Kagarlitsky which appeared in the *TLS* of 25–31 December 1987, and of the *London Review of Books* for permission to reprint Robin Blackburn's interview with Kagarlitsky which appeared in the *LRB* of 24 November 1988.

We are grateful to Dr Nick Lampert and to Tamara Deutscher for editorial help with this volume; and we would also like to thank Brian Pearce, who translated 'The Thinking Reed' and the essay in NLR 164, for tracking down English versions of works cited in the endnotes.

Preface

'Manuscripts don't burn!' These words from Mikhail Bulgakov's novel *The Master and Margarita* were destined to prove prophetic. For several generations of the Soviet Russian intelligentsia they became a kind of formula for hope: what has been written will return to us, thought cannot be killed.

The history of our culture provides some wonderful examples to confirm the truth of what Bulgakov wrote. Vasily Grossman's outstanding novel *Life and Fate* was seized from its author as far back as in Khrushchev's time. It was supposed that all copies of the manuscript had been confiscated, and the chief state ideologist of those days could tell the writer, with absolute conviction, that this work would not be published for the next two hundred years.

Grossman indeed did not live to see the publication of his novel. Nevertheless, even in Suslov's lifetime, at the beginning of the 1980s, a copy of Grossman's manuscript which had secretly been saved from destruction was in the hands of foreign publishers, and in the summer of 1987 the Moscow periodical *Oktyabr'* announced its intention to publish the novel in its pages. 'Manuscripts don't burn!'

This is also true, to some extent, of the present book, most of which was written as long ago as in Brezhnev's time. I was arrested in April 1982 just as I had, as I thought, completed the work, and had handed it over to be read by my friends. And so while I was in prison under Brezhnev, while, under Andropov, they were deciding whether to release me, and while, in Moscow's kitchens, people were arguing about how long Chernenko could survive, my manuscript was passing, through channels unknown to me, in and out of several publishing houses, to end up, in Gorbachev's time, in the hands of the editors of *New Left Review* – one of the periodicals for which I have the greatest liking and esteem.

Those five years saw more changes in the USSR than just the succession of four General Secretaries. The social situation altered, with the emergence of a new generation for whom changes were just as natural as 'stability' had been for their predecessors. When I wrote the first chapters of my book an intense propaganda campaign was being waged in our country against 'Eurocommunism'; the newspapers were full of praise for Brezhnev's wisdom and literary talent; and drunkenness had become the only permitted form of protest against the demoralizing official reality. The epoch of stagnation was an epoch of drunken stupor.*

Five years later, when I learned from my British friends that *The Thinking Reed* was about to be published, I was able to rejoice not just on my own account. Interest in our country and demand for books about it had been evoked by the real changes that had taken place in the USSR. Whatever may have been the social and political basis for these changes, they are reflected directly in people's lives. Books formerly banned are being published and heretical ideas discussed. Left-wing groups are allowed to function openly. In August 1987 these groups were able to organize, on their own, an actual conference at which an All-Union association of left-wingers was set up – the Federation of Socialist Public Affairs Clubs (FSOK). In October representatives of the Federation were able to hold a press conference for Soviet and foreign journalists, on the premises of the official news agency *Novosti*, and at the end of that month a gathering of editors of literary and political *samizdat* periodicals took place openly in Leningrad, and was attended by correspondents of the official press.

Izvestiya has published an interview with the surrealist Salvador Dali, whose pictures were until recently treated as an example of 'the decadence of Western culture'. In the subway at Pushkin Square tickets are being sold for performances at the *avant-garde* Skazka Theatre, which has put on plays by French exponents of the 'Theatre of the Absurd'. All this is becoming part of everyday life, although only recently it would have seemed unthinkable. Nobody is surprised when poets from the 'Direct Speech' club, which has joined the FSOK, call for the reorganization of that 'offspring of Stalin', the Writers' Union of the USSR. Students collect signatures to a petition calling for the rehabilitation of Aleksandr Galich, a poet and playwright who died in emigration. Representatives of Central Television film the assemblies of unofficial groups.

To many people the changes that have taken place seemed a miracle they had never expected to happen. However, miracles do not occur in

---

*Here I've done my best with an untranslatable pun – *trans*.

history. We were able to convince ourselves of that in November 1987, when the fall of the First Secretary of the Party's Moscow City Committee resulted in a real political crisis. Speakers at the plenary meeting of this committee accused their former leader of all the mortal sins, resorting to the rhetorical methods of the period of Stalin's purges. Millions of people who read the report in *Pravda* felt that behind the speeches of many participants in the plenum lay a real Stalinist threat.

Activists of the FSOK who were collecting signatures in the streets for a perfectly loyal letter about the granting to citizens of access to political information found themselves arrested by the militia. A gathering of the Club for Social Initiatives (KSI), one of the leading elements in the Federation, was broken up at the very moment when the television people were filming it. Some activists and leaders of the clubs complained that they were being closely shadowed.

By the end of November, of course, the situation had been stabilised, and the activity of the Left clubs resumed its normal path. After a fortnight's crisis *glasnost'* had come into its own again. The attempt to force the left-wingers back into the underground, or to make political 'outsiders' of them, had not succeeded. Yet the November crisis demonstrated once again the contradictory character of the processes under way, the tenacity of the forces of Stalinism and their readiness to oppose any democratic initiative.

A few days before the events connected with the Yeltsin affair, the *Financial Times* correspondent in Moscow, Patrick Cockburn, wrote that, to all appearances, the intelligentsia's influence in the life of our country was 'likely to diminish at the very moment when they have largely obtained the freedom of expression denied them for so long' (3 November 1987). Actually, the rise in the level of education and political awareness of the Soviet population has perceptibly quickened in recent years. The Soviet Union of the mid-1980s was already not what it had been under Stalin or even under Khrushchev. The profound modernization of society which went on throughout the Brezhnev period constituted, in fact, one of the most important social preconditions for Gorbachev's *perestroika*. However, this does not mean, in the least, that the Stalinist past has been completely overcome. As before, there exist in our country influential forces which are interested in a return not just to the state of affairs under Brezhnev but, so far as possible, to the way things were in Stalin's time. The struggle going on in society assumes, to a considerable extent, the form of a cultural confrontation between those groups which appeal to traditional authoritarian 'values' and the supporters of socialist democracy. In these circumstances a very important role on the Left is being played, as before, by the 'intelligentsia factor'. Society is changing, and culture with it. New problems and new possibilities are arising. But it is quite clear that the mission of Russia's radical intelligentsia, traditionally hostile to authoritarian and bureaucratic structures, and coming forward as custodians of democratic and socialist ideals, is far from exhausted.

Without a radical design for the future there can be no revolutionary practice. And such a design is, in its turn, impossible without the development of a new political culture, without a change in social consciousness. This task cannot be accomplished by politicians and social activists alone. Without help from writers, playwrights and poets they will not win their battle.

The intelligentsia is changing along with society. The future of culture is the future of the country. Many generations of Russia's best people have given their labour and their lives so that this country should be free. A defeat for the present movement for socialist democracy would not only be a catastrophe for our society, it would mean the downfall of all Russian culture, with its historic values, its continuity and traditions. The outcome of this struggle is by no means dependent on the intelligentsia alone, but, as before, the role they have to play is an important one.

Boris Kagarlitsky, 1987

PART ONE

The Thinking Reed

Introduction

This work is an attempt at an examination, as objective as possible, of some pressing problems of the cultural-political process in our country. The reader may judge the degree of objectivity attainable by someone who is not a detached observer or a historian of remote periods, but a contemporary.

However, this question may be asked at the outset: What does the author actually mean by 'cultural-political process', or, in other words, what is the book about? This very question confronted me while I was writing, and only, it seems, when I had finished the book did I find – more or less – the answer to it. Consequently, I might quite naturally invite the reader to seek the answer in the book itself, but it would be too cruel to force him or her to traverse, even in a shorter time, the entire path which the author had to follow. So some very important explanations are called for right at the start.

Culture is itself one of the most complex of concepts. Some American scholars who have analysed the different points of view that exist where this question is concerned have arrived at the not very comforting conclusion that there are 'plenty of definitions but too little theory'.[1] Culture is an 'evasive' concept – like time, man, or nation. To begin this book with yet another 'formula' would be not only hopeless conceit but also a futile procedure. Instead of engendering definitions, a better idea would be to take a closer look at the essence of the problem which is studied in this book.

What interests me in this matter is not the 'cultural sphere' in its entirety (philosophy, art, to some extent science and learning, traditions, and so on) but only what in Western sociology is linked with the concept 'political culture'.[2] This means that the 'cultural sphere' as such will consequently be looked at from a definite, narrow standpoint.[3]

3

Archie Brown, who has written interestingly on this subject, says that 'political culture', in the true sense of the term, 'is not divorced from a "culture" in the widest social sense. On the contrary, it is closely related to cultural values and orientations more generally.'[4] It is quite natural, therefore, to consider political culture as a part of culture in general, and political ideology as a part of the total spiritual life of our society – and, contrariwise, to study general-cultural processes in the context of political conflict. 'Political culture', writes the American historian R. Tucker, means 'politics as a form of culture, and political activity related to the larger culture of a society', and this might

> be taken as the central subject-matter of the discipline. Instead of treating political culture as an attribute of a political system, we would then view the political system of a society in cultural terms, i.e., as a complex of real and ideal cultural patterns, including political roles and their interrelations, political structures, and so on.[5]

Such an approach seems to be highly productive when studying certain processes which have taken place in our society, but unfortunately Western experts (1) analyse political culture as something fairly stable and static, paying less attention to how it evolves, and (2) are much more interested in the culture of the official upper circles of our society than in the oppositional and semi-oppositional trends. For this reason I think it appropriate to use – instead of the Western expression 'political culture', which is associated with studies of that sort – the expression 'cultural-political process'. By this I mean the whole process of spiritual life, in which politics forms a natural constituent element.

Art, criticism, philosophy, history and politics do not exist in isolation from each other. They constantly come into contact and interpenetrate. At the same time they can be regarded, in the broad sense, as constituting a single process of spiritual life and, in the narrow sense, as a cultural-political process.

In my view the different forms of legal – and to a considerable extent also illegal – 'dissent' (as the Anglo-American theoreticians call it) belong to the sphere of cultural phenomena, and (still more importantly) a number of processes in legal art, philosophy, history, criticism and the 'cultural sphere' in general become politically significant in our country. This 'political culture' of the Russian intelligentsia – together with the 'cultural opposition' as a whole – deserves systematic study. And although works on this subject also exist in substantial numbers (in their time they helped me considerably), the subject cannot be seen as having been exhausted.

The importance of politics as an object of reflection, as a world-view and as an objective factor in spiritual life has increased steadily since, perhaps, the epoch of the Reformation. There is nothing surprising about this, for society itself has become politicized. This has been particularly marked in the twentieth century. George Orwell wrote:

> This is a political age. War, fascism, concentration camps, rubber truncheons, atomic bombs, etc., are what we daily think about, and therefore to a great extent what we write about, even when we do not name them openly. We cannot help this. When you are on a sinking ship your thoughts will be about sinking ships.[6]

In theory there can be two ways out of this conflict. Either, in a totalitarian society, politics absorbs and completely subjects to itself all forms of spiritual life; or, in a society of democratic socialism, politics itself is, in the last analysis, dissolved in the general 'ideological' process (I do not, of course, refer to political ideology in the narrow sense). For Marx, already, political activity, both theoretical and practical, was a kind of applied philosophy.

In the present work, therefore, we are concerned not to consider politics 'and' culture, but to study politics as *part of culture* or, contrariwise, culture and art as *political factors*. Finally, we have the question of the evolution of the political culture of our society as a whole. The cultural-political process is such that we cannot draw a precise line of demarcation between politics and philosophy, politics and religion, art and politicized philosophy, and so on. In the frontier zone at which we are looking they do not only interact: they interpenetrate, becoming transformed into a single entity; furthermore, one of them can appear in the form of another.

The significance of the cultural-political process for the life of society, for its future, is much greater than could be supposed on the basis of vulgar Marxist or positivist schemas. Marx's general formula to the effect that social consciousness, belonging to the sphere of the 'superstructure', reflects and interprets the 'base' – that is, the relations which take shape in the process of production – is absolutely correct as a fundamental law; but it explains particular cases just as little as the universal law of gravity explains the trajectory of the flight of a shell travelling at such and such a speed, with such and such a wind blowing, and fired from such and such a gun, and so on. In every case many laws and factors come into play. Merely referring to a general historical law means no more than refusing to explain. This is all the more so because in society it is living people who are acting, and they cannot be reduced to any schemas. Thus consciousness, as one of Marx's happiest formulations has it, does not merely reflect the world, it also creates it.

This means, incidentally, that the 'superstructure' does not simply influence the 'base': it penetrates and sometimes becomes it. For man, with his illusions, his political views and even his aesthetic preferences, is himself a very important productive force. Marx and Engels understood this very well. Lenin appreciated it too, and for Gramsci it possessed central significance. H.H. Holz, in his work on present-day socialism, wrote:

> The basis is in Marxist theory defined through production. The latter consists, however, not only of material things, embodied in productive forces, but also of the people who work with the aid of these productive forces, and these productive forces are organized in accordance with those people's ideas. These ideas are defined, naturally, by the development of the productive forces, but they are also formed by traditions of theory and practice, prevailing usages, the philosophical and religious doctrines assimilated by the people concerned, the works of art that they like – in short, people's self-awareness as objectified in culture.[7]

The truth of this can be judged, for example, by the many failures suffered by European (especially Soviet) specialists in the countries of the Third World when they have tried to make local workers use up-to-date equipment. This attempt failed (or did not fully succeed) because the necessary level of culture was absent or, more precisely, because the workers' *type* of culture was different from what the engineers required.

As can be seen from its subtitle, the present work makes no claim to be an all-embracing and exhaustive examination of the problem of cultural-political development in the USSR. That would be quite impracticable given the huge amount of material, the many aspects of the problem and the extremely few serious (especially Marxist) studies that have been devoted to it. The task of this work is to pose and formulate the questions in a clear-cut way rather than to provide a conclusive answer to them.

It is well known that it was the intelligentsia of the humanities who, between the 1950s and 1970s, were the principal – or among the principal – bearers and exponents of social protest against bureaucracy in Soviet society. It is not accidental that Wolfgang Leonhard, in his article on the development of the class struggle in the USSR, where he lists the potential gravediggers of the bureaucracy, puts the artistic intelligentsia second after the scientific and technical intelligentsia, while the working class appears only in fourth place.[8] This schema does not, of course, reflect the real power of any social group or class, but indicates the level of its political activity.

Leonhard writes that writers and poets play a bigger political and moral role in the USSR than in the West, and are taken more seriously there.[9] As M. Agursky has pointed out, 'no serious analysis of Soviet society is possible without profound study of present-day Soviet literature and art, which have become the field of political battles.'[10] This situation is to be expected in a country where the cultural-political process was almost the only form of political development over many years. The Russian tradition of independent oppositional thought has its roots in the nineteenth century, and perhaps even in a much more distant past. In the post-Stalin epoch many Russian intellectuals have made heroic efforts to revive this tradition. We may now hope that in future the democratic tradition will not be extinguished and that critical thinking will find the correct answers to the burning problems of our society.

It is customary to end a preface with thanks to people who helped the author in his work on the book. I, alas, am unable, for a number of reasons, to name the many friends, comrades and colleagues without whom my work would have been simply inconceivable. It remains only to express the wish that a time will soon come in Russia when scientific research and political discussion will no longer be treated as anti-state 'sedition'.

Notes

1. A.L. Kroeber and C. Kluckhohn, *Culture: A Critical Review of Concepts and Definitions*, Cambridge Mass., p. 357.

2. The concept 'political culture' was introduced into Soviet sociology by F. Burlatsky, but he gave it an extremely narrow significance: as meaning the aggregate of 'political knowledge and notions' (F. Burlatsky, *Lenin, gosudarstvo, politika* [Lenin, the State and Politics], Moscow 1970, p. 55). In his later work he defined it more precisely as the 'historical experience' embedded in culture (F. Burlatsky and A. Galkin, *Sotsiologiya. Politika. Mezhdunarodnye otnosheniya.* [Sociology. Politics. International Relations], Moscow 1974, p. 113).

3. There is a great deal of research material available on 'political culture', including the Soviet variety, most of it in English. See Archie Brown and Jack Gray, eds, *Political Culture and Political Change in Communist States*, 2nd edn, 1979; Archie Brown, *Soviet Politics and Political Science*, 1974, pp. 89–104; L.W. Pye and S. Verba, *Political Culture and Political Development*, Princeton 1965; Dennis Kavanagh, *Political Culture*, Indiana 1972; Louis Schneider and C.M. Bonjean, eds, *The Idea of Culture in the Social Sciences*, Cambridge 1973, pp. 65–76; A, Bauer, A. Inkeles, C. Kluckhohn, *How the Soviet System Works: Cultural, Psychological and Social Themes*, Cambridge Mass. 1956; R.C. Tucker, 'Culture, Political Culture and Communist Society', *Political Science Quarterly*, vol. 88, no. 2, 1973. See also: R. Fülöp-Miller, *The Mind and Face of Bolshevism*, New York 1928; R. Solomon, *Mao's Revolution and the Chinese Political Culture*, Buckley 1971; R.R. Fagen, *The Transformation of Political Culture in Cuba*, Stanford 1969.

4. Brown and Gray, *Political Culture and Political Change in Communist States*, p. 1.

5. Tucker, p. 182.

6. 'Writers and Leviathan', in *Selected Writings*, ed. George Bolt, 1958, p. 90.

7. H.H. Holz, *Strömungen und Tendenzen in Neomarxismus*, Munich 1972, p. 16.

8. Wolfgang Leonhard, 'In welcher Verfassung ist die Sowjetunion?', *Zukunft*, Heft ll, 1980, p. 30.

9. Wolfgang Leonhard, 'Are We Moving Towards A Post-Communist Era? The Soviet Empire in Crisis', *Encounter*, November, 1980, pp. 24–5.

10. M. Agursky, *The New Russian Literature*, Hebrew University of Jerusalem, Russian Research Centre 1980, Paper No. 40, p. 64.

1

The State and the Intelligentsia in Russia

'For a people deprived of civic freedom, literature is the sole tribune from which it can make heard its cries of indignation and conscience,' wrote A.I. Herzen. 'The influence of literature in such a society acquires a dimension long since lost in the other countries of Europe.'[1] Nearly a century later, Roy Medvedev's *Politicheskii Dnevnik* [Political Diary] repeated Herzen's words almost verbatim:

> Under conditions where political thought is deprived of free expression, where political discussion and argument are impossible, the role played by literature and art is inevitably enhanced: these more complex forms in which reality is reflected enable the questions which interest and worry society to be posed all the same.[2]

The coincidence of the two quotations is not accidental.

Those words spoken in the middle of the nineteenth century continue to be applicable, in their fullest extent, to present-day Soviet society, especially in the 1960s and early 1970s. This fact leads us to two kinds of reflection. First, that Russian culture in general and literature in particular are rich, to this day, in living traditions of social criticism. Second, that these traditions, founded in one period of history – the early and middle years of the nineteenth century, when Herzen wrote 'On the development of Revolutionary Ideas in Russia' and 'The Russian People and Socialism' – have blossomed in another period in a state which has proclaimed, at least in words, a break with that past which so angered Herzen. General references to the fact that suppression of individual freedom is characteristic of both regimes are not enough. A number of circumstances were needed for the social-critical tradition in culture to revive almost unchanged after several

9

decades. First and foremost, the structure of the ruling power against which persons of culture set themselves must have retained a certain element of continuity. What and why?

The Asiatic State

Before we concern ourselves with the critics, we must form a more precise idea of what it is they criticize. 'Autocracy' and 'Stalinism' are concepts too general for use as scientific terms. A degree of concreteness and precision is needed here: what do you understand by these words? In *Strömungen und Tendenzen in Neomarxismus*, Holz wrote:

> The term 'Stalinism' confuses the question, because it personalizes a particular phase in the development of the Soviet Union and the international Communist movement. Analysis, leaving aside the personality of Stalin, must be objective in character in order that we may understand what is meant by 'Stalinism'.[3]

The history of the Russian state and the Russian intelligentsia begins, as we all know, not in 1917 but much earlier, and anyone who studies Russia's autocracy discovers here some very serious differences from the history of the other countries of Europe.

Marx used the concept 'the Asiatic mode of production'. At first, following Hegel, he distinguished Asiatic despotism as a purely political phenomenon. Only later, in the 1850s, did he come to the conclusion that what was involved was a more profound difference between Europe and Asia. Above all, private property in the European sense was almost unknown in Asia. Engels explains this by arguing that the huge expanses of territory and the need to organize large-scale irrigation and other public works entail the necessity of a strong state. Such a state can arise and develop only if it has economic support in the form of a state monopoly of land, which in the given conditions is the principal means of production (or some sort of mediated state ownership of the principal means of production – including, of course, human beings). In short, the despotic ruling power appears as both the supreme property-owner and as an economic power. Marx noted features of this Asiatic mode of production in Russia as well.

Russian serfdom cannot be equated with European feudalism. In the West the development of feudal relations first gave rise to decentralization, and then absolutism consolidated political authority while allowing a certain economic autonomy to both the feudal landlords and the bourgeoisie. In the economic sphere both groups were able to operate not as subjects of the state but as free property-owners (although the degree and type of freedom they enjoyed varied in different countries and for different estates); in any case, as independent individuals. The state did not subordinate the entire life of society but dominated the political sphere alone. In Russia, however, as a result of the Tatar yoke and the general backwardness, there arose a system akin to the Asiatic type. Here the landlord appeared also in the role of local representative of the central authority. 'Every landlord', writes Herzen, 'played the part of the Grand Prince of Muscovy in miniature.'[4] The state, the landlord class and the sadly celebrated Russian bureaucracy formed a single entity. 'The privileges of officialdom in Russia represent another side', wrote Lenin, 'of the privileges and agrarian power of the landed nobility.'[5] While Marx's formula about the state expressing the interests of the ruling class is correct for the West, in Russia this class was *itself* the state. Similarly, there was never any 'free' capitalism in Russia – not only in the sense of the absence of bourgeois democracy but also in that of the absence of free competition and the other features of liberal capitalist economics. The Russian state was itself the biggest entrepreneur; it had its own 'state factories', it constantly intervened in business life, regulating relations between capitalists and workers (in such a way, moreover, that both parties lost by this interference). A notable example of this was the creation of the 'Zubatov trade unions' with official support. The Bolshevik historian M.N. Pokrovsky recalls:

> In that same year, 1903, when the fight against Zubatovism was being waged, on the initiative of some large-scale entrepreneurs they were working in the Ministry of Finance on the question of freedom of combination – under the peculiar conditions characteristic of Russia, of course, but all the same, with freedom to strike, in the European style. When they were regaled with such an Asiatic method of solving the labour question as a class organization of the proletariat functioning under the aegis of the police, but directed against the immediate economic interests of the capitalists, the entrepreneurs naturally groaned with dismay.[6]

In short, Russian Tsardom retained features of Asiatic despotism even at the beginning of the twentieth century. The autocracy was unlike any other monarchy in Europe, its rule far more all-embracing than even the Western absolutisms of the seventeenth and eighteenth centuries. But for this very reason the conflict between the state and the civil society that was coming into existence – between the government which strove to subject to itself as completely as possible all spheres of economic, political and spiritual life, and the developing intelligentsia, asserting its independence – could not be other than all-embracing, acute and chronic. In a society where the state tries to control each and every activity, any independent action, even if it has no conscious political content, turns out to be an act of rebellion. A social group which is engaged in creative activity will inevitably, from the standpoint of the authorities, behave 'suspiciously' or even 'defiantly'.

Pre-Petrine Russia had a popular church-and-state culture, but it lacked a stratum of professional intellectuals. In the West, as Gramsci pointed out, the Church and its apparatus engendered such a stratum even in the Middle Ages. Russia's priests, however, were for the most part 'civil servants in the department of spiritual affairs', and the Orthodox Church, unlike the Catholic Church, created no intelligentsia. Characteristic was the complete absence of even the embryo of university education. 'In Muscovite Russia,' wrote Nikolai Berdyaev, 'there existed a real fear of education. Science aroused suspicion as being "latinising".'[7]

The Emergence of an Intelligentsia

Towards the end of the seventeenth century, however, mastery of the basics of Western civilization became for Russia, in the words of P. Milyukov, 'a question of self-preservation – not moral or national but simply physical'.[8] The Russian intelligentsia came into being thanks to Peter's reforms: to the partial Europeanizing of society. Having entered the European political sphere, Russia made contact with European civilization, with a certain type of culture and certain cultural tasks; an inevitable result was the appearance of a social stratum occupied with the performance of those tasks.

One must not conclude from this that the intelligentsia was an 'alien' phenomenon in Russia, introduced from without, and so on. Successful intellectual activity proved possible in Russia only because the cultural tasks common to Europe were coped with on our national soil, in a Russian manner. On the one hand the Russian intelligentsia faced towards the West; on the other it became firmly rooted in its native soil. Herzen's English biographer wrote: 'The Russian intelligentsia as a whole would draw from foreign thinkers those elements which helped them to solve their own problems. When they were enamoured of a whole body of these ideas, they interpreted them in accordance with their predilections.'[9]

The fact that a European-type intelligentsia developed in the setting of an Asiatic state had enormous importance for Russia's history. The basic features of European culture can be defined in a few words: it is secular, humanist and universalist, and therefore democratic. The Asiatic state in Russia, for its part, was closely linked with the Church; its ideology was religious, nationally narrow, anti-humanist and, naturally, authoritarian. On the one hand, Tsardom needed a certain level of European enlightenment, without which it could not function as a world-class power. On the other, it needed European enlightenment without European culture, and especially without 'Western' ideas. 'This is the dilemma', writes the American historian Marshall Shatz, 'that has confronted every Russian government from the eighteenth century down to the present.'[10] He makes an exception for Peter I alone, calling him 'the first Russian *intelligent*'.[11] This description is not, however, correct. Peter was the first – and perhaps, up to now, the only – Russian technocrat in power who saw in the West 'civilization, but not culture'. Precisely for this reason the Europeanized Petersburg monarchy of the Romanovs was never able to find a common language with the intelligentsia it had engendered. 'We shall see', wrote Berdyaev, 'that the intelligentsia which took shape as the result of Peter's work was to adopt his universalism and his looking to the West, and to overthrow the empire.'[12]

The new intelligentsia of Petersburg Russia – European in its occupations, its views and its way of thinking – came into conflict with the Asiatic autocracy, even though the latter had in its time engendered this intelligentsia through its reforms. In Milyukov's words, the Russian intelligentsia 'was almost from its beginning anti-government and counterposed to the historical state the concept of law'.[13] To the political reality of Russia it opposed the political ideal of Europe.[14] Criticism of the established order became the principal content of Russian art; the whole of spiritual culture (in the persons of its most outstanding representatives, of course, not in those of hired hacks like Bulgarin) came to be politicized and orientated towards revolution. Even those writers who (like Dostoevsky and Tolstoy) argued against the revolutionaries were obliged to concern themselves with the problems of revolution. For this reason Herzen, having undertaken to compose a history of revolutionary ideas in Russia, wrote what was essentially a history of literature.

The first revolutionary revolt in Russia – 14 December 1825 – was exclusively the affair of an intellectual minority. The intelligentsia from the nobility who came out on to Senate Square were not at all motivated by their own social interests. Their protest was of an exclusively ideological and, in its own way, cultural character. Men who had received a Western education could not refrain from opposing their country's own 'native' tyranny. It was a movement inspired by philosophical ideas, not by class interests. This revolt was a turning point in the history of the Russian intelligentsia despite the fact that it ended in utter defeat, both politically and militarily. It is with the Decembrists that the Russian tradition of revolutionary struggle begins. The old Russian state had, of course, had its 'dissidents' already, centuries before them. Historians can argue as to who was the first Russian dissident – Prince Kurbsky, who fled to the West from the tyranny (a real totalitarian hell) of Ivan the Terrible, or Radishchev and Novikov, who criticized Catherine II. There were always people in Russia who opposed their humanistic ideals to Asiatic despotism, but the Decembrists were something different. This was the first attempt to go over, in Marx's phrase, 'from the weapon of criticism to criticism with weapons' – or, more precisely, not merely to condemn the system but also to try to change it. These men were no longer dissidents, they were revolutionaries. 'The Decembrists were much more effective as martyrs than as insurrectionaries. Thus, their historical contribution is ambiguous,' writes the American historian Philip Pomper. 'The direct and overt effect of their activity was reaction and repression. The other momentous consequence was the birth of a revolutionary tradition that survived for a century.'[15]

It must be acknowledged that the cultural-ideological results of 14 December 1825 were more important than the political results. This cultural tradition has remained in our memory to the present day. 'With the Decembrists', writes Shatz, 'the Russian intelligentsia finally crystallized, and the movement of political and social dissent associated with it would now become a permanent feature of imperial Russian history.'[16] The history of the Russian intelligentsia begins in 1825, for before that one can speak only of its prehistory.

At this point, however, we must define somewhat more precisely the actual concept of the intelligentsia. Today the Russian word *intelligent*, which was made current by P. Boborykin, is often employed as a synonym for the Western word 'intellectual'. There are, as we shall see later, some grounds for this, but originally the concept *intelligentsia* was almost the direct opposite of the concept 'intellectuals'. It is much easier to clarify the term 'intellectual'. This means (in common usage) a person engaged in mental work, an expert. There is no moral or ideological content in the concept. *Intelligent* is a different matter. Berdyaev quite rightly protested against treatment of the two concepts as identical: 'Our intelligentsia were a group formed out of various social classes and held together by ideas, not by sharing a common profession or economic status,' he declared.[17] What was the important distinctive mark of the intelligentsia? Not only formal occupation with mental work, but also exceptional concern with European culture. But even this definition may prove inexact. Originally the word *intelligent* was clearly marked with moral evaluation. Polonsky wrote in the 1920s that from Boborykin's time what was meant by the intelligentsia was 'a historical group of people who promoted the self-awareness of Russian society.'[18] He considered that as a Marxist he was obliged to treat such a definition ironically, but he recognized that in nineteenth-century Russia, the *intelligent* 'was a spiritual leader, a worker on behalf of social ideals.'[19]

It is obvious that a 'purely functional' definition of the *intelligent* is quite inadequate, unless it is supplemented with a 'cultural' definition.[20] On the other hand, the contradiction between these two definitions can be seen as a contradiction between phenomenon and essence. Apparently, the Russian intellectuals of the nineteenth century discovered and developed within themselves some important characteristics of which their Western colleagues had, up to that time, no suspicion. This was due, however, not to 'the mysteriousness of the Russian soul' or to 'divine grace' but to the specific sociohistorical and historico-cultural peculiarities of the Russian intelligentsia's being. Plekhanov's biographer, Samuel Baron, observed that it was quite natural for the intelligentsia to produce revolutionaries: 'This social group had no exact parallel in Western society; yet, paradoxically enough, it was itself a consequence of the Western impact upon Russia. The intelligentsia was the product of cultural contact between two unlike civilizations. ...'[21] It found itself on the frontier between two worlds and its thinking could not but be critical.

From the very beginning of the nineteenth century the Russian intelligentsia was to a certain extent outside the system. Already quite numerous it found, in the words of Brym, that it 'had no functional role to play in Russian society: *intelligenty* originated as, and remained, "superfluous men".'[22] This indefiniteness in their social role made them 'marginals', compelled to look upon the given society 'from without'.[23] They became radicals and 'ideologues' in the sense that their behaviour was determined more by ideas than by social interests. Such 'ideologism' is, of course, typical of all intellectuals, but in Russia the objective conditions caused it to develop with exceptional vigour. Members of the Russian intelligentsia were given no specific function in the framework of their country's social organization and their spiritual rights were trampled on by the autocratic government. At the same time, a typical feature of Russia – with its academic institutions which grew proportionately to the state's ambitions but disproportionately to the real requirements of a backward country – was a great overproduction of *intelligenty*. In a country where there were not enough schools, there was no shortage of universities. What could the new-baked *intelligenty* do? Entry into the bureaucracy meant then, as now, either breaking or at least weakening the ties with one's intellectual milieu: going into the quite different world of the state apparatus. The state could find no other employment for the educated youth, and private enterprise never really developed (except in the short period 1909 to 1913). The new Russian bourgeoisie had as yet no need of *intelligenty*.

The lack of correspondence between the ideals and values which the intelligentsia acquired and the ways of the Russian state, and the inability of this state to 'integrate' the *intelligenty*, to include them in its system, making them a necessary part of official society – these were the conditions that created the Russian intelligentsia, a peculiar social stratum of 'educated critics of the Russian political and social order'.[24] Consequently, a struggle for democracy became to an important extent the content of the history of Russian culture and the Russian intelligentsia. 'The belief that literature and art, and to a somewhat lesser extent scholarship and science, had a primary responsibility to society became axiomatic in Russian left-wing circles,' writes Pipes.[25] Hence the special attitude of writers, critics, artists and scholars towards their work, and their conception of the role of art as part of social ideology and a weapon in the social struggle. In Russia the *intelligent* was necessarily the bearer of a certain system of ideas – radical-democratic, anti-serfdom, anti-bourgeois and, later, socialist. This radical left-wing ideology did not come from nowhere but was due to the social position of the Russian intellectuals. However, the 'exceptionality' of Russia's *intelligenty* was only relative. As early as the beginning of the twentieth century Tugan-Baranovsky wrote that in the West, too,

> under the influence of the natural course of development of social relations, an 'intelligentsia' in our Russian sense of the word is appearing, which in many of its features resembles our Russian intelligentsia, an intelligentsia which not only is not affiliated by virtue of its interests to the bourgeois class but actually fights against that class.[26]

Subsequently, Gramsci and Sartre tried to rethink the concept 'intellectual', treating it as very similar to the Russian concept *intelligent*.[27] With Sartre, who rejects the 'purely-functional' conception of the intellectual, what – on the contrary – is put in the foreground is the moral content of spiritual activity:

> The intellectual's most immediate enemy is what I will term the *false intellectual* and what Nizan called a watch-dog – a type created by the

dominant class to defend its particularist ideology by arguments which claim to be rigorous products of exact reasoning.[28]

Sartre, too, regards an oppositional attitude and left-wing radicalism as characteristics of the true intellectual.[29] To distinguish this notion from the traditional one he introduces the concept 'new intellectual', with essentially the same meaning as Russian *intelligent.*

If the oppositional attitude, criticism, rejection of the state's values are predicated by the concept *intelligent,* then there is some foundation for the paradoxical thought of G. Pomerants: 'that the intelligentsia as a special social stratum came into being first of all in Russia ... and only later began to take shape in Western Europe and the USA.'[30] The exceptionality of the Russian intelligentsia consisted, therefore, not in the non-existence of anything similar in the West (as P. Struve claimed in *Vekhi*) but in the fact that Russia's intelligentsia 'arrived too soon' — that it took shape as a special stratum in historical conditions that were extremely unfavourable to it. In this lies the tragic element in its history.

Westernists and Slavophils

This tragic element is especially evident in the views of P.Ya. Chaadaev, our intelligentsia's first ideologue, Russia's first original thinker. In Berdyaev's words, his 'philosophical letters' marked for Russia 'the first awakening of independent thought'.[31] And that voice with which, perhaps, began our entire real spiritual history was already a voice of despair. Chaadaev's revolt, wrote Berdyaev, was not only directed against the established order, it was a 'revolt against Russia's history'.[32] To Chaadaev, Russia's past seemed to be a sort of endless marking time:

> While the Christian world marched on majestically along the road marked out for it by its divine Creator, carrying along generations, we, although called Christians, stuck to our place. The entire world was being rebuilt, while we built nothing: as before, we hibernated in our hovels built of logs and straw.[33]

Berdyaev wrote that 'Chaadaev came out decidedly as a Westernizer, and his Westernism was a cry of patriotic anguish.'[34] The author of the 'philosophical letters' already felt keenly that he was standing at the frontier of two worlds, unable either to accept Russia completely or to reject her. 'His rejection of Russia, of Russia's history,' Berdyaev comments, 'was a typically Russian rejection.'[35]

With Chaadaev begins the development of 'Westernist' thought in

Russia, and at the same time the spiritual history of the Russian *intelligent*. He it was who first asked the questions to which Belinsky and Gogol, Chernyshevsky and Dostoevsky, Martov and Lenin, Trotsky and Bukharin, Lakshin and Solzhenitsyn were to give their different answers, questions which are to this day debated fiercely: What was, is and will be Russia's role in Europe? What is the road to the Europeanization of Russia? The Westernists were not merely men who had had a European education. Their interest in the West led them to master quickly all the innovations of European thought, so that the Russian intelligentsia was undoubtedly the bearer of the most up-to-date and advanced Western ideas in a very backward semi-Asiatic country. This only intensified its tragic isolation.

Different thinkers evaluated differently their isolation from the people. On the one hand, as V. Polonsky noted, 'its isolation in battle positions' gave the intelligentsia grounds for

> feeling that it was the sole bearer of advanced, progressive missions for the nation, the defender of the interests of the oppressed people, and their leader. The very deep conviction of the Russian intelligentsia that its destiny was to be the teacher and guide of the masses was given brilliant expression in Russian literature.[36]

We can find this idea in many thinkers, starting with Herzen, but it was expressed with special clarity by the young Lenin when he wrote in his book *What Is To Be Done?* that the revolutionary consciousness of the proletariat can be elaborated only by the intelligentsia and then 'brought to them from without'.[37] At that time Lenin said that 'the intelligentsia are so called just because they most consciously, most resolutely and most accurately reflect and express the development of class interests and political groupings in society as a whole.'[38] Plekhanov even blamed Lenin for such statements, saying that for him 'the masses are merely inanimate raw material, upon which the intelligentsia, signed with the seal of the sacrament of the Holy Ghost, carries out its operations.'[39]

On the other hand, it may be that awareness of the isolation of the intelligentsia and its separation from the people was one of the causes of the Slavophil reaction. It is important to understand that Slavophil thought appeared in Russia considerably later than Westernist thought. A contemporary scholar, A. Yanov, has tried to prove that Slavophilism existed from Peter I's time, albeit in unrealized form, as a sort of 'ideology in itself' and that its proponents were the Streltsy who revolted against Peter's reforms.[40] This view completely fails to stand up to criticism. It is a curious fact that many who have written about the Slavophils forget that this trend was not only a reaction against the Europeanization of Russia but also a product of that process. Many of the Slavophils were men with a European education, and – most importantly – their ideology was formed under the explicit influence of German Romanticism and German classical philosophy. 'The Slavophils', wrote Berdyaev, 'absorbed the Hegelian idea of the vocation of peoples, and what Hegel applied to the German people they applied to the Russian. They applied the principles of Hegelian philosophy to Russian history.'[41] The wave of revival of national cultures which swept over all Europe in the age of Romanticism gave rise, when it reached Russia, to the Slavophil movement. Furthermore, the initial aims of both Westernists and Slavophils were the same – progress and the emancipation of the people. Slavophilism in its original form was a sort of liberal opposition to the Petersburg government: often, it was not so much against Western culture as *for* what was distinctively Russian. For that very reason Herzen, the spiritual leader of Russia's Left, was ready to offer his hand to the champions of Russian 'originality'. The first Slavophils, Berdyaev points out, were 'opposed to the state. There was even a strong element of anarchism in them. They considered the state an evil and government a sin.'[42] But they drew their own conclusion from the isolation of the Westernist intelligentsia. They endeavoured to return to the nation's roots, to 'the sources', to the true Russia, to the pre-Petrine tradition. In addition, they shut their eyes to Western humanism and turned their faces to the past, away from future prospects. Berdyaev wrote that 'the freedom-loving Slavophils' idealized, through misunderstanding, the Moscow period, which was 'the worst in Russian history, the most stifling, of a particularly Asiatic and Tatar type'.[43]

The Slavophils' road was a dead end. They did not find a way to the masses: they were, after all, not representatives of *traditional* popular culture, but only 'repentant Europeanists'. At the same time, they broke with the intelligentsia. Slavophilism, Herzen considered, 'did not set free, it bound, did not move forward, it pushed back.'[44] This was why Russian nationalism, in its ever-sharper conflict with Westernism, became an anti-democratic, anti-humanist ideology, increasingly supported by the authorities and with decreasing influence on Russia's intelligentsia. As a whole, the intelligentsia rejected Slavophilism completely. Closeness to the masses would have to be attained, sooner or later, as civilization developed in Russia: as the masses themselves became Europeanized and intellectualized. But this was a very slow process, and in the meantime the *intelligenty* remained in isolation. Thanks to the influence of German philosophy, British liberalism and French democratism, revolutionary ideas took shape in Russia earlier than revolutionary class forces, and for a long time the intelligentsia remained the country's sole bearer of the democratic principle. Russia's regime, wrote Gredeskul,

> stifled thought and speech above all, that is, the very 'essence' of the intelligentsia, and the intelligentsia had to wage a desperate struggle for the people's rights while the people itself stayed right outside that struggle, quite failing to understand why it was being waged.[45]

The Revolutionary Tradition

Everyone knows Lenin's famous statement in his article 'From the History of the Workers' Press in Russia':

> The emancipation movement in Russia has passed through three main stages, corresponding to the three main classes of Russian society, which have left their impress on the movement: (1) the period of the nobility, roughly from 1825 to 1861; (2) the *raznochintsi* or bourgeois-democratic period, approximately from 1861 to 1895; and (3) the proletarian period, from 1895 to the present time.[46]

Schoolchildren have to learn that quotation by heart, but all the same, one should take a closer look at it. Lenin indicated the three periods quite correctly, but his linking of them with three classes of Russian society must raise doubts. Most of the nobles and bourgeois in the years 1825 to 1895 were quite alien – even hostile – to the freedom movement. The Decembrists expressed whatever other interests you care to mention, but *not* the interests of the landlord class. The Narodniks, being socialists, were pretty remote from the bourgeoisie, even from its democratic wing.

But if we compare the periods in the development of the freedom movement with the periods in the development of Russian literature, then with a few corrections – Lenin's precise dates need not be taken too seriously – we observe a remarkable coincidence. The first period is the period of Pushkin, Lermontov, Belinsky and Gogol. The second is the period of Turgenev, Chernyshevsky and Dostoevsky. To the third period – let us describe it for the time being by the conventional expression 'the age of Lenin and Chekhov' – we shall return later.

Thus in the famous quotation we see listed three periods in the development of the Russian intelligentsia and Russian culture. Undoubtedly the social composition of the intelligentsia changed during that time. The intelligentsia of the first period was predominantly of noble origin; that of the second was petty-bourgeois. Consequently the intelligentsia's ideas changed, and also its relation to other classes of society. Nevertheless, there can be no doubt that the bearer of the revolutionary principle in Russia, right to the end of the nineteenth century, was not any definite class, still less the weak Russian bourgeoisie, but the intelligentsia. It was that very intelligentsia whose entire conditions of existence impelled it to struggle against despotism: it simply could not become reconciled to the rulers of Russia without ceasing to be an intelligentsia. The fight against the government went on, even though the ideals of the intelligentsia changed.

The change in political principles took place, of course, not only through the appearance of new, predominantly petty-bourgeois young people, the *raznochintsy*, but also through meditation on past experience and the latest ideas from the West. What continued unchanged was the tradition of opposition, social criticism, radical-democratic endeavour. Even though the gap between the *intelligenty* and the 'lower orders' persisted, there was every reason to hope that it would be overcome. 'Although they belong by origin to the modernized minority of the society, they identify with the oppressed majority,' writes Robert C. Tucker of *intelligenty* 'of the Russian type'. 'And despite the fact that it is only a minority of a minority in terms of numbers, the intelligentsia has – as it had in Russia – a potentially very large revolutionary constituency among the masses of the population.'[47]

The intelligentsia itself became more numerous, and members of the working classes joined its ranks. Some intermediate 'semi-intelligentsia' strata began to emerge. Although education, as always, lagged behind modernization, it did at any rate accompany the process. Impatient desire to speed up this process gave rise to the Narodniks' propaganda, to the 'going to the people' and, in the last analysis, even to terrorist acts which were intended by their organizers to advance the political enlightenment of the masses. Revolutionary socialist parties were formed – 'Land and Liberty', then 'The People's Will' and 'Black Redistribution'. A psychological type of Russian *intelligent* came into being, and has remained the model even for many dissidents under the Soviet regime. 'The fate of all educated people in Russia', writes the Leningrad socialist M. Bodkhovsky in his *samizdat* essay on Plekhanov,

> was in a certain sense predestined by the fate of this, the most politically active group. And it is extremely important to understand the path it took, the height of its ascent and the depth of its fall, so that, in our own day, we may correctly estimate the prospects before our country's development.[48]

The preparation and realization of the Reform of 1861, which emancipated the peasantry, helped public opinion to take shape in

Russia – especially because the government, which feared opposition from its traditional backers, began to flirt with liberalism. When, however, it became clear that the authorities would not proceed beyond half-measures, conflict arose between the reform-minded intelligentsia, who had been roused by the promises recently given by the rulers, and the actual policy that the latter pursued. This clash was, as we have seen, typical of Russian history down to our own time. Paradoxically, a reforming government always finds itself up against a stronger left-wing opposition than a conservative government because, to its misfortune, through its reforms it awakens hopes in society which it is incapable of satisfying. Belief is engendered that something can change in our country, in a general way, and not after five hundred years but 'here and now' (we shall find a similar situation when we come to look at the 'Khrushchev era'). In attempting to cope with social discontent and put an end to the hopes which official policy had just aroused, the government resorted to repressive measures which led to the development of an underground press and clandestine organizations. The logic of the struggle carried the intelligentsia further and further to the left. Europeanism was at first understood in a liberal spirit, then in a democratic spirit, and from the middle of the nineteenth century in a socialist spirit. Later, in 1910, Tugan-Baranovsky wrote: 'The socialist sympathies of the Russian intelligentsia constitute one of its most characteristic distinguishing features.'[49] Moreover,

> a Russian *intelligent*, if he is interested at all in social problems, is usually more or less inclined towards, and sometimes is even fanatically committed to socialism. This is so plain to see that it hardly calls for proof.[50]

On this basis Pipes considered that in general, acceptance of socialism 'in some one of its several forms' was a necessary feature of all Russian *intelligenty*.[51] In my view it would be more correct to say that for the Russian intelligentsia of the nineteenth century, socialism became the embodiment of the humanist ideals of the Westernist tendency.

Marxists were later to abuse the Narodniks, the first Russian socialists, for their insufficiently 'European' views (especially their idea that Russia's road to socialism lay not through up-to-date industry but through the village commune). Then, still later, the Mensheviks among the Marxists were to attack the Bolsheviks for returning to Narodism (with their idea of a socialist revolution in backward Russia, their preference, in practice, for centralized organizations of intellectuals rather than the spontaneous movement of the workers, their conspiratorial methods, and so on).[52] In both cases such criticism was probably correct, but somewhat exaggerated. For example, the

Bolsheviks saw the Russian road to socialism differently from the Narodniks; according to the statements of Trotsky and Lenin, it proceeded by way of what Trotsky and Parvus called the European 'permanent' revolution.[53] On the other hand, the Narodniks' views were more complex than is indicated in present-day official history books. It is to their credit that they were the first *to formulate the problem of non-capitalist development*. Furthermore, their approach can be regarded as the more fruitful in that they alone linked this path of development with democracy and political freedoms. It is this, I think, that explains why Marx, unlike the Russian Marxists, treated the theoretical views of the Russian Narodniks quite seriously, as an interesting hypothesis, refusing either to endorse them or to reject them 'out of hand'.

Although their subsequent transition from Narodism to Marxism was very painful for many *intelligenty*, it was a perfectly logical and natural continuation of the evolution of Russian Westernism. The common feature of both these socialist theories was, as Lenin observed, 'their defence of democracy by appealing to the masses'.[54] Marxism, however, was a more consistent variety of Westernism. 'The first Russian Marxists', Berdyaev notes, 'were more European, more Western folk than the Narodniks.'[55]

The success of Marxism was bound up with the fact that this more finished theory provided answers to the problems Narodism was trying to solve. Marxism took a step towards liberalism in so far as it recognized bourgeois democracy as a necessary transitional stage towards socialism – a stage which might, in Russia as in other countries, occupy an entire epoch of history.[56] At the same time, Marxism became in Russia precisely what Narodism had tried to be – the ideology of modernization.[57] Many people both then and later saw the victory of Marxism over Narodism as the final victory of Westernism over what remained of Slavophil ideas in the thinking of the intelligentsia. 'It was necessary', Trotsky wrote a quarter of a century later, 'to overcome the homegrown revolutionary prejudices of the Russian intelligentsia, in which the arrogance of backwardness found its expression.'[58]

Through Marxism Russian social thought entered the mainstream of all-European social thought, as many people quite remote from Marxism recognized at the time. Lenin wrote:

in Russia the theoretical doctrine of Social Democracy arose altogether independently of the spontaneous growth of the working-class movement; it arose as a natural and inevitable outcome of the development of thought among the revolutionary-socialist intelligentsia.[59]

Thus the victory of Marxism over Narodism meant, in the first place, the beginning of a new stage in the evolution of Westernist ideology.

Important also was the change in the situation in the country at the turn of the century. Even the half-hearted reform of 1861 had given a considerable stimulus to industrialization and modernization. Its consequences began to make themselves felt especially in the 1890s. By the beginning of the twentieth century about a third of the inhabitants of the Russian Empire were literate. A militant working class was rapidly increasing: their hard living conditions not only stirred the compassion of the intelligentsia but also angered the proletarians themselves, who until recently had been easily reconciled to their lot. The intelligentsia itself grew to massive proportions; in the countryside, for example, there were now, besides landlords and peasants, what was called 'the third element' – doctors, teachers and so on. But most importantly the intelligentsia now had an extensive audience: educated strata had emerged in the towns who could serve as intermediaries between the Europeanized democratic elite and the masses. 'There arose and in our day became especially large a semi-intelligentsia milieu which could no longer be left out of account', wrote Ovsyaniko-Kulikovsky.[60] The situation had changed.

In the article by Lenin we considered earlier we find the following facts: in the years 1827 to 1846, 76 per cent of the political prisoners were intellectuals of the noble class. In the second period 'intellectuals accounted for the overwhelming majority (73.2 per cent) of participants in the democratic movement.'[61] As we can see, the percentage proportion remains almost the same. But then in 1901–03 workers already made up 46.1 per cent of the prisoners and *intelligenty* 36.7 per cent – by 1905–08 no more than 28.4 per cent. The percentage is still, as before, very large when one considers that the entire intelligentsia made up only 2.2 per cent of the population[62] – which means that the political activity of the intelligentsia 'exceeded' its social mass by more than a factor of 12, whereas the corresponding figure for the working class, which was also active out of proportion to its small numbers, was only 4. But already the working class was playing the decisive role.

Thus, on the eve of the Russian Revolution the proletariat was the vanguard of the freedom movement. The intelligentsia, although retaining its democratic sympathies and critical attitude to the autocracy, was yielding up its position at the forefront. 'Revolution', wrote Trotsky, 'was no longer a privileged avocation in intellectual circles. The number of workers arrested was increasing. It was easier to breathe in the prisons, despite the overcrowding.'[63] The revolutionary *intelligenty* were already acting as representatives of the workers: they not only spoke in their name but were indeed strong in the strength of the working class and its consciousness. Their ideas were already shared by the masses. At the same time another section of the intelligentsia was withdrawing, to a considerable extent, from the revolutionary movement and becoming depoliticized. Although this section did not become alien to politics or revolution, these were no longer the matters it saw as fundamental. That is why the most characteristic figures of the period are Lenin and Chekhov. The writer and the social leader were no longer united in one person.

Nevertheless, the intelligentsia played no small role in our twentieth-century revolutions. 'Lenin, Trotsky and other *intelligenty*', writes Brym, 'loom large in accounts of the Russian Revolution; the worker and peasant often disappear from sight as we make our way through the web of political intrigue and ideological conflict in which the intelligentsia was entangled.'[64] The Social Democrats undoubtedly relied upon working-class support; without that support they would have achieved nothing. But, wrote Pokrovsky, 'even when the idea of a workers' party had come into existence and this party was being built, the leading role nevertheless belonged to the revolutionary intelligentsia.'[65] When the twentieth century began, 'the intelligentsia found the masses', but the masses were only beginning to act as an independent political force:[66]

> The fact that before 1905, despite Comrade Lenin's demand that the committees should be made up of two intellectuals and eight workers, the committees still consisted of eight intellectuals and two workers, is something that cannot be denied. Comrade Lenin was a thousand times right when he called for the proportions to be revised, but this reversal was a postulate, was what he wanted, while reality was such that Akselrod had some grounds for calling our party in that period a party of boy and girl students.[67]

It was important, though, that all these students were already able to find support among the workers. As for the overwhelming majority of the *intelligenty*, who remained outside the Social Democratic Party (or, more precisely, parties, for the Russian Social Democrats split into Mensheviks and Bolsheviks in the very period when they were trying to create a united organization), they supported other left-wing parties. A large section of the intelligentsia followed the Social Revolutionaries, while another group formed the left wing of the Constitutional-Democratic Party (the 'Cadets'). It was typical of the time, too, that even among members of this essentially 'left-centre' party there were many supporters of socialism who while considering, in Milyukov's words, the socialization of industry and the nationalization of the land 'to be beyond the bounds of practical politics', yet did not reject these ideas in principle. Milyukov himself, speaking of the socialists, said:

'like them, we stand on the left wing of the Russian political movement.'[68] Thus intellectual liberalism in Russia was altogether unlike the usual bourgeois liberalism. This is recognized also by Western writers. Tompkins writes:

> We are inclined to use the term 'liberal' casually, as if we knew exactly what it means. It is sometimes associated with the bourgeoisie, as though the middle class had a monopoly on 'liberalism'. It may at times be equated with radicalism, or even with socialism.[69]

Something like that happened with the Left Cadet intelligentsia which was fighting against Russian Tsarism.

Vekhi and the Crisis of the Intelligentsia

Perhaps the years 1904 and 1905 were the golden age of the Russian intelligentsia, the time when it seemed that all its hopes were being fulfilled and everything it had been fighting for over several generations was being realized. However, the intelligentsia found that it could not act independently in the revolution. 'There arose even then as a confused idea', Pokrovsky recalls, 'the notion of a political strike of the intelligentsia – in the end, the only effective weapon was the one used by the proletariat. But that was not put to use till the working class gave the example of how to use it.'[70]

The results of the 1905 revolution, which failed to smash the monarchy or even to force it to accept any sort of reasonable constitution (for even the Manifesto of 17 October 1905, which 'granted' some political rights to the people, was not put into effect) caused dismay and a real 'spiritual crisis' among many Russian *intelligenty*,[71] who asked themselves whether the path they had been following was the right one. This produced a crisis among the left-wing Radicals: to use the expression of an American historian, 'a crisis of identity'.[72]

The symposium *Vekhi* [Waymarks] was first and foremost an expression of this crisis. It was issued by a group of former left-wing Cadets among whom were also men who had done much to propagandize Marxism in Russia – P. Struve, N. Berdyaev, S. Bulgakov and others. The publication of *Vekhi* was a most important episode in the history of the Russian intelligentsia and of Russian social thought. Essentially, this was the only serious attempt to 'revise' the consciousness of the intelligentsia and turn it rightward, breaking it away from the revolution. The unexpectedness and exceptional nature of this attempt focused society's attention upon *Vekhi* and made it the centre of a serious political debate. A great deal has been written about *Vekhi* both then and since, and the problem of *Vekhi* remains topical to this day for many people of Solzhenitsyn's type. To understand it, however, one needs to analyse, as Berdyaev did later, the events of those years and to look at the history of Russian idealism.

The question of Russia's Christian intelligentsia was badly muddled by Lenin, who was quite unwilling to investigate the concrete problems of Russian religious thought, which seemed to him utterly reactionary. He saw 'traitors', 'reactionaries', 'counter-revolutionaries', 'poltroons', 'gasbags' and 'layers-out of corpses' who 'did not even destroy the monarchy' in all intellectuals who took up moderate positions in politics.[73] The subsequent Soviet-Stalinist interpreters of Lenin aggravated his mistake by declaring all the Christian intellectuals of the early years of this century to be if not direct then indirect supporters of the autocracy (it is interesting that Solzhenitsyn's admirers usually hold the same view). In reality, however, matters were very much more complicated. The Russian intelligentsia in the nineteenth century was to a very large extent *opposed to the Orthodox Church* (and has remained so down to the most recent times); this, however, did not prevent some circles of the Slavophil intelligentsia from taking up arms on behalf of 'true' Orthodoxy against the bureaucratic, 'Petersburg' Orthodoxy of official Russia. These attempts met with no success.

The religious revival in Russia at the turn of the century was part of a reaction against positivism throughout Europe, which led to the appearance of various forms of philosophical idealism. Moreover, 'dead positivism' was regarded, as D. Merezhkovsky put it, as one of the weapons of 'autocratic conformism'.[74] In this situation the religious ideas of the Russian philosophers were not only not 'reactionary' but were in the highest degree productive, and their attacks on positivist schemes were in many respects similar to the anti-positivist pronouncements of the latest Western Marxists. Of course, the positivist treatment of Marxism which was widespread in the parties of the Second International could not but become a target of criticism, and it must be admitted that it often failed to stand up to this criticism. At the same time the political views of many 'mystics and God-seekers' were , at first, not at all as 'right-wing' and 'reactionary' as Lenin described them. Recalling the cultural and religious revival of those years, Berdyaev wrote later: 'There was nothing reactionary in the cultural renaissance of the beginning of this century: many of its active spirits even sympathized very definitely with revolution and socialism.'[75]

The first, and perhaps the most important, of the Russian religious philosophers was V. Solovev, who asserted that in modern times the divine spirit lay rather with unbelievers than with believers. Solovev, of course, was never a supporter of the Russian autocracy and his ideas can properly be called the Christian justification of the political opponents of the official Orthodox state. Solovev's attitude to the socialists was very contradictory, but he considered it impossible either to denounce them (they were right to attack modern capitalism) or to unite with them (they put forward a positive programme which was unacceptable to him).[76] From this one can easily conclude that whether or not the political ideas of the Lefts were correct, Solovev's philosophy justified destructive activity directed against the old order. According to his logic the Narodovoltsy, the Marxists and all those atheistic socialists were bearers of the divine spirit. Consequently, even the terrorist acts of the Social-Revolutionaries could be justified morally. True, Solovev did not draw that conclusion, but Merezhkovsky did it for him. A present-day Soviet thinker of the 'new right', M. Agursky (who is probably the most profound theoretician of that tendency) was quite justified, in his own way, when he remarked maliciously that 'Merezhkovsky and Zinaida Hippius rejected Bolshevism, without recognizing that it was their own godchild.'[77]

In Merezhkovsky's opinion, the revolution had to come down from the sociopolitical plane 'into the religious depths, which, however, include that plane as well, just as the third dimension includes the second.'[78] Political emancipation must be combined with spiritual, religious renewal – that was Merezhkovsky's basic idea, which determined his political sympathies and antipathies and explains his disagreement with the subsequent Bolshevik revolution, which was absolutely alien to the Christian renaissance. However, was not the Bolshevik ideology itself a peculiar sort of atheist or, rather, anti-God religiosity? 'Up to now,' wrote Merezhkovsky, 'revolution has been the religion of the Russian intelligentsia. It is not a long step from this to religion becoming revolution.'[79] Something like that did happen, perhaps, but the only *revolutionary* religiosity proved, in practice, to be the atheistic variety.[80] Was Merezhkovsky mistaken, though, in his prophecies? Perhaps in this case, too, he 'failed to recognize his own godchild'?

We can appreciate the difficulties of official Soviet historians of social thought when they try to depict such pronouncements as 'reactionary'. In the end, for example, V.A. Kuvakin,[81] in his book on Russian religious philosophy published by the *Mysl'* publishing house, is obliged to write: 'In the period when it came into being, the "new religious consciousness" represented a conservative camp only in the person of V. Rozanov.'[82] The specific nature of Kuvakin's language, of course, enables him to speak of a whole 'camp' consisting of one man. But it becomes clear that in this case, too, one cannot get by without a reservation, since Rozanov 'was close to Merezhkovsky in some points of his modernistic religious programme'.[83] Actually, Rozanov's religious utopianism was to a large extent simply outside the realm of politics. He could be called conservative, or even reactionary, only if he had not been so remote from life. Rozanov's dream was to 'extinguish the political bonfire' completely,[84] not to bring about the triumph of any particular political ideas. His immediate interests lay in another direction altogether – the field of religious reform. Furthermore, his criticism of the official Church (and even of Christianity itself) was radical enough to create a fairly large audience for him among the Russian intelligentsia.

Before the beginning of the twentieth century idealist philosophy was not very popular in intellectual circles. In *Vekhi* Berdyaev admitted that 'the Russian intelligentsia did not read or know Solovev: it failed to recognize him as its own.'[85] It was Rozanov and Merezhkovsky together who in 1901 made the first attempt to reconcile religion and the intelligentsia, by organizing meetings to discuss religion and philosophy. The aim of such a reconciliation, however, was to bring about a modernization of the Orthodox Church itself, which in its current form could offer no attraction to the intelligentsia. The official Church's attitude to this initiative was extremely unfriendly, for 'Orthodox conformism' came under sharp criticism in these meetings. The *intelligenty* put questions to the church dignitaries which the latter could not and did not want to answer. 'These religious and philosophical gatherings were interesting principally for the questions that were asked rather than for the answers that were given,' Berdyaev recalled.[86]

The movement for church reform smacked very definitely of oppositional politics and we are surprised to find that Lenin, contrary to his custom, reacted quite favourably to this liberal 'new Orthodoxy' as he called it, a follower of which he saw in the 'sincere Christian socialist' G. Gapon.[87] In his opinion the

> discontent among the clergy, the striving among them after new forms of life ... the appearance of Christian Socialists and Christian Democrats ... this all serves the purpose of the revolution and creates exceedingly favourable conditions for agitation for the complete separation of the Church from the State. The allies of the revolution, voluntary and involuntary, conscious and unconscious, are growing and multiplying hour by hour.[88]

Experience showed – and this, evidently evoked Lenin's enthusiasm –

that the call for church reform had a much greater effect among the intellectual or radical circles of the clergy than among members of the intelligentsia themselves. On the whole, the first attempt to reconcile the intelligentsia and religion was not a success. The second attempt – in the same direction, formally, but in essence quite unlike the first – was made by a group of former 'legal Marxists' – Berdyaev, Bulgakov, Struve, Izgoev and others – in the symposium *Vekhi* after the failure of the 1905–07 Revolution, when the intelligentsia's disappointment had created favourable soil for radical self-criticism.

It was by no means accidental that the authors of *Vekhi* were former Marxists. The entire evolution of the ideas of Berdyaev and, to a lesser extent, of his co-authors testifies to this. At first they launched a critique against the Social Democrats which cannot be dismissed as lacking foundation. They attacked the Russian Socialists for their vulgar materialism, for their scorning of spiritual values, for their insufficient interest in the individual: 'Neither soul nor body should be affirmed,' wrote Berdyaev in 1905, 'but the individual as a whole and the distinctiveness of his being.'[89] Without suspecting this himself, he was here almost repeating the basic idea of the young Marx. He could not have known that, because the *Economic and Philosophical Manuscripts of 1844* had not then been published either in Russian or in German.[90] Nevertheless, it must be admitted that twentieth-century Russian (and not only Russian) idealism owed much to Marxism. It was no accident that the greatest representatives of idealist dialectics in our century, Croce and Berdyaev, were men who had been trained as Marxists. It was through Marx that they came to know Hegel's dialectic which, had it not survived in the setting of Marxism, would have been completely ousted from the scientific method of the positivists. Berdyaev never denied his link with Marx: 'However strange it may be at first sight, yet it is actually Marxism – at first critical rather than orthodox Marxism – which has supplied us with an idealist, and later on a religious current of thought.'[91]

The periodical *Voprosy zhizni* [Problems of Life], which was published by the idealists in 1905, 'belonged to the left, the radical school of thought, but it was the first in the history of Russian periodicals to combine that sort of social and political ideas with religious inquiry, with a metaphysical outlook and a new tendency in literature.'[92] However, this periodical survived for one year only – amid the turmoil of the first Russian Revolution – and then ceased to appear. 'In the heat of battle,' its writers, as Berdyaev himself admitted, 'often attached insufficient value to that social truth and right which was to be found in the left intelligentsia and which retained its power.'[93] This impelled them further and further away from the democratic and socialist line that they had originally proclaimed. In itself the appearance of the Russian idealists was, as I have already said, a logical reaction to positivism and the positivistically treated vulgar Marxism of European Social Democracy. The trouble was that, lacking support from the mass of the intelligentsia, the idealists moved more and more to the right: 'these cultural and idealist tendencies began to lose their connection with the social revolutionary movement; more and more they lost the broad social standpoint.'[94] Later, Berdyaev was to say that this departure from the revolution was 'fatal'. And it was just this shift to the right, intensified by disappointment with the failure of the 1905 movement, that gave rise to the *Vekhi* symposium, with its openly reactionary programme. Berdyaev subsequently complained that *Vekhi* had been misunderstood – that it was not, on the whole, a political act but a 'struggle for the spirit' and only through misunderstanding, 'in accordance with the ancient tradition of the Russian intelligentsia, the struggle for the spirit was taken as reactionary, almost like a betrayal of the struggle for freedom.'[95]

Nevertheless this interpretation of *Vekhi*, after the event (in a period when Berdyaev had again become a left-winger, a personalist[96] and a Christian socialist) raises doubts. Above all, the tone adopted by all the contributors to *Vekhi* was extremely aggressive and uncompromising. There were no sins with which they did not charge the intelligentsia. While condemning them, they simultaneously tried to preach to them. 'There is no word more unpopular in the intelligentsia milieu than the word "humility",' complained S. Bulgakov.[97] 'A swarm of sick men isolated in their native land – this is the Russian intelligentsia,' declared M. Gershenzon.[98] 'The intelligentsia's consciousness demands radical reform,' concluded Berdyaev.[99] The same idea is developed by Struve, too, when he affirms that 'it is mandatory that the intelligentsia re-examine its entire world-view, and this includes subjecting its chief buttress to radical re-examination – the socialist repudiation of personal responsibility. ...'[100]

Not surprisingly, such attacks produced an outburst of indignation within the Russian intelligentsia. Until then such voices had been heard only from the governmental camp and the appearance of *Vekhi* was regarded as an act of betrayal, as 'a stab in the back by persons who had always stood in their [the intelligentsia's] own ranks'.[101] The bulk of the intelligentsia repudiated the 'revisionism' of *Vekhi*. 'Opposition to the views of *Vekhi*', wrote Leonard Schapiro, 'was strong not only among the avowed radicals such as the Social-Revolutionaries, the heirs of the nineteenth-century Populists, but even more so among the Kadets, a party with an avowedly liberal programme.'[102] The collection of essays by Struve and his friends was reprinted several times, and everyone read it, but only as a 'scandalous' book.[103]

Nevertheless, *Vekhi* gave rise to a serious polemic. The Social-Revolutionaries and the Cadets even published two symposia in reply.[104] Lenin wrote a special article 'Concerning *Vekhi*'. It must be said that he used the appearance of *Vekhi* to compromise the Cadet Party, to which its authors belonged. Consequently, he did not so much argue against the ideas expressed in the symposium as denounce the Cadet Party, calling it 'the party of *Vekhi*' with a criminal connection with the authors of that book, which the Cadets themselves disowned in every possible way.[105] Lenin had a poor understanding of the essence of the dispute and did not even discuss it, declaring that 'it is not the intelligentsia that *Vekhi* is attacking. This is only an artificial and misleading manner of expression.'[106] In his own way he was even glad about the publication of *Vekhi*, for Berdyaev, Bulgakov and Struve unknowingly helped him considerably in his fight against Russian liberalism by discrediting their own party: 'working-class democrats should welcome *Vekhi*.'[107]

The fact is that it was rather difficult to see *Vekhi* as a manifesto of the Cadet party, and Lenin himself acknowledged that on the whole the programme of *Vekhi* was similar to that of the conservative 'October 17th' Party. But precisely the fact that Struve and the other contributors to *Vekhi* belonged to the Cadets showed, according to Lenin, that there was no great difference between the liberals and the conservatives. This view can be more or less justified where the right-wing Cadet politicians were concerned but not in relation to the Left-Cadet intelligentsia, upon whom Lenin fell no less vigorously than did the *Vekhi* contributors themselves (with this difference only: that the Left-Cadet *intelligenty* were for Struve almost Bolsheviks, whereas for Lenin they were almost conservatives). 'The Cadet polemic with *Vekhi*', he wrote, 'and the Cadet renunciation of *Vekhi* are nothing but hypocrisy, sheer idle talk.'[108]

In fact, however, the Left Cadets were arguing with *Vekhi* about essential matters. They wrote that the 1905 Revolution, despite its failure, had helped the country to progress and one could not talk of the bankruptcy of the Russian intelligentsia who had prepared the revolution, for in 1905 the gap between the intelligentsia and the people had been closed for the first time. The people had supported the ideas of the intelligentsia. 'The autocracy', wrote N.A. Gredeskul, 'is now consciously "rejected" in Russia not by the intelligentsia alone (as had been the case before 1904–1905) but also by the people as a whole. The brunt of the fight against the absolutism is borne no longer by the intelligentsia but by the people.'[109]

The tragic gap between the ideologues and the masses had been overcome; the prophecy had been fulfilled: 'The nation has been spiritually reborn, or, more correctly, only now has it come to spiritual birth.'[110] This crisis of the movement was a crisis of growth. *Vekhi* anticipated in grotesque fashion the present official propaganda which accuses the oppositionist intelligentsia of 'renegacy' from the state and the generally accepted ideology, and also of 'cosmopolitanism'.[111]

From the standpoint of the Lefts there was nothing reprehensible in being, in those days, 'isolated from the people', from the 'soil' which was not yet ready for their work of liberation: 'In Russia the clash between the thinking of the intelligentsia and popular tradition had a special character not because our evolution was irregular or immoral but because the heresy of the intelligentsia found the masses at too low a level of development.'[112] Milyukov observed that by condemning 'nihilism' the *Vekhi* contributors had themselves acted towards the tradition of the intelligentsia as 'real "nihilists"'.[113]

The Cadets' onslaught on *Vekhi* was no less furious than Lenin's. They refused even to have discussions with the contributors themselves:

Where is there any battle of ideas here, when they proclaim that we are moral lepers? Is it appropriate to talk of a battle of ideas when they preach to us humility, repentance and renunciation of our errors? This is more in the nature of a sermon, but would it not be better to leave that sort of thing to the Church?[114]

By their action the contributors to *Vekhi* had put themselves outside the ranks of the Russian intelligentsia. Essentially, their task was doomed from the start because the ideology of the intelligentsia was already fully formed and could not be remade by a series of articles. Theoretical questions, wrote Tompkins, had already 'given way to practical ones, so that the effort of Struve to turn the clock back and re-examine the ideology was quite useless.'[115] Ideas for which generations of Russian revolutionaries had gone to penal servitude and to the gallows could not be simply disaffirmed. 'Neither the "God-seekers" nor the "God-builders",' wrote K.K. Arsen'ev, 'were able to rouse any broad, deep movement. None of them spoke "a word to set men's hearts on fire".'[116] Berdyaev, too, acknowledged this failure when he said that the preaching of *Vekhi* had 'no influence on the wide circles of Russian society'.[117]

The *Vekhi* writers were wrong, but the optimism of the Left was also premature. After 1905 they hoped that one more shove would suffice to bring down the old regime, and nobody doubted that what would follow then would be the triumph of freedom. Besides, could it have been known beforehand that 'near the end of the play' the Tsar's government would get involved in a world war and bring Russia to such a monstrous catastrophe that what would be at stake would be not a transition to democracy but the salvation of the people and the state, the mere survival of society? ... In 1910 nobody suspected that, not the *Vekhi* writers not the Liberals nor the Socialists.

The *Vekhi* writers suffered not only political defeat (in the sense that the intelligentsia did not follow their lead) but also philosophical defeat. In the last analysis Merezhkovsky was quite right, in his polemic against *Vekhi*, when he said that the spiritual revolution cannot be separated from the social revolution. In a country where there is no political liberty, spiritual rebirth can come only through a struggle for democracy. And that, in turn, implies that social consciousness must be renewed in forms quite different from those proposed by the 'God-seekers' – including Merezhkovsky himself. However, history was to outwit not only the *Vekhi* writers, the 'God-seekers' and the 'God-builders', but, as we shall see later, the Bolsheviks as well. ...

Notes

1. A.I. Herzen, *Sobranie Sochinenii v tridtsati tomakh*, Moscow 1956, vol. 7, p. 198.

2. *Politicheskii Dnevnik, 1964–1970*, Amsterdam 1972, vol. 1, p. 179.

3. *Strömungen und Tendenzen in Neomarxismus*, Munich 1972, p. 7.

4. Herzen, vol. 7, p. 68.

5. Lenin, *Collected Works*, 4th edn, English version, vol. 18, p. 48.

6. M.N. Pokrovsky, *Ocherki po istorii revolyutsionnogo dzheniya v Rossii XIX–XX vv*, Moscow 1924, p. 133.

7. Nikolai Berdyaev, *The Russian Idea*, 1947, p. 12.

8. P. Milyukov, *Intelligentsiya v Rossii*, St Petersburg 1910, p. 156.

9. Edward Acton, *Alexander Herzen and the Role of the Intellectual Revolutionary*, Cambridge 1979, p. 9.

10. Marshall S. Shatz, *Soviet Dissent in Historical Perspective*, Cambridge 1981, p. 11.

11. Ibid., p. 16.

12. Berdyaev, *The Russian Idea*, p. 17.

13. *Intelligentsia v Rossii*, p. 128.

14. Israel Getzler, Martov's biographer, analyses in detail the views of this important Russian Marxist on the problem of the relation between the intelligentsia and the autocracy. He writes that Martov regarded the intelligentsia 'as the vanguard in the struggle for the modernization of Russia' (I. Getzler, *Martov*, Cambridge 1967, p. 34).

15. Philip Pomper, *The Russian Revolutionary Intelligentsia*, New York 1970, p. 30.

16. Shatz, p. 35.

17. N. Berdyaev, *The Origin of Russian Communism*, 1937, p. 17.

18. V. Polonsky, *Krasnaya Nov'*, no. 1 (18), January–February 1924, p. 190.

19. Ibid.

20. In my book *The Dialectics of Hope* I have tried to look more closely at this question (in the chapter entitled 'The Intelligentsia and the Establishment').

21. Samuel H. Baron, *Plekhanov, the Father of Russian Marxism*, London 1963, p. 3.

22. Robert J. Brym, *The Jewish Intelligentsia and Russian Marxism. A Sociological Study of Intellectual Radicalism and Ideological Divergence*, London 1978, p. 4.

23. This was especially evident in the case of the Jewish intelligentsia, whose members

were able to obtain education yet lacked civil rights. Owing to the 'Pale of Settlement' and absence of political rights, the Jewish *intelligent* embodied, so to speak, in concentrated form the contradictions of the Russian *intelligent*. He was doubly marginal (and if he got his education in the West, doubly a 'Westerner'). Besides, he had already ceased to feel that he was a Jew and considered himself a Russian *intelligent*. Clearly the Black Hundreds' conception, in which 'Jew' was a synonym for *intelligent*, had in its way a certain foundation.

24. Shatz, p. 13.

25. R. Pipes, *Russia under the Old Regime*, 1974, p. 280.

26. *Intelligentsiya v Rossii*, p. 254.

27. See A. Gramsci, *O literature i iskusstve*, Moscow 1967, pp. 25–47.

28. Jean-Paul Sartre, *Between Existentialism and Marxism*, London 1983, p. 252.

29. Ibid. See also Sartre, *Du Rôle de l'intellectuel dans le mouvement révolutionnaire*, Paris 1971.

30. G. Pomerants, *Obshchestvo, elita i byurokratsiya v razvivayushchikhsya stranakh Vostoka*, Book 2, Moscow 1974, p. 357.

31. Berdyaev, *The Origin . . .*, p. 24.

32. Berdyaev, *The Russian Idea*, p. 35.

33. P. Ya. Chaadaev, *Filosofskie pis'ma*, Moscow 1913, pp. 18–19 (*Philosophical Letters*, Knoxville 1969, p. 43).

34. Berdyaev, *The Origin . . .*, p. 25.

35. Ibid.

36. 'Zametki ob intelligentsii', *Krasnaya Nov'*, no.1, 1924, p. 199.

37. Lenin, *Collected Works*, vol. 5, p. 375.

38. Ibid., vol. 7, p. 45.

39. G.V. Plekhanov, *Sochineniya*, Moscow and Leningrad 1926, vol. 13, p. 125.

40. See A. Yanov, 'Zagadka slavyanofil'skoi kritiki', *Voprosy literatury*, no.5, 1969, pp. 91–116. For more details about this article and the discussion around it, see Chapter 5 below.

41. Berdyaev, *The Russian Idea*, p. 40.

42. Berdyaev, *The Origin . . .*, p. 29.

43. Berdyaev, *The Russian Idea*, p. 3

44. Herzen, p. 234.

45. *Intelligentsiya v Rossii*, p. 21.

46. Lenin, *Collected Works*, vol. 20, p. 245.

47. Robert C. Tucker, *The Marxian Revolutionary Idea*, 1970, pp. 120–21.

48. M. Bodkhovsky, 'Through the Swamp' [Cherez top'] *Samizdatovskii sbornik*, Leningrad n.d., p. 23.

49. *Intelligentsiya v Rossii*, p. 235.

50. Ibid.

51. R. Pipes, ed., *The Russian Intelligentsia*, New York 1961, p. 48.

52. Such views were expressed from other quarters as well as from the Menshevik camp. See Berdyaev, *The Origin . . .*.

53. The term was borrowed from Marx but used in quite a different sense. Although Lenin did not employ it, he expressed similar ideas. See the original publication of his speeches in *Severnaya Kommuna*, no.58 (14 March 1919) and the stenographic reports of the Moscow Soviet of Workers', Peasants' and Red Army Men's Deputies, Bulletin 15.

54. Lenin, *Collected Works*, vol. 16, p. 128.

55. Berdyaev, *The Origin . . .*, p. 127.

56. Even in 1919, at the 8th Congress of the RCP (B) Lenin was calling the October Revolution a bourgeois revolution. In 1905–07, but especially in 1917–22, Lenin and the Bolsheviks reconsidered the idea of inevitable bourgeois development for Russia, affirming that in Russia the proletarian revolution fulfilled objectively a number of the tasks of the bourgeois-democratic revolution but did this, of course, not in a bourgeois-democratic way but by other means. This interpretation of the historical process accounts for some important aspects of Bolshevik policy. See Lenin, *Collected Works*, vol. 33, pp. 465, 470, etc.

57. Similar processes can be observed today in many developing countries, where the local variant of 'Marxism' has ousted revolutionary populism. In Russia Marxist ideas fell upon ready-prepared soil. 'Russian thought will always be concerned with the transformation of the actual state of affairs,' writes Berdyaev. 'Recognition of the latter will go hand in hand with the changing of it' (*The Russian Idea*, p. 29). This conception of the tasks of social thought corresponds to the very important principle of Marxism: 'The philosophers have only *interpreted* the world in various ways, the point, however, is to *change* it' (Marx and Engels, *Sochineniya*, vol. 3, p. 4: 11th Thesis on Feuerbach) (*Collected Works*, English edn, vol. 5, p. 8).

58. *Pod znamenem marksizma*, 1922, no. 5–6, p.5 (Trotsky, *Portraits Political and Personal*, New York 1977, p. 36).

59. Lenin, *Collected Works*, vol. 5, pp. 375–6.

60. *Intelligentsiya v Rossii*, p. 194.

61. Lenin, *Collected Works*, vol. 20, p. 247.

62. See *Vsemirno-istoricheskve znachenie Velikoy Oktyabr'skoy sotsialisticheskoy revolyutsii*, Moscow 1957, p. 65.

63. Trotsky, *Moya Zhizn'*, Part I, Berlin 1930, p. 147 (*My Life*, Universal Library, New York 1960, p. 123).

64. Brym, p. 1.

65. Pokrovsky, *Ocherki...*, p. 103.

66. Ibid.

67. Ibid., pp. 107–8.

68. Pokrovsky, *Brief History of Russia*, vol. 2 (1933), p. 245.

69. S.A. Tompkins, *The Russian Intelligentsia, Makers of the Revolutionary State*, Norman 1957, p. 175.

70. Pokrovsky, *Russkaya Istoriya*, pp. 126–7 (Partly given in *Brief History of Russia*, vol. 2, p. 130).

71. The mood of the Russian *intelligenty* after 1905 is splendidly depicted in Boris Savinkov's book *To, chego ne bylo* ['What Never Happened'], which is above all a most interesting psychological document of the period.

72. Martin Malia, 'What is the Intelligentsia?', in Tompkins, p. 17.

73. Lenin, *Collected Works*, vol. 33, pp. 52 ff.

74. See D. Merezhkovsky, 'The Boor who is Coming', *Poln. sobr. soch.*, Moscow 1914, vol. 14, p. 37.

75. Berdyaev, *The Origin...*, p. 131.

76. See Vl. Solovev, *Sobr. soch.*, vol. 8, pp. 368 and also 362 (*The Justification of the Good*, 1918, pp. 327–33).

77. M. Agursky, *Ideologiya natsional-bol'shevizma*, Paris 1980, p. 36.

78. Merezhkovsky, 'The Revolution and Religion', *Poln. sobr. soch.*, vol. 13, p. 96.

79. Merezhkovsky, 'Once more on "Great Russia"', *Poln. sobr. soch.*, vol. 16, p. 59.

80. Berdyaev wrote that Bolshevism 'adopted primarily not the determinist, evolutionary scientific side of Marxism, but its messianic myth-creating religious side, which gave scope for the stimulation of the revolutionary will, and assigned a foremost place to the proletariat's revolutionary struggle as controlled by an organized minority, which was inspired by the conscious proletariat [*sic*] idea' (*The Origin...*, p. 125). While this description cannot be applied to such rationalists as Lenin, Sverdlov, Trotsky and Bukharin, it is fully applicable to the rank-and-file Bolsheviks who put the Party line into practice. Even in Bukharin's case Marxist determinism bears a marked resemblance to religious fatalism; Bukharin himself felt this and tried, not very successfully, to defend his ideas from possible accusations of that sort (see N.I. Bukharin, *Historical Materialism*, 1926, p. 51).

81. Valery Aleksandrovich Kuvakin: not to be confused with Vsevolod Kuvakin, the leader of the Soviet free trade unions!

82. V.A. Kuvakin, *Religioznaya filosofiya v Rossii: Nachalo XX veka*, Moscow 1980, p. 46.

83. Ibid., p. 47.

84. V. Rozanov, *Opavshe list'ya, Korob Vtoroy* ['Fallen Leaves. Bundle Two'], St

Petersburg 1915, p. 29 (checked from the edition *Vasily Rozanov: Izbrannoe*, Munich 1970, p. 230).

85. *Vekhi*, Moscow 1909, p. 17 (*Landmarks*, ed. B. Shragin and A. Todd, New York 1977, p. 17).

86. Berdyaev, *The Russian Idea*, p. 227.

87. Lenin, *Collected Works*, vol. 8, p. 106.

88. Ibid., p. 448.

89. Berdyaev, 'On the New Religious Consciousness (D. Merezhkovsky)', *Voprosy zhizni*, no. 9, 1905, p. 167.

90. This leads to the paradoxical conclusion that Marxist philosophy in the exact sense of the word did not exist at all before the 1930s and began to be developed as an independent scientific current in the works of Lukács, Gramsci, Adorno and Marcuse, and then Fromm in the 1930s and 1940s. Berdyaev read Lukács at that time and discovered, along with everyone else, the young Marx, in whose works he found ideas that were important for him – 'an element of genuine existential philosophy' (*The Origin* ..., p. 116). We can say, therefore, that Marx influenced Berdyaev twice – first through his economic works and then, much later, through his philosophical works.

91. Ibid., p. 128.

92. Berdyaev, *The Russian Idea*, p. 246.

93. Ibid., p. 221.

94. Berdyaev, *The Origin* ..., p. 129.

95. Ibid., p. 133.

96. The term 'personalist' is as a rule unfamiliar to the Soviet reader, and not at all associated with politics. In France, where Berdyaev lived as an *émigré*, personalism became the ideology of the left-wing Catholics who founded the journal *Esprit*, an ideology which influenced the programme of the French socialist movement (the *Parti Socialiste Unifié*, the *Parti Socialiste Français* and, especially, the trade-union centre associated with the socialists, the *Confédération Française Démocratique du Travail*). To the French Left Catholics are due some important ideas in the sphere of the theory of property and workers' self-management which are shared by many Marxists. In Russia Berdyaev's ideas could serve as an excellent basis for a dialogue between progressive Christians and the Marxist opposition. Unfortunately, many who call themselves admirers of Berdyaev are totally uninterested in what he actually said and thought.

97. *Vekhi*, p. 49 (*Landmarks*, p. 45).

98. Ibid., p. 87 (ibid., p. 79).

99. Ibid, p. 21 (ibid., p. 21).

100. Ibid., p. 171 (ibid., p. 151).

101. *Intelligentsiya v Rossii*, p. 11 (Gredeskul).

102. Leonard Schapiro, 'The Pre-Revolutionary Intelligentsia and the Legal Order', in Pipes, ed., *The Russian Intelligentsia*, p. 30.

103. S.A. Frank, *Biografiya P.V. Struve*, New York 1956, pp. 83–4.

104. See *'Vekhi' kak znamenie vremeni* (1910) and *Intelligentsiya v Rossii*.

105. Lenin, *Collected Works*, vol. 16, p. 123.

106. Ibid., p. 125.

107. Ibid., p. 123.

108. Ibid., p. 131.

109. *Intelligentsiya v Rossii*, pp. 48–9.

110. Ibid., p. 50.

111. See *Vekhi*, pp. 171, 172 (*Landmarks*, pp. 152–4).

112. *Intelligentsiya v Rossii*, p. 119.

113. Ibid., p. 170.

114. Ibid., p. xii (Petrunkevich).

115. Tompkins, p. 223.

116. *Intelligentsiya v Rossii*, p. 3 (K.K. Arsen'ev).

117. Berdyaev, *The Origin* ..., pp. 129–130.

2

Revolution and Bureaucracy

The Party of Revolution and Order

The events of 1917 in which the old Russia perished proved to be a turning point in the history of the intelligentsia, of culture, of the freedom movement and of the state system. In circumstances of general breakdown and collapse, when the country was threatened with complete disintegration and reversion to barbarism, the Bolshevik Party and the organized working class were together the only force capable of establishing some sort of order in Russia and saving it as a civilized state.

The Bolsheviks were at one and the same time 'the party of revolution' and 'the party of order'. Because they constituted the sole militarily disciplined and centralized organization amid the general ruin and chaos, when even the army was without the slightest discipline, it was inevitable that they should come to power. On the day of the October Revolution the independent Social-Democratic newspaper *Novaya Zhizn'* acknowledged that the Bolsheviks were probably the only force that could bring back order in Russia. Unlike the 'good wishes' of the intelligentsia, the decisions of the Bolshevik workers' organizations 'do not remain on paper'. The paper wrote that 'the Bolshevik working-class intelligentsia, who played the leading role in the trade unions, the factory and works committees and the other practical organizations of the proletariat, have carried out an immense amount of cultural work during recent months.'[1] The Bolsheviks alone managed to maintain labour discipline in the factories.

The actual seizure of power on 7 November was received fairly calmly by the intelligentsia. The Provisional Government which the Bolsheviks drove out had been elected by no one and possessed no authority. 'The Provisional Government', observed *Novaya Zhizn'*, 'did not perish, did not fall in battle, it dissolved.'[2] A shock for the intelligentsia, however, was the series of measures taken by the new rulers which restricted democracy, such as the suppression of a number of right-wing newspapers, which *Novaya Zhizn'* called an 'anti-socialist and stupid measure'.[3]

The cause of the October 1917 revolution is not to be sought in the 'evil will' of the Bolsheviks but in the objective situation, which left no room for any other solution. The Russian bourgeoisie, weak and involved with the old regime, had from the very beginning of the revolution, in February 1917, taken up extremely reactionary positions. Even if the proletariat which carried out the revolution had not put forward socialist slogans, large-scale industry would have had to be nationalized, for purely political reasons, as a measure of struggle against bourgeois reaction. In this case socialist ideology provided justification for what was a matter of political necessity. Despite the view generally accepted later, the Bolsheviks were not free 'creators' of history but rather the slaves of objective necessity which, as a rule, left them no choice. They could have repeated the words of Saint-Just: 'La force des choses nous conduit peut-être à des résultats auxquels nous n'avons point pensé.'[4]

Indeed, Lenin, Trotsky and other 'wise heads' in the leadership of the Bolshevik Party[5] had no intention of introducing socialism forthwith. Their general policy was aimed not at establishing socialism but at defending – by revolutionary-socialist methods – industry, transport, civilization and the Russian state itself in conditions of collapse and anarchy. The prospect of socialism was bound up with the victory of the proletariat in Germany. 'The job of construction', wrote Lenin, 'is completely dependent on how soon the revolution will succeed in the more important European countries. Only after it succeeds there can we seriously get down to the job of construction.'[6] This way of presenting the problem did not seem at all utopian at that time. Although Rosa Luxemburg, observing from Germany the struggle in Petrograd, was highly critical of Lenin and Trotsky she saw 'proof of their farsightedness' precisely in the fact that 'the Bolsheviks have based their policy entirely upon the world proletarian revolution.'[7]

It was clear that the class foundation for socialism did not exist in Russia; the working class was too small and industry undeveloped. This gave N. Sukhanov grounds for saying:

> the Bolshevik regime is doomed to perish not through armed force but through the inner defect which has corroded it from the first moments of the Bolsheviks' 'state' activity. This defect is the absence of objective conditions for their rule.[8]

In an agrarian country a regime which tried to base itself on the working-class minority, ignoring the will of the other groups in the population, was bound to degenerate and give place to something different. However, Sukhanov could not know in advance the form that this process would take. Another Russian Marxist, B. Avilov, declared that a socialist revolution was possible only on the basis of a highly developed industrial capitalism, 'and not as an amateurish creation based upon small-scale economy and ruined capitalist industry', and he considered a transition to socialism unrealizable in practice.[9] In his paper *Novaya Zhizn'*, which in 1917–18 became the mouthpiece of the left-wing intelligentsia, Gorky described – perhaps more realistically than did many socialists in the West – the attempt to accelerate the world revolution by using the Russian Revolution to urge it on, as 'a cruel experiment which is doomed to failure beforehand',[10] and warned that the working class itself would suffer as a result: 'And if the working class is crushed and destroyed, that means the best forces and hopes of the country will be destroyed.'[11]

Lenin and his comrades were aware that there was no majority in favour of socialism in Russia, that they lacked sufficient support in this peasant country, that the conditions for socialism had not matured. They realized, too, that 'the only stable power is the one that has the backing of the majority of the population.'[12] Nevertheless, they regarded it as their duty to take power. 'It does not occur to any of them,' Lenin wrote in reply to Sukhanov and his comrades,

> to ask: but what about a people that found itself in a revolutionary situation such as that created by the first imperialist war? Might it not, *influenced by the hopelessness of its situation*, fling itself into a struggle that would offer it *at least some chance* of securing conditions for the further development of civilisation that were somewhat unusual? [emphasis added][13]

And later, on the same page of his notes (written not long before his death) on *Our Revolution*, he asks again:

> What if the *complete hopelessness of the situation* by stimulating the efforts of the workers and peasants tenfold, offered us the opportunity to create the fundamental requisites of civilization in a different way from that of the West-European countries? [emphasis added][14]

Lenin understood no less than Sukhanov or Gorky that Russia was not ready for the transition to socialism. Trotsky solved this problem very simply, by supposing that proletarian revolution in the West would help the Bolsheviks to overcome the backwardness of Russia. Lenin also hoped for revolution in the West (not realizing that the Bolsheviks' dictatorial methods scared off the Western proletariat from the revolution, thus postponing socialism rather than bringing it nearer). On the whole, though, Lenin's thinking was incomparably more profound than Trotsky's for, while appreciating Russia's backwardness, he saw the task before Bolshevism in the years immediately ahead as precisely to correct that situation and thereby create the possibility of socialism. Anyone who reads the statements made by Lenin after 1917 with an unprejudiced mind will easily perceive that what the Bolsheviks saw *as their immediate task* was not 'the construction of socialist society' but, on the contrary, the strengthening in Russia of civilization and state capitalism in the German manner, because this state capitalism was 'a complete *material* preparation for socialism, the threshold of socialism'.[15]

In aiming directly at state capitalism Lenin, at the same time, made no attempt whatsoever to present this as socialism, but on the contrary reacted against any such verbal deception.[16] State capitalism was what, in his view, would make possible the creation of those foundations of civilization which were necessary preconditions for socialism:

> Is it not clear that from the *material*, economic and productive point of view, we are not yet on 'the threshold' of socialism? Is it not clear that we cannot pass through the door of socialism without crossing 'the threshold' we have not yet reached?[17]

As I said earlier, the Bolsheviks interpreted Marxism, in a certain sense, as the ideology of modernization and Europeanization. In this lay both their strength and their weakness, for this simplified ideological treatment of Marxism, while rendering socialism more intelligible to many people in Russia, at the same time obliged them to shut their eyes to some very important scientific conclusions that followed from its discoveries. But this was not the main problem. Berdyaev wrote that Peter I was 'a Bolshevik on the throne'.[18] One can also make this comparison the other way round. Politically, Lenin's party was to a greater degree the party of Peter I than the party of Karl Marx, since it strove first and foremost to ensure that Russia imitated contemporary forms of Western organization. Lenin said that his followers should

> not shrink from adopting *dictatorial* methods to hasten the copying of [state capitalism as in Germany]. Our task is to hasten this copying even more than Peter hastened the copying of Western culture by barbarian Russia, and we must not hesitate to use barbarous methods to hasten the copying of it.[19]

The Bolsheviks were the party of revolution and of order by virtue of their discipline, their unity and their conviction. They were the only party capable of defending the vestiges of European civilization in Russia, modernizing the country and preserving Russia as an independent and unified power. In 1918 *Novaya Zhizn'* noted with irritation that very many people, even those who did not agree with Bolshevism, were pleased with the way the Bolsheviks were 'gathering up the land of Russia', and compared Lenin with Ivan Kalita, unifying the disintegrated Russian state 'through an unflinching civil war'.[20] Socialist democrats of both the Marxist and the Narodnik tendencies were alienated and fragmented and, in general, could not constitute a serious political force in this backward country. The Social-Revolutionary Party existed, as a united party, only on paper. The Whites, despite their use of methods even harsher than those of the Bolsheviks, were unable to establish a unified political order even in the territories which they occupied.

The Bolsheviks and the Socialist Intelligentsia

The programme of eradicating barbarism by barbarous methods was objectively engendered by Russian conditions. But this programme concealed within itself an unresolved contradiction, for means always possess this dangerous property: that they may alter the end pursued. In their fight against barbarism by such methods the Bolshevik Party increasingly degenerated, and barbarism, Asiaticism and anti-democratism entered more and more into their ideology – into the consciousness of the mass of Party members, which grew in numbers but not always in moral stature. The Tenth Congress, by prohibiting factions in the Party, barred the last path to a democratic development of Bolshevism. The centralism of their organization, which gave the Bolsheviks cohesion, at the same time predetermined the decline in inner-Party freedom. Yet Asiaticism got its own back on them – not at once but only by degrees.

N. Sukhanov wrote that at first Bolshevik rule was 'a peculiar sort of democratic absolutism', but from the earliest days it was in danger of degenerating into bureaucratic absolutism.[21] In her book *The Origins of Totalitarianism* Hannah Arendt very aptly compared the Bolsheviks' rule in 1917 with enlightened absolutism.[22] Its principal task was to save civilization in Russia – although it must be remembered that in this respect railways were for Lenin much more valuable than spiritual culture, for understandable reasons. The original plan of the Russian Communists was – relying on the power of the working class – gradually to advance towards a new society: democratic, socialist and delivered from the hated Asiaticism. That might have happened, had there not been the civil war. In the words of Giuseppe Boffa, 'Lenin's calculation was, to win the majority by unreservedly accepting the most important and widespread demands of the people at the moment when the Party took power.'[23] But the new government was unable to avert the civil war, and events passed completely out of its control. The war compelled the Bolsheviks to take a number of measures which they thought would be only temporary but which soon were made permanent. Trotsky later recalled:

> Democracy had been narrowed in proportion as difficulties increased. In the beginning the Party had wished and hoped to preserve freedom of political struggle within the framework of the Soviets. The civil war introduced stern amendments into this calculation. The opposition parties were forbidden one after the other. This measure, obviously in conflict with the spirit of Soviet democracy, the leaders of Bolshevism regarded not as a principle but as an episodic act of self-defence.[24]

For Rosa Luxemburg the dictatorship of the proletariat ought to have manifested itself as a new '*manner of employing democracy*, not its *elimination*'.[25] Kautsky stressed that 'we cannot mean by the dictatorship of the proletariat anything other than its rule on the basis of democracy.'[26] These ideas corresponded fully to those of Marx and Engels. The latter declared that 'the specific form for the dictatorship of the proletariat' was 'a democratic republic'.[27] The Bolsheviks, while not repudiating democratic ideas in principle, saw the dictatorship of the proletariat differently: on the one hand they stressed its temporary and transitional character; on the other, they associated it with severe restrictions on democracy. 'In its essence', Trotsky wrote, 'the dictatorship of the proletariat is not an organization for the production of the culture of a new society, but a revolutionary and military system struggling for it.'[28] If victory for the revolution requires that the state become like an army in the field, there is no time for thoughts about freedom and democracy.

It was these anti-democratic measures, and not their revolutionary ideas, that caused the breach between the Bolsheviks and the intelligentsia. *Novaya Zhizn'* declared more than once that attempts to introduce socialism otherwise than by democratic means could only 'compromise the idea of socialism'.[29] The first clashes between the left-wing intelligentsia and the new rulers were over the question of press freedom. On 28 January 1918 a 'Revolutionary Press Tribunal' was established, with the task of dealing with 'crimes and misdemeanours against the people committed through use of the press'.[30] This tribunal was empowered to inflict very severe penalties. However, compared with present-day Soviet notions, what prevailed at the beginning of

1918 was absolute liberalism in censorship matters, for the creation of the tribunal assumed the existence of independent newspapers which would be subject to control, and the absence of preliminary censorship. Regulations for the press were also issued by the Soviets of different towns, and in most of this legislation such disorder reigned that it was impossible to ensure a consistent censorship policy. The activity of the newspapers was governed by a mass of rules and regulations, of which *Novaya Zhizn'* wrote that they were 'senseless and contradictory decisions which offered incredible scope for arbitrariness'.[31] Such gagging of the press, in the view of the intelligentsia, could only delay 'the triumph of radiant socialist ideals'.[32] But real suppression of press freedom was yet to come.

The first attempt to bring in preliminary censorship, in Moscow in winter 1917, miscarried. A decree establishing it was not put into practice and on 2 January 1918 the censorship was revoked. However, inroads to press freedom continued to be made, creating antagonism against the Bolsheviks among the democratic intelligentsia who had fought so long for this freedom. 'Truly, those whom the gods wish to punish they first make mad,' wrote the Mensheviks' paper. 'Bolshevism's worst enemy could not have done it more harm than is done by this wretched decree on censorship.'[33] Besides, the first attempt to impose a censorship was not the last, and all independent oppositional newspapers were eventually suppressed both in Soviet Russia and in the territories where the counter-revolution was victorious for a time. Independent 'thick journals' continued to appear until the mid–twenties, but that was no substitute for a free press.

The question arises: How was it possible for the Bolsheviks, who had themselves emerged from the Russian intelligentsia and the freedom movement, to renounce democratic liberties? Boris Souvarine, who knew Lenin personally, explains it by referring to 'cette aberration désastreuse, d'après laquelle est moral tout ce qui sert la révolution.'[34] In fact, the revolution had to some extent been transformed from a means to the conquest of freedom into an end in itself. This religious attitude to the revolution, of which Merezhkovsky and Berdyaev spoke, was developed by the Russian intelligentsia itself in the pre-revolutionary period, and Lenin's way of thinking undoubtedly embodied one aspect of the intelligentsia's mentality.

Despite later fantasies, none of the Bolsheviks was opposed in principle to pluralism and a multiparty democracy. When he became chairman of the Petrograd Soviet, Trotsky said: 'The hand of the Praesidium will never oppress the minority.'[35] Apparently he was sincere in saying this. At any rate – according to Sukhanov – three years later, in 1920, Trotsky, when reminded of this speech, exclaimed:

'What a happy time!'[36] The American historian Abraham Asher wrote that even as late as 1919 Kautsky, who knew the Bolshevik leaders well, spoke 'with remarkable naïveté' of their possible return 'to the path of democracy'.[37] One of the leading figures in the Bolshevik political police wrote, at about this same time, that arrested members of the left-wing parties 'must not be regarded as undergoing punishment but as temporarily isolated from society in the interests of the revolution. The conditions of their detention must not have a punitive character.'[38] Even W. Scharndorf, in his crudely anti-Bolshevik booklet, admits that in the early days the Party leaders were tormented 'by pangs of democratic conscience'.[39]

Reading the newspapers of those days, including the anti-Bolshevik ones, one observes at once that the suppression of opposition parties and the restriction of press freedom were unexpected not only by the Mensheviks and the democratic opposition but also by the Bolsheviks themselves. These measures had not been planned beforehand. It can be said, though, that they followed inevitably from the position of a minority party which had taken power in a period of revolutionary crisis. However, this is only part of the truth. Measures of this sort are often reversible. The Bolsheviks did nothing to ensure that their prohibitions remained merely 'temporary' and did not become permanent. Restriction of democracy had its limits, beyond which one must speak not of 'restriction' but of annihilation. With regret, it has to be said that the Bolsheviks went beyond those limits with amazing ease. It was this which predetermined their relations with the intelligentsia. Moreover, taking a long view, it was precisely these fatal mistakes in 1917–18 that marked the beginning of the bureaucratic degeneration of the revolutionary regime. The path of the revolutionary dictatorship was not doomed in advance to failure and, as Stephen Cohen has rightly observed, mass terror, the Stalinism of the thirties, was not 'the logical, irresistible outcome of the Bolshevik revolution',[40] but the possibility of such an outcome was great from the very beginning. The path Lenin had taken was extremely risky, and the mistakes of 1917–18 predetermined the subsequent fate of the revolution, marking the start of the bureaucratic degeneration. Rosa Luxemburg warned at that time:

Without general elections, without unrestricted freedom of press and assembly, without a free struggle of opinion, life dies out in every public institution, becomes a mere semblance of life, in which only the bureaucracy remains as the active element.[41]

The force of political inertia carried the Bolsheviks from restricting the freedom of the press to dispersing the Constituent Assembly, from that to suppression of the opposition, and from that to terror. And each of these measures, far from uniting the nation around the regime, engendered new enemies, so making necessary a fresh series of repressive measures.

The results of the civil war were tragic for the Russian intelligentsia. The suppression of bourgeois-democratic institutions dealt a heavy blow to its hopes for a new, free Russia. The conflict between Reds and Whites, the cruel terror on both sides, could not but evoke its protests. Part of the intelligentsia adhered to the Bolsheviks; many joined the Whites; the majority tried to find some third way. Characteristic of the feelings of that majority is the diary of V.G. Korolenko, which was published in the second number of *Pamyat'*. 'Utter brutalization,' he wrote. 'And each side denounces the other's atrocities. The Volunteer Army denounces the Bolsheviks, the Bolsheviks denounce the Volunteer Army. ... But brutality enters in everywhere.'[42] These words were written under Bolshevik rule; but then a few months later, after the arrival of the Whites, we find: 'Eager informers, often the same who previously cried: "There's a counter-revolutionary!", have now taken to crying: "There's a commissar!"'[43]

'Mutual brutality is increasing,' said Lenin's former intimate Martov, as he watched the raging of the White and Red terrors.[44]

> Under Nicholas Romanov it was sometimes possible, by pointing to the monstrous severity of a sentence, to prevent its execution and to wrest a victim from the hangman's grasp. Under Vladimir Ulyanov this is not possible.[45]

Violence engendered violence, bloodshed provoked bloodshed, and those who had raised the banner of Red terror would, Martov prophesied, sooner or later themselves perish:

> But we cannot wait for that moment. Already now the counter-revolution rules, under the protection of German bayonets, on the Don and in the Crimea, in the Ukraine and in the Baltic provinces. And to every volley of Bolshevik rifles fired *here* at the political opponents of the Soviet power we hear the answering tenfold echo *there* of other rifles, shooting down the local revolutionary workers and peasants.[46]

V.M. Doroshevich also noticed the striking similarity of the Red and White terrors:

> Just as, with the Reds, the word 'bourgeois' is applied to everyone who does not wear a Russian shirt, so, with the Whites, the word 'socialist' is applied to

everyone out of military uniform. Mensheviks and SRs [Socialist Revolutionaries] are 'second-grade Bolsheviks', and are shot.[47]

The Whites studied closely the methods of the Red terror, and the Bolsheviks had only to introduce some 'novelty' for the Whites to begin applying it, only on a larger scale – 'simply because the "Reds" do it'.[48]

Korolenko tried to stop the Red terror, as also did Kropotkin, who returned from abroad specifically for this purpose. The latter even met Lenin. Trying to persuade Lenin, he 'referred to the French Revolution, which was "killed", in his view, as a result, *inter alia*, of the policy of terror adopted as a weapon by the revolutionaries of 1793.'[49] Even earlier he had warned Lenin in a letter: 'The terror practised in the French Revolution held back its influence for fifty years.'[50] When he had heard and read all this, Lenin proposed the publication, 'at once and in the largest number of copies,'[51] of Kropotkin's book on the French Revolution, in which the writer's attitude to the terror is as indulgent as could be. Korolenko addressed letters to Lunacharsky with equal lack of success, reminding him that the advance to socialism must rely

> on the best side of human nature, presupposing courage in direct struggle and humanity shown even to opponents. Let cruelty and blind injustice remain wholly with the outlived past, not finding any place in the future. ....[52]

Martov, who was no less an intellectual than Korolenko and no less a revolutionary than Lenin, was utterly shaken by what had happened. He wrote of the 'vicious encroachment by Lenin and Trotsky' upon the principles of socialism and democracy[53] and of the impossibility for him, or for any who had fought in previous years against the autocracy, to accept such a revolution.[54] What had happened was for him above all a tragedy for the socialist movement. 'Shame on the party', he exclaimed, 'that tries to sanctify with the name "socialist" the vile work of the hangman.'[55]

In justifying the Red terror, the Bolsheviks – Trotsky, Lenin, and ex-Menshevik Larin – referred to the French Revolution. Martov reminded them of the sad end of the French revolutionaries to whose shades Larin appealed. After all it was the Jacobin terror, the execution of the deputies to the Convention, the disrespect shown to the people's will, that eventually led to the failure of the revolution and the establishment of the Thermidorian dictatorship. That same path, Martov foretold, would be trodden by the Bolsheviks who abandoned the principles of Marxism in favour of Jacobinism. They would share the fate of the French revolutionaries, for whoever is unable to learn from the past is fated to repeat it:

Had Danton and Robespierre lived to see that moment when, out of a series of 'surgical operations' performed on the Convention and later on the Legislative Assembly, Bonapartism emerged, they might perhaps have bequeathed the advice to Larin not to copy slavishly all the 'primitives' of previous revolutions.[56]

The dissolution of the Constituent Assembly, the terror and the introduction of the censorship were actions that the left-wing intelligentsia could not excuse *under any conditions*:

We may agree with Larin that every great political revolution has been accompanied by foul deeds, and by the flourishing of rascality in the camp of the victors. But Larin is cruelly mistaken if he thinks that, contrariwise, an abundance of foul deeds and a flourishing of rascality always proves that what it happening is a great revolution.[57]

Such warnings as these did not go unremarked, but they produced no results except an increasing hostility among the members of the ruling party towards Marxist criticism coming from the ranks of the socialist intelligentsia. Pokrovsky wrote with irritation that 'a "strictly Marxist" line leads straight into the swamp.'[58] Not only the activists of the opposition parties, who were subjected to 'temporary isolation', but also many critically minded people in the worlds of science and art fell victim to repression. Zhores Medvedev writes:

The larger part of senior research and academic personnel backed the anti-Bolshevik forces, and during the first waves of 'Red terror' 'professors' and 'academicians' were almost automatically considered to be enemies of Soviet power. A large number of scientists and technical experts were harassed, arrested, sentenced and even executed during the beginning of the civil war in 1918–1919.[59]

Among those executed was the outstanding poet N. Gumilev.[60] The gulf between the intelligentsia and the new government widened. 'For the revolution', writes Boffa, 'this was a difficulty, for the intelligentsia it was a tragedy.'[61]

Refusing to accept the revolution, which had betrayed their expectations, while still – as before – hating the reaction, members of the intelligentsia found themselves at a parting of the ways. Stankevich noted during the civil war, among the intelligentsia of Moscow, 'a fanatical hatred of the Bolsheviks' together with not the slightest sympathy with the Whites.[62] For him the choice was agonizingly hard. 'Where am I to go?' he pondered.

To Denikin, the representative of the military and national idea with which I worked all through the war, fighting along with most of my friends against the Bolsheviks, because they perverted the idea of revolution? ... Or, finally, to the Bolsheviks? After all, they are what is left of Russian freedom and revolution, I should have greater scope with them, and even among their military I should find men with whom I could deal with complete respect.[63]

In 1925 Bukharin admitted that 'in the initial period of the October Revolution it was the worst section of intelligentsia who came over to us,' whereas 'the majority of the honest intelligentsia were against us.'[64] To some extent Bukharin was exaggerating, for among those who supported the Bolsheviks were not only oddities and careerists but also some prominent and prestigious members of the intellectual elite. Nevertheless, only a few 'accepted' the revolution: Mayakovsky, Blok, Bely. The Bolsheviks were joined also by the 'extreme left' of the aesthetes, who were totally alien to their ideology but felt a psychological kinship with them. Thus, for example, the idealist philosopher Vyacheslav Ivanov wrote some super-revolutionary articles, hailing in what had happened the rebirth of *sobornost'* [sense of community] and denouncing his opponents for their lack of loyalty to 'the spirit of the present-day socialist movement'.[65] The decadent N. Evreinov actively organized triumphal performances in honour of the revolution, which was destined, according to Ivanov, to be the expression of 'the effective power of the artistically formulated masses'.[66] The Futurists also attached themselves to the Bolsheviks and enjoyed the protection of the authorities in the person of A.V. Lunacharsky (and some other leading figures). Futuristic designs were even offered for the emblem of the Russian Federation and, later, of the Soviet Union.[67] Only later did the rulers' sympathy with the aesthetic 'leftists' fade away, when the latter became very disappointed with the new order. This mood is expressed, perhaps, in Malevich's 'enigmatic' picture 'Black Square'.

Much has been written about Blok's support for Bolshevism, but it must be remembered that this support was of a rather peculiar kind. To begin with he was close to the Left SRs rather than to the Bolsheviks, and was even arrested after the Left SRs' revolt in July 1918. All his well-known articles about the revolution were printed by the Left SRs. That is not, however, the essential point. Blok considered, not without justification, that since all the previous activity of the intelligentsia had been directed towards preparing for the revolution, now, when the revolution had taken place, *intelligenty* had no right to disavow it, even if this revolution turned out to be not at all as they had expected. In fact, the idea of the coming revolution permeated Blok's poetry long before 1917. These vague expectations and hopes can be found even in the quite 'non-political' plays of Chekhov. Blok's idea was not without inner logic.

In his notes Gorky quotes, *inter alia*, this remark by Blok:

> Having invoked the spirit of destruction from the darkness, it is not honest for the intelligentsia to say: this was not done by us but by those people over there. Bolshevism is the unavoidable result of the work of the intelligentsia in various pulpits, in editors' offices, and in their 'underground' teachings.[68]

One ought probably to agree with Gorky, who shared this idea of Blok's, which he introduces with the words: 'he remarked very justly ...'.[69] The value of this note of Gorky's is especially great if we take into account the fact that he published it in Berlin in 1924, at a time when he had not yet become an obedient tool of the Soviet government. Berdyaev later voiced a similar idea when he wrote: 'The whole history of the Russian intelligentsia was a preparation for Communism.'[70]

It must be said that both the acceptance and the non-acceptance of the 1917 Revolution by the Russian intelligentsia had their tragic aspects, and Blok felt this keenly and gave it expression. The Bolshevik revolution was that social revolution of which they had dreamed, yet it had not brought the democracy for which they had hoped. The Soviet scholar V. Orlov, author of a very fashionable biography of Blok, writes that, with him, 'his faith in the future was at odds with his trust in the present.'[71] He blames the poet for this:

> His morbid feeling, that what was happening in the world and in Russia was a drop into a 'chink of history' (in other words, a gap in the historical process) indicated that his awareness of complete accord with the spirit of the times, without which, he held, a poet could not write, had become fatefully blunted.[72]

In reality it was Blok, perhaps more than anyone else, who felt the tragic character of what was happening around him. The failure of the revolution as a democratic revolution ominously foreboded its future failure as a social revolution. That was why Blok *could not write*. After 'The Twelve', indeed, the great poet wrote remarkably little. How few verses! To be sure, he wrote articles and gave lectures, but he almost completely stopped writing poetry. This tragedy of a great Russian poet expresses the tragedy of the Russian intelligentsia.

A search for a third way and neutrality in conditions of civil war can seldom be successful, in any case, if its implies some sort of active position. A substantial section of the neutral intelligentsia were obliged to emigrate. Among those who left Russia were the prominent scientists

I. Sikorsky, V. Korenchevsky, G. Kistyakovsky, P. Sorokin and V. Leont'ev, and such notable members of the creative intelligentsia as I. Bunin, I. Stravinsky, S. Rakhmaninov, A. Pavlov and F. Chaliapin. The ranks of the *émigrés* included also the 'proletarian writer' Maxim Gorky. Those who stayed in Russia were to a considerable extent demoralized.

The NEP Period

In the period of the New Economic Policy, in connection with the transition from 'war Communism' to a more moderate economic line, there was not only a quickening of economic activity in both the state and the private sectors and an improvement in living conditions, but also a certain revival of the Russian intelligentsia: a cultural upsurge. Nobody can deny that for Russian literature, painting, art criticism and spiritual life generally, the twenties were an extremely fruitful epoch. Under the NEP a neutral position towards Bolshevism and the revolution was quite tenable: it entailed no personal catastrophes or inevitable repressions, at any rate so long as only the sphere of culture and science was affected.

The first attempts to induce the intelligentsia to come over to the Bolsheviks had been made already during the war with the Whites. Zhores Medvedev writes:

> The real danger of the 'brain drain' as a result of civil war and emigration became all too apparent as soon as the Bolsheviks began to take measures to restore industry for military purposes in order to fight the dangerously prolonged civil war. Any large-scale war needs technological support, and civil wars are no exception. The change of attitude towards military and scientific experts became evident from the beginning of 1919 and particularly at the Eighth Congress of the Bolshevik Party.[73]

In this particular case the Bolsheviks were interested primarily in the scientific and technical intelligentsia, whose work began to be supported by the state:

> A historian of science might well be astonished by the number of new educational and research institutions created during the most dramatic period of the civil war when the very existence of the Soviet system was seriously at stake.[74]

The Bolsheviks were justly proud of the material support that they gave to the intelligentsia, despite the difficult conditions prevailing. 'A professor's ration', wrote Pokrovsky, 'was 136 per cent of that which a worker had to make do with without any supplements, and it was issued with "academic" regularity, more regularly than any others.'[75]

The Bolshevik Party's effort to preserve and restore modern civilization, to save it from perishing in Russia, the new rulers' relative tolerance in matters of artistic creation, the traditional links between the Bolsheviks and the old anti-monarchist movement (to which the left-wing Cadets belonged) and the *rapprochement* between the state and a section of the 'experts' could not fail to influence the main mass of the democratic intelligentsia, mitigating its oppositional attitude to the new regime. But the chief factor here was that the experience of the civil war proved once and for all that the Whites were *even worse than the Reds*. Compared with Denikin, Lenin clearly appeared as 'the lesser evil'. Furthermore, after the civil war a considerable part of the intelligentsia saw the Bolshevik Party as having been 'chosen' by the majority of the people. Stankevich, who was in the White camp during the conflict, wrote: 'This was not now a mere one-tenth of the nation, as at the beginning of the revolution, but the most numerous party, with the greatest influence among the masses. It was obviously stupid to wage armed struggle against this party.'[76] The very fact that Bolsheviks were now supported by substantial masses of the working people gave cause for hope that the regime would evolve towards democracy. If the government was a people's government, then sooner or later it would become a democratic government: the possibility that it might develop in the opposite direction was not given sufficient weight. If the people recognized the Bolsheviks as the lesser evil – and the peasantry, after some hesitation, supported the Reds against the Whites, at whose hands they suffered *even more* – then advanced members of the scientific and cultural communities thought it proper to follow their example. Science developed more or less freely. 'At this stage,' writes Zhores Medvedev, 'there was still nothing to suggest the future long isolation of Soviet science. All the tendencies were against it.'[77]

In those days, writes Loren R. Graham,

> almost no one thought seriously that the Communist Party's supervision of intellectuals would extend from the realm of political activity to that of scientific theory itself. Party leaders neither planned nor predicted that the Party would approve or support certain viewpoints internal to science; indeed, such endorsement was fundamentally opposed by all the important leaders of the Party.[78]

Zhores Medvedev even calls the years 1922 to 1928 'the golden years of Soviet science'.[79] (However, the 'hundred flowers' that bloomed in that period were soon 'uprooted' by the Stalinist bureaucracy.)

Culture, no less than science, became in the twenties a sort of politically neutral zone. This was not because it had no connection with politics – on the contrary, politicization of culture in the twenties went a long way – but because at that time in the cultural field it was not obligatory to take up a position on one side or the other of the barricades. Culture was a 'no-man's-land', not in the sense that 'no man' was there but simply that everyone could be there, and there was no 'boss'. A third way, though impossible in politics, was possible in spiritual life. Censorship existed but was still fairly liberal, so that a neutral position was permitted in *this* sphere.

Literary groups with different aesthetic and philosophical platforms began to appear. A definite quickening of social life undoubtedly occurred, and discussion was carried on pretty openly. Independent and semi-independent journals were published: *Mysl'*, *Ekonomist*, *Golos Minuvshego*, *Novaya Rossiya*, *Russky Sovremennik*, *Sovremennik*, *Byloe*, *Novaya Epokha*, *Vol'naya Zhizn'*, *Slovo Istiny*, *Vestnik Literatury* – and also almanacs: *Krug*, *Kovsh*, *Zhizn' Iskusstva*. The Petrograd philosophical journal *Mysl'* freely published the writings of idealists and positivists who made no pretence at all of loyalty to Marxism. 'Our journal', wrote the editorial board,

> will serve quite impartially all and every tendency in philosophy, provided only that in these tendencies there is a sense of living search for truth and living thought, not inert marking time in abandoned and outlived positions.[80]

No political restrictions were imposed. To be sure, *Mysl'* and *Ekonomist* were soon suppressed, but some of these journals survived right down to Stalin's victory and the complete crushing of every form of opposition. Symbolic, in a way, of the twenties were the journals and newspapers produced in the prisons. Numerous unreliable people continued to be held in custody, but they were still allowed freedom of speech and of the press. Journals appeared with expressive titles: *Mysl' za reshetkoi* [Thought Behind Bars] (Irkutsk), *Mysl' zaklyuchennogo* [Prisoners' Thought] (Vitebsk, Omsk and elsewhere), *Golos zaklyuchennogo* [The Prisoners' Voice] (Kharkov, Penza, and elsewhere), and others. Quite critical views were expressed in the pages of these journals (and where could the writers be sent for such views?).[81] All this compels most historians, even those with a very hostile attitude to the revolution, to write of the 'situation of relative freedom' that existed in Russia in the twenties.[82]

'After the revolutionary storm came a lull,' wrote I. Lezhnev in the independent journal *Novaya Rossiya*, the bloody fog of war and revolution lifted and went away. The face of the earth could be seen again, and we were at last given our first favourable opportunity to comprehend events in their true historical perspective.[83]

The new situation enabled one, as was thought at that time, 'to meditate calmly and historically upon what had happened, to clarify for oneself the lessons and indications of the revolution, and to draw from these appropriate conclusions.'[84]

Relations between the Bolsheviks and the intelligentsia were, as before, uneasy, but also extremely ambivalent and contradictory. They could be defined as 'conflict plus co-operation'. The new rulers strove to come to an understanding with members of the intelligentsia, to win their confidence, offering them the maximum of creative freedom within the limits of the revolutionary dictatorship. But their intention was itself contradictory, and it was quite natural that the *intelligenty* viewed the Bolsheviks with a distrust which was sometimes well founded.

It must be said that the attitude of the Bolsheviks themselves towards the Russian intelligentsia was sometimes condescending, sometimes contemptuous, sometimes condescending with a nuance of contempt. 'The Russian intelligentsia', wrote Meshcheryakov in 1922,

> did not love the autocracy. Before the 1905 Revolution they even hated it, and fought against it heroically, not sparing their lives. In this struggle they drew together with the proletariat. Along with this the intelligentsia acquired some elements of a socialist world-view. They wrote the word 'socialism' on their banner. But in the great majority of cases they intepreted 'socialism' purely in their own, 'intelligentsia' way. They dreamt of socialism as something very far away, and saw it as beautiful, dazzlingly white and pure, just as, from a distance, the snow-covered Alpine peaks seem virginally pure.[85]

All this evokes not the slightest sympathy so far as the Bolshevik Meshcheryakov is concerned: he is a man of practical action, with no time for sentiment. For him the intelligentsia is merely a variety of the petty bourgeoisie:

> They do not work for wages but independently of the entrepreneur, receiving payment for their labour either directly from the person they serve or from the capitalist to whom they sell not their labour-power but the finished results of their labour. This circumstance renders such strata of the intelligentsia close ... to the petty bourgeoisie.[86]

Consequently, they are drawn to socialism, not by class interests but by 'study or moral feeling'.[87] This last-mentioned fact not only fails to win

Meshcheryakov's approval, it even seems to him suspicious. For Pokrovsky the intelligentsia's sacrifices in the past inspire no respect: if it did not support the Party in 1917–18, it is nothing but a 'swamp' and there is nothing to respect it for.[88]

The Bolsheviks did not consider themselves native sons of the Russian intelligentsia. Revolutionary democracy had somehow been able to combine practical action with humanistic idealism.[89] True, this was difficult even then (we remember Dostoevsky's criticism of the Narodnik socialists) but nevertheless it was to a certain extent achieved. In general, combining humanistic idealism with *Realpolitik* is an extremely difficult task; although, perhaps, the future of mankind depends on the success of the attempt.

Be that as it may, we have seen that at the turn of the century the intelligentsia's loss of its special role as the political vanguard meant that the 'practical men', associated with the working class, became separated, in the main, from the 'humanists', and the political movement from the movement of ideas. Everything that followed seemed to confirm the rightness of the 'practicals'. Even then, however, the moral superiority of the 'idealists' remained indubitable – in their own eyes, at any rate. Subsequent experience showed that the Bolsheviks were wrong to disdain the warnings of the 'petty-bourgeois' humanists (among whom were such major Marxist theoreticians as Martov). But at the beginning of the twenties there were few who were able to conceive that after the revolution of 1917 there could come the terror of 1937. For most people, the bloody upheavals were all behind them and what lay ahead was a process of reaping the results thereof.

Lenin, Trotsky, Bukharin and the *Intelligenty*

In those years the Bolsheviks argued amongst themselves a lot about the intelligentsia. Some rejoiced that 'the Russian intelligentsia will rise no more. ... Its culture will not rise again. ... And within twenty or thirty years the tribe of *intelligenty* will have vanished from the surface of the Russian land.'[90] Others regretted the fate of the intelligentsia but declined to take responsibility for what had happened, saying that the breach between the intelligentsia and the revolution was due either to the former's petty-bourgeois nature or to a 'tragic misunderstanding'.[91] Lenin also often thought about this problem. Voytolovsky even claims that 'concern about the historical role of the Russian intelligentsia had for a long time given Lenin no rest.'[92] But Lenin was nevertheless unable to work out a unified conception of this role. 'We are startled by his sudden shifts from praise to blame,' admits Voytolovsky[93] when he summarizes a number of Lenin's statements on the subject. He explains this by Lenin's drawing a sharp line between the bourgeois and the socialist intelligentsia. That may be so, but it shows, then, that he, unlike younger Marxists – Martov and, later, Gramsci – did not perceive the intelligentsia as an integral entity, as an independent social stratum which, despite the complex and even motley nature of its composition, was able to elaborate a common 'intelligentsia' culture, ideology and psychology.

Among Lenin's comrades the one who took most interest in the problem of the intelligentsia was N.I. Bukharin. He returned to the theme on several occasions, recognizing that the Russian intelligentsia had 'experienced a very great tragedy',[94] but he was unable to determine the causes of this tragedy. He refused to blame his party in any way, not understanding where the essence of the tragedy lay. He saw this in a contradiction between the intelligentsia's integrity and love of the people on the one hand, and on the other their refusal to support the people's revolution. Treating the matter in this way meant that he had not grasped the most important thing. The Bolshevik revolution, which the *intelligenty* had done so much to prepare, trampled upon the very ideals that had led them to fight against Tsardom in the preceding decades. This was due, of course, not to any 'evil will' on the part of the Bolsheviks, who were themselves 'hostages of history', but to the objective conditions of the development of Russian society, conditions which in 1917 left no room for democratic decisions. What happened was therefore a tragedy, and one in which the fatal role was played by objective forces. That was something which Bukharin, still upwardly mobile after coming to power, did not yet understand. ...

No less contradictory was the Bolsheviks' attitude to culture. This, for example, was what Trotsky wrote on this subject in 1924:

> All this brings to my mind a worker of the name of Vorontsov who just after October was detailed to guard Lenin's person and to help him. As we were preparing to evacuate Petrograd, Vorontsov said to me gravely: 'If it so happens that *they* take Petrograd, *they* might find quite a lot that's useful. ... We should put dynamite under the whole city and blow it all up.' 'Wouldn't you regret Petrograd, Comrade Vorontsov?' I asked, admiring his boldness. 'What is there to be regretted? When we are back, we shall build something much better.' I have not invented that brief dialogue, nor have I stylized it. Such as it was, it remained engraved on my memory. That was the correct attitude towards culture.[95]

What startles us here is not what the Petrograd worker said, but Trotsky's delight at it.

It is difficult, of course, to require of the people who are creating their destiny through revolution that they show concern for objects the meaning, importance and beauty of which their former masters did not trouble to explain to them,

wrote *Novaya Zhizn'* in 1918. 'But we not only can, we must require this of the people's leaders, of the worker and peasant intelligentsia, of the government organizations and institutions.'[96] In reality, however, Trotsky's remark was typical of the intelligentsia. None other than the singer of 'the Beautiful Lady', Alexander Blok, issued this appeal in the revolutionary years:

Do not be afraid of the destruction of the Kremlin, of palaces, pictures and books. They should have been preserved for the people: but, in losing them, the people have not lost everything. A palace which has been destroyed is not a palace. A Kremlin which has been wiped off the face of the earth is not the Kremlin.[97]

This nihilism was part of a peculiarly 'intelligentsia' social idealism, carried to extremes, which enabled a Europeanized *intelligent* to *like* the way the peasants, out of ignorance, destroyed buildings which later they themselves, perhaps, would regret having destroyed. For Blok and Trotsky the act of destruction was itself transformed into an aesthetically creative act. However, no actual palace was being demolished, no actual book burnt. They conceived destruction very abstractly and speculatively, as the pure *idea* of 'creative' destruction rather than as practical activity.[98]

Obviously the ideologues of Bolshevism, who were themselves *intelligenty*, rejected the value of the culture of the past not out of ignorance but because they regarded themselves as the bearers of more important values. When reproached for not wanting Shakespeare or Molière, they protested: 'But how can you put it like that? Shakespeare and Molière fulfilled their historical mission, and now they are of interest to the proletariat mainly from the historical standpoint.'[99] We shall see later that Lenin – probably the first to do this among the party theoreticians – began to concern himself with the ideological rehabilitation of culture: at first, to be sure, in its role as a social instrument.

The final *débâcle* of the intelligentsia and the impoverishment of spiritual culture threatened to destroy the foundations of Russian civilization, and it was precisely these foundations that Lenin and his comrades were striving, above all, to preserve and defend. Accordingly, Lenin, Trotsky and Bukharin barred the way before their left-radical colleagues who tried to finish off the Russian intelligentsia so as to have a clear space on which to erect a 'proletarian culture'. Lenin categorically opposed those efforts, saying:

> we hear people dilating at too great length and too flippantly on 'proletarian' culture. For a start, we should be satisfied with real bourgeois culture; for a start, we should be glad to dispense with the cruder types of pre-bourgeois culture, i.e., bureaucratic culture or serf culture, etc.[100]

After all, Lenin observed, 'At a time when we hold forth on proletarian culture and the relation in which it stands to bourgeois culture, facts and figures reveal that we are in a very bad way even as far as bourgeois culture is concerned.'[101] Trotsky spoke out no less resolutely:

> There can be no question of the creation of a new culture, that is, of construction on a large historic scale during the period of dictatorship. The cultural reconstruction which will begin when the need of the iron clutch of a dictatorship unparalleled in history will have disappeared will not have a class character. This seems to lead to the conclusion that there is no proletarian culture and that there never will be any, and in fact there is no reason to regret this. The proletariat acquired power for the purpose of doing away for ever with class culture and to make way for human culture.[102]

In another place this same Trotsky – who, not long before, was ready to love those who would have blown up Petrograd – said that 'the development of art is the highest test of the viability and significance of every epoch.'[103] Trotsky's line was that writers who accepted the revolution should be allowed 'complete freedom in the sphere of artistic self-determination'.[104] Later on he was very proud of that phrase, uttered at a time when he was in power, evidently considering it important as a refutation of the view that he began to defend freedom only after he found himself in opposition.[105] And in fact, despite his sometimes 'appalling' statements, Trotsky remained one of the defenders of maximum toleration in the sphere of literature and an opponent of vulgar-sociological methods in the theory of art. His views, however, were far from being fully shared by Bukharin, who supported the idea of 'proletarian culture'. As for Zinoviev and Stalin, they thought in altogether different categories. Joel Carmichael writes: 'In cultural life, too, Trotsky was without a faction! He was simply the spokesman, once again, for abstract ideas, in a situation where such ideas had found no embodiments.'[106] This generalization, like most of Carmichael's generalizations, is quite incorrect. The line advocated by Trotsky was supported by Lenin and for a certain period continued to be official Party policy in the cultural sphere, but within the Party opposing tendencies were already gathering strength.

The liberal Bukharin wrote: 'We need to have the cadres of the intelligentsia trained ideologically in a definite way. Yes, we must turn out intellectuals mechanically, produce them just like in a factory.'[107] According to him, what the Party needed was not an independent group of creators of cultural values but disciplined intellectual functionaries, transmitters of state policy, without any personal initiative. True, in those same years Bukharin spoke in defence of freedom of artistic creativity, but these contradictions merely show his inability to grasp the problem of individual freedom and spiritual independence as a whole.[108] Some Bolsheviks came out with anti-individualist statements that were a great deal sharper. 'For us the individual personality is merely that apparatus through which history acts,' we read in the works of Pokrovsky. 'Perhaps these apparatuses will one day be created artificially, just as we now make electric accumulators artificially.'[109] This prospect reminds one forcibly of the gloomy picture given in Aldous Huxley's anti-utopia *Brave New World.* Familiarity with this sort of statement evidently inspired Zamyatin's melancholy jests of a few years later:

I do not know how many decades it will take, but some day the first pages of all the newspapers will be filled with reports on the international Geneva conference on problems of state anthropoculture: just as now one argues about the calibre of instruments, so in the future one will argue about the calibre of mothers and fathers permitted to bring children into the world. Having organized the material basis of life, the state must inevitably concern itself with problems of eugenics, the perfection of the human race. ...[110]

However,

the trouble is that with the use of the machine one can very easily manufacture as many Oedipuses, as much raw material for tragedy, as he likes, but for the manufacture of rare, complex apparatuses, capable of processing this material and its would-be Shakespeares, the machine civilization does not suffice.[111]

The contradictions between the above-quoted statements by prominent Bolsheviks – Trotsky, Pokrovsky, Bukharin – are not accidental. They reflect the contradictoriness of the Bolsheviks' actual attitude to culture (and also to democracy, individual freedom, and so on). On the one hand, culture (like democracy) was recognized as a very important, fundamental social value; while on the other the very logic of the class struggle made it permissible for the sake of future democracy, future culture, future freedom, to destroy the elements of culture or democracy that actually exist today. Regarding these contradictions in the ideas of Trotsky or Lenin one can, of course, moralize and engage in talk about 'doublethink' and so on. But that would be to contradict Russian history itself. We should not launch into reflections on whether the Bolsheviks were right or wrong, concretely, in this or that action, but observe that the choice before them was not easy. In any case the Russian Communists, who considered civilization and education to be very important preconditions for socialism, had need of an intelligentsia.

On the one hand attempts were made to start a dialogue with the old intelligentsia, while on the other they quickly began to create a new one. In 1925 there were more students in the USSR than in 1914 – 167,000 as against 112,000.[112] The revolution had opened wide access to cultural activity for the children of the workers and for members of the national minorities. The relative freedom of the press and a certain degree of trade-unions independence give grounds for Giuseppe Boffa's description of the NEP period as a time when 'germs of pluralism' appeared.[113] There was not only a revival of spiritual life in the country after the bloody nightmare of the civil war, but a new upsurge. The elements of civil society were taking shape in Russia, and the sphere in which the greatest individual and social freedom prevailed was that of culture.

Smena Vekh

In the 1920s there appeared among the *intelligenty* who were co-operating with the new rulers a special ideology of their own: 'left-wing Smenovekhism'. The authors of the symposium *Smena Vekh*, published in Prague, criticized the pre-revolutionary publication *Vekhi*. One of them, Yu. Potekhin, declared that if members of the intelligentsia were guilty before Russia it was not for 'their excessive revolutionariness' but on the contrary for 'their inability to accept the great Russian Revolution in the popular forms which were alone available to it.'[114]

Although the symposium *Smena Vekh*, which gave a name to a whole tendency (or, more precisely, to two tendencies at once), was published abroad, it very quickly became well known to the public in Russia. 'Smenovekhist ideas were popular among the intelligentsia and military men who were obliged to serve under the Bolsheviks,' writes Agursky in his work on 'national Bolshevism'.

Already at the very outset of the revolution they needed an ideology to justify this service. The appearance of *Smena Vekh* proved to be a powerful catalyst in the relations of this group with the Soviet power. ... the journal

Smena Vekh and the newspaper *Nakanune* were freely sold in Russia, and sold well. Soviet sources which have no interest in overstating the influence of Smenovekhism provide us with the following facts. Out of 230 engineers who were questioned in 1922, 110 held Smenovekhist views – which does not mean that the remaining 120 did not share those same views, merely that 110 persons considered it necessary to announce the fact.[115]

Smenovekhism, moreover, received official encouragement. *Pravda* wrote that the Smenovekhists retained their old prejudices, but 'life teaches, and they are capable pupils. The logic of life will compel them to advance farther and farther along the road of *rapprochement* with the revolution.'[116] The new tendency received all the more support from the Bolsheviks, writes Boffa, because 'in the frightful isolation of 1921 the declaration of the *Smena Vekh* group had to be welcomed as a positive fact.'[117] Consequently the Bolsheviks recognized at once that the symposium published in Prague was 'a major event not only in literature but in life itself'.[118]

The ideas of the *Smena Vekh* group were somewhat heterogeneous, having in common only the principle of collaboration with the Soviet power for the good of Russia. However, they were sharply split into a left and a right wing, though neither Agursky nor Soviet scholars show the true significance of this split. The ideas of the left-wing Smenovekhists are summarized clearly enough by Trotsky. They understood that

> Russia's salvation lies in the Soviet power, that, in present historical conditions, no power but the Soviet power is capable of preserving the unity and independence of the Russian people against aggression from without.[119]

Without the Bolsheviks Russia would simply have ceased to exist as a unified state in 1917 or 1918.

The right-wing Smenovekhists reasoned a little differently, for *their* aim was to transform the Bolshevik dictatorship into a nationalist one. It is clear that while for former 'White' ideologues and monarchists *Smena Vekh* was closely linked with their hope for a nationalistic degeneration of the Soviet power (a hope which was to some extent fulfilled), for many liberal *intelligenty* Smenovekhism was above all an appeal for collaboration with the Bolsheviks on a national – that is, non-party – basis. In his study Agursky pays insufficient attention to this contradiction between the 'ideologues' and the 'masses' of the intelligentsia, the dual nature of Smenovekhism (which also explains why Trotsky's support for *Smena Vekh* in 1921 mystifies him). In this matter, strange as it may seem, the semi-official publicist Kuvakin turns out to be somewhat more profound than Agursky when he notes that the doctrine proclaimed by the ideologues of right-wing Smenovekhism – Ustryalov and others – coincided with in many ways, but in many other ways differed from, the new tendencies 'which were noticed among the broad "lower" groups of the intelligentsia who ensured a degree of popularity for Smenovekhism at the beginning of the 1920s.'[120] However, Agursky shows us something which Kuvakin does not wish so much as to mention: that while left-wing Smenovekhist ideas were taken up by certain strata, right-wing Smenovekhism, with its aggressive nationalism, evidently influenced the views of Stalin and the Party bureaucracy which followed him. To each his own. ...

Pokrovsky pointed to the many-sidedness of *Smena Vekh* immediately after the symposium appeared: 'their psychology is more or less the same, but there are several ideologies among them.'[121] Willingness to collaborate with the Bolsheviks united them, but their aim and ideals differed. Isai Lezhnev, who was then one of the leaders of the left-wing Smenovekhists inside Russia, wrote frankly that *Smena Vekh* was trying to reconcile and unite positions that were 'diametrically opposed to each other not only in ideas but even in their basic feeling'.[122] Undoubtedly the left Smenovekhists also hoped to see the Soviet power evolve, but they, unlike the rights, believed that this evolution would run in the direction of a gradual democratization, and certainly not towards a nationalistic Thermidorian dictatorship. These ideas of the left Smenovekhists were not at all to the liking of Zinoviev, who organized a persecution of Lezhnev's *Novaya Rossiya*, trying to get it suppressed, but was unable to succeed in this owing to Lenin's opposition. As a result, the publication was renamed and restarted in Moscow. Nevertheless, despite even the indirect support given to Lezhnev's tendency by Lenin and Trotsky, the democratic hopes of *Novaya Rossiya* could not fail to irritate many activists who spoke in the Party's name. N. Meshcheryakov, comparing the right-wing Smenovekhists of the Ustryalov type and the left-wingers of *Novaya Rossiya*, wrote that the former no longer believed in the 'fetish' of democratic liberties, whereas the latter were 'full of yearning for those constitutional liberties',[123] for which Meshcheryakov, of course, sharply rebuked them, presenting Ustryalov as the example to be followed. Ustryalov was, indeed, a nationalist – that was his shortcoming – but as Meshcheryakov put it, 'shortcomings have their merits', and this nationalism of his was not so bad if his desire for Russia to be a great power 'helps him to abandon the camp of counter-revolution'.[124]

The left-wing Smenovekhists often emphasized that their support for the Bolshevik government ought not to involve a loss of independence. Lezhnev wrote:

> Collaboration with the Soviet power has already ceased to be a watchword. For a long time now it has been a reality for the whole of Russia's intelligentsia. But collaboration does not mean absorption.[125]

They protested when the official press, 'in the style of a sort of comical caricature', depicted them as 'repentant' whiners who had at last understood the truth of Bolshevism. No, their attitude had resulted 'from thinking about the general ideological collapse – which was general, that is, without any exception.'[126] The intelligentsia might still have a lot to teach the Bolsheviks. They protested also against being identified with the nationalism of the right-wing Smenovekhists. Essentially, *Novaya Rossiya* sought to find a third way between nationalism and Communism, proclaiming the slogan: 'Neither Third Rome nor Third International'.[127] Such efforts were very fruitful on the theoretical plane. Thus long before Brzezinski there was formulated in the pages of *Novaya Rossiya*, in broad terms, a particular 'theory of convergence' which contemplated an inevitable *rapprochement* between capitalism and Communism: 'As a result we shall get neither Communism nor a revival of the old (capitalist) type of industry, but a completely new economic formula.'[128] Their principal interests, however, lay in the political field.

'The swords of the revolution,' wrote Lezhnev, 'before being beaten into ploughshares, are being transformed into the blades of a guillotine. And the guillotine, like any other machine, is subject to the law of inertia.'[129] According to Lezhnev, however, the frightfulness of the terror had been left behind. The Bolshevik regime was moving towards liberalization – the New Economic Policy and the cessation of the Red terror proved that this was so – and what was now necessary was to halt the momentum of the civil war. They believed in gradual democratization, in the quickening of free discussion in the Soviets:

> The local Soviets will become municipal organs, the All-Union Central Executive Committee will turn into a Parliament, the trade unions will be transformed from general compulsory schools of Communism to voluntary associations of workers and the whole state apparatus, right up to the Council of People's Commissars, will be emancipated from the Party.[130]

One cannot say that such a development of events was impossible in principle, but by 1922 it was already improbable. The dominant tendency was towards bureaucratization, not democratization.

The New Bureaucracy

During the civil war a new stratum emerged on the social scene and immediately asserted its rights. This was the Party and state bureaucracy. The early attempts to create a democratic organization of authority in the localities and free elections to Party organs failed to 'take' under war conditions. Moshe Lewin writes:

> The constantly alarming nature of the situation and the extension of the state of emergency required a constant mobilization of the cadres, their transfer from one front to another, or from a military task to an economic one and vice versa. No democratic procedure would have made these solutions possible, but only authoritarian ones: orders, appointments and dismissals made them possible. These methods, which were sanctioned in no way either by theory or by statute, but which had been practised for three years, became a reality of Party life.[131]

As early as 1919 the Bolshevik leaders felt that the development of a bureaucratic dictatorship in the period of war Communism constituted a menace to the fundamental aims of the revolution, but the changes made were by that time irreversible. Democratic life had died in the soviets and the omnipotent bureaucracy, in complete fulfilment of Rosa Luxemburg's prophecy, had taken possession of all real power – if not in Moscow, at least in the provinces. 'The Soviet bureaucracy in the localities', wrote Martov, 'simply ignores the "liberal" instructions received from above.'[132] Thus in 1919 the central leadership was unable to implement its important decision to bring the Mensheviks back into the Soviets. Lenin came up against bureaucratic sabotage which he had no means of combating.

After the civil war ended, bureaucratization not only did not decrease – on the contrary, it was intensified. NEP was not only a period of economic and cultural liberalism, it was also a period of intensified Party dictatorship. Cohen writes:

> At the same time that the Party-State began relinquishing its control over much of the country's economic life, it moved to solidify its political monopoly. Dangers inherent in the economic concessions were to be counterbalanced by political safeguards.[133]

Whereas during the civil war, despite all the restrictions, the Mensheviks and some small opposition parties still enjoyed some opportunities for legal – or semi-legal – activity, in 1921–22 they were completely suppressed. Lenin and his comrades considered that if they allowed a degree of freedom to alien class elements in the spheres of economics and culture, they must at the same time restrict still further the political freedom of these elements – otherwise, after gaining strength, they would overthrow the Bolsheviks, and that would mean another civil war and a real catastrophe for Russia.

Clearly, this meant restrictions on freedom for the proletariat as well. The Bolsheviks did not take into account the indivisibility of democratic principles, the fact that *one cannot restrict the political freedom of one class of society without at the same time restricting that of the others.* However, the workers were in no position to protest. Although some small proletarian groups such as 'Rabochaya Pravda' did appear at the beginning of the 1920s, they played no role in politics. The Bolsheviks themselves acknowledged that 'our working class has been atomized'[134] and called for measures to combat this situation, but the political steps proposed were hardly such as to bring about a real consolidation of the proletariat. A. Voronsky, for example, speaking of the need to combat 'the weariness and apathy of the worker masses', considered that what was necessary for this purpose was, first and foremost, to shut for good and all the mouths of the Menshevik comrades who were declaiming in favour of freedom of the press, and so on. If the workers put political demands to the Bolsheviks, he argued, this was due to 'apathy' (!), but if they obediently trudged along whithersoever the Party ordered, without asking any questions, that signified that their 'spiritual impoverishment' had been 'overcome'. Here everything is stood on its head, yet Voronsky himself reproaches the Mensheviks for setting everything 'topsy-turvy'.[135]

At first Lenin underestimated the fact that in crushing the freedom of those enemies of the proletariat who had already been vanquished he was at the same time strengthening a new and more dangerous enemy – the bureaucracy. As a result the Bolsheviks, who had regarded themselves as the party of the proletariat, very soon found themselves hostages in the hands of alien social forces. Lenin soon frankly recognized this when he spoke of the relations between the Bolsheviks and 'the bureaucratic heap': 'I doubt very much whether it can truthfully be said that the Communists are directing that heap. To tell the truth, they are not directing, they are being directed.'[136] As he admitted, the number of bureaucrats not only did not decrease after several 'cuts' (!) but even increased. And it was not only a question of numbers.

From the time when Stalin came, first *de facto* and then formally, to head the Party's bureaucratic apparatus, the new officialdom was transformed into an *independent* social and political force. This development was more or less logical. Gramsci wrote later:

The prevalence of bureaucratic centralism in the state indicates that the leading group is saturated, that it is turning into a narrow clique which tends to perpetuate its selfish privileges by controlling or even by stifling the birth of oppositional forces – even if these forces are homogeneous with the fundamental dominant interests. ...[137]

The contradictions in the revolutionary government became more and more acute. 'The Party-State apparatus,' writes Carmichael,

rapidly solidifying in Stalin's embrace, was creating its own momentum: this fundamental process no doubt underlay a poignant metaphor coined by Lenin at the Eleventh Party Congress in 1922 – the strange feeling he had at the helm of the Soviet government like that that of a driver who suddenly notices that his 'machine has got out of control' ... Lenin was doubtless preoccupied by 'bureaucratism' toward the end of his short life.[138]

Not long before his death, Trotsky recalls, Lenin 'was systematically preparing to deliver ... a crushing blow at Stalin as personifying bureaucracy, the mutual shielding among officials, arbitrary rule and general rudeness.'[139] It was Stalin whom Lenin saw, not without justification, as the embodiment of all these 'qualities'.

Lenin's criticism of bureaucracy has armed later generations of anti-Stalinist Communists with a number of important ideas, but first of all we need to mention the important defects in his approach to the problem. Moshe Lewin writes:

The continual increase in the number of civil servants and in their hold on the life of the country was facilitated by a conjunction of factors inherent in a backward country that had a real need for new administrative bodies and additional administrators, if it was to develop the economy along planned, centralist lines. But this meant – and Lenin did not realize it – that the bureaucracy would become the true social basis of power. There is no such thing as 'pure' political power, devoid of any social foundation. A regime must find some other social basis than the apparatus of repression itself. The 'void' in which the Soviet regime had seemed to be suspended had soon been filled, even if the Bolsheviks had not seen it, or did not wish to see it.[140]

The new bureaucracy was created out of various elements. It included both former officials and Communist workers, but the majority of its members came from the petty bourgeoisie. 'The demobilization of the Red Army of five million played no small role in the formation of the bureaucracy,' wrote Trotsky later.

The victorious commanders assumed leading posts in the local Soviets, in economy, in education, and they persistently introduced everywhere that regime which had ensured success in the civil war. Thus on all sides the masses were pushed away gradually from actual participation in the leadership of the country.[141]

The same process went on inside the Party as well. In 1923 Trotsky wrote:

> However exaggerated were the forms it sometimes assumed, the bureaucratism of the war period was only child's play in comparison with present-day bureaucratism which grew up in peacetime, while the apparatus, in spite of the ideological growth of the party, continued obstinately to think and decide for the Party.[142]

Although Lenin wrote and spoke a good deal about bureaucratization, only Bukharin raised openly the question of the threatening degeneration of the revolutionary government:

> The working class is not homogeneous in its composition, in the level of culture, political maturity, technical skill and so on of its members, its component parts. Consequently, it cannot rule, either in political life or – what interests us here – in economic life, as a 'Novgorod Veche' with millions of hands: inevitably, it rules through its *vanguard*, through its *administrative cadre*, through its leaders.[143]

Consequently, the working class has to be subordinated to the apparatus. This is necessary, but not without its dangers. 'If', writes Stephen Cohen,

> during the transition period, a slowly maturing but largely undeveloped proletariat remained politically, culturally and administratively subordinate to a host of higher authorities, then the danger of a perversion of the socialist ideal was very great.[144]

Bukharin emphasizes that this does not necessarily lead to the restoration of capitalism. He frankly fears that under these conditions 'a new ruling class' and a new form of exploitation may emerge, based not upon private but on state property. This honest self-warning, however, constituted only part of Bukharin's theory. While his general hypothesis was to some extent confirmed by history, his concrete analysis proved quite erroneous.

In the first place Bukharin, in the manner typical of the Bolsheviks, 'absolutizes' the Russian situation of his own time. The backwardness of Russia's working class – its inability, after the revolution, to create an independent democratic organization in the sphere of production – seems to him a law of universal history. If that were so, the danger he mentions would be absolutely insuperable and socialist revolution would be pointless. Experience has shown, however, that in industrially developed countries the workers are capable of creating their own non-Party organizations, that they are fully capable of democratic participation in the management of production, and so on. Bukharin could not know, of course, about workers' self-management in present-day Yugoslavia or about Poland's 'Solidarity', but in Turin as early as 1920 Italian workers had created their factory committees, which functioned much more effectively than the corresponding Russian organizations of 1917.

Bukharin, while not doubting the need for the working class to be completely subject to the government apparatus and the Party 'vanguard', rests his hope entirely on the culture which later on, many years after the victory of the revolution, will enable the workers to 'mature' into independent activity. Cultural development is indeed, as we shall see later, one of the most important preconditions for a democratic organization of society, but it is only a precondition. Nobody can learn to swim without jumping into the water, nor can any people become 'mature' enough for democracy otherwise than by establishing democracy among themselves, nor can workers be prepared to participate in management except by beginning to participate in it. In general, culture is not some sort of 'condition' which one has to attain, but a historical process: 'developed' culture of the masses is possible only as *both* a precondition *and* a consequence of democracy. And at the same time, as Marcuse wrote, without democracy 'the revolution is bound to reproduce the very antagonisms which it strives to overcome.'[145]

Another – and no less dangerous – mistake made by Bukharin sadly confirms Lenin's opinion of him: that 'he has never made a study of dialectics and, I think, never fully understood it.'[146] Bukharin sees the danger to the revolution's future not in the Party bureaucracy but in the old intelligentsia, especially the technical intelligentsia. He thinks that the enlistment of intellectual forces educated in capitalist society is 'quite inevitable and historically necessary', but that it is 'fraught with very great danger'. It is from the direction of the intelligentsia that the threat of 'degeneration of the proletarian state and the proletarian party, comes.'[147] He writes:

> We must not forget that the intellectual forces which are obliged to work with the proletariat, and even those among them who work conscientiously, bringing essential benefits, nevertheless represent (here I stress: at a particular phase of development) the experience of the *old* culture. ... For them socialism is not the regulating principle of their work.

And finally, while recognizing the danger that even that section of the administrative cadre which is drawn from the working class may become separated from the masses, he sees this as happening only under the influence of their colleagues from the old intelligentsia.[148] Only through the fault of intellectuals of the old type can the apparatus degenerate 'into the embryo of a new ruling class.'[149] This way of presenting the problem actually prepared the ideological and psychological arguments for Stalin's subsequent massacres of the old intelligentsia and the Party's old guard, including Bukharin himself: for he, after all, embodied ('at a particular phase of development', of course) 'the experience of the old culture'. It was precisely the inability of the Bolshevik theoreticians to counterpose, against advancing Stalinism, a consistent programme based on a critical analysis of the experience of the revolution that rendered them quite helpless before the bureaucracy. Those who, in 1921, could not break out of the theoretical dead end were in 1937 thrust against the wall for execution. Both Lenin and, later, Trotsky also saw one of the principal causes of the increasing bureaucratization in the low cultural level of the masses. Although one cannot refrain from pointing to the defects in Lenin's analysis of 'the bureaucratic phenomenon', it does call for special attention because it constitutes the point of departure from which any analysis of present-day Soviet society must begin.

'Our state apparatus is so deplorable, not to say wretched,' wrote Lenin in his last article,

> that we must first think very carefully how to combat its defects, bearing in mind that these defects are rooted *in the past, which, although it has been overthrown, has not been overcome*, has not reached the stage of a culture that has receded into the distant past. I say culture deliberately, because *in these matters we can only regard as achieved what has become part and parcel of our culture, of our social life, our habits*. We must say that the good in our social system has not been properly studied, understood and taken to heart; it has been hastily grasped at; it has not been verified, or tested, corroborated by experience, and not made durable, etc. Of course, it could not be otherwise in a revolutionary epoch, when development proceeded at such breakneck speed that in a matter of five years we passed from Tsarism to the Soviet system. [emphasis added][149]

We can follow the motif as it is repeated from one of Lenin's writings to another. Bureaucracy is the fundamental danger, and the principal antidote to it is culture. Lenin argues roughly like this: Why are the workers and peasants in a dependent position in the first workers' and peasants' state? Why is even the ruling party under the control of a bureaucratic apparatus? First and foremost because the proletariat needs this apparatus; cannot get by without it. The workers and the Communists cannot solve their own problems by themselves, because they lack the necessary level of consciousness. Therefore they put themselves in a position of dependence on the bureaucrats.

In themselves the bureaucrats are by no means bearers of high culture: 'Their culture is miserable, insignificant, but it is still at a higher level than ours.'[150] In more civilized countries there are traditions of independent thought, self-government and democracy. Even when the economic base for workers' democracy has been undermined by ruin or war, these traditions go on existing in people's heads. That enables democracy to 'hold out' for a certain time and – relying on culture, tradition and so on – to restore its own economic basis. In Russia there is neither economic basis nor culture. Consequently the political power of the Bolsheviks must be used to develop both, in rapid tempo. Culture is the most decisive link. To raise it is the hardest task. Without that, the task of economic construction will be very difficult to accomplish. Finally, the cultural level must be raised as quickly as possible, so as to counteract bureaucratization.

In his day Marx, looking at the problem of bureaucracy, warned: 'In the case of an irrational people one cannot speak at all of a rational organization of the state.'[151] But what does one have to do in order that the people may become 'rational', in Marx's broad sense of the concept? 'Widely disseminated education and training of the people', said Lenin, 'is a decisive factor for overcoming and eradicating bureaucracy.'[152] One can repeat the objection that 'education', by itself, is not enough – that what is needed is democratic organization, or at least some developed elements thereof – that culture alone will not solve the problem. Yet Lenin understood very well the actual historical logic which is revealed with particular clarity in the history of Russia: that the only rational basis for bureaucracy lies in the inadequacy of culture. *Culture and bureaucracy are incompatible. They are antipodes. A fight against bureaucracy therefore cannot but be a fight for culture.*

What did Lenin mean by culture? We have to remember that he did not draw a sharp distinction between civilization and culture, and this somewhat confused his thinking. First and foremost, naturally, the people had to be taught to read and write. But that was a precondition for culture rather than culture itself. For Lenin the main thing was, evidently, the culture of thought. The workers and peasants had to be taught to think for themselves. Art, political education, self-teaching – all these means were good, provided they led to this result. But the need to raise the level of culture presupposed a bearer of this culture, on whom the state would have to rely. The bureaucrat was not fit for this role because he had a vested interest in *not* letting the masses attain to culture in Lenin's sense – to the culture of independent thinking. This meant that one was left with the intelligentsia. On its members one had to count for the fulfilment of this task. But Lenin did not draw that conclusion. He was simply unable to, because he died before he had managed finally to decide what course to follow or what action to undertake. Lenin lost the power of speech in the very heat of his struggle against Stalin and the Party bureaucracy. In the last eleven months of his life he was unable to write a single line. His last articles represent only a beginning – the preparation for a great work, both theoretical and practical, which he could not carry out.

Notes

1. *Novaya Zhizn'*, 25 October (7 November) 1917.
2. Ibid., 26 October (8 November) 1917.
3. Ibid., 28 October (10 November) 1917. It is amusing that the expression 'anti-socialist activity', which Soviet propaganda employed in relation to the 'Solidarity' movement of 1980–81 in Poland, was first employed by the Mensheviks to describe the policy of the Bolsheviks in 1917–18.
4. Saint-Just, *Discours et rapports*, Paris 1957, p. 145.
5. An expression of Rosa Luxemburg's.
6. *Severnaya Kommuna*, 58, 14 March 1919. In the *Collected Works* this passage is truncated. [The omitted passage follows the sentence in vol. 29, p. 21, which ends 'and regulate them in proper time' – *trans*.] On the distortion of quotations from Lenin in present-day Soviet publications, see R.A. Medvedev, *Let History Judge*, 1971, p. 45.
7. M.A. Waters, ed., *Rosa Luxemburg Speaks*, New York 1970, p. 368.
8. *Novaya Zhizn'*, 29 October (11 November) 1917.
9. Ibid., 25 April (8 May) 1918.
10. M. Gorky, *Untimely Thoughts*, New York 1968, p. 106. See *Novaya Zhizn'*, 10 (23) December 1917.
11. Ibid.
12. Lenin, *Collected Works*, 4th edn, English version, vol. 24, p. 418.
13. Lenin, *Collected Works*, vol. 33, p. 478.
14. Ibid.
15. Ibid., vol. 27, p. 342; cf. vol. 25, pp. 357–9.
16. His dispute with Bukharin is interesting in this connection. See *XI s'ezd RKP (B)*, *Stenograficheskii Otchet*, Moscow 1961, pp. 139–41; also *Krasnaya Nov'*, 1925, no. 4, p. 265; and Stephen Cohen, *Bukharin*, 1974, p. 134 ff.
17. Lenin, *Collected Works*, vol. 27, p. 342.
18. N. Berdyaev, *The Russian Idea*, 1947, p. 15.
19. Lenin, *Collected Works*, vol. 27, p. 340.
20. *Novaya Zhizn'*, 26 January (8 February) 1918.
21. Ibid., 5 (18) April 1918.
22. Hannah Arendt, *The Origins of Totalitarianism*, 1958.
23. G. Boffa, *Storia dell' Unione Sovietica*, Milan 1976, vol. 1, p. 57.
24. Trotsky, *The Revolution Betrayed*, New York 1945, p. 96.
25. *Rosa Luxemburg Speaks*, p. 394.
26. K. Kautsky, *Demokratie oder Diktatur*, Berlin 1920, p. 38.
27. Engels, 'Contribution to the Critique of the Social-Democratic Programme of 1891 (The Erfurt Programme)', in Marx, *Critique of the Gotha Programme*, Moscow n.d. p. 58.

28. Trotsky, *Literature and Revolution*, New York 1957, p. 190.
29. *Novaya Zhizn'*, 26 (13) March 1918.
30. *V.I. Lenin i V Ch K. Sbornik dokumentov (1917–1922gg.)*, Moscow 1975, p. 53.
31. *Novaya Zhizn'*, 20 (7) February 1918.
32. Ibid., 2 March (17 February) 1918.
33. *Vpered!*, no. 257, 20 December 1917.
34. Boris Souvarine, *Autour du Congrès de Tours*, Paris 1981, p. 13.
35. Joel Carmichael, *Trotsky*, 1975, p. 182.
36. Ibid., p. 183.
37. Abraham Asher, *Pavel Axelrod and the Development of Menshevism*, Cambridge Mass. 1972, p. 355.
38. R.A. Medvedev, *Let History Judge*, 1971, p. 274 (quoted from M.Ya. Latsis (Sudrabs), 'Chrezvychaynye Komissii po bor'be s Kontrevolyutsiei', Moscow 1921).
39. W. Scharndorf, *Istoriya KPSS*, Moscow 1962.
40. Cohen, pp. xvi–xvii.
41. *Rosa Luxemburg Speaks*, p. 91.
42. *Pamyat'*, no. 3, Paris 1979, p. 388.
43. Ibid., p. 395.
44. L. Martov, *Doloi smertnuyu kazn'!*, Moscow 1918, p. 8.
45. Ibid., p. 7.
46. Ibid., p. 12.
47. *Novaya Rossiya*, 1922, no. 1, p. 75.
48. E.V. Starostin, 'K istorii izdaniya knigi', in P.A. Kropotkin, *Velikaya Frantsuzskaya Revolyutsiya*, Moscow 1979, p. 500.
50. Ibid.
51. Ibid.
52. V. Korolenko, *Pis'ma Lunacharskomy*, Paris 1922, p. 16.
53. *Vpered!*, 13 (26) December 1917.
54. When we discuss the Red terror we are dealing with one of the principal points of dispute between socialists and Communists. 'Humane' revolutions which sought to avoid bloodshed – and especially acts of repression – were crushed by counter-revolutionaries. 'Harsh' revolutions which did not shrink from bloodshed and terror, from open political dictatorship, degenerated and were crushed by Thermidorians. The Paris Commune was put down. 'Popular Unity' in Chile was put down but Bolshevik Russia degenerated, as also did Castro's Cuba. The Communards and Allende were killed by reactionaries, while Bukharin, Trotsky and the old Bolsheviks were killed by the punitive organs they themselves had created. This is really a 'sore subject'. In my view, however, Martov and Allende were right, not Lenin. A revolution that falls under the blows of reaction remains at the very least a moral victory and a new generation retains belief in its ideas, readiness 'to begin again from the beginning', 'to try once more'. Degeneration of a revolution inspires aversion and demoralizes the working people. The death of Allende was glorious; the death of Bukharin shameful. But real history is not reducible to the hard choice, 'either-or'. If that were so, all revolutions in the world would have ended with counter-revolution or Thermidor. But it is not so. The real problem is to find a 'middle way' or, more precisely, a democratic way – a path leading to the new society whereon the Lefts can be both politically strong and morally pure: to ensure the stability of the revolutionary government under conditions of class struggle without restricting democracy and resorting to terror. The humanization of society can be achieved by humanistic means alone, but these means must be effective. What the new society will be like depends on the means we employ in fighting for it, but this question can be answered only in practice. Where and when? Will the Nicaraguan revolution prove an example of such an answer? We shall see. As for theory, the problems of revolution are studied very seriously in the works of Fernando Claudín and of our own G. Vodolazov. In *The Dialectics of Hope* I have tried to touch on some of these problems, in the chapters entitled 'The Tragedy of Bolshevism' and 'Elements of Hope'.
55. Martov, *Doloi smertmuyu kazn'!*, p. 9.
56. *Vpered!*, 13 (26) December 1917 (in I. Getzler, *Martov*, 1967, p. 173).

57. Ibid.
58. *Intelligentsiya i revolyutsiya*, Moscow 1922, p. 75.
59. Zhores Medvedev, *Soviet Science*, 1978, p. 6.
60. Lists of those executed were at that time published in the newspapers. See, for example, *Petrogradskaya Pravda*, no. 181, 1 September 1921.
61. Boffa, vol. 1, p. 281.
62. V.B. Stankevich, *Vospominaniya 1914–1919*, Berlin 1920, pp. 344–5.
63. Ibid., pp. 351–2.
64. *Pechat' i revolyutsiya*, 1925, no. 3, p. 3.
65. Preface by V. Ivanov, p. xii, to Romain Rolland, *Narodny teatr*, TEO Narkomprosa, Petrograd and Moscow 1919.
66. *Vestnik teatra* no. 62, 1920, p. 5.
67. See V.S. Drachuk. *Rasskazyvaet geral'dika*, Moscow 1977, p. 226, plate XXXI, design no. 5; also p. 231, plate XXXIV, design no. 1; and the less extravagant project on p. 231, design no. 2, which, however, gave rise to certain 'suspicions' with regard to Futurism.
68. M. Gorky, *Fragments from my Diary*, 1924, p. 216.
69. Ibid.
70. N. Berdyaev, *The Origin of Russian Communism*, 1937, p. 145.
71. Vl. Orlov, *Hamayun: The Life of Alexander Blok*, Moscow 1980, p. 459.
72. Ibid., p. 459. [The English version abridges the original, in which Orlov writes of the poet having 'met the revolution with such spiritual courage and civic dignity' – *Trans.*]
73. Zh. Medvedev, p. 9.
74. Ibid., p. 10.
75. *Intelligentsiya i revolyutsiya*, p. 73.
76. Stankevich, p. 291.
77. Zh. Medvedev, p. 17.
78. Loren R. Graham, *Science and Philosophy in the Soviet Union*, 1973, p. 10.
79. Zh. Medvedev, p. 13.
80. *Mysl'*, no. 1, 1922, p. 3.
81. A review of prison periodicals was included in the first issue of the historical miscellany *Pamyat'*.
82. See Agursky, *Ideologiya natsional-bol'shevizma*, Paris 1980, p. 104.
83. *Novaya Rossiya*, no. 1, 1922, p. 63.
84. Ibid., p. 57.
85. *Intelligentsiya i revolyutsiya*, p. 51.
86. Ibid., p. 90.
87. Ibid., p. 92.
88. Ibid., p. 80.
89. Idealism here, of course, means idealism in the moral, not the philosophical sense.
90. M. Levidov, 'Organizovannoe uproshchenie kul'tury', *Krasnaya Nov!*, no. 1, January–February 1923, pp. 311, 318.
91. P. Kogan, 'Russkaya literatura v gody Oktyabr'skoy revolyutsii', *Krasnaya Nov'*, no. 3, 1921, p. 239.
92. L. Voytolovsky, 'Lenin ob intelligentsii', *Pechat' i revolyutsiya*, Book 2, 1925, p. 1.
93. Ibid.
94. N.I. Bukharin, 'Sud'by', in ibid., Book 3, p. 8.
95. *Pravda*, 7 October 1924. (Trotsky, *On Lenin*, 1971, p. 176. In the *Pravda* version, instead of 'admiring his boldness', Trotsky says: 'for I was fond of this "Piter" proletarian.').
96. *Novaya Zhizn'*, 19 (6) February 1918.
97. A. Blok, *Sobr.soch.*, Moscow and Leningrad 1962, vol. 6, p. 16. [He goes on to explain that the Kremlin, etc., continue to live 'in our hearts and minds'. – *Trans.*]
98. Just like the French 'new lefts' who called for the *Mona Lisa* to be set fire to, while doing nothing to put that idea into practice. What mattered was the 'renunciation', not any concrete deed.

99. *Sovremennik*, no. 2, 1923, p. 89.

100. Lenin, *Collected Works*, vol. 33, p. 487.

101. Ibid., p. 462.

102. Trotsky, *Literature and Revolution*, pp. 185–6.

103. Trotsky, *The Revolution Betrayed*, p. 179.

104. Ibid., p. 181 (in the 1924 preface to *Literature and Revolution*, p. 14: 'complete freedom of self-determination in the field of art'. Originally published in *Krasnaya Nov'*, no. 7, 1923, p. 274).

105. Trotsky, *The Revolution Betrayed*.

106. Carmichael, p. 322.

107. Bukharin, 'Sud'by', p. 6.

108. I must observe here that in my opinion the 'Bukharinism' and the 'Trotskyism' of the 1920s were alike both preparations for Stalinism and alternatives to it, and consequently are full of inner contradictions. Bukharin and Trotsky put forward many ideas which Stalin took into his armoury, while at the same time also advancing a number of anti-Stalinist ideas. See *The Dialectics of Hope*, Part I.

109. *Pod znamenem marksizma*, no. 2, 1924, p. 63.

110. *Russian Literature Triquarterly*, Fall 1973, p. 433 (English trans. p. 438), 'Evgeny Zamyatin's "The Future of the Theatre".'

111. Ibid., p. 432 (English trans. p. 437).

112. *Istoria SSSR s drevneishikh vremen do nashikh dnei*, Moscow 1968, vol. 8, p. 276.

113. Boffa, pp. 289–91.

114. *Smena Vekh*, Prague 1921, p. 170.

115. Agursky, pp. 103–4.

116. *Pravda*, 14 October 1921.

117. Boffa, p. 283.

118. *Intelligentsiya i revolyutsiya*, p. 117.

119. *Pravda*, 27 October 1921. (Trotsky, *How The Revolution Armed*, 1981, vol. 4, pp. 43–44. [The last words of the quotation – *i chto nuzhno ei pomoch'* – do not appear in the book version – *Trans.*] In connection with Trotsky's attitude to *Smena Vekh*, see Agursky, pp. 159–161. It can be objected here that Trotsky is speaking of the Smenovekhovtsy generally, but undoubtedly his interpretation of *Smena Vekh* is closer to the left wing of the movement.

120. Kuvakin, *Religioznaya filosofiya v Rossii: Nachalo XX veka*, Moscow 1980, p. 121.

121. *Intelligentsiya i revolyutsii*, p. 80.

122. *Novaya Rossiya*, no. 1, 1922, p. 63.

123. *Krasnaya Nov'*, no. 1, 1922, p. 339.

124. *Intelligentsiya i revolyutsii*, p. 115.

125. *Novaya Rossiya*, no. 1, 1922, p. 65.

126. Ibid., p. 3.

127. Ibid., p. 13.

128. Ibid., p. 7.

129. Ibid., p. 64.

130. *Novaya Rossiya*, no. 2, 1922, p. 71.

131. M. Lewin, *Lenin's Last Struggle*, 1969, p. 13.

132. *Mysl'* (Kharkov), no. 1–2, 1919, p. 13.

133. Cohen, p. 125.

134. *Intelligentsiya i revolyutsiya*, p. 153.

135. Ibid., p. 154.

136. Lenin, *Collected Works*, vol. 33, p. 288.

137. *Selections from the Prison Notebooks of Antonio Gramsci*, ed. Q. Hoare and G. Nowell Smith, 1971, p. 189.

138. Carmichael, pp. 274–5.

139. Trotsky, *My Life*, Universal Library, New York 1960, pp. 480–81.

140. Lewin, p. 124.

141. Trotsky, *The Revolution Betrayed*, pp. 89–90.
142. Trotsky, *The New Course*, 1956, p. 16 (*Pravda*, 29 December 1923).
143. *Pod znamenem marksizma*, no. 7–8, 1922, p. 65.
144. Cohen, p. 142.
145. H. Marcuse, *Soviet Marxism*, New York 1958, p. 98.
146. Lenin, *Collected Works*, vol. 36, p. 595.
147. *Pod znamenem marksizma*, no. 7–8, 1922, p. 79.
148. Ibid., pp. 80–81.
149. Lenin, *Collected Works*, vol. 33, p. 488.
150. Ibid., p. 288.
151. Marx and Engels, *Collected Works*, vol. 3, 1975, p. 58.
152. Klaus Zetkin, *My Recollections of Lenin*, Moscow 1956, p. 22.

3

The Bureaucratic Labyrinths, or The Rules of the Game

After Lenin's death the Party bureaucracy, dealing blow upon blow at the Communist opposition, gradually seized more and more power. A period began, in Trotsky's words, 'of the intense but still silent stifling and routing of the Bolshevik Party',[1] a period which ended, however, in noisy show trials and mass repression of Communists. Trotsky called what happened 'the Soviet Thermidor', meaning a regime which was both the heir born of the revolution and also its gravedigger, its strangler. From the historico-cultural standpoint this was how barbarism, Asiatic despotism, got its own back on the Western political tradition in Russia – 'the Eighteenth Brumaire of Ivan the Terrible'.[2]

The dictatorship of Stalin and his successors, wrote Pomper, 'perpetuated the very evils that the intelligentsia had struggled against so desperately in the nineteenth century.'[3] A time came for the arts 'when singers were killed and song was put away in museums.'[4] Paradoxically, the Russian Revolution proved the accuracy of the prophecies of classical Marxism. When he watched the first steps being taken by the revolutionary movement in Russia, Engels expressed serious fears as to the consequences that might follow an attempt at socialist transformation in a backward peasant country which retained features of 'Oriental despotism'. From this revolution, carried out

> by a small revolutionary minority there follows the necessity of a dictatorship after the successful outcome of the revolt – a dictatorship, of course, not of the whole revolutionary class ... but of the small group of persons who carried out the revolution and who themselves ... are already subject to the dictatorship of one or a few persons.[5]

Earlier still he had said that a revolutionary class which is obliged to take power prematurely, when the economic conditions are not yet ripe, does not liberate itself but merely creates the conditions for rule by some other class, even though the leaders of the revolutionary class sincerely believe the contrary.[6] Later, Plekhanov reiterated that 'the Russian socialist party merely provides a fresh historical example to confirm the idea expressed by Engels ...',[7] and that its victory would result in a 'political monstrosity similar to the ancient Chinese or Peruvian empire, that is, to a renewal of Tsarist despotism in communist dress.'[8]

The Statocracy

The revolutionary dictatorship was replaced by a new system which was qualitatively different. This could hardly be called socialism, despite its pretensions, for it did not grant elementary rights to the working people.

When Stalin announced in 1936 that socialism had been built in the USSR, he referred to the fact that in our country there were no longer any bourgeois, landlords or kuląks. The groundlessness of such an argument is obvious. As Wolfgang Leonhard later pointed out, the fact that the old exploiting classes have been destroyed testifies to the appearance of a post-capitalist or non-capitalist society, but certainly not necessarily to the victory of socialism.[9] In a subsequent period the nature of the official argument changed somewhat, and today the ruling ideologists speak of the building in the USSR of 'developed socialism', referring mainly to the predominance of state property in the country's economy.

For state property to be really 'property of the whole people' it is not enough to write fine words in a constitution. What is needed is democratic social control over the means of production and the public administration, with wide participation by the masses in the discussion and implementing of decisions. This, in turn, is not possible without definite democratic institutions of people's power, both indirect (Parliament, a multiparty system, a free press, free elections) and direct (a system of participation by trade unions in the application of economic-administrative decisions, local and economic self-government, and so on). Marxists always distinguished between socialization (real collectivization) of the means of production and their formal nationalization. 'The basic criterion of socialization of the means of production, therefore, in our understanding,' writes the eminent Marxist economist Wlodzimierz Brus, 'is the criterion of democratism.'[10] This is why 'there can be no victorious socialism that does not practise full democracy.'[11] How 'full' present-day 'Soviet democracy' is can best be judged by the fighters for civil rights who are now behind bars. It is a pity that we cannot ascertain the opinion of the twenty million Soviet people who were tortured by Stalin. ...

Some democratic and socialist institutions do exist in the USSR, but only formally: they do not work! One can point to this unquestionable fact, if to nothing else: that in the entire history of the USSR there has never been a single referendum or testing of the views of the nation as a whole concerning political problems. Consequently, talk by official ideologists about 'full democracy', and still more about 'developed', 'mature' and 'victorious' socialism in the USSR appears rather comical.[12]

The new order established by the Stalinist bureaucracy is often called – not without reason – an 'industrialized Asiatic mode of production', or a 'statocracy'. Here once more, as in ancient Asia, the state appears as the organizer of production and supreme property-owner, but it is now faced with new tasks. The attitude of the ideologists of the Stalinist bureaucracy to the concept of the Asiatic mode of production obliquely confirms the correctness of this analogy. In 1930–31 this theory of Marx's was subjected to systematic criticism, although Marx's name was not mentioned, and eventually it was condemned and 'cancelled'. 'The simplest explanation for this', writes the Italian scholar Gianni Sofri,

> would refer to the climate of dogmatism which existed in the Soviet Union in those years, but that answer is inadequate, for all that it explains is how the ground for such an event was prepared – no more than that. In reality, the Asiatic mode of production was once more the subject of a sharp and serious political discussion. ...
>
> In the first place one must not underestimate the fact that the 'Asiatic' interpretation of Russian history could be very well applied to the forms that Soviet power had gradually begun to assume after Lenin's death. The idea of a new Leviathan-state and a new caste of bureaucrats was, as has already been mentioned, a central feature of the criticism which various oppositional groups, and especially the Trotskyists, directed against Stalin and the Party apparatus. This criticism was, naturally, engendered by reflection upon the everyday development of the Party and the Soviet state, but it was highly reminiscent of what Marx and Engels had written about Asia. That the opposition might make use of those ideas was more than obvious.[13]

In *The Revolution Betrayed* Trotsky came to the conclusion that in the twentieth century there could be no capitalist road to overcoming a country's backwardness.[14] One should probably qualify this statement to read that it is impossible for a capitalist country to overcome its backwardness if its relies on its own internal forces alone. Otherwise, perhaps, by importing capital, rapid growth can be ensured, but as a result the country concerned will fall into a state of extreme economic dependence (as we see from the cases of South Korea, Brazil, Taiwan and other countries of the 'Third World'). Concentration of the means of production in the hands of a despotic state makes it possible to achieve relatively rapid industrial and scientific technological growth (at least in the period which might be called that of primary growth, until the centralized bureaucratic organization comes into contradiction with the new productive forces which it has created). Statocratic society has some of the outward signs of socialism and also of State capitalism, but in reality it is a quite distinct system of relations. Society is here divided into two basic groups – the 'collective producer' (the proletariat: workers, engineers, scientists and scholars, and all the exploited working people) and the 'collective exploiter', the statocracy. In addition there are intermediate middle strata whose position is extremely contradictory.

The statocracy was studied by Trotsky, Deutscher, Djilas and, in his own way, by Orwell, as well as by many others.[15] Berdyaev was one of the first to write that 'the new Soviet bureaucracy is more powerful than that of the Tsarist regime. It is a new privileged class which can exploit the masses pitilessly.'[16] The difficulty in the position of Marxist critics of 'the new class' lies, however, in the fact that this qualitatively new phenomenon cannot be adequately described by using the categories of the capitalist mode of production. For example, the problem arises as to whether, in this case, political power results from economic power or vice versa. Djilas inclined towards the latter view, thereby casting doubt on the validity of Marx's main idea that politics is the concentrated expression of economics. The Eurocommunists – Johnstone, Elleinstein, and others – are in general disposed to treat economics and politics quite separately.[17] In fact, as more recent studies have shown, the question has been posed quite wrongly, through analogy with capitalism. In statocratic society economic and political power are simply identical. The one cannot give rise to the other, for the one already is the other. Power exists here only as complete political and economic power, and can exist in no other form.

There are a number of theories current in the West which see the statocracy as a sort of administrative bourgeoisie.[18] This view seems to me to be mistaken in principle, because the historical specificity of the bureaucratic 'estate' is not taken into account in the given case. According to Andras Hegedüs, himself a former Stalinist bureaucrat, bureaucracy has always appeared and developed where the formal property-owner was no longer able to perform directly the management functions which derived from the fact of his ownership, and he was thus forced to share his power with a hierarchically and professionally organized social group qualified to perform these tasks. This group became, however, not only the executor of specific management functions but simultaneously acquired specific interests of its own.[19]

In 1917 the workers became, formally, the collective owners of Russia's industry but could not manage this industry directly and were obliged, under pressure from the Bolshevik Party, to yield part of their 'proprietorial rights' to a bureaucracy. Brus has specially studied this phenomenon in his book. He notes that the bureaucracy is parasitic upon the gap between formal nationalization and real socialization, appropriating for itself *some* of the rights and privileges of the owner. Here, however, we find a vital difference between the bureaucracy and the bourgeoisie. The bourgeoisie can appropriate and control the use of the surplus product, because it is the formal owner of the means of production. The statocracy (in the narrower sense, the bureaucracy[20]) can control and partly appropriate the surplus product of labour precisely because it is *not* the formal owner thereof. Hence the inability of a statocracy to become a hereditary class, its need to reinforce itself by co-optation of new members, and so on.

Another specific feature of the bureaucracy – in contrast to a bourgeoisie of any sort – is that its organization is based almost exclusively upon vertical ties: that it is hierarchical. Hence its specific mentality, in which 'not only is prestige aligned with the hierarchical order, but so too is knowledge. The higher one stands in the hierarchy, the more one knows, or at least ought to know.'[21] In the last analysis, as Marx wrote, it all comes down to the notion that the officials possess '*superior* knowledge'.[22] This makes bureaucratic organization unified, discipline, stable – and ineffective. Unlike the bourgeois, or even the bourgeois administrator in the Western sense, the statocrat is not an independent economic and political subject. As for the top leadership, which possesses '*superior* knowledge', it receives only such information as is supplied by its subordinates, and they *unconsciously and involuntarily* manipulate their own leaders.

For many Marxists the awkward problem is that of property. As Cohen writes, 'the narrow association of class dominance with legal ownership of property would later hamper the critiques of anti-Stalinist Communists for decades.'[23] Djilas and the Leningrad Marxists V. Ronkin and S. Khakhaev arrived at about the same time at the conclusion which had already been drawn in Orwell's *Animal Farm* and *Nineteen Eighty-Four*: that the bureaucracy is the collective owner of the instruments and means of production. Similarly, Voslensky says that 'socialist property is the collective property of the *nomenklatura*.' The *nomenklatura* (Voslensky uses here the name by which the top section of the statocracy call themselves) 'holds all the means of production of the society at its proprietorial discretion. Under real socialism the *nomenklatura* is the collective employer.'[24] This statement is highly abstract and imprecise, because it is a judgement formed by analogy. Here, once more, capitalism remains the only pattern of an exploitative social formation. Paradoxically enough, however, under statocracy property appears in the form of state power (and vice versa), losing independent existence. It was Trotsky, perhaps, who offered the most interesting formulation: 'The means of production belong to the state. But the state, so to speak, "belongs" to the bureaucracy.'[25] This situation does not seem so very peculiar if we remember the role played by the state and its property-ownership in the countries of Asia and in pre-revolutionary – especially pre-Petrine – Russia. The property-owner is the state, but the state is inseparable from the ruling class. If Louis XIV could say 'L'Etat, c'est moi', in the USSR the ruling statocracy can say, with equal justification, 'The state is us'.

Marx never gave a definition of class, and Lenin by no means always reduced his concept of class to the question of property-ownership. Classes, he wrote, are distinguished 'by their position in the social structure of production', and are distinguished in such a way 'that one group can appropriate the labour of another.'[26] So broad a definition makes it possible to raise the question whether the statocracy is a 'new class' in the USSR. But we need to bear in mind that, as a whole, the classical Marxist concept of class, elaborated on the basis of material from nineteenth-century Britain and France,[27] is in need of serious re-examination if we want to apply it to present-day society, whether Soviet or Western. Property-ownership is a key category only under capitalist conditions (under neocapitalism its role is markedly reduced, even though not to the extent supposed by supporters of Galbraith or right-wing Social Democrats); in other formations it loses its significance, becoming a formal or even fictitious concept. The concept of property-ownership can be applied to early feudal Europe, to the India of the Great Mogul or to present-day Afghanistan only conditionally, by analogy with capitalism. In the USSR property-ownership cannot be treated as a class category and attempts to define the 'new class' through property-ownership are fruitless. The categories of 'classical Marxism' cannot be applied mechanically to the USSR, as Voslensky has done. From this it is not to be concluded that such categories as class, property-ownership, and so on are false 'in general', but they have to be made more precise in relation to concrete reality.

Many Western Marxists speak of the statocracy as 'a class of a new type', and even 'a political class of a new type'.[28] Many Soviet sociologists consider it problematic whether the concept of property-ownership can be applied at all to Soviet society. A similar idea was expressed by Rakovski when he pointed out the 'ownership functions are distributed between the various parts of the administrative apparatus and are, at the same time, impossibly intertwined with their non-ownership functions: for example, the tasks of ensuring political stability and macroeconomic balances.'[29]

A more general Marxist category is that of 'the surplus product'. Production of a surplus product and its appropriation by the employer, whether capitalist or state, is a necessary condition for exploitation. At the same time, production of surplus-value is in itself a necessary feature of any profitable economic process. Under socialism the surplus product must actually be put at the disposal and under the control of society as a whole – the collective producer. Thereby surplus-value would become, essentially, an alienated portion of necessary value.[30] Since surplus-value *is* extracted in the USSR – as *all* economists have acknowledged since Stalin's death – but there is no social control over its utilization, the statocracy is able to appropriate the labour of others, using this to satisfy its own collective and individual requirements.

It can do this, however, only because it is inseparable from the state: its structure is the structure of the state apparatus and it has no 'class structure' of its own. Marc Rakovski has written: 'In Soviet type societies, none of the social classes is in a position to organize itself, not even the ruling class, although this does not mean to say that this does not have a greater cohesion than the class it rules over.'[31] M. Cheshkov, a Soviet Marxist who has studied the economics of developing countries, the general problems of overcoming backwardness, the structure of state proprietorship and cognate problems, has defined this peculiarity of the statocracy by means of the concept 'state-class'.[32] In so far as the statocracy as a whole is markedly different from the ruling classes known to European history, Cheshkov rightly says that it would be more exact to speak not of a 'new class' but of 'a community of the class type'.[33] Important characteristics of a class are not visible here, and from the formal standpoint the Soviet *nomenklatura*-bureaucracy is an *estate* rather than a class. In this respect we observe a similarity between it and the old Russian nobility, which also replenished itself to a large extent – unlike its Western counterparts – not so much through heredity as by co-option (when he attained a certain position in the state apparatus, a man became a nobleman for life). One could call the statocracy 'a class in itself' but never 'a class for itself'. Its interests cannot be directly expressed. Its position as heir of the revolution provides it with ideological advantages, making it more attractive to the masses inside and outside the country, but this position is not such that it can pursue its group and class interests *to the end.* Consequently, the term 'new class' can be employed here only with serious reservations.

The statocracy exploits the working people in quite a different way from the bourgeois, being itself, outwardly, just another group of wage-workers. The outward appearance is, of course, deceptive. 'The contradictions between its class nature and its immanent social funct-ions constitute the fundamental contradiction of the statocracy', writes Cheshkov.

> By virtue of the indicated social function of the statocracy it seems that it, the collective ruler, is at the same time a particular variety of the collective worker. What is illusory is not the social functions performed by the statocracy, but the interpreting of these functions without regard to the class nature of the statocracy.[34]

As a result, it often seems to the statocracy itself that it is indeed the bearer of socialism and Communism, but that does not prevent it from using exclusive shops and living at the expense of the exploited workers. To the country's leaders it seems that they act on behalf of society, but this is nothing but an illusion. Voslensky wrote:

> In the Soviet system the members of the Politburo and the secretariat of the Central Committee of the CPSU are not independent rulers, but only representatives of the ruling class, the political bureaucracy known as the *nomenklatura.* ... The USSR's policy expresses the interests and ideas of this class, and that is what makes it consistent and transparent, despite all attempts to turn everything into a secret.[35]

The privileges of the statocracy have not risen out of nothing. They are engendered by the actual situation of the 'class-state' in the social division of labour, in the economic system as a whole.

What is characteristic of the statocratic upper circles is, to use G. Lisichkin's expression, 'payment in accordance with the office held', and not in accordance with work done or with the value of labour-power.[36] 'The distribution and redistribution of the surplus product', wrote Cheshkov,

> is effected in such a way that part of the statocrats' income (in particular, of state revenue) takes the form of collective income, and part of it the form of individual income; including that which takes the form, on the one hand, of expenditure on collective needs and, on the other, of expenditure on individual needs (in the form of salaries and wages). These forms, which arise

not in the process of the creation of the statocrats' income but in that of its distribution, make it appear that the statocracy, with the individuals who compose it, is a variety of the collective producer. This appearance is reinforced by the fact that individuals' unearned income takes the same form here as earned income, although wages are, in essence, no longer the price of the commodity labour-power, but an income. In statocratic society wage–labour relations appear to be universal, applying both to the producers and to the exploiters.[37]

From this ensue some important peculiarities of the society in question. Let us begin with the fact that the ruling class entertains an extraordinary number of illusions about itself owing to the contradictoriness of its position, as mentioned earlier. These class illusions are no less real than class interests, but they can lead the class in a quite different direction. The consequence is that we can speak of an extraordinary 'ideologization' of society which penetrates into every sphere of social activity, including culture.

The main characteristic of this ideology,[38] as Charles Bettelheim and Bernard Chavance rightly observe in their study of Stalinism, is 'fetishism of the state, in which the latter appears as a "supernatural force".'[39] Analogous to this is 'fetishism of the Party', expressed in the celebrated formula 'the Party is always right.' One of the first to put into ideological circulation this notion of the Party's infallibility – absolutely alien to Lenin – was Trotsky (incidentally, when he had already been ousted from power). 'I know', he said, 'that one cannot be right against the Party. One can be right only with and through the Party, for there is no other way of realizing history's task.'[40]

The ruling statocracy tries to impose these illusions upon society, and does this not least by means of art. The ideologization of consciousness means that the governing circles look on all forms of intellectual activity, in the last analysis, as varieties of propaganda. Naturally, members of the *nomenklatura* can see art in no other way than as one form of ideological agitation. They impose this role upon it by every means available. 'But art as a political force is art only in so far as it preserves the images of liberation,' wrote Marcuse.[41] By trying to oblige artists to sing the praises of slavery, the Stalinists actually come into conflict with the essential nature of art. Sometimes the official ideology wins this battle: 'It wants art that is not art, and it gets what it asks for.'[42]

The second most important aspect of social development is connected with the incredible plenitude of power. The class-apparatus, which is itself the ruling class, concentrates in one centre the entire administration of social life in all its manifestations. One must of course allow for the fact that as the crisis of the system deepens, one sphere of social activity after another escapes from bureaucratic control. Nevertheless, the tendency is maintained. In consequence there is constant pressure by the state upon culture, as a sphere which is not thoroughly subject to this centralized control. Similarly, constant pressure is also brought to bear on the individual. How successful this pressure is, and what it leads to, we shall see later, but it is obvious that it exists. On the whole we can say that there is obvious domination of civil society by the state. Moreover, it must be remembered that, as Cheshkov has written, this domination

> results not from a growth in the economic functions of the state in general, but from its concrete socioeconomic nature, or, in other words, from the nature of the ruling class, whose basis is the growing state sector, from the character of its relations with the working classes and with the masses as a whole.[43]

Finally, statocratic society is a super-alienated society. According to Marx the individual who sells his labour-power, and to whom the process and result of his own labour does not belong, is an alienated personality. In so far as every member of society in the USSR is in the situation of a wage-worker – at least formally – every stratum of the population, including the topmost, is subject to alienation of the personality. The various forms of democratic self-management and initiative which could lead to the elimination of alienation are completely absent. Moreover, owing to the tendency – already mentioned – towards full control, the state, striving to subject people to itself outside as well as within the sphere of production, subjects their personalities to additional alienation, imposing obligatory norms, obligatory ideas, and so on. This leads – apart from anything else – to an incredible flourishing of social hypocrisy, both 'upstairs' and 'downstairs', with neither the ruling circles nor their subjects able to voice their actual thoughts. Just as Marx wrote:

> It is not possible for either [the slave or the ruler] to say what he wants: the slave cannot say that he wants to become a human being, nor can the ruler say that he has no use for human beings in his country. To be silent, therefore, is the only way out.[44]

One-Dimensional Man and the Politicization of Culture

It is perfectly logical that art and, in general, the whole sphere of culture should prove refractory to the system. Artistic activity assumes free self-expression by the artist. A good novel cannot be written nor a good picture painted, to someone else's orders. Consequently art, as an unalienated activity, confronts the world of total alienation. Here it is not irrelevant to recall Herbert Marcuse's books *Soviet Marxism* and *One-Dimensional Man*.[45] To employ Marcuse's terminology, the 'social universal' of Soviet industrialized society has a tendency to shut itself up in 'one–dimensional space', excluding all freedom for the individual. The state's aim is, precisely, to create a one-dimensional man who can easily be manipulated. However, the manipulators are themselves one-dimensional, too, and in Sartre's words are 'manipulés par leurs manipulations mêmes'.[46] The cultural sphere, though, is less easy than any other to confine to one-dimensional space: on the contrary, new dimensions begin to appear in it as a result of the specific nature of artistic activity, every time external pressure slackens even a little. As soon as a crack is perceived in the system of control, or there is softening of totalitarian authority,[47] a struggle spontaneously begins for 'the recovery of intellectual space' (to use the excellent expression of the Italian Marxist A.L. De Castris[48]), when one cultural zone after another is emancipated from ideological control. The bureaucracy then tries to get its own back, tightening once more the screws of censorship. It must be said, though, that it is finding this harder and harder.

The authorities endeavour to submit to themselves the entire life of the Soviet citizen and to supervise everything he does. But cultural creativity, as I have said, is less submissive than anything else to external control. How can one control a poetic image or an actor's gesture? It is easy to control the worker at the bench, for the production process is regulated and the result known beforehand. But how is one to control the artist before his canvas, if the result of his work is not known in advance even to the artist himself? Adequate criteria and methods of control do not exist for this purpose, and the bureaucratic mentality is incapable of inventing them; this is true not only of art but of all branches of culture. The art critic, the art historian, the culturologist and the philosopher can easily be censored, but here too there are difficulties. The chief complication consists in the fact that the meaning of the part often differs from that of the whole. In cultural creativity the whole not only cannot be regarded as the sum of the parts (such an approach to any problem leads to very defective and inaccurate conclusions), but is also sometimes a negation of those parts. Any current, 'running' control has to be a control of parts. Suppression of the whole is a repressive measure which shows that running control has suffered fiasco: it reveals the presence of a conflict and proves that manipulation has failed; that the object of manipulation has escaped from control or has simply refused to submit.

It is natural that the cultural sphere, being 'remotest from the reality', the least controllable, and consequently the freest, becomes the last (or first) refuge for opposition to the regime.[49] The process of constant politicization of art goes on, as a rule, independently of the will of either the rulers or the ruled. Striving to subject culture to itself, the statocracy intensifies its pressure, imposing obligatory norms, and the result is that a mere attempt to evade this control – to ignore these norms – is seen as a political protest: 'When independent political opinions are suppressed, it is aesthetic value judgements, abstract problems of philosophy and social theory and the evaluation of the remote historical past which assume political significance.'[50]

Antonio Gramsci drew, in his *Prison Notebooks*, the very important conclusion that such processes are to be observed in countries 'where there is a single, totalitarian, governing party.' There,

> the functions of such a party are no longer directly political but merely technical ones of propaganda and public order, and moral and cultural influence. The political function is indirect. For, even if no other legal parties exist, other parties in fact always do exist and other tendencies which cannot be legally coerced, and, against these, polemics are unleashed, and struggles are fought as in a game of blind man's buff. In any case, it is certain that in such parties cultural functions predominate, which means that political language becomes jargon. In other words, political questions are disguised as cultural ones, and as such become insoluble.[51]

In this way the political struggle is shifted to the sphere of art and culture generally, where it becomes 'chronic', because for the contradictions to be resolved, real, non-mystified political activity is needed and the intelligentsia finds itself in constant, chronic opposition. There is another aspect to this. A number of concrete problems need to be studied by the social sciences, but owing to the censorship they cannot be studied completely enough. Art then begins to reflect upon these problems – employing, of course, its own specific methods. As a result some very distinctive artistic productions make their appearance, marked by a special analytical approach to the subjects they describe.

Thus the conflict between state and intelligentsia, government and culture, traditional in Russia, is revived at a different level. In this connection it is worth recalling once again Lenin's thought concerning the incompatibility between culture and bureaucracy. The Stalinist *nomenklatura*, like the Tsarist government, cannot exist totally without civilization. In order to achieve its aims, in order that the country as a whole may be up to contemporary standards and aspire to the role of superpower, civilization is needed. Needed also, consequently, is an intelligentsia. But once more, as in the case of Tsarist Russia, what the state needs is European enlightenment without European democratic ideas. The conflict between the Stalinist statocracy and the new intellectuals is a continuation of the conflict, historically typical of Russia, between an Asiatic ruling power and a European intelligentsia.

In the nineteenth century people spoke of the two Russias. That dualism returned under Stalin. 'Russia had again become a dual entity,' writes Tucker.

> Despite the spread of literacy and education in the Soviet period, the country experienced a revival of the cleavage of cultures. The culture of official Russia, with its apotheosized autocrat in the Kremlin, its aristocracy of rank, its all-powerful bureaucracy, its pervasive atmosphere of police terror, its regimentation of all activities, its rituals of prevarication, its grandiose 'construction projects of Communism', its great new foreign empire, its official friendships and enmities, its cold and hot wars – this was one thing. There was also a suppressed and little-known unofficial Russia with a life of its own.[52]

The traditions of Gogol and Shchedrin could not fail to come back to life under such conditions. Even in Stalin's time a small flame of spiritual opposition flickered among the intelligentsia:

> For the artist, thinker and writer it often meant an underground creative life over which the state had no control, an escape from the dreary official culture to real self-expression in secret. Among some youthful elements there was a revival of evangelical religion, carried on underground, and the old Populist tradition came alive again when university students at Moscow, Leningrad and elsewhere formed secret circles to discuss among themselves oppositional political ideas with an anarchist tinge.[53]

Later this flickering flame of protest was to blaze up, startling people who were unfamiliar with Russian tradition. 'The rebirth of dissent in Russia astonished many observers,' writes Shatz.[54] In the 1950s Western scholars noted that between the old intelligentsia and the new,

> a residual element of continuity was much greater than they expected, for the situation of the Soviet intelligentsia was, objectively, in many respects similar to that of the *intelligenty* in pre-revolutionary Russia.[55]

The new conditions merely revived an old tradition:

> Once again, an embattled little minority of intellectuals is determinedly resisting the power of a mighty state; the hallowed tradition of literature as an instrument of dissent has been resurrected; lives are being shattered by prison, exile and emigration. Even such specific government responses as the detention of dissidents in lunatic asylums have their historical precedents, for

this approach to nonconformist thought was foreshadowed as far back as the 1830s by Nicholas I's treatment of Peter Chaadaev. With justification, many parallels have been drawn between dissent in Tsarist times and in the post-Stalin period.[56]

Old debates were renewed and old problems came up again.

The Terror

It has to be said that the old tradition of Russian culture – its humanistic, critical and anti-authoritarian (and so anti-governmental) political tendency – contributed to no small extent to the acuteness of this conflict. It is well known that tradition in general matters more to the intelligentsia than to any other social stratum. The question to be asked, though, is a different one: How had Russia's intellectual tradition been preserved after the intelligentsia had suffered, first the severe consequences of the civil war, and then the ferocious repression under Stalin? Between 1917 and 1937 the old Russian intelligentsia had been literally destroyed.

The strictly Stalinist attack on the intelligentsia was waged systematically, beginning at the end of the twenties. One can even distinguish several stages in it, each with clearly defined tasks. The first mass-scale blow ('partial' repressions, not aimed against a particular stratum in its entirety, went on all the time, almost without interruption) was struck at the old engineers, the technical intelligentsia, those whom Bukharin had once suspected of dangerously propagating 'the old culture' within the new society. They were now openly accused of being 'wreckers'. Roy Medvedev writes:

> The serious mistakes made during collectivization and industrialization lowered the workers' standard of living, disrupted the supply of food and manufactured goods, and weakened the alliance between the city and the country. Strict rationing had to be reintroduced in the cities. Discontent grew. It was hard to ascribe all these shortcomings only to kulaks and 'subkulaks'. Another scapegoat had to be found for Stalin's faults. And such a scapegoat was found: the specialists, the intelligentsia, who had been tainted before the Revolution.[57]

There began a real witch-hunt of the old specialists. The official organs wrote that 'between 90 and 95 per cent of the old engineers must unquestionably be regarded as having a counter-revolutionary attitude.'[58] But not only the engineers were involved. The second edition of the *Great Soviet Encyclopaedia* asserted plainly that wrecking 'is possible not only in the economic sphere but also in the spheres of science, literature and art.'[59] A group of Ukrainian intellectuals were even charged with 'wrecking on the front of the development of the Ukrainian language, its terminology, spelling and alphabet'.[60] The matter did not stop at accusations. Sentences duly followed. ...

The Communist historian Boffa, who has carefully studied the material on the trials of the 'wreckers' which appeared in the Soviet press, came to the conclusion that *not one* of the charges brought was justified:

> Today it is quite clear ... that the cases were faked. As in the later ... trials, no documentary evidence against the accused was produced apart from their own confessions. Much subsequent testimony has since exposed these methods of physical torture and moral coercion by means of which they were forced to slander themselves.[61]

And yet, to this day, none of the big 'wrecking' trials has been revised. Even after the 'exposure of the cult of personality' in 1956 and condemnation of the unlawful repressions carried out in the Stalin era, the Soviet government continues to maintain that the policy of the 1920s in relation to the intellectuals was correct and the arrests justified.[62] On the other hand, the thesis of the universal 'counter-revolutionariness' of the old intelligentsia has been quietly abandoned. The official textbook on the history of the CPSU acknowledges that 'the overwhelming mass of the old specialists worked honestly.'[63] Dr S. Fedukhin states that the intelligentsia did not approve of the Bolshevik revolution; 'but', he goes on judiciously, 'these intellectuals who did not agree with the new government, and denounced it, did what the republic mainly required of them – they worked.'[64]

We thus get a curious picture. The thesis according to which 90 per cent of the engineers were counter-revolutionaries was evidently wrong, yet the arrests carried out on the basis of this thesis were right. This same book on the Party's history approves of the persecution of the engineers in the fabricated Shakhty case. The textbook published under B.N. Ponomarev's editorship continues to affirm that 'they were wreckers'.[65]

Most of the official historians prefer to say nothing about the Shakhty case, but their silence is also interesting because it implies unwillingness to clear the intelligentsia who were persecuted. Thus, reviewing a monograph on the history of the Soviet intelligentsia,[66] *Voprosy Istorii* complained that the book dealt inadequately with 'the process of re-educating the old intelligentsia'.[67] It is quite clear that if this 'process' were to be 'dealt with' in greater detail it would show a significant picture of mass repressions and 're-education' in the camps. But it is curious that the writer in *Voprosy Istorii*, a certain V.N. Sheyko, was apparently unable to understand, almost two decades after Stalin's death, that these intellectuals were not thieves or juvenile delinquents who needed to be re-educated.

On the whole, Stalin's 'solution of the problem of the intelligentsia' had much in common with his solution of the peasant problem and that of the workers. Collectivization and industrialization had as their most important consequence the destruction of firm bonds within all classes of society. The peasantry lost their old social structure and millions of declassed peasants rushed to the towns, eroding the small working class. During the five years of collectivization and industrialization the numbers of industrial workers almost doubled, owing, as Roy Medvedev writes, to 'the mass exodus of peasants to the cities because of the bad situation in the countryside, and failure to achieve the planned increase in the productivity of labour'.[68] In consequence, the old working-class cadres were diluted in the marginal mass of former peasants, who had lost their own traditions, work habits and social ideals. In a country where the whole population had been turned, to a considerable extent, into a declassed mass, the bureaucracy remained the only socially organized force. The terror was to play the same role in relation to the intelligentsia as collectivization played in relation to the peasantry. The more or less united old intelligentsia was replaced by a declassed mass of 'new specialists'.

Altogether, in spite of everything, the intelligentsia was, it seems, always an object of particular hatred on Stalin's part. The specific character of intellectual labour presumes, as has been said, a certain degree of independence for every person who participates in it, and this made the intelligentsia particularly dangerous. 'The fundamental problem', observed the French socialist historian Gilles Martinet, in a discussion with Boffa on Stalinism, 'is to prevent the rise of cadres possessing a measure of autonomy. Hence the need for special attention and particular repressions where the intelligentsia are concerned.'[69] This 'special attention' accounts for the incredible ferocity of the repression of Party intellectuals, most of whom had by 1937 reconciled themselves to the ruling order. 'The educated elite found itself', notes Shatz,

> in the unenviable position of displaying to the greatest degree the characteristics that most aroused Stalin's suspicions. ... It cannot be said that the Great Purge deliberately set out to annihilate the educated elite inherited by the Stalin regime from the Tsarist era, but as it snowballed it came close to doing precisely that.[70]

After the 'purge' of the intelligentsia in 1928–32 came the inner-Party repressions of 1936–37, and then the new 'purge' of intellectuals in 1937–39. The historian M.N. Pokrovsky was accused posthumously of having, with his 'school', 'carried out wrecking work in the field of history',[71] and this was followed by a witch-hunt among historians:

> In the pages of *Pod znamenem marksizma* [Under the Banner of Marxism] accusations of philosophical mistakes – mechanism, idealism, agnosticism, subjectivism, Machism, sophistry – quickly turned into various kinds of political accusations, and then to fashionable and highly effective charges of hostile and even terrorist activity.[72]

Later, after Stalin's death and the exposures of the Khrushchev period, it became known 'that in the mid 1930s nearly all the most capable Soviet Marxist philosophers, no matter of which trend, fell victim to political repression. Most of them died.'[73] In 1937–38 the devastation of the People's Commissariats of Education in several of the Union Republics involved the deaths of thousands of teachers.

Mere repressive measures, however, were obviously not enough where the intelligentsia was concerned. Ideological and cultural control over its activity was required. It must be said, to the credit of the Bolsheviks, that in the twenties such control was very slight. In February 1925 Bukharin, who spoke at that time as the Party's chief theoretician and was at the zenith of his fame, came out categorically against attempts to subject literature to Party control:

> I said that no Politburo gave Pushkin any directives on how to write his verses. And if that was so, then think what it means. I said that the question of a new style is a very important and very specific question. It can be settled only when the Party does not clutch everybody in one fist, but allows free competition.[74]

Bukharin advocated 'a tolerant attitude', reminding his readers that 'there is no need to inflame passions', and that the Bolsheviks 'ought to allow maximum scope for competition.'[75] He conceived this competition in a rather broad way:

> Let there be a thousand organizations, two thousand, let there be ... as many circles and organizations as you like. Do you think that the Politburo ought to chase after everyone and attach him to the Agitation Department?[76]

Accordingly, official recognition was given to the autonomy of art. Bukharin's position, which was at that time completely official, was summed up in this formula: 'the problem of culture cannot be solved by means of mechanical coercion', and in general, the solution was to be found only through 'free competition between creative forces'.[77]

But at the same time voices made themselves heard demanding the abolition of the autonomy of culture, and most importantly, precisely this view – akin to Stalin's conception of art as a form of political propaganda – became increasingly widespread in the Party, ousting the liberal ideas of Trotsky and Bukharin. In 1925, when the Bukharinists were still in power, the Central Committee's resolution 'on Party policy in the sphere of belles-lettres' mentioned the need for a 'tactful and cautious attitude' to non-Communist literature, but at the same time condemned inadequate attention to 'the struggle for the ideological hegemony of proletarian writers'.[78] While the trend of the resolution was liberal, the very fact that the Party was now concerning itself with a number of questions with which it had not previously dealt was ominous.

Supporters of a hard line invoked Lenin's idea about 'partnership' in literature. This was, however, unsound. For Lenin there was no contradiction between freedom for the writer or the journalist (what he said obviously had no bearing on fictional writing) and his partisanship, for what he had in view was adherence to an opposition party in a society with elements of a multiparty system.[79] It is characteristic that during the period when he was in power Lenin *never once* referred to the idea of 'Party literature'. His article had been written in a different period and in a different connection. But Stalin and his henchmen were extremely clever at making use of Lenin's casual remarks. 'Thus, a year and a half after Lenin's death, his successors brought to triumph a point of view he had expressed in 1910,' writes a Canadian historian, 'although he himself, on coming to power, had not thought it appropriate to confirm that approach by decree.'[80]

The final crushing of Trotsky, whose line was declared to be 'anti-Leninist', 'counter-revolutionary' and 'reactionary-capitulatory not only on questions of literary policy but also on creative matters',[81] and then the fall of Bukharin in 1928–29 led to the final establishment of totalitarian rule by the statocracy, in the cultural sphere as in others. Literary groups were dissolved and a single Writers' Union formed, which was absolutely subject to the Party and even spoke of 'the fruitfulness of the Party's guidance' in the very years when the persecution of the intelligentsia was well under way, with the badgering of Bulgakov, the exiling of Zamyatin, and so on.[82] Other 'creative unions' were formed, on the pattern of the Writers' Union, with the task of controlling every aspect of creative activity. These professional associations were not in the least supposed to protect the interests of their members although, it must be admitted, something was nevertheless done in that direction. Their main task was to organize creative 'production' under state control. They wrote quite frankly about this, speaking of the creation of 'a single production-creation collective'.[83]

In 1936–39 the Writers' Union willingly sanctioned the extermination of its own members. 'It is impossible', writes Roy Medvedev, 'to list all the writers arrested and destroyed in 1936–39. Some calculations put the number in excess of 600, almost one-third of the Union's total membership.'[84]

The Limits of Control

Despite these measures, the intelligentsia managed to retain a certain cultural continuity with the democratic and humanist Russian tradition of the nineteenth century. At first sight there is even something mysterious in this. 'Tyranny', writes Edward Shils, in a study of the laws of development of the intellectual tradition in different countries,

> may crush men physically, it can thrust them into outer darkness where they are unable to do their work, it can silence them, and it can corrupt them, it can rule its society with the aid of the police and the army; but it cannot destroy the intellectual tradition unless it also annihilates those who bear it. Modern tyrannies have never succeeded in doing this – though they have exiled many and sent many others to concentration camps.
>
> As long as totalitarian regimes allow creative personalities who have had contact with the great intellectual traditions to work in libraries and laboratories, to have pupils, and to be in touch with each other through their published writings and through conversation, the continuity and growth of intellectual traditions are not seriously in danger. Somehow the mind finds its way and the stream flows onward.[85]

In fact, although the repression was very severe, not all bearers of the tradition were exterminated and many continued to work. Although they, too, often had to include in their books some absurd passages in praise of 'Comrade Stalin', the Party and the government; although they, too, had to participate in the universal hypocrisy; although they, too, despite that, suffered persecution as 'cosmopolitans', 'bourgeois scholars', and so forth, they nevertheless went on contributing to culture. The most important thing was that they had pupils. Many of them were no longer able to do anything important themselves, but they passed on the tradition, their way of thinking, the European type of education. And that was very important.

One of these figures who probably linked together the old and the new intelligentsias in Russia was M.M. Bakhtin, the literary critic, culturologist and philosopher. Although he began his work in the twenties it was only in the seventies that he became widely popular. Bakhtin was persecuted for a long time; many of his works remained unpublished for decades, and some he published under other people's names. But not long before he died his books began to be published and his name became fashionable. People learnt from Bakhtin and he became the founder of a whole school of culturology and literary criticism. He passed on his humanist and democratic ideal to members of the new intelligentsia and gave them a lesson in original, non-standardized, undogmatic thinking.

Besides this there exists and cannot be destroyed the objective bearer of the tradition – the great Russian literature of the nineteenth century. This determined, and will go on determining, the cultural orientations of the Russian intelligentsia. It must not be forgotten that the categorial apparatus of Russian literature – its elements, its language – are European. That Russian literature is distinctive is beyond dispute, but this is a distinctiveness within the framework of a common cultural archetype, like the distinctiveness of English, French or Spanish literature. In philosophy and art every new generation, as Marx and Engels themselves remarked, has to use the material bequeathed by its predecessors. Whatever efforts have sometimes been made to separate Russian literature of the Petersburg period from Soviet literature, and counterpose the one to the other, this is objectively impossible.

Finally, Marxism itself, with its universalism and its critical orientation, could not but educate the minds of Soviet intellectuals in a way that was highly undesirable for the authorities – that is to say, in the spirit of the radical-critical ideas of Western left-wing culture. In the USSR and in the world Communist movement Marxism became, of course, degraded under the influence of Stalinism. Fernando Claudín wrote that from the beginning of the 1930s until 1956, 'Marxism suffered from prolonged theoretical paralysis.'[86] This is not entirely correct so far as the West is concerned. In those very years the famous 'Frankfurt School' was formed, and Gramsci's *Prison Notebooks* and Trotsky's *The Revolution Betrayed* were written. In the Soviet Union itself, however, Marxism was replaced by a set of ideological dogmas which had little in common with the 'critical philosophy'. Its most important and valuable ideas (the theory of the state, the concept of the Asiatic mode of production, and so on) were revised and replaced with new ones devised by the authority of the 'great teacher' to justify the concrete facts of statocratic society. The trouble was that the Stalinists' practice was sorely reminiscent of those theoretical utopias of 'barracks-Communism' with a sharp criticism of which Marx had begun to form his own revolutionary-democratic and later socialist ideas. From this standpoint, as Marcuse noted, 'the problem of Soviet "revisions" of Marxism' possesses special interest,[87] for the ruling group was adapting revolutionary theory to suit its own needs, and each of these 'revisions' is instructive in its own way. Dialectics suffered especially, being banished from analysis of the historical process after the 'critical philosophy' had been arbitrarily divided into two parts: 'historical materialism', alien to dialectics, and 'dialectical materialism', 'free' from historicism. Under Stalin even the dialectical law of negation, the foundation of foundations of the 'critical philosophy', was eliminated and then, under Khrushchev, 'rehabilitated' (but, it would seem, only posthumously: in any case, it has still not been 'restored to its rights'). On the whole, the Italian Communist Umberto Cerroni expressed the essence of what happened when he said that 'we witnessed a dogmatization of Marxism which can also be defined as the replacement of scientific socialism by utopian socialism.'[88]

Nevertheless, one can concur with Marcuse when he wrote of 'the difficulties which the regime creates for itself by constantly teaching and publicizing Marxian ideas'.[89] Although in the schools and institutes they still teach, in the guise of Marxism, the dogmatic utopia of 'state socialism' and barracks-Communism, that same utopia which Marx constantly combated, they have not yet forbidden people to read *The German Ideology,* or to study *The Economic and Philosophical Manuscripts of 1844,* or to become acquainted with Gramsci's *Prison Notebooks* – books that are shaping the minds of the intelligentsia in the West.

In general, history has shown that however strange this may be, it is considerably easier to preserve the spiritual property of the past than to destroy it. Shils writes:

> Intellectual work is sustained by and transmits a complex tradition which persists through changes in the structure of the intellectual class. One could almost say that if these traditions did not confront the intellectual as an ineluctable inheritance, they could be created anew in each generation by the passionate disposition of the 'natural' intellectual to be in contact ... with symbols of general scope. They are traditions which are, so to speak, given by the nature of intellectual work. They are the immanent traditions of intellectual performance, the accepted body of rules of procedure, standards of judgement, criteria for the selection of subject matters and problems, modes of presentation, canons for the assessment of excellence, models of previous achievement. ...[90]

This is positive material accumulated during centuries and worked out as a result of the practice of many generations, and in it are expressed the most general laws of modern culture. Tradition lives on in present-day scientific methods, in accessible works of art, in language, in history. And sometimes the mightiest and harshest of states proves helpless in the face of it.

The Proletarianization of the Intellectuals

Furthermore, traditions revive when the situation favours this. The seed has to fall on good soil. The critical protest of the intelligentsia is not only due to its special role in the bureaucratic state, where it is at once a necessary part of the system and extraneous and alien to it. This protest is evoked also by social and professional factors.

The political role of the intelligentsia in the USSR (and in the countries of Eastern Europe which have copied the Soviet model) is somewhat specific, so it would be best to begin with this. But it is no secret that Russia is not the only country where, in the last thirty or forty years, the intelligentsia has come into conflict with the state. This conflict has quite profound social roots. There are numerous problems which are the same in all present-day societies, and among them is the problem of the intelligentsia.

In the twentieth century, and especially after the Second World War, a process of proletarianization of the intelligentsia has been observable practically everywhere. Their numbers have sharply increased, but their social status has simultaneously declined even more rapidly. It is noteworthy, though, that this fall in social status has not as a rule been accompanied by a decline in moral authority. On the contrary, this has remained as before and has sometimes even increased. All this created the complex and confused mass of problems which gave rise to the student movement of 1966–68 in the West. '*Nous n'étions autrefois qu'une petite minorité de futurs privilégiés nécessairement intégrables. Nous sommes maintenant une trop grande "minorité" non assimilable mais gardant le statut de l'ancienne minorité*', wrote the students of the Sorbonne during the youth disturbances in Paris in May–June 1968, '*Nous ne sommes plus assurés de devenir des futurs dirigeants. ... Nous sommes dorénavant des travailleurs comme les autres.*'[91] The proletarianization of the intellectual workers, accompanied by the massive increase in their numbers – outstripping, as often happens, the actual needs of economic and academic institutions – placed the Western intelligentsia in the situation of the Russian intelligentsia in the nineteenth century. Tugan-Baranovsky's prophecy was fulfilled. Furthermore, though, exploitation of the intelligentsia was intensified and its members experienced in person what is meant by alienation of labour, unemployment, and so on. In 1966–68 the student youth in the West discovered that they were 'in the classic proletarian position'.[92] The general situation in the USSR was similar, even though it developed differently. Moreover, these same processes sometimes found more striking expression here.

The traditional intelligentsia belonged to the privileged strata of society. The term 'bourgeois intelligentsia' used by Marxists, provided it is not as a term of abuse, defines very precisely the position of that stratum. 'Workers by brain' lived on the profits of the bourgeoisie, and thus on the surplus product produced by the workers. This idea calls for some refinement lest the present-day reader, who feels a proper repugnance for the schemas of vulgar sociology, should suspect the author of trying to 'insult' Chekhov or Stanislavsky. The intelligentsia was bourgeois (or petty-bourgeois) in the way it got its income. Its world-view, however, could not but be wide rather than narrow. Later, when the intelligentsia's social position began to change while it still retained many important privileges, this contradiction became especially marked. Sartre describes the situation of the intellectual:

> The dominant class attaches no importance to him: all it is willing to acknowledge is the technician of knowledge and the minor functionary of the superstructure. The underprivileged classes cannot engender him since he derives from the specialist in practical truth who in turn is created by the options of the dominant class, which allocates a fraction of surplus value to produce him.[93]

All this made the situation of the intelligentsia rather complex, and it was beaten right and left – undeservedly, as a rule. The question of the social status of the intellectual in traditional bourgeois society is extremely difficult, for the intelligentsia is heterogeneous. This heterogeneity is also a serious social and psychological problem. The intelligentsia often shows itself dissociated, wavering, and so on. But Gramsci observed, quite rightly, that there is always some stratum or group of the intelligentsia which, to a certain extent, determines the ideas of its whole mass. In the society of the late nineteenth century, that stratum was undoubtedly bourgeois.

We know that the surplus product received by the industrial capitalists is subsequently redistributed among the different strata of the bourgeoisie. A share – a very small one, of course – was also received by the intelligentsia. If we take, for example, the position of an engineer in a nineteenth-century factory – even if he was not the head of the firm – or a professor in a university, we discover without difficulty that they were in a privileged position: that their salaries were much higher than the wages of the ordinary workers, in factory or office. Their privileged position enabled them to appropriate part of the surplus product, even though they themselves did not directly exploit anyone. Finally – and this is the main thing – the intellectual was not, as a rule, obliged to sell labour-power; he or she did not work for wages but kept their independence, controlled their own labour, and their personality was not subjected to alienation. The very concept of a 'free profession' reflected this independence of the intelligentsia, especially that of the intellectuals working in the humanities and the arts.

All this made people like N. Meshcheryakov see the intellectuals as a variety of the petty bourgeoisie, but that was in the past. In the West, scientific and technological progress has led to a marked increase in the number of intellectuals, transforming them from an elite into a mass and causing intensified competition among them as a result. A consequence of this has been the transformation of a considerable section of the intellectuals into wage-workers – proletarians. And what matters here is not only that their incomes have fallen, but also that the way they get them has changed. In the nineteenth century many intellectuals broke with the bourgeoisie because their mental horizon was considerably wider than the bourgeoisie's: their very speciality made them think about the interests of humanity and the needs of society as a whole. In the 1960s the intelligentsia found itself objectively in conflict with the bourgeoisie, while possessing – thanks to its specific professional activity – a higher level of consciousness than the traditional working class, so that there now exist theoreticians for that class who can elaborate moral, cultural and political ideas. There emerges what the French socialist Chevènement has called 'the contradiction of the educated slave'.[94] The intellectual still occupies a special place in society, but for this reason he or she feels even more acutely oppression by the ruling class. This has made the left-wing intelligentsia the vanguard of the socialist movement, orientated towards its ultimate aims.

Serious conflicts arise from society's inability to make use of the knowledge it imparts to intellectual workers. In the West this contradiction takes the form of mass unemployment among graduates and in the Soviet Union, where unemployment is not a problem of the first order (though there are rather a lot of unemployed intellectuals), engineers and specialists of various kinds are very often obliged to work at jobs outside their particular field. 'In the Porshen factory,' *Pravda* reports,

> there are twenty-five persons with higher-educational diplomas who wear the overalls of manual workers. ... If we look at this branch of industry as a

whole, we find that there are hundreds in a similar situation. Thus, in the enterprises of the Ministry of Non-Ferrous Metallurgy of the Kazakh SSR, last year, 906 specialists with higher education were employed as ordinary manual workers. In the republic's Ministry of the Meat and Dairy Products Industry there were 169, and in the Ministry of Power Engineering and Electrification no fewer than 584 graduates similarly placed.[95]

Pravda has reviewed the situation in one republic, Kazakhstan, which is not as highly industralized or rich in institutions of higher education as (for example) Russia, but for this reason the overall situation appears even more dramatic. The newspaper notes a social fact of enormous importance: 'a number of professions are being depreciated.'[96]

Thus, in the Soviet Union the process of proletarianizing the intelligentsia, while happening in a different way, has led to the same results as in the West. The statocracy has transformed an entire mass of working people into wage-workers. The 'free professions' have ceased to exist. Even those workers in the field of art who have retained a certain degree of independence have been subordinated to particular organizations – the trade-union committee of cultural workers, the 'creative' unions, and so on. These organizations frequently stand, in relation to their members, in the role of employers. The narrow specialization of our publishing houses, for example, means that a writer whose work concerns a particular subject becomes, *de facto*, an unestablished employee of one particular publishing enterprise, since there is nowhere else – or almost nowhere – he can turn to. His independence has become purely formal. Henceforth he is obliged to carry out someone else's orders and perform tasks set by others. This situation is not, of course, favourable to artistic creativity. The worker in the field of art is consequently placed in a position where he must resist – indeed, cannot refrain from resisting – exploitation if he wants to retain even a fragment of his self-respect and personal independence.

Marc Rakovski, comparing Eastern with Western Europe, came to the general conclusion that in the twentieth century *creative activity has been proletarianized*:

> The times when the so-called 'free' intelligentsia formed the greatest part of the intelligentsia have passed. The free intellectual used to have financial resources unconnected with his professional activities, or, if he did not, it was not his labour-power that he sold but the product of his labour. ... But by the middle of this century the free intelligentsia had become a minority even in the sphere of social science and of humanist culture in the strictest sense. In Soviet-type societies this process has been even more vigorously intense than it has been under capitalism.[97]

At the same time social pressure on the intelligentsia has increased and this has to a certain extent promoted its consolidation, its development of group-consciousness. Furthermore the intellectuals, feeling that they belong to the oppressed and exploited masses, increasingly claim the right to speak in their name. They enjoy greater access to information (even in the USSR, and other societies of the Soviet type, learned publications offer the reader many facts and ideas which are excluded from popular publications) and consequently are better able to express themselves. This is why, incidentally, oppositions first take shape in the setting of legal culture and only later does the logic of the movement, the barriers of censorship, and the impossibility of saying everything one wants to say impel the intelligentsia to take the path of activity which is 'illegal' from the standpoint of the official bureaucrats. '*Samizdat*' appears, together with underground universities and clandestine seminars. This 'illegal' culture[98] is always a prolongation and product of legal culture.

It is precisely the pressure exercised by the authorities upon an intellectual in the course of his quite legal professional activity that first evokes his protest. Workers and engineers have to carry out tasks imposed by others, eight hours a day. Their personality is subjected to alienation during their work, and they try to make up for that in their leisure time. The creative process of the scientist or the writer is uninterrupted (purely technical work in the laboratory or at the desk is only part of it). But this being so, if the process in question is subject to control by an exploiting bureaucracy (and control of the result implies control of the process), the writer's personality is even more alienated than that of the worker, and it is even harder for him to 'remain himself'.

The statocratic master tells the intellectual in advance what is wanted from him, what he must reveal, what he must write about, what he must depict. Consequently – at any rate, so long as he resigns himself to submitting to the will of the 'boss' – the intellectual's activity is determined not by the objective logic of science or art, not by society as a whole, but merely by the administrative job he has to perform. In the post-Stalin period, moreover, this problem has become even more acute for writers than it is for scientists. Marat Cheshkov wrote quite correctly that under statocratic rule, and in general in present-day industrial society, alienation of the product of the intellectual's labour becomes transformed into direct alienation of his personality.

But of course, it is not only protest against alienation and proletarianization that motivates intellectuals. Their actual exploitation grows steadily more severe. The statocratic state is in the position of a monopolist who can dictate conditions to the wage-workers. As a result the material position of most scientists, writers, actors and intellectuals in the USSR has become worse – as a whole, that is, of course – than that of their colleagues in the West. An exception must be made, however, for those bureaucrats of culture or science who perform official propaganda functions, completely accepting the rules of the game and refraining from independent creative work. Although these people contribute nothing of practical benefit to society, their books, which nobody reads, are printed in many thousands of copies. For the sake of propaganda the state accepts losses. Such pseudo-intellectuals are for practical purposes integrated into the lowest level of the ruling statocracy, with all the consequences this entails. But it must be realized that in this field there are always fewer vacancies than applicants. The result is that many of these people get thrown overboard, even though they have accepted the rules of the game. Unfortunately, talentless people and mediocrities are more numerous in our country than the bureaucratic posts for them to fill.

At first, until the mid 1930s, although the intelligentsia were in the position of wage-workers they retained some economic privileges. It was typical that when the onslaught on the old specialists began, as Roy Medvedev writes, 'their material position was, for the most part, better at the time of their arrest than before the Revolution.'[99] The intelligentsia was not yet very numerous; the rulers had need of it and shared with it a part of the statocratic surplus product. But the increase in the number of people with higher education meant also that the position of remaining members of the traditional intelligentsia was undermined. It was no accident that the wave of Stalinist repression broke over them at the end of the thirties. By that time the ruling *nomenklatura* had a sufficient *number* of new specialists to replace those who were now ousted.

And so we see in the USSR, as in the West, a social degradation of the intelligentsia, but we must consider also the fact that this is happening against a background in which new middle strata are being formed. While the bulk of the intellectuals are being turned into simple proletarians, certain groups of them, directly connected with the statocratic upper stratum, are on the contrary strengthening their position and obtaining fresh privileges. On the one hand these new middle strata confront the intelligentsia, but on the other they form part of it. In relation to the mass of the intelligentsia they can be seen as a sort of aristocracy of labour. In the ideological struggle they perform an important function in defence of the existing order, but their relation to the ruling circles is also heterogeneous. These middle strata consist not only of the upper circle of the ideological and repressive apparatus but also of technocrats, business managers, some scientists and also the auxiliary personnel of the *nomenklatura* and the 'commercial aristocracy' – people who enrich themselves by battening on our economic difficulties. This entire motley mass is certainly linked very closely with the Party bureaucracy but it also possesses its own interests – professional ones included – which it sometimes has to defend against its own protectors.

Furthermore, these middle strata retain fairly close links with 'the lower orders', who frequently influence them. Where the intelligentsia working in the humanities are concerned, the rulers constantly strive to integrate their leading representatives into the middle strata. At the same time the reverse tendency operates, with a section of the middle strata constantly drifting down to the level of 'the lower orders', sinking to their position. The political ideal of the middle strata is a very moderate reformism, but a political ideal does not determine all one's thinking, even one's thinking about politics. Consequently the middle strata, as the intermediate link between the statocracy and the intelligentsia, form that field in society where a bitter struggle is constantly being waged, 'for the souls of men', between the government ideologists and the dissidents.

These, broadly speaking, are the social conditions in which the cultural-political process is advancing in the USSR. Before immediately proceeding to expound ideas and events, we must say something about the role of another factor which has had an important influence on the character of social thought: censorship.

On Censorship

It would really be more correct to speak not of censorship but of the censors. Formally the censor's function is performed by 'Glavlit', but it is also carried out by editorial boards themselves. In addition, a variety of higher organizations constantly intervene in the work of those subordinate to them, granting 'approval', making observations and, in short, playing the part of censors. What matters, however, in the last analysis is not so much the structure of the censorship apparatus as the influence it exercises on the country's spiritual life.

The well-known historian A. Nekrich wrote: 'Censorship, which was introduced by Lenin as a "temporary measure", has become one of the pillars supporting the edifice of the Soviet regime.'[100] What we are concerned with, though, is not only the bans and administrative controls but the combined effect of many different phenomena connected with the censorship – its influence on culture as a whole. The most important feature of the Soviet censorship (one mentioned by A.

Sinyavsky) is, perhaps, that it '*forbids silence.* It not only prescribes what you should write and how, it also insists that you do write. Pasternak, for instance, fell silent; Babel was silent; and this was a crime [emphasis added].'[101] It is this which ultimately renders the censorship all-powerful in its way, for it leads to the practice of *self-censorship.*

In connection with Solzhenitsyn's letter to the Fourth Congress of the Writers' Union, in which he demanded that belles-lettres be at last allowed creative autonomy, V. Sosnora wrote: 'The censor-in-chief, like Jesus Christ, has his twelve apostles, who watchfully protect and stoutly defend this responsible personage. We do not have just one guilty censor. We have twelve.'[102] These are the author himself, the editors at different stages, the reviewers, and so on. It often happens that by the time a work reaches Glavlit there is nothing in it to be censored. Self-censorship flourished especially in the Stalin era when, essentially, no ordinary censorship was needed. People were on the one hand so frightened, and on the other so indoctrinated by systematic propaganda, that they not only wrote but thought as the government wanted. It was typical of the time that the 'thick' literary journals such as *Novy Mir* were, generally speaking, not censored under Stalin. A piece of fiction or poetry which had been approved for printing by the editor-in-chief could not be deleted by Glavlit. This arrangement explains how V. Ovechkin's sketches on the Soviet countryside could appear in print, and later, after Stalin's death, the articles by V. Pomerantsev, F. Abramov and M. Lifshits which aroused the fury of conservative-bureaucratic circles. On the contrary, however, under Khrushchev it was necessary for Tvardovsky, as editor-in-chief of *Novy Mir*, to wage a running fight with the censorship, which was openly unwilling to recognize his authority. The curious 'liberalism' of the Stalin era was possible only given the conditions of a totalitarian regime when all free thought was stifled and *there was nothing left to stifle.*

Marx, who devoted several articles to establishing the principle of press freedom, considered this situation the most dangerous of all:

Among the *special* obstacles to the press we must include not only *individual difficulties dues to censorship,* but equally the *special circumstances* which made censorship itself superfluous because they did not allow the object of censorship to come into being at all, even tentatively. When the censorship comes into obvious, persistent and sharp conflict with the press, it can be concluded with a fair certainty that the press has achieved vitality, character and self-assurance, for only a perceptible action produces a perceptible reaction. When, on the other hand, there is no censorship because there is no press, although the need for a free and therefore censorable press exists, one must expect to find a *pre-censorship* in circumstances which have suppressed by fear the expression of thought even in its more unpretentious forms.[103]

The history of the Soviet state fully confirms Marx's view that censorship and any attack on the freedom of the press is a form of 'the *most frightful terrorism*'.[104]

It was the series of unorthodox works published in *Novy Mir* after Stalin's death that led to the tightening of the censorship, for only then did ideas appear in our society which needed to be hunted down in the press. The Stalin era, being a period of complete lawlessness, was also a period of relatively liberal legislation. Only later, in connection with the quickening of public life, were the prohibitory laws made increasingly precise, as though to confirm Marx's words:

> The law against a frame of mind is *not a law of the state* promulgated for its *citizens* but the *law of one party against another party*. . . . Laws against frame of mind are based on an unprincipled frame of mind, on an immoral, material view of the state. They are the involuntary cry of a bad conscience.[105]

Censorship is introduced by those who fear public opinion, but the very existence of censorship is a sign that oppositional thought is alive and cannot be eradicated – that alongside the ruling bureaucratic 'party' there is also a *de facto* democratic party.

It must be remembered that Russian culture has always been subject to censorship. Nevertheless, the system established by the statocracy was extraordinarily refined even by Russian standards. One can distinguish three levels of censorship. The first of these is, of course, the political level. The authorities are concerned to ensure that nothing 'hostile' shall appear in print, on television, on the cinema screen, on the stage or on an artist's canvas – that is, anything which goes beyond the limits of 'reasonable criticism'. These limits are, of course, constantly widening. Under Stalin it was risky to say even that there were bad people among us, but in the sixties and seventies many highly critical works were published. However, it is the very existence of these limits that is of most decisive importance. Legal culture is allowed to develop only within frontiers laid down beforehand. It is constrained by the limits of the censorship.

The political censorship influences the development of culture in its own way. The works that suffer from it most of all, of course, are not works of fiction but theoretical writings in the social sciences. 'The censor's sway is felt most acutely in the social sciences,' wrote Nekrich, especially in the sphere of history. Soviet censorship begins in the head of the historian. When preparing to research some topic he must imagine not only the difficulties he will face because of a shortage or primary sources, and because he is unlikely to be able to work in foreign archives, etc., but he must also assess the 'acceptability' of his topic from the point of view of the censor. There are themes which to this day remain taboo for a historian whose field is Soviet society – for example, the history of working-class and peasant parties other than the Bolshevik Party. Even the real history of the CPSU is impossible to research because the ban on the works of Trotsky, Bukharin, Kamenev, Zinoviev, the 'Bulletins of the Opposition', the 'Socialist Herald' and many other sources,[106] dooms any such attempt to complete failure. This is why it is something of a heroic feat when a Soviet historian manages to 'drag out' a new document under some pretext or other.[107]

As a result Soviet sociologists, historians and political scientists have developed a special sort of associative thinking. They study the actual problems of their own country, but to discuss – or sometimes even to mention – these problems is forbidden. All that remains is to examine similar problems on the basis of the material of other countries and other periods. However, this does not mean in the least that, for example, G. Vodolazov (about whom I shall have more to say later), when dealing with problems of the history of the Russian socialist movement in the nineteenth century, is really writing about present-day ideas or political processes. It is all both more complicated and simpler. Take, let us say, the studies of statocracy mentioned earlier. M. Cheshkov's task was not to analyse Soviet reality under the guise of discussing the 'Third World': he did not attempt that. But, using 'Third-World' material, he constructed a model which is applicable *also* to our understanding of Soviet society. This was felt by the censorship, too, and for a long time they obstructed publication of his article.

This is where we find the answer to the question. Theoreticians study the actual history of or the actual relations existing in other countries. The relevance to Soviet reality of their researches appears not in the garbling or mixing-up of some phenomena with others – that is done by the authors of official textbooks – not in any sort of camouflage, but merely in the choice of material. Here it is hard for the authorities to find fault with the researcher. One cannot forbid study of nineteenth-century Russian society, or Mexico in the 1960s. The censor is not himself a theoretician and cannot know beforehand what will be written. When the learned work is ready, it is not easy to cavil at it – especially as this would not be to the authorities' advantage, for it would mean that they recognized themselves and were the first to strip off the camouflage. As a rule they do not go that far, though there have been some cases. In one way and another, the censors face a complicated task in attacking objective studies of other societies which are 'not ours'. Thus topicality and relevance are manifested in the choice of those countries and periods in which problems similar to ours are to be found. This feature of the development of the social sciences determines also the nature of the interest taken in them. The best people are engaged, as a rule, in studying not our own country or our own period, but subjects far away in time and space. This should, at any rate, save them from the need to lie.

But the censorship remains the censorship. In these works the reader is always aware of some reticence and he pays attention not so much to what is written as to what is between the lines – what cannot be written in legal publications. He himself draws the conclusions and makes the analogies which were not possible for the author. Yet all the same something remains hidden even from him, something understated. Such books raise questions rather than answer them. Illegal material is available only to a relatively small circle of people and cannot, at least for the time being, effectively supplement the legally published literature.

Hence the special role played by art as a means of cognition and generalization. As I have already said, a work of art is less easy to censor. The specific feature of art lies precisely in the fact that its content is never on the surface: that it is not formulated but shaped. It is 'encoded' in artistic images. This is a law of creativity which has nothing in common with the censor's rules, but that makes it all the easier, consciously or unconsciously, to get round those rules. The reader or the viewer draws his conclusions under the influence of the artistic whole. The censor can delete a phrase from a book about the history of the 'Third World', but it is much harder to correct a novel or a play. There may be nothing 'seditious' in any particular line. A work of art influences through its mood, its atmosphere, and here even the most skilful censor is helpless. As the saying goes, you can't leave any words out of a song. This strange ability of some works of art to resist censorship was noticed as early as the nineteenth century. 'La censure', wrote Herzen, 'est une toile d'araignée qui prend les petites mouches et que les grandes déchirent.'[108]

The censorship does not allow political conflicts to be directly depicted in art, but that does not mean that the artist is any the less politicized. Without wishing to, the censor does art a good service. For an idea to 'get across' it must be expressed in the most generalized form possible. Thoughts about society, a picture of our country's life, must be presented to the reader as a story about one household, or to the viewer as a film about the work of one brigade. But this is a truly artistic task! The law of art proclaims that social and political conclusions have to be drawn at the level of high philosophical generalizations, for otherwise what we have is not art but, at best, illustrations to theoretical works. Well, the censor always keeps that law in mind. The state censorship has not only ruined our literature: as Sinyavsky observed, 'up to a certain point it has also helped to make that literature more interesting.'[109]

We should not, however, see the censor as the artist's friend. Bureaucratic restrictions cannot avoid constraining creative people. But the censorship is not confined to politics alone – its second level is the censorship of subjects. A former Soviet newspaper editor, L. Finkelshtein, has spoken in the West of 'a 300-page index of banned subjects, known informally as the Talmud'.[110] Glavlit takes its decisions on the basis of this list.

Western scholars are often puzzled as to why a certain work has been banned. After all, some things that are sharper politically have been published! Many speak of a bureaucratic lottery, explaining such phenomena by mere chance. As a rule, though, bans are well motivated. There is method in this madness.[111] 'In most cases,' writes Claude Frioux, author of one of the best works on the Soviet intelligentsia published in the West, 'these works do not contain direct attacks on the regime. But they contain evidence of those aspects of history and reality which the censorship does not allow to be mentioned.'[112] As an example we can take the play *The Sailor's Rest*, by Alexander Galich, in which there was nothing anti-Soviet. The subject was the persecution of the Jews by the Nazis during the Second World War. For some time this had been a proscribed subject for writers, as the authorities considered that mention of such facts would arouse sympathy for the Jews and so hinder the pursuit of their anti-Semitic policy (restriction of access to institutions, to jobs, and so on). The play was banned. Galich became a dissident, and died in emigration.[113]

The censorship of subjects – or, more precisely, the index of forbidden subjects – decides what can and cannot be talked about. This 'taboo' often affects art more painfully than direct political censorship. But there is yet a third censorship – the censorship of form. The state declares that art must be accessible to the masses. Since the masses are unable – because they are not allowed – to express their views for themselves, the *nomenklatura* speaks on their behalf. In this way the aesthetic concepts of the ruling elite become the general norm. Accessibility to 'the masses' is in reality accessibility to the ruling circles, although it must be said that the artistic taste of the actual masses changes and develops rapidly, whereas the ruling statocracy shows bureaucratic conservatism in this sphere as well. This means that what is pursued in the guise of a struggle for 'popularity' in art is an anti-popular policy, a policy of imposing certain aesthetic norms and views on the people. Ilya Ehrenburg wrote of the bureaucrats that 'the tastes of the pre-revolutionary petty bourgeoisie seemed to them to be the canons of beauty.'[114] There is nothing surprising in that if we consider the petty-bourgeois origin of the present ruling elite. The stability of the statocracy's artistic principles is also quite natural, for owing to its well-defined organizational structure and artificial selection (only 'people of the same sort' are accepted into the *nomenklatura*), the mentality of this class has changed a great deal less in forty years than the consciousness of society as a whole. This results in exacerbated conflict between the higher and lower orders, in the cultural sphere as well.

The bureaucracy has its own notion of ideal form and of accessibility – of what is more and what is less admissible, both for artists and for viewers or readers. Consequently, the creative intelligentsia (except for the bureaucrats' servants who consciously work to please them) fight for their rights in constant conflict with the censorship of form. It is in this very sphere that the bitterest battles have been waged. In the post-Stalin period this censorship has weakened considerably, but this was achieved only after prolonged struggle.

In the Stalin era the attitude to art was totalitarian in the most precise sense of the word. Not only content and ideas but also style, form and artistic images were subjected to control. If an artist was allowed aesthetic independence, then he might later demand political independence as well. There could therefore be no concessions to creative individuality, or it would escape from control. As subsequent experience has shown, this attitude was, in its way (from the standpoint of the bureaucracy's interests), the only correct one. 'If we start from such premises,' a Canadian scholar has rightly observed, 'any policy which claims that a little artistic nonconformity does no harm to anybody appears foolish and suspicious.'[115] The Stalinist bureaucracy's endeavour to reduce art to politics, ignoring the specific character of artistic creativity, was capable of engendering only unartistic works. Theodor Adorno wrote, in his time, that essentially it was as unthinkable – or, rather, fruitless – for art to be devoted exclusively to problems of social and political struggle as for art to try to ignore that struggle. Artistic creativity can develop only 'between the two poles of involvement and non-participation, inclining now to one pole, now to the other, but never coinciding with either'.[116] The failure of the bureaucrats' attempts to make the question of form a political question – and thereby to create a state literature which should be reliable *in all respects* and yet which should really be *literature* – proves the correctness of this idea *a negativo*. The statocracy was compelled increasingly to lift its control, allowing greater freedom for intellectual activity and retreating from Stalin's totalitarian principles. But this process was slow and painful.

A peculiarity of totalitarian society is the existence of official ideals and norms applicable to every sphere of life. These ideals and norms are proclaimed by the ruling statocracy and guarded by the state, and deviation from them incurs sanctions. As Soviet society has evolved from the totalitarian to the authoritarian phase, 'free zones' have appeared where such norms and principles are absent. In these zones an opposition is formed. Most of these 'free zones' appeared after Stalin's death, in everyday life and in art, because it was hardest to pursue a unified policy in these spheres. Stalin, incidentally, understood this; that was why he tried to submit these hard-to-control spheres as much as possible to the state. 'The great leader' was quite right, from his point of view, to distrust the intelligentsia. However, in the policy of the statocracy towards the intelligentsia there were always two closely interconnected aspects. On the one hand the intellectuals had to be made to serve the regime; on the other, their independence had to be undermined by all possible means.

The 'Stratum' Concept

The bureaucracy fostered in every way an image of the intellectual as an inferior being compared with the worker and, still more, with the official – a 'whimperer', a 'crybaby', an unstable and cowardly person who needed to be looked after. Ushakov's dictionary gives this definition of the intellectual: 'a person whose social conduct is marked by weakness of will, waverings, doubts . . .'[117] The weak-willed 'intellectual' needed, as has been explained, to be guided by the bureaucrat.

At the theoretical level this policy was expressed especially in the concept of the 'stratum'. The *Great Soviet Encyclopaedia*, second edition, tells us: 'Being a stratum and not a class, the intelligentsia cannot play an independent role in social life.'[118] The illiteracy of this formulation is obvious. In the first place, we wonder what is meant by a 'stratum'? What is the class nature of the intelligentsia? If it is not itself a class – which is correct in principle – then to what class does it belong? After all, social strata exist *within classes*. If the intelligentsia exists only 'between' other classes, then it must be an independent class. Thus the 'stratum' theory is inherently contradictory, a circular square, and such a formulation is absolutely contrary to the very elements of Marxist theory.

The question of the class essence of the intelligentsia is, as we have seen, not an easy one to answer if we take into account the complex way the intelligentsia is formed. It was not by chance that Gramsci devoted considerable time to examining this problem to which Stalin had given, in two ticks, the answer quoted above – an answer which has since been quoted, with some variations, in all Soviet textbooks. But without going into details we can say that the twentieth century has seen a process of change in the class essence of the intelligentsia: its transformation from a petty-bourgeois to a proletarian stratum. At the same time, naturally – being a particular, distinct stratum – the intelligentsia could not but play an *independent* role in relation to the class with which it was connected. All this is elementary Marxism. But these were precisely the conclusions Stalin feared to draw: his task was to avoid them at all costs.

The Stalinists referred to a phrase of Lenin's about the intelligentsia not being an independent force. But in the first place, that does not mean that the intelligentsia has no special political role to play in social life. It has such a role, and Lenin wrote about it in *What Is To Be Done?* Secondly, Lenin was talking about the intelligentsia at the beginning of our century, which was small. Since the scientific-technological revolution, thanks to the transformation of science into a force of production, the many-millioned intelligentsia of today has become an independent social stratum, capable not only of formulating its aims but often of achieving them.

It was impossible for Stalin not to know this. The first signs of the scientific and technological revolution were already felt at the beginning of the 1950s. Why did he need to say, deliberately, such absurd things? Behind curious theoretical constructions it is not difficult to perceive real political aims. Let us examine his argument:

> The intelligentsia has never been a class and never can be a class – it was and remains a stratum, which recruits its members from among all classes of society. In the old days the intelligentsia recruited its members from the ranks of the nobility, of the bourgeoisie, partly from the ranks of the peasantry, and only to a very inconsiderable extent from the ranks of the workers. In our day, under the Soviets, the intelligentsia recruits its members mainly from the ranks of the workers and peasants. But no matter where it may recruit its members, and what character it may bear, the intelligentsia is nevertheless a stratum and not a class.[119]

We perceive at once that Stalin is consciously devising a theoretical sleight of hand. He replaces the question of the intelligentsia's role in the social division of labour (that is, of its class essence) with the question of how it is formed. Yet it is well known that every class and every social stratum 'recruits' its members from among other classes and social strata. Alongside the hereditary intellectuals there are people who have sprung from the working class, just as alongside the hereditary workers in the factories there are people of peasant origin, and also ruined bourgeois. The conclusion which Stalin was trying hard to avoid was that the Soviet intelligentsia formed part of the proletariat – that alongside the traditional working class, a new proletariat of mental labour had emerged. These now constitute two sections of one and the same class. Why was this conclusion unacceptable to Stalin? Precisely because his aim was to counterpose 'the intelligentsia' to 'the working class'.

His idea was roughly this. The intelligentsia must work under the leadership of the working class, *for* the working class, and so on and so forth. But since the workers also lack a voice of their own, the intelligentsia must work under the leadership of the 'Party' – that is, of the bureaucracy, which falsely substitutes itself for the working class. If Stalin had recognized the intelligentsia as part of the proletariat, he would have been obliged to recognize also its right to speak for itself. His entire construction would then collapse. Moreover, if it were a part of the proletariat the intelligentsia would be as close as possible to the workers in social position and fundamental interests, and would have no need of a mediator in the shape of the bureaucracy: it would itself be the vanguard of the proletariat.

Recognizing – even if only formally – the independence of the intelligentsia would mean, ultimately, recognizing also the independence of the workers themselves in relation to the statocracy. Stalin needed to see the intelligentsia 'side by side with the workers and peasants, *pulling together* with them'.[120] The role of driver of this *troika* fell to the bureaucracy. They decided the direction to be taken, they wielded the whip, and they got all the pleasure from the ride. The masses subject to the statocracy had to be separated from each other and deprived of independence. This was the political aim of the ruling circles. The 'stratum' concept helped to justify it.

'Socialist Realism'

A special theory was worked out for the sphere of art, establishing a sort of normative aesthetic code which could not be deviated from without incurring penalties. This was the famous 'socialist realism' (both words should be in inverted commas, since this aesthetic was in fact neither socialist nor realist).

In 1932 the Party functionaries in the sphere of literature (I.

Gronsky and V. Kirpotin) began to affirm this newly invented dogma. At the Writers' Congress in 1934 the formula 'socialist realism' was, for the sake of prestige, put into the mouth of Gorky, to whom its authority was ascribed. Later, and until 1956, Stalin himself was named as creator of the theory (which was evidently not far from the truth). Gorky's novel *Mother* was, as is well known, designated as the first example of 'socialist realism'. All of which, however, tells us nothing about the essence of the theory in question. Every definition of it in the textbooks, given in deliberately unintelligible bureaucratic jargon, is extremely abstract and can be interpreted in any way one likes. *Mother* was a phenomenon wholly rooted in the Social Democratic propaganda tradition of the beginning of the century, and comparison with it provides no answer. From the standpoint of style and distinctive artistic features *Mother* is a typical product of turn-of-the-century European naturalism, and a very imperfect and second-rate one at that. A much better example of such writing is Zola's novel *Germinal.* Consequently, neither the artistic nor the ideological features of Gorky's novel (which contained a few well-realized episodes) can be regarded as innovatory in any way. There is not the slightest basis for seeing in it a new 'artistic method'. Western literary critics therefore conclude, as a rule, that the official theory of 'socialist realism' is not to be taken literally, since its 'demagogic aspect' is too strongly marked.[121] But there is in it an element which cannot be left without comment or overlooked: the idea of 'partisanship' as officially interpreted. This is the key concept in normative aesthetic of 'socialist realism'.

As I have said already, Stalin's interpretation of 'partisanship' had little in common with Lenin's, although he claimed continuity. This contradiction was to be noted by critical intellectuals at the beginning of the 1960s, when they protested that 'partisanship in literature is now understood quite differently from the way Lenin understood it.'[122] However, it is the very 'originality' of Stalin's idea of partisanship that interests us here.

First, this doctrine assumes that 'the Party' – in the form of the bureaucratic leading circles, of course – has the right to give an artist guiding instructions, to supervise his work, to 'direct' him. Such instructions are published periodically either as special decisions (on the journals *Zvezda* and *Leningrad,* or, comparatively recently, on literary and art criticism, and so on) or as advice given to artists by the Party leaders (in every report he made to every congress, Brezhnev gave the creative intelligentsia their due share of advice and, as has been observed even in official circles, the advice handed out on different occasions is inconsistent). All these instructions are given, of course, in the name of 'the people', 'the Party', and so forth which, however, alters nothing. Such instructions can be comically detailed. Thus in the summer of 1954 writers were told to write books that would depict

> the splendid image of Soviet people – advanced workers in production, masters of agriculture, people who have brought the virgin lands under cultivation and by their inspired shock-work have created plenty in foodstuffs and other material benefits.[123]

In Stalin's time 'partisanship' was understood above all as meaning eulogy of 'the great teacher'. And they did eulogize him. In A. Surov's play *Dawn over Moscow*, the hero said of him: 'It seems to me that, every morning, he switches on the dawn over Moscow with his own hand.'[124] It would seem that one could not go further than that. ...

While freedom to create has been recognized by the official ideologists, very strict limits have been laid down for this freedom (fortunately, as time goes by, these limits are widening). The essence of 'socialist realism' as a whole is the subordination of artistic creativity to the tastes and purposes of the ruling statocratic class. These tastes and aims, however, have changed. The degree of subordination has also changed. For this reason 'socialist realism' can not simply be treated as a whole, as a consistent 'artistic' phenomenon. Analysis of concrete works also tells us little here. It has to be said that 'socialist realism' in the strict sense existed for a very short time, in the Stalin era alone. Where those years were concerned, one can speak of a more or less harmonious system of principles laid down by the ruling statocracy as the basis for any artistic creation. As the prominent Soviet historian A. Ya. Gurevich has said, every social phenomenon has to be studied 'in the phase when the potentialities contained within it are revealed most fully'.[125]

The first distinctive feature of Stalinist aesthetics is that it is centred on literature. This characteristic of socialist-realist theory can be explained from the historico-cultural and also from the sociopolitical standpoint. In the first place nineteenth-century Russian culture, on which theoreticians of Soviet art have based (and have continued to base) themselves really was, to a large extent, 'literature-centred'. This tradition has its roots in the depths of history. Secular literature took shape in Russia much earlier than secular art or music, even before Peter's time. Here it may be objected that eighteenth-century Russian painting was better than the literature of the same period. But we must remember that at the level of *world classics* it was Russian literature, the works of Pushkin and Griboedov, that came to the fore, while the turn of Russian painting and music arrived only later. Continuity and national originality were most strongly marked in literature, and that made it the reference point for Russian art as a whole. Symphonic music and secular painting came to Russia from the West, and in their search for identity the national schools of painters and composers (the 'Itinerants', the 'Mighty Handful', and so on) based themselves above all upon the successes of literature.

Consequently, there is nothing bad about 'literaturocentrism' in itself. It is bad only if it is made into an obligatory norm for all the arts. The literary mode of thought was proclaimed the model for all artistic thinking. The entire terminology and all the categories of 'socialist realism' were drawn not from the arts as a whole, but from literature alone. The aesthetics of the Renaissance, Classicism, Romanticism, the great epochs in the history of art, expressed something vital which united all the genres. The term 'critical realism', applied to nineteenth-century Russian and Western art but invented later, was used only in relation to literature – in its pure form, indeed, only to prose. The theory of 'critical realism' in Soviet art criticism was developed under the influence of the 'literaturocentrist' dogma and transformed into the 'historical element' in the socialist-realist construct. Attempts to discover 'critical realism' in art amounted to mere speculation. Instead of looking for *common features* in Courbet and Balzac, or in the Itinerants and Tolstoy, Courbet and the Itinerants were simply reduced to Balzac and Tolstoy, forced into the framework of literary aesthetics. (The question arises: What *is* realism in music or, for heaven's sake, in architecture?)

The concepts of 'critical' and 'socialist' realism were ideological twins, created in bureaucratic offices. Although they belong to different epochs, their coincidence revealed very well an approach which identified the history of art with the development of literature. This principle survived Stalin's death. It is interesting that between the 1950s and 1970s there were very few *artistic* disputes between the state and writers, even though there were plenty of *political* disputes. On the other hand, however, the constantly recurring disputes with composers and painters were exclusively artistic in character, although sometimes they were treated later as having been political. The reason was that the aesthetics of 'socialist realism' is in general potentially hostile to painting and music as art forms. Every new phenomenon in these fields, if it is original at all, is quite impossible to fit into the categories of 'literaturocentrist' aesthetics. The revolt against 'socialist realism' was, for painters, mainly a revolt against 'literaturocentrist' norms. The painters' refusal to let themselves be guided by literature aroused the indignation of the 'socialist realists', who accused their opponents of modernism, formalism and other sins. But the real issue was different: not between 'realism' and 'formalism', an antithesis thought up by the socialist-realists themselves, but between 'socialist realism' and painting.

With 'literaturocentrism' went an extremely suspicious attitude to the producer in the theatre. For the classical socialist-realist, a theatrical performance is a play which is read from the stage 'in character'. Everything else is from the Evil One. Campaigns were waged against 'distortion of classical plays' periodically throughout the sixties and seventies. The theoretician of 'socialist realism' cannot understand that what is being shown on the stage is not a play but a performance – that is, a totally new work, even a work of a different art. Naturally, an attempt to subject one art to the laws of another can have no good outcome. It is therefore not surprising that when, immediately after Stalin's death, the restrictions of the normative aesthetic were slightly loosened, Soviet literature achieved great successes, but painting developed with great difficulty.

But the orientation upon literature has social causes as well. Words are easiest to control. The strokes of a paintbrush, gestures, harmonies – these are less submissive to censorship. All existing methods of censorship are applicable chiefly to written texts. They can be cut – as also, though less successfully, can cinema film. Any narrative can be shortened, but it is difficult to 'cut' a picture without destroying it completely. Considerations of the censor's convenience played no small part in the establishment of 'socialist realism'.

Another important feature of 'socialist realism', as in any normative aesthetic, is orientation upon past examples. Again, there is nothing dangerous in this, provided that such orientation is not made binding on everyone and is not ensured (literally) by a repressive police apparatus. Here we also see the artistic conservatism of the ruling class, its inability to turn itself towards the future or even the present, as is the way with every anti-democratic ideology.

There were models of the first order – the masterpieces of Russian realist art of the nineteenth century and the beginning of the twentieth: Tolstoy, Turgenev, Chekhov. In painting, the Itinerants. In music, the Mighty Handful. In drama, the Moscow Art Theatre and Stanislavsky. But along with these genuine peaks of artistic achievement there were also models of the second order, in 'socialist realism' itself. These were, so to say, models of the correct imitation of models. Consequently, the ordinary painter was supposed to base himself not directly upon the models offered by Russian classical art, but upon them in the form in which they served as reference points for the creation of models of the second order. Then there were models of the third order – models of correct imitation of the imitators, and so on. If the chain were not broken, the degradation of art would continue. Plastov bases himself upon the Itinerants, and the next generation of artists base themselves on Plastov, for he himself has been canonized already. In each generation we see new canonized models. It is the same in the theatre. After Stanislavky, Kedrov becomes the classical model for everyone.

The actual development of art, however, took a different path after 1956. The contradiction between obligatory schemas and the real processes going on in culture gave rise to conflict after conflict over many years.

Finally, we must look at the bureaucratic concept of realism. Essentially, as I have already explained, for the conservative thinking of the bureaucrat, 'realism' means what resembles the work of Tolstoy, Turgenev, Gorky, and so on, so that what does not resemble it is not realism. This is a sort of artistic criterion which, again, is not without foundation. At the basis of such thinking, however, lies a deliberate rejection of any new form of realism. Along with the artistic criterion there is also an extra-artistic one which is no less important. This is the judging of a work of art according to the principle: is it like my idea of life (more correctly, is it 'lifelike' or 'not lifelike')? This criterion has been assiduously drummed into the heads of the mass of Soviet viewers and readers, right down to the 1970s. It continues to be an important theoretical stereotype.

In this connection it is very interesting to recall a study by a group of Soviet sociologists – G. Dadamyan, D. Dondurei and L. Nevler – who researched, with a group of students as their material, 'the ordinary way of perceiving art' as taught by official propaganda, the schools and the socialist-realist aesthetic. Those interrogated had to give their opinion of a super-realistic fresco in one of the rooms in their institute. Literal correspondence between the picture and its actual subject was the first and most important criterion. 'For some sections of the students,' the sociologists write,

the 'correctness', the exactness of 'what is painted on the wall' is the chief indicator which decides whether they accept or reject a painting. 'It shows a men's hostel, but there are women in it, and that's wrong, because we have segregated hostels,' they say: 'nobody wears overalls in our engineering workshops,' and so on. One viewer, after examining a painter's work, 'looking at everything in it', noted 'several mistakes' and declared that 'It's not like that,' for 'everything is sort of lifeless, static dummies with stony faces, identical figures': 'the artist has botched it, because he didn't study the way we live thoroughly enough: the faces and the buildings are not ours, and the teachers aren't like that.' The painter was said to have 'depicted our life untypically: for instance, all the students look very serious, but they are like that only at lectures,' and 'the girls are, for some reason, shown as very middle-aged-looking, as though they were teachers.'[126]

It is interesting that the viewer judged the fresco in accordance with the socialist-realist stereotype and his ideas were expressed in the language of the newspapers, of officialdom! The same interrogatees were convinced 'that the purpose of painting is, basically, practical. ... This thinking in terms of utility,' the sociologists comment, 'this assignment to a painting of a practical, functional purpose eliminates any possibility of perceiving its uniqueness as a work of art.'[127] Finally, their thinking was also marked by normativeness: 'In their judgements they often used such expressions as "the artist ought to be", "he should have shown", "it was necessary to depict", "it oughtn't to be done like that", and so on.'[128]

It is important to remember that this research was carried out at the end of the 1970s. Students are, as a rule, very well informed about matters related to the popular and narrative arts – the stage, literature, the cinema, television. Generally speaking, it must be said, an old ideology does not collapse all at once but 'departs bit by bit', losing its foothold in one sphere while still keeping it in another. The socialist-realist way of seeing things was shown here, first and foremost, in an obvious inability to understand contemporary painting, and that is very significant. Of course, by no means all the students who were questioned answered like those quoted above. Moreover, the socialist-realist perception of images was already by the 1970s not completely orthodox, having been partly depoliticized. The stereotypes of the 1930s and 1940s were much stricter. Interesting also was the presence of a large number of inside-out socialist-realists, who said that 'real' art is when everything is 'unlike life', when everything is the other way round.

Perhaps this concrete sociological investigation reveals the essence of 'socialist realism' better than any theoretical criticism. Every system of art has its 'model viewer', and this model tells us more about the given system than any statements made by its supporters and opponents. Social changes bring about the death of old aesthetic dogmas, because the actually existing 'model viewer' begins to change, and then no declarations, threats or bans can save what has outlived itself. Here, however, we are anticipating somewhat.

In concluding our discussion of the Stalinist conception of artistic creativity we must describe one more of its characteristic features. According to this theory, art must be free from conflict (this was said openly), or else the conflicts or real life must be replaced by invented, illusory or secondary ones. Typical of the classical 'socialist realism' of the 1940s was a conscious utopianism, the creation of a 'second reality', of what André Malraux called 'a fictitious world'.[129] Art's task here was not the cognition of reality by artistic means but the fashioning of an anti-reality while trying in every way to present this fictitious world as the only real one. For this reason 'socialist realism' was frequently and correctly described as 'utopia in lifelike forms'.

What is true is not what actually exists but what ought to exist, what is 'correct' from the standpoint of official ideology. Lunacharsky spoke frankly on this point:

> Imagine that a house is being built, and when it has been built it will be a splendid palace. But the building of it has not been finished yet, and you depict it in this unfinished state and say: 'There's your socialism for you – it's got no roof on it!' You will, of course, be a realist in saying that, you will be telling the truth: but it is immediately obvious that this truth is actually a lie.[!] Socialist truth can be spoken only by one who understands what sort of house is being built and how it is being built, and who knows that it *will* have a roof. A person who does not understand the course of development will never perceive the truth, because truth is not like its actual self [!!], it does not sit still, truth takes wing, truth is progress, truth is conflict, truth is struggle, truth is tomorrow, and it has to be seen like that. Whoever does not see it in that way is a bourgeois realist and therefore a pessimist, a moaner, and frequently a scoundrel and a falsifier – in any case, willingly or unwillingly, a counter-revolutionary and wrecker.[130]

Such an attitude as this fully justifies the persecution of Mikhail Bulgakov, the hushing-up of actual facts, the practice of censorship, and so on. There is really nothing else to be said on this matter. The division of truth into 'harmful' and 'useful', 'needed' and 'not needed', 'big' and 'little' is false in itself. Moreover, we have to bear in mind that it is the ruling class that has appropriated for itself the monopoly right to decide which truth is 'needed' and which is not. This approach to the 'reflection' of reality illustrates better than anything else the radical break with Marxism at which the Stalinist bureaucracy arrived. For comparison one can only quote Lenin, when he wrote: 'We need *full* and *truthful* information. And the truth should not depend on whom it has to serve.'[131]

Socialist realism was therefore not realism at all but, so to speak, promises in the form of art. This art performed very important functions in the Soviet society of the 1930s and 1940s. The Stalinist ideology was not without solid foundations: it was based upon a particular type of psychology, social and individual, which had been formed by a totalitarian regime over two and a half decades. L.S. Vygodsky was quite right when he said that 'no sociological investigation which is not supplemented by a psychological investigation will ever be able to reveal the most important cause of ideology, namely, the state of mind of social man.'[132] In the last analysis, as

Plekhanov observed, 'All ideologies have a common root in the psychology of the epoch to which they belong.'[133]

Stalinist art served a well-defined purpose – to create the 'optimum' moral and psychological climate for subjecting the masses to barracks-'Communism'. It had to embellish people's lives in a society suffering from poverty, repression and war, to create a utopian counterpoise to reality, and thereby to help people find the peace of mind that was desired.[134] This was an art of promises in a period of great promises. In a country which was moving further and further away from socialism it had, along with propaganda, to create the illusion of 'socialist construction'. 'Socialist realism' was, in the strictest sense, opium for the people, sedating and stupefying them. Finally, this same art had to educate people for totalitarian collectivism. Architecture had a special role to play here. At a time when many families were huddled together in 'communal' flats, the state was building enormous edifices which were then thought beautiful. The function of this architecture was to make the citizens' collective life more attractive than their individual lives. More than that: the poorer, harder, more squalid their individual lives were, the more attractive would their official, collective life become. This second life was no less real than the first, perhaps even more so. In Moscow they built a magnificent Metro, with stations like the halls of palaces, although their décor was excessively luxuriant in accordance with the taste of the *nomenklatura*. Soviet skyscrapers were built in the 'Stalinist baroque' style. The same purpose was served by organizing demonstrations on public holidays, bringing everyone together in a mood of celebration. The same sentiments had to be fostered by the theatre, films, painting and literature. It was an idea that spread from one work to another.

The utopian world of pseudo-art had its own laws and its own heroes. Characteristic of it was, as V. Kardin wrote later in the journal *Teatr*, 'a cold pomposity'. One was shown 'a significant conflict between a beardless worker-innovator and a grey-bearded conservative professor'. There appeared on the stage 'intellectuals poisoned by the venom of grovelling [before Western achievements? – *Trans.*] and restored to new life through a talk with a wise housewife or a shrewd Party organizer.'[135]

Constant lying and toadying corrupts people. Stalinist 'socialist realism' did not create a single significant work of art, nor did Stalinism create anything valuable in any other branch of culture. Bureaucratic totalitarianism and spiritual creativity proved incompatible. Stalinism, as one of the critics grouped around *Novy Mir* wrote later,

dried up the scholar as well as the writer. The system of literary prizes, the pre-determined analysis and evaluation of works, the impossibility of disputing the aesthetic standards laid down from 'on high', the dogmatism, the ostentation, the verbosity, all gradually destroyed the scholar's personal, subjective approach to literature. And without this there can be neither love for art – one can love only in one's own way and not otherwise – nor creative thinking about it: one can reveal only what is 'one's own', it is impossible to 'reveal' another person's ideas.[136]

One can, however, argue against this view. If things did not go too well as regards innovations in art, in science Stalin's favourites 'revealed' a great deal which later had to be quietly 'covered up'. 'Pseudoscientific approaches became dominant,' writes Zhores Medvedev, 'or at least prominent, in soil science, silviculture, zoology, botany, evolution, agrochemistry and many other areas.'[137] It was characteristic that theories which ran counter not only to scientific facts but even to simple logic became especially firmly established in just those branches of knowledge that were connected with agriculture, where they could do the greatest *practical* damage. There reigned in biology in those days the woefully renowned T. Lysenko, who was personally responsible for the persecution and death of a number of scientists and became notorious for the falsifying of experiments and other similar 'exploits'.[138] Towards the end of his career Lysenko was even intending to undertake, in the spirit of Zamyatin's sombre prophecy, the improvement of the human race on the basis of scientific humanity.

What most interests L. Graham, in analysing 'the Lysenko affair', is the fact that this orgy enjoyed state approval: 'The support that Lysenko won from Stalin was doubtless very important in his continued rise. But it is difficult to find the reason for this sympathy in Stalin's theoretical writings.'[139] The explanation, however, seems to be discoverable not in theory but in the psychology of the ruling circle in Stalin's time. The attitude of the statocracy to art largely explains its attitude to science also. The logic is the same in both cases. The essence of policy in science and the arts at the end of the 1930s and in the 1940s was this: it was necessary to bring the creative thinking of the intellectual – whether scientist, scholar or artist – down to the level of ordinary bureaucratic thinking, as this would make total control of them possible and effective. Fortunately the need to develop industrial, and especially military, technology checked this tendency towards the bureaucratization of science. The physicists could, on the whole, consider themselves lucky. The social sciences and biology suffered immeasurable harm.

To explain the Lysenko affair it is not enough to talk about Stalin, since Khrushchev, the exposer of Stalin, was an admirer of Lysenko too. What was involved here was not any sympathies or antipathies but the type of consciousness that was predominant in the ruling statocracy of those years. The fact, mentioned by Graham, that Lysenko's ideas were essentially anti-Marxist and even anti-materialist is far from accidental. It was quite natural for the ruling circles of the Stalin era to give their approval to such ideas. Lysenko's notion that acquired characteristics are inherited was fully consonant with Stalin's slogan: 'There are no fortresses that Bolsheviks cannot overcome.' If 'socialist realism' was 'an art of great promises', Lysenko tried to create 'a science of great promises'. The absolute power of the statocracy created the illusion of absolute possibility, unrestricted by any laws – and that meant that the laws of nature could not withstand Lysenko's work in selection, 'approved by the Party and the Government'. A similar situation arose in economics, where doubt was cast on the very idea that objective economic laws applied in the Soviet 'planned economy'. In this sphere retreat was sounded, though, and Stalin himself produced his famous *Economic Problems of Socialism in the USSR*, in which he acknowledged the objective character of economic laws under socialism.[140] To be sure, the 'laws' designated by him were in fact no more than ideological slogans and had no scientific meaning. Regardless, however, of this unimportant 'side effect' of Stalin's work, on the whole it meant a step forward for Soviet economic science, since this science can exist only if the objective character of economic laws is recognized. The catastrophic experience of some 'lawless' experiments by the Stalinist statocracy in the period of the first 'Five Year Plan' had taught somebody something. Economic 'laws' received permission to exist, if only formally.

The Lysenko affair was thus not accidental but a logical outcome of bureaucratic voluntarism, no less than 'socialist realism' in aesthetics. 'The situation in the arts in these years', writes Graham, 'was only indirectly related to that of the sciences, but it was none the less a significant aspect of the general environment of the Soviet intellectual.'[141] The standardization of art deepened the psychological hopelessness of the scientist – affected his or her consciousness – while the crisis in science, in its turn, could not but have its effect upon art. And processes of a crisis nature undoubtedly developed in several fields of scientific knowledge, albeit with varying intensity.

All critical thinking died away, and the spiritual life of the Stalinist state increasingly offered 'a suggestive resemblance to the classic church-state' of the Byzantine type.[142] Such were the first results of the bureaucrats' onslaught upon culture and the intelligentsia.

Notes

1. Trotsky, *My Life*, Universal Library, New York 1960, p. 488.
2. An expression of M. Bolkhovsky's (*Cherez top'*, p. 48).
3. Philip Pomper, *The Russian Revolutionary Intelligentsia*, New York 1970, p. 196.
4. Roman Jakobson (1930) in R. Jakobson and D. Svyatopolk-Mirsky, *Smert' Vladimira Mayakovskogo*, Paris 1975, p. 34.
5. Marx and Engels, *Sochineniya*, 2nd edn, vol. 18, pp. 511–12 (Émigré Publications 1874–75: The Blanquists' Programme).
6. Engels, *The Peasant War in Germany* (Marx and Engels, *Collected Works*. vol. 10, pp. 469–70.)
7. G.V. Plekhanov, *Nashi raznoglasiya*, in *Izbrannye filosofskie proizvedeniya*, Moscow 1956, vol. 1, p. 345.
8. Ibid., p. 323.
9. See Wolfgang Leonhard, *Was ist Kommunismus? Wandlungen einer Ideologie*, Munich 1976 (? 1978), pp. 41–2. Cf. Trotsky, *The Revolution Betrayed*, New York 1945, p. 255.
10. Wlodzimierz Brus, *Socialist Ownership and Political Systems*, 1975, p. 30.
11. Lenin, *Collected Works*, 4th edn, English version, vol. 22, p. 144.
12. A somewhat different view is maintained by Roy A. Medvedev. He, of course, regards democracy as one of the distinguishing features of socialism, but says that the absence of one of these features by no means signifies the absence of socialism (see, for example, his interview in *Paese Sera*, 13 February 1977). To my mind, however, the trouble is not that one of the distinguishing features of socialism is 'absent' but that it is hard to find any important distinguishing features that *are* present. There is no political democracy, there is no workers' self-management in production, and so, consequently, there is no social ownership. The abolition of illiteracy, the creation of a more or less developed system of social security – not to mention the industrialization and the immense growth of the productive forces in the former colonial borderlands of Russia – are undoubted achievements by the ruling regime which nobody will deny; but what is there in them that is specifically 'socialist'? In the advanced capitalist countries too, as is well known, there has been economic and social progress in the last sixty years. Besides, what is vitally important is something different: that *democracy is not just a distinguishing feature of socialism, but its essence* – as Engels, incidentally, pointed out long ago.
13. Gianni Sofri, *Il modo di produzione asiatico: storia di una controversia marxista*, Turin 1974 (1969), pp. 104, 105.
14. Trotsky, *The Revolution Betrayed*, pp. 5, 20.
15. For a survey of Marxist views on the Soviet bureaucracy, see René Ahlberg, *Die sozialistische Bürokratie: Marxistische Kritik am etablierten Sozialismus*, Stuttgart 1976.
16. Berdyaev, *The Origin of Russian Communism*, 1937, p. 153.
17. See Monty Johnstone, 'Conflicts between socialist states', *Marxism Today*, vol. 23, no. 8, August 1979; W. Granow and M. Krütke, 'Zwei Stalinismus-Debatten in der K.P. Grossbrittaniens', *Das Argument*, 1/8, 1979; J. Elleinstein, 'Sur le phénomène Stalinien, la démocratie et le socialisme', *Esprit*, no. 2, February 1976. For criticism of this type of theoretical notion, see the review of works by Elleinstein, Garaudy and other writers in the special number of the Paris review *Critique*, no. 392, 1980, under the heading: 'Le comble du vide'.
18. Such views have been expressed by Charles Bettelheim and C. Castoriadis. The best work of this kind, in my opinion, is G. Chaliand's *Mythes révolutionnaires du Tiers Monde*, Paris 1979. For an exposition and critique of these ideas, see M. Cheshkov, *Kritika predstavlenii o pravyashchikh gruppakh razvivayushchikhsya stran*, Moscow 1979.
19. Andras Hegedüs, *Socialism and Bureaucracy*, 1976, pp. 9–10.
20. We must define the difference between the terms 'statocracy' and 'bureaucracy'. By a bureaucracy is meant an exclusive apparatus of officials, composed by the method of appointment. A statocracy is a community of the class type, which a bureaucracy may not

be. In any case, bureaucracy is found practically everywhere. It exists in present-day Britain and America and it existed in the France of Louis XIV and in the Germany of Marx's time. Statocracy, however, exists only in societies of the Soviet type and in a number of countries of the Third World (for example Mexico) which have developed their own variety of the statocratic mode of production.

21. Hegedüs, p. 170.

22. Marx and Engels, *Collected Works*, vol. 1, p. 344.

23. Stephen Cohen, *Bukharin*, 1974, p. 143.

24. M. Voslensky, *Nomenklatura: Anatomy of the Soviet Ruling Class*, 1984, pp. 112, 118.

25. Trotsky, *The Revolution Betrayed*, p. 249.

26. From Lenin's notes on Bukharin's book *Economics of the Transformation Period*, in *Leninsky Sbornik*, vol. 11, 1929, p. 357. [This passage is mistranslated in the 1971 New York translation of Bukharin's book, where – on page 214 – the phrase meaning 'appropriate the labour' is rendered as 'take on the work' – *Trans.*]

27. It is noteworthy that when he wrote about countries outside the sphere of European capitalism, Marx used these categories with extreme caution.

28. See Ahlberg, p. 108.

29. Marc Rakovski, *Towards an East-European Marxism*, 1979, p. 85.

30. If this conjecture is valid, then consequently alienation and the social problems connected with it will continue to exist under socialism: alienation in general cannot be completely eliminated. What is involved is merely the elimination of present-day social forms, which threaten *total* alienation of the personality, in favour of more human forms which will ensure the systematic removal of alienation.

31. Rakovski, pp. 47–8.

32. M.A. Cheshkov, 'Metodologicheskie problemy analiza gosuklada: tip obshchestvennogo vosprizvodstva i sotsialnyi nositel', in *Ekonomika razvivayushchikhsya stran: teorii i metody issledovaniya*, Moscow 1979, p. 336.

33. Ibid.

34. Ibid., p. 339.

35. *L'Express*, no. 1532, 1980, p. 27.

36. G. Lisichkin, *Chto cheloveku nado?*, p. 120.

37. Cheshkov, p. 329.

38. We must make clear that in this book 'ideology' is not, of course, to be understood in the spirit of Stalinism but also is not to be interpreted as Marx's 'false consciousness'. Marx's interpretation – science is true, ideology is false – is thoroughly polemical. We are well aware that in scientific work, too, some false information can appear (owing to imperfect equipment, inadequate methods, mistakes by oneself and others, and so on). The watershed does not run there. In my view, science is distinguished from ideology by the fact that the former is based upon knowledge and the second upon belief. One and the same scientific fact can be an ideological fact, and vice versa. For some Marxism is a science, for others an ideology, depending on how they understand and perceive Marxism (and so both are right, each in their own way). As for the official Soviet interpretation of ideology, based on Stalin's interpretation of Lenin's thesis that there are 'only two ideologies' ('bourgeois' and 'Soviet'), its consistent exposition must bring any rationally thinking person to quite absurd conclusions. If the 'two ideologies' contradict each other on all points and have nothing in common, then of course peaceful coexistence between ideologies is impossible and dialogue, discussion, debate between them unthinkable. In order to debate one must be agreed on something, otherwise the very subject for debate disappears. But for this same reason (the impossibility of ideological discussion) ideological struggle is also impossible. War between ideologies, therefore, can be concluded only by force of arms – not by 'the weapon of ideas' but by real weapons. All this is, of course, unreal. There are not only two classes and there are not only two ideologies. Furthermore, every social class is heterogeneous. The ideology of a class expresses not just its interests but also its illusions, its traditions and its mood at each actual moment. And if being does indeed determine consciousness, then a society's ideology must be changeable and diverse, like life itself. Finally, the Stalinists recognize

only the ideology of blind faith. In real life faith may waver, and may be tested by knowledge. In reality we find both ideological struggle and coexistence between ideologies. For example, semi-official Soviet internationalism has always coexisted peacefully with unofficial Russian chauvinism and anti-Semitism. Ideology, therefore, is to be understood here as the totality of ideas about society which are engendered by certain real interests and conditions. These ideas may, of course, be remote from the truth, especially if that suits somebody's interest.

39. C. Bettelheim and B. Chavance, 'Le stalinisme en tant qu'idéologie du capitalisme d'état', *Les Temps Modernes*, no. 394, May 1979, p. 1736.

40. *XIII S'ezd R.K.P. (b.), stenografichesky otchet*, Moscow 1924, p. 167. (In the 1963 reprint, p. 158.)

41. H. Marcuse, *Soviet Marxism*, 1968, p. 132.

42. Ibid., p. 131. To be sure, official ideologists do sometimes speak out in defence do criticism and satire. At the Nineteenth Party Congress, in 1952, Malenkov said that we needed Soviet Gogols and Shchedrins. These statements, made in the midst of an anti-intellectual and anti-Semitic terror, were for some reason not taken seriously. Moscow wits joked that 'we need Shchedrins and Gogols all the more so that they'll leave *us* alone.'

43. Cheshkov, p. 165.

44. Marx and Engels, *Collected Works*, vol. 3 (1975), pp. 140–41.

45. *One-Dimensional Man*, 1964.

46. Jean-Paul Sartre, *Situation IX*, 1972, p. 235.

47. The term 'totalitarian authority' is used here only in relation to Stalin's rule, the period 1928 to 1953. Contrary to the view taken by many Soviet and East European socialists (e.g. Kuron), I do not regard the post-Stalin regimes as being totalitarian. They are, rather, transitional between the totalitarian and the authoritarian type. (This transition was completed in Poland, Hungary and Yugoslavia by the end of the 1970s, and it is ridiculous to speak of totalitarianism in the Poland of 1979.)

48. A.L. De Castris, *Egemonia e paseismo*, Bologna 1981, p. 117.

49. Marcuse, *Soviet Marxism*, p. 125.

50. Rakovski, p. 46.

51. Gramsci, *Selections from the Prison Notebooks*, ed. Quintin Hoare and Geoffrey Nowell Smith, 1971, p. 149. Cf. Gramsci's *Elementi de Politica*, Rome 1978, p. 51.

52. Robert C. Tucker, *The Soviet Political Mind: Stalinism and Post-Stalin Change*, 1972, pp. 138–9.

53. Ibid., p. 139.

54. Shatz, *Soviet Dissent in Historical Perspective*, Cambridge 1981, p. 1.

55. Leopold Labedz, 'The Structure of the Soviet Intelligentsia', in Pipes, p. 75.

56. Shatz, pp. 1–2.

57. R.A. Medvedev, *Let History Judge*, p. 110.

58. *Klassovaya bor' ba putem vreditel' stva*, Moscow and Leningrad 1930, p. 9.

59. *Bol' shaya Sovetskaya Entsiklopediya*, 2nd edn, Moscow 1951, vol. 9, p. 262.

60. R.A. Medvedev, *K sudu istorii*, p. 239 [apparently not in *Let History Judge* – trans].

61. Boffa, vol. 1, pp. 447–8.

62. The *Great Soviet Encyclopaedia*, 3rd edn, repeats the Stalinist version, according to which 'an active, organized wrecking campaign' was carried out in the USSR (vol. 29, Moscow 1978, p. 307). (In the English translation of the *Encyclopaedia* [1982] this passage appears in vol. 29, p. 530). And in 1976 the journal *Chelovek i Zakon*, no. 10, published an article by D. Golinkov on the Shakhty case which repeated all the old propagandist fabrications.

63. *Istoriya KPSS*, 4th edn, ed. B.N. Ponomarev, Moscow 1975, p. 383.

64. *Vecherniy Tbilisi*, 18 November 1981, p. 4.

65. *Istoriya KPSS*, p. 383.

66. *Sovetskaya intelligentsiya. Istoriya formirovaniya i rosta, 1917-1955*, Moscow 1968.

67. *Voprosy istorii*, no. 8, 1970, p. 148.

68. R.A. Medvedev, *Let History Judge*, p. 106.

69. G. Boffa and G. Marinet, *Dialogue sur le stalinisme*, Paris 1977, p. 175.

70. Shatz, p. 88.

71. *Protiv istoricheskoy kontseptsii M.N. Pokrovstrogo*, Part I, Moscow 1939, p. 5.

72. R.A. Medvedev, *Let History Judge*, p. 224.

73. Stephen F. Cohen, ed., *An End to Silence*, 1982, p. 124.

74. N. Bukharin, 'Proletariat i voprosy khudozhestvennoy politiki', *Krasnaya Nov'*, no. 4, May 1925, p. 272.

75. Ibid.

76. Ibid.

77. *Literaturnaya Entsiklopediya*, Moscow 1930, vol. 1, p. 693.

78. *Kratkaya Literaturnaya Entsiklopediya*, Moscow 1968, vol. 5, p. 893.

79. See, for fuller discussion of this, Ernst Fischer and Franz Marek, *Was Lenin wirklich sagte*, Vienna–Munich–Zurich 1969, pp. 174–6.

80. Chaké Der Melkonian-Minassian, *Politiques littéraires en URSS: Depuis les débuts à nos jours*, Montreal 1978, p. 19.

81. *Literaturnaya Entsiklopediya*, Moscow 1935, vol. 9, p. 144.

82. Ibid., p. 150.

83. Ibid.

84. R.A. Medvedev, *Let History Judge*, p. 231.

85. Edward Shils, *The Intellectuals and the Powers, and other essays*, Chicago and London 1972, pp. 92–3.

86. Fernando Claudín, *Vida y obra de Marx y Engels*, 1979, p. 95.

87. Marcuse, *Soviet Marxism*, p. 11.

88. Umberto Cerroni, *Crisi ideale e transizione al socialismo*, Rome 1977, p. 65.

89. Marcuse, *Soviet Marxism*, p. 39.

90. Shils, p. 15.

91. *Mouvement Social*, no. 64, July–September 1968, p. 239.

92. *International Socialist Journal*, vol. 5, no. 25, 1968, pp. 42, 43.

93. Jean-Paul Sartre, *Between Existentialism and Marxism*, p. 246.

94. Jean-Pierre Chevènement, *Le Vieux, la crise, le neuf*, Paris 1974, p. 149.

95. *Pravda*, 14 November 1981.

96. Ibid.

97. Rakovski, p. 44.

98. Let me stress that the term 'illegal' activity is used in this work conventionally, only in the sense of activity not approved of by the official authorities. 'Illegal' activity is not necessarily 'against the law'. The actions of dissidents are often more legal, even in relation to Soviet laws, than those of the authorities, who continually violate their own ordinances. This is very clear from the documents of the human-rights movement in the USSR.

99. R.A. Medvedev, *Let History Judge*, p. 118.

100. A. Nekrich, 'Rewriting History', in *Index on Censorship*, vol. 9, no. 4, 1980, p. 4.

101. A. Sinyavsky, 'Samizdat and the Rebirth of Literature', in ibid., p. 8.

102. *An End to Silence*, p. 253.

103. Marx and Engels, *Collected Works*, vol. 1, p. 354.

104. Ibid., p. 119.

105. Ibid., pp. 120–21.

106. Russian works published abroad are especially difficult to get sight of. A high reputation among historians of the Soviet period is enjoyed by the 'special store' of Tartu Library, where pre-war *émigré* publications are extensively available. (Before the war, Tartu was 'abroad'.) But even if you manage to find something and read it, a second problem then arises: how can this be communicated to the reader?

107. Nekrich, p. 5.

108. Herzen, *Sobranie Sochinenii v tridtsati tomakh*, Moscow 1956, vol. 7, p. 87.

109. Sinyavsky, p. 8.

110. Ronald Hingley, *Russian Writers and Soviet Society, 1917–1978*, 1979, p. 210.

111. The journal *Index on Censorship* has published a great deal of information which throws quite a lot of light on the workings of the Soviet censorship. See: L. Vladimirov, 'Glavlit: How the Soviet Censor Works' (no. 3–4, 1972); J. Jurasas, 'Censoring Shakespeare in Moscow' (no. 3, 1975); M. Jonson, A. Vinograde, 'Censoring Böll's books in the USSR' (no. 2, 1976); 'Reprisals against *Metropol* authors and *Poiski* editors' (no. 2, 1980).

112. *Révolution*, no. 14, 1980, p. 28.

113. More details about the affair of *The Sailor's Rest* and of the struggle against censorship in the theatre are given in A. Tamarchenko, 'Theatre censorship', in *Index on Censorship*, vol. 9, no. 4, 1980.

114. *Novy Mir*, no. 4, 1962, p. 35.

115. Der Melkonian-Minassian, p. 256.

116. Theodor W. Adorno, *Zur Dialektik des Engagements*, Frankfurt-am-Main 1973, p. 8.

117. D.N. Uskakov, ed., *Tolkovyi slovar' russkogo yazyka*, Moscow 1935, vol. 1, p. 1214.

118. *Bol'shaya sovetskaya entsiklopediya*, 2nd edn, vol. 18, p. 270.

119. Stalin, Speech, 25 November 1936, on the Draft Constitution of the USSR (*Leninism*, 1940, p. 581).

120. Ibid., p. 567.

121. Der Melkonian-Minassian, p. 128.

122. *Politichesky dnevnik*, vol. 1, p. 178 [apparently not in *An End To Silence* – *Trans.*]

123. *Novy Mir*, no. 12, 1954, p. 219.

124. Quoted in *Novy Mir*, no. 9, 1964, p. 236.

125. A.Ya. Gurevich, 'M. Blok i "Apologiya istorii"', in M. Blok (Marc Bloch), *Apologiya istorii*, Moscow 1973, p. 185.

126. G. Dadamyan, D. Dondurei, L. Nevler, 'Vospriyatie monumental'nago iskusstva', in *Voprosy sotsiologii iskusstva. Teoreticheskie i metodologicheskie problemy*, Moscow 1979, pp. 218–19.

127. Ibid., p. 215.

128. Ibid., p. 214.

129. *Sovremennaya burzhuaznaya estetika*, Moscow 1978, p. 201.

130. Lunacharsky, 'Sotsialistichesky realizm' (1933) in *O teatre i dramaturgii*, Moscow 1958, vol. 1, pp. 735–6.

131. Lenin, *Collected Works*, vol. 42, p. 339 (Letter to E. Varga, 1 September 1921).

132. L.S. Vygodsky, *Psikhologiya iskusstva*, Moscow 1969, p. 26.

133. G.V. Plekhanov, *Fundamental Problems of Marxism*, 1930, p. 73.

134. W. Brus notes, for example, that real wages in the USSR 'according to detailed Western research, reached in 1952 barely 66–68 per cent (depending on the prices used in the calculation) of the 1928 level'. (Brus, p. 107.)

135. *Teatr*, no. 5, 1957, p. 47.

136. *Novy Mir*, no. 9, 1956, p. 248.

137. Zh. Medvedev, *Soviet Science*, p. 55.

138. There is an extensive literature on Lysenko. Among the *émigrés* this subject has been studied with greatest thoroughness by M. Popovsky and Zhores Medvedev. See Zhores Medvedev, *The Rise and Fall of T.D. Lysenko*, London 1969: also Dominique Lecourt, *Proletarian Science? The Case of Lysenko*, 1977.

139. Graham, p. 214.

140. *Bol'shevik*, 1952, no. 18.

141. Graham, p. 15.

142. Tucker, in *Political Science Quarterly*, p. 181.

4

The Thaw

The Late Stalin Period: Anti-Intellectualism and Russian Nationalism

The growth of the new intelligentsia during the 1940s, in both quantity and quality, was bound to worry Stalin. In the 1930s members of the old intelligentsia and the revolutionary intelligentsia had suffered from his repressive measures, but those same years saw the formation of the nucleus of a new intellectual stratum. A considerable proportion of these people belonged to national minorities, especially the Jews, to whom exodus from the Pale of Settlement had given access to the intellectual professions, which from the nineteenth century onwards enjoyed particular prestige in that community. The thirties were not only the period when the old intelligentsia was crushed, but also the period of the formation on a mass scale of a new intelligentsia which was partly Jewish. During the twenties a certain cultural potential had accumulated in Jewish families and they had turned 100 per cent towards Russian culture. The Jews who joined the intelligentsia in the 1930s took up the banner of the Russian Westernizers of the nineteenth century. Had the Jews remained within the ambience of their own 'national culture' and not become assimilated, they would have given the rulers no great cause for alarm. However, instead, they reinforced to a certain degree the most progressive wing of the Russian intelligentsia and Russian culture.

It is therefore not surprising that the campaign launched by Stalin against the new intelligentsia was at the same time an anti-Semitic campaign. I. Kon wrote later that for the anti-Semite 'the Jew symbolizes the intellectual in general.'[1] The hatred of 'Yids, students and intellectuals' which was a traditional characteristic of the Russian bureaucracy was revived, so to speak, at a new level. 'Stalin', observes Roy Medvedev,

> showed clear signs of anti-Semitism even before the war, when many centres of Jewish culture were eliminated and a great number of Jewish organizations suppressed. Hitler watched his harassment of Jews with considerable satisfaction. After the war, persecution and repressive measures against Jews were resumed with mounting intensity and brutality, until Stalin came up with his plan for a 'final solution' of the Jewish question, which envisaged the deportation of all Soviet Jews to the northern regions of Kazakhstan.[2]

Nevertheless, the struggle against the new intelligentsia which began at the end of the forties cannot be reduced to anti-Semitism alone. In Russia anti-Semitism was always clearly linked with anti-intellectualism.

The period 1945 to 1946 was a time of great expectations. After the victory in the Second World War people hoped in a vague way for some changes such as those which did actually come about in 1953–54. 'Immediately after the Second World War,' writes Graham,

> many intellectuals in the Soviet Union hoped for a relaxation of the system of controls that had been developed during the strenuous industrialization and military mobilizations. Instead, there followed the darkest period of state interference in artistic and scientific realms. This postwar tightening of ideological controls spread rather quickly from the fields of literature and art to philosophy, then finally to science itself. Causal factors already mentioned include the prewar suspicion of bourgeois science, the extremely centralized Soviet political system, and the personal role of Stalin. But there was another condition that exacerbated the ideological tension: the Cold War between the Soviet Union and certain Western nations, particularly the United States.[3]

The American writer underestimates the most important factor. From the standpoint of Stalin and his closest collaborators, the growth of hope for a softening of the regime was at that time of extremely negative significance, and they had to put an end to such 'weakness' and 'complacency'. Boffa mentions also that the statocracy necessarily feared 'the new unity between the intelligentsia and the people which had come about during the war'.[4]

The attack on the creative intelligentsia was headed by Stalin's 'loyal pupil and comrade-in-arms', Andrei Zhdanov. His task was to organize a showdown with what remained of the intellectuals who still preserved continuity with tradition. For this purpose he made a speech at the Central Committee Plenum on 14 August 1946, after which the CC adopted its pogrom-resolution 'On the Journals *Zvezda* and *Leningrad*'. The victims of the persecution that followed included Zoshchenko, Akhmatova and Shostakovich and, later, Eisenstein,

Pudovkin, Kozintsev, Trauberg, Prokofiev, Khachaturian and many others. The task before Stalin and company was more complex than this, however: it was to destroy, once and for all, the last shoots of genuine cultural life, seen, in Boffa's words, 'as a sphere in which critical thinking might emerge'.[5]

The witch-hunt spread. From literature it moved to music, the new composers being charged with underappreciating Russian national folk melodies. Zhdanov's death in 1948, at the height of the anti-intelligentsia hysteria, did not check it in the least. The crushing of the writers and musicians, which went ahead against the background of the Lysenko debauch in science and the Cold War in politics, led to a final break in cultural ties with the West. 'It was dangerous even to quote foreign sources,' writes Roy Medvedev, 'to say nothing of corresponding with foreign scholars.'[6]

Zhdanovism and Lysenkoism went hand in hand. The bureaucratic onslaught on spiritual life began with the attack on the journals *Zvezda* and *Leningrad* and ended ... it is hard to say with what or where it ended, because until Stalin's death no end to this onslaught was in sight. The fight against 'kinless cosmopolitans' in literary criticism was accompanied by the rooting-up of 'bourgeois genetics', and the attacks on Zoshchenko's stories were echoed by curses directed at 'the pseudoscience of cybernetics'. By 1952 the agenda even included a fight against the theory of relativity, referred to as 'reactionary Einsteinism'. It was typical that this new campaign was headed by A. Maksimov, who had written very favourably about Einstein in the 1920s,[7] and by G. Naan, who later became a defender of the theory of relativity.[8] However, Einstein's theory managed to withstand the attacks upon it, thanks to the resistance put up by the physicists. After Hiroshima the development of physics was connected with the increase of military might, and the statocracy valued above all others the scientists working in this field. The change of psychological climate in the discussion about the theory of relativity, as Graham notes, 'began to occur even before Stalin's death in March 1953.'[9] The main blow was struck at literature and the social sciences.

At this time the ideological basis of the bureaucratic reaction became open nationalism. In his pamphlet *Concerning Marxism in Linguistics*, published in 1950, Stalin divided languages into two categories, the strong and the weak, and wrote, about the crossing of languages:

> As a matter of fact, one of the languages usually emerges victorious from the cross, retains its grammatical system and its basic word stock and continues to develop in accordance with its inherent laws of development, while the other language gradually loses its virtue and gradually dies away.[10]

He added, as though casually, that the Russian language 'always emerged the victor'.[11]

It is important that this was mentioned as an example; Stalin did not ascribe any special qualities to the Russian language; these were simply assumed. This is, in general, a notable feature of the statocratic ideology: the main thing lies between the lines; the main thing is not said, only implied. But the significance of such 'slips of the tongue' at the beginning of the 1950s can hardly be overestimated. 'In this way,' as the Austrian Scharndorf observes, 'Great-Russian chauvinism received its theoretical foundation.'[12] The Soviet statocracy, born of the Bolshevik Revolution, had hitherto concealed its nationalism behind 'internationalist' phraseology. After the war the ideological situation changed. 'From defence,' writes Boffa, 'nationalism went over to the offensive.'[13]

The 1940s saw an intensive rethinking of history on Russian nationalist lines. As an example we may take *the struggle for priority*: the attempt to show that everything had always been first invented by Russian craftsmen. Even serious academic publications were obliged to repeat this blatant falsehood. There were even quite anecdotal items, such as the story about 'Kryakutnoy of Nerekhta', who was said to have risen into the air in a balloon long before the Montgolfier brothers. ... An article about the daring balloonist appeared in *Izvestiya* on 16 July 1949 and four years later, in 1953, Kryakutnoy, 'eighteenth-century Russian inventor, who built the first hot-air balloon in the world', already figured in the *Great Soviet Encyclopaedia*.[14] All this, as L. Reznikov wrote later in *Voprosy Literatury*, was 'fantasy of the first water'. The fact was that 'Kryakutnoy had been invented by the well-known nineteenth-century forger A. Sulukadzev.'[15] It is strange that exposure of this falsification had to wait until 1981, when Reznikov published his article.[16] Everyone knew perfectly well about Sulukadzev in 1949 and 1953, but contempt for truth was so great in Stalinist society that even the sedate *Great Soviet Encyclopaedia* did not shrink from printing a notorious lie, provided it corresponded to 'Party directives' – in this case the fight for 'priority'.

All the peoples of the USSR had to acknowledge that they were 'younger brothers' of the Russians, although some of them (for example, the Tadzhiks and the Armenians) went back a thousand years earlier. It was suddenly discovered that the cultural traditions of all the peoples of our country had been linked with Russia long before the conquest of these peoples by the Muscovite Tsars and that everything that was best (!) in their history and culture was due to the Russians. Thus, for example, in Tadzhikistan in the 1950s a certain Radzhabov specialized in working up this idea. Firdousi's poetry would never have

been written, according to him, had the poet not been influenced by ...
Kiev Rus. Through provincial backwardness this sort of 'research'
continued in some places even after Stalin's death.[17]

But it was the historians who made the most impressive effort. In
order to justify Russian nationalism a special theory of 'the lesser evil'
was elaborated, according to which the conquest of Caucasia and
Central Asia by the Russians was not at all a misfortune for the
subjected peoples but really a stroke of luck, in a way, for they thus
avoided 'something very much worse': the British yoke. Inclusion in the
Tsarist state enabled these peoples to get to know their Russian 'elder
brother' and to wage a struggle for freedom alongside the Russian
proletariat. The crass absurdity of this theory is obvious, if only because
it presents as the great good fortune of the Uzbeks and the Georgians
the fact that, having fallen under the rule of the autocracy, *they were
then in a position to fight against the autocracy*. It was as though an
arrested person were to be told that he was lucky to be in prison,
because he could now try to escape. As for the comparison between
Russian and British colonialism, the only advantage ascribed to the
former was that it was Russian, and here we should mention a point
which is objectively correct. As Marx observed in his writings on British
rule in India, colonialism actually led to progress in the development of
the productive forces of Asia and brought about the only real social
revolution the East had known. However, Marx and Engels considered
Russian Tsarism a greater evil in Asia (and in Europe) than British
imperialism. It is important that while acknowledging the objective
advance made in the sphere of the productive forces, they nevertheless
did not justify colonialism morally.[18] The theory of 'the lesser evil', on
the contrary, amounted precisely to a moral justification of the Russian
state. Fighters for independence like Shamil were depicted as villains
and reactionaries (just as the official press does today when writing
about Eritrea or Afghanistan). The new version of history was finally
established during a discussion in 1951–52 which followed a letter by
M.V. Nechkina to *Voprosy Istorii* in April 1951. The textbooks were
urgently revised, popular heroes being transformed into agents of
British imperialism.[19]

Along with the 'Russian orientation' in the historiography of the
Union Republics, the latter also developed their own 'little nationalism',
which at that time could still coexist with Russian chauvinism. Thus B.
Gafurov, in Tadzhikistan, wrote that the Tadzhiks were the most
enlightened people in Asia, that Persia was a cultural periphery of
Tadhikistan, and that the Greeks and Chinese of Antiquity were
influenced by the Tadzhiks.[20] In Armenia the same role was played by
G. Goyan. The minor nationalism of the Tadzhiks, the Armenians or

the Uzbeks coexisted happily with and supplemented the major nationalism of the Russians. It was clear that the greatest people of all was the Russian people. Its superiority was not contested. On the next rung down stood all the other peoples of the USSR, and beneath them, as the lowest of the low, all the other peoples in the world. As experience showed, playing with 'little nationalism' was playing with fire: the 'younger brothers' grew up quickly. But in the forties and at the beginning of the fifties the principal concern of the Russian statocracy was to put an end to internationalism.

The decisive onslaught on the internationalist ('cosmopolitan') intelligentsia began in January 1949, when *Pravda* devoted an entire page to an unsigned article 'On a Certain Anti-Patriotic Group of Dramatic Critics'. By a strange coincidence, almost all the 'anti-patriots' and 'cosmopolitans' turned out to be Jews. The newspaper declared that if a play with an ideologically correct theme was put on it must not be criticized severely, even if it was 'poorly performed'.[21] When they criticized such plays art critics were committing anti-state acts:

> In the field of dramatic criticism there has been formed an anti-patriotic group of trailers after bourgeois aestheticism, who have wormed their way into our press and are most at their ease in the pages of the journal *Teatr* and the newspaper *Sovetskoe Iskusstvo*.[22]

Examples were given of the disgraceful statements made by the 'cosmopolitans'. For instance, the critic Gurevich had said somewhere that 'complacency is not alien to Russian people.' That might not seem offensive, but *Pravda* argued otherwise:

> This is a slander on Russian Soviet man. A foul slander. And just because complacency is profoundly alien to us, we cannot refrain from branding this attempt to calumniate the Soviet national character.[23]

Here is another example, from an article by A. Gerasimov: 'For Soviet Patriotism in Art' – in this case the subject was painting, for the 'cosmopolitans' were doing their fell work in every sphere of cultural activity:

> Beskin's malicious attack and conscienceless persecution compelled the artist A. Yar-Kravchenko to withdraw from the exhibition hall of the Moscow Artists' Association his talented painting 'Maxim Gorky reads his story *Death and the Maiden* to Comrades Stalin, Molotov and Voroshilov', for which in 1940 he was awarded a Stalin Prize.[24]

The other 'crimes' of our 'cosmopolitans' were of the same order. In general, they did not understand how to carry out the task of depicting 'man of the Stalin epoch', they were given to 'cringing before the decadent art of the bourgeois West', and so on.[25] At the same time, the reader was informed that the Soviet fine arts were on an incomparably higher level than anything created in the capitalist countries in the previous half-century, 'which servile Efros and his like try to present as the last word in art.'[26]

In France Chagall and Picasso were painting; in Soviet Russia Plastov reigned supreme. However, in the forties it was senseless to argue with *Pravda*, and today those who participated in the witch-hunts of that time disavow what they said then. It would be boring to rehearse a lot of articles about 'cosmopolitanism' which contain nothing but monotonous abuse and unfounded accusations. It is worth drawing attention only to a couple of important details. *Pravda* devoted more space to articles about 'cosmopolitanism' than to the most significant international events. The fight against a group of dramatic critics, to deal with whom it would have been enough to summon a meeting of the All-Russia Dramatic Society (VTO), or to write two or three lines, was transformed into an affair on the all-national scale. Clearly, what was at stake was not just some ideologically 'incorrect' article in the journal *Teatr* but state policy, the struggle against the creative intelligentsia generally. Significant, too, was the fact that among the 'cosmopolitans' there were hardly any members of the old intelligentsia. They were all people who had come up under Soviet rule, bearers of the new traditions. What was at stake was not just errors committed by writers in *Teatr* but something bigger.

'The campaign against "cosmopolitanism" embraced at the end of the 1940s not only dramatic criticism and literature', Roy Medvedev wrote later, 'but also all the social and natural sciences.'[27] On 24 March 1949 I. Gladkov launched an attack in the Academic Council of the Institute of Economics against 'cosmopolitan economists', calling for a showdown: 'This is not the time', he said, 'or the place to argue with the cosmopolitans. ... We have to talk with those people by other means and in another language.'[28] The 'cosmopolitans' – Academician Varga, Trachtenberg, Eventov, Rubinshtein, Lif, Roitburd, Bokshitsky, Berdnikov – were, again somehow, mostly non-Russians. True, in each successive list the representatives of 'these people' – in plain words, Jews ('the concepts "Jew" and "cosmopolitan"', writes Boffa, 'actually coincided'[29]) always had one or two Russians 'mixed in' with them, but that had no particular political significance since the anti-Semitic campaign was closely interwoven with a campaign against intellectuals in general. Not only 'the Jewish question' but the problem of culture as well was threatened with a 'final solution'.

In 1949–53 the destruction of culture – or, more precisely, of what was left of it – was in full swing, and we cannot tell what the end would have been had Stalin lived two or three months longer. In any case, the incompatibility of culture with the bureaucracy had never been more obvious. The personalist Emmanuel Mounier wrote: '*Il y a des gens qui sont "aveugles à la personne" comme d'autres sont aveugles à la peinture ou sourds à la musique.*'[30] If Mounier had had to deal not with the French bourgeoisie but with the Stalinist statocracy, he would have expressed himself more harshly. Those who destroyed millions of people in the concentration camps were fully capable of trying also to destroy culture as such. Of course it was necessary to retain some *appearance* of culture, and when even that appearance vanished the statocracy got worried. Hingley writes that the crisis in culture in 1949–53 was so striking that even Stalin and his clique 'began to show mild signs of dissatisfaction with what they had wrought.'[31] It was not accidental that Stalin had issued quite a liberal constitution. We were to have everything – a parliament, elections, guaranteed rights. But not real ones, just shams. In the same way we now had to have Soviet satire, Soviet lyric poetry, Soviet comedy and even Soviet tragedy. It was on the basis of the contradiction between the formally existing laws and what actually happened that there arose later among us the movement for civil rights, which claimed to uphold ... the Stalin Constitution of 1936. Similarly, the official willingness to permit the writing of satirical verses or tragic plays created an ideological chink through which dissidents soon contrived to push themselves.

Paradoxically, through Stalin's death in March 1953 the struggle against 'cosmopolitanism' had a final effect which differed from what had been intended. Without having destroyed the new intelligentsia it prepared them for a future clash with the rulers, aroused discontent, and engendered doubt in the minds of people who had grown up under Stalin and believed his dogma.

The Quest for Sincerity

Stalin had not succeeded in carrying through his anti-intellectual campaign to the end. He died at the very moment when the anti-Semitic hysteria had reached its climax in connection with the case of the doctors who were supposed to have been going to kill him ('a group of corrupt Jewish bourgeois-nationalists', recruited 'by a branch of American intelligence, the international Jewish bourgois-nationalist organization "Joint"', who attempted to murder prominent political personalities,[32] and so on). After Stalin's death the case was immediately discontinued and the investigator shot. The difference between this frame-up and other Stalinist cases which were no less frame-ups was merely that this time the organizers suffered fiasco. But because it had exacerbated relations between the rulers and the intelligentsia, this campaign prepared and facilitated the rapid movement of the bulk of the intellectuals into definitely anti-Stalinist positions in 1955–56.

This turn did not, however, make itself felt immediately. After the dictator's death *Novy Mir*, edited by Tvardovsky, published an article by A. Fadeyev with the expressive title 'The Humanism of Stalin'. In this article it was said that, even against the background of Stalin's splendid achievements in the political sphere, his contribution to the development of culture was incredibly important. 'Comrade Stalin's role was absolutely exceptional', wrote Fadeyev,

> in the development of Soviet art and literature. More than anyone else, Stalin defined the great humanistic significance of literature as a force for the education and re-education of man in the spirit of Communism, calling writers the engineers of the human soul. Stalin discovered and established theoretically the method of socialist realism in Soviet literature, and developed Lenin's teaching on the partisan character of Soviet literature. Stalin inspired all the Party's decisions on questions of literature. He directed the progress of Soviet literature, animating it with ever new ideas and slogans, and exposing its enemies, while carefully fostering cadres of writers, criticizing and inspiring them.[33]

This passage was by no means something put in for the censor's benefit, or a product of hypocrisy. In this sense the eulogy of Stalin was categorically different from the subsequent, thoroughly hypocritical panegyrics to Khrushchev and Brezhnev. Fadeyev actually said what was thought by a considerable section of the intelligentsia and the overwhelming majority of the people. Stalin still seemed sinless: propaganda had done its work. It was not accidental that V. Bukovsky – the same Bukovsky who was later to devote his whole life to combating the system – wrote that in 1952 'for every single one of us, Stalin was greater than God.'[34] But 'cosmopolitanism' had sowed doubt in the minds of the intellectuals. This doubt did not yet touch Stalin, but later events quickly clarified the picture. Even before the exposure of Stalin at the Twentieth Party Congress a large number of cultural figures, who were to play no small role in the next decade, had already taken up their position in relation to Stalinism. Strictly speaking, even before March 1953 many intellectuals felt no particular love for Stalin, but they respected him. The general grief which followed the news of his death involved even many critically thinking people. As early as

1953, however, a vague sense of change was in the air.[35] The attitude to Stalin became cooler and cooler, and early anti-Stalinism began to take shape. As we shall see later, this position was not entirely consistent, but nevertheless one can say that a patent break in Russia's spiritual history happened in the 1950s. 'The death of Stalin,' writes Tucker,

> like the death of Nicholas I, was the end of an era and posed the problem of internal change and reform. In both instances the autocratic system revolved around the autocratic personality, and the situation towards the end of the reign assumed the aspect of a profound national crisis, a crisis of paralysis and compulsion.[36]

The first wave of liberalization, which began after the fall of Beria, created a paradoxical situation, when it seemed impossible to make out what was still forbidden and what was already permitted, what was punishable and what would merit encouragement by the authorities. The statocracy itself had not yet decided on its new line, and a struggle for power was going on at the top. At that moment there appeared in *Novy Mir* V. Pomerantsev's brilliant article 'On Sincerity in Literature', which marked the beginning of a spiritual break with the past.

Tvardovsky was later to suffer a good deal for that article and was even temporarily removed from the editorship of the journal. The article had been published by I. Sats in the absence of the editor-in-chief, and it was approved by Tvardovsky only *post facto*. Like many others he was not yet anti-Stalinist; his position was undefined. New ideas made their way into literature by degrees, casually or accidentally, so to speak. But a logical historical tendency was cutting a road for itself by way of these 'chance cases'.

In the first place, Pomerantsev directed attention to the almost complete absence of truth and sincerity in the literature of the Stalin period. 'Insincerity does not necessarily mean lying',[37] he wrote. It meant everything artificial, contrived, made up and not born in the creative process, not achieved through suffering. Writers had not been speaking their own thoughts – they had been, as it were, making statements 'in the name and under the instructions of'. Genuine art is not only preaching, it is confession.

The simple idea that a writer has the right to speak in his own name and set forth his own thoughts became the subject of a most impassioned discussion during the period of liberalization, immediately after Pomerantsev's article appeared. Such a principle, it became clear, subverted the very foundations of the system of 'socialist realism', but precisely this fact that 'socialist realism' had proved inimical to the elementary laws of art said a great deal. When, later, the Stalinists reacted against Pomerantsev and his followers, they revealed once more their hostility to culture in general – to any culture at all.

Pomerantsev called for an end to the prettifying of reality:

> Life is embellished in a dozen different ways, and not always deliberately. These ways are so firmly established that some people employ them almost unconsciously: they have become, so to speak, a style of writing.[38]

These ways amounted, briefly, to the pretence, in the first place, of all-round well-being. In a period when the whole country was going hungry, films were made such as *Kuban Cossacks, Tales of the Siberian Land,* and so on, 'in which people were seen banqueting on plentiful and tasty food, whole collective farms of them.'[39] Another device that was used was elimination. 'Nothing' was added to life, but instead all unpleasantness was removed. A third way was the selecting of 'safe', serene subjects. The heroes of the socialist-realist novel were typical one-dimensional people such as the bureaucrats wanted everyone to resemble: 'Their very dreams were always consistent. Ordinary chaotic dreams were out of the question for them.'[40]

It is interesting that Pomerantsev, whom we must assume to have been perfectly sincere, spoke out at the same time for 'Party truth', against 'subjectivism', and saw his article as merely giving support from below to the official self-criticism which some groups in the leadership needed to initiate in the course of their struggle for power. The subsequent charges against Pomerantsev, accusing him of being almost an enemy of the Party and the regime, were absolutely false. In fact, Pomerantsev and the other liberal intellectuals of the Khrushchev period regarded themselves as supporters of the system, and hoped merely to promote its evolution towards greater democracy. The fact that Stalinism was being criticized from above filled them with many hopes and illusions.

At the same time, Pomerantsev attacked quite sharply the bureaucrats' policy in the sphere of literature and the established institutions in that sphere. He criticized the editorial and publishing apparatus of the Writers' Union, but showed that responsibility for the crisis in art lay chiefly with the workers in that field themselves, who submitted to this apparatus:

> As for the apparatus of the Writers' Union, the 'creative sections' and the rest, what has all that got to do with me, as a reader? Things are in a bad way in the Union? Well, change them. I'm only afraid that, in your Union, though everybody thinks the present system is bad, nobody knows what improvement should be made. And I don't understand why this prevents you

from writing interesting books. I've heard that Shakespeare did not belong to any union, yet he wrote pretty well.[41]

Some changes, said Pomerantsev, could already be observed, but these were by no means always for the better. Interest in the individual, which was being proclaimed officially with increasing frequency, sometimes implied a new form of 'absence of conflict': 'Will not the importunate whispers of lovers prove irritating to me, even as hitherto I have been deafened by the sound of tractors?'[42]

The critics, too, received Pomerantsev's attention. Their articles ought to have constituted a programme, but instead they provided only a list of facts – and that was true only of the best of them. There was also another breed of critic: 'These are professional unmaskers, nit-pickers, exposers.'[43] In any case, criticism was not fulfilling the most important task:

> What is wanted is not the creation of literary Highnesses, not selecting for immortality, nor the passing of sentences without right of appeal, but study of the characteristic features of our writers' creativity, their role in the progress of literature – and telling the truth about all this.[44]

In place of standardized and empty literature there should come a new sort – truthful, individual, variegated: 'The writer will clarify life for us, and change it.'[45] What was needed was to tell the truth, only the truth, nothing but the truth. Under conditions of liberalization the officials sometimes allow art to show the dark sides of life, but call for 'a sense of proportion'. On that point Pomerantsev observes:

> People who *introduce* 'an element of the negative' into their books do not deserve respect. One can, of course, find the equilibrium between 'prettifying reality' and 'a gloomy picture', but the very quest for that, the mere calculation, condemns a work to lack of artistic merit. That way of looking at things can produce compilations, but not writings, because it is not the viewpoint of art. When a writer takes to calculating what is in his novel – a third of this, a half of that, a quarter of the other – he is not giving his artistic heart to the work.[46]

In Pomerantsev's view the literature of the Stalin era was bad primarily because the spirit of the age is not discernible in it. On that he was, of course, not altogether correct. It is precisely in the soulless socialist-realist novels and plays, in their lack of artistry and their monotony, that the 'spirit' of the Stalin era is best discernible. On the whole, though, Pomerantsev's idea was quite correct. Literature can reflect the spirit of a new age, can feel the breath of the wind of freedom. The age of Stalin had passed away, and with that age its art. After 1953 one needed to write differently. 'Only what is actual is lasting,' said Pomerantsev, 'but what is actual is not what is fleeting. True actuality does not fade with the passing of time.'[47]

I have dealt with Pomerantsev's article in so much detail because it was undoubtedly the first manifesto of the post-Stalin liberal intelligentsia, and was seen as that by friends and foes alike. Mark Perakh wrote that Pomerantsev's work also influenced the young people who, at the end of the 1950s, formed the first underground socialist groups.[48]

The influence of Pomerantsev's article on the ideological protest of the late fifties and early sixties was indeed very great. It gave expression to something very important for an entire cultural epoch. Its ideas retained their significance to the end of the Khrushchev era, as the distinctive minimum progamme of the radicals. The universal favourite of those years, Yevtushenko, answered a question about 'the voice of the young writer' by saying that 'this voice must, above all, be sincere. It is not a matter of sounding sincere but of being sincere, being honest. The young poet and writer must write as he thinks, as he feels.'[49] It was just that simple honesty that compelled Tvardovsky to support Sats in the Pomerantsev affair. Honesty became the *initial* principle of the democratic ideology. Sincerity, as we see, can be not only an artistic but also a political category. The article evoked many responses. *Komsomolskaya Pravda* published a letter from students, supporting the writer. (Later on, that put the paper in an awkward position.) The Stalinists, too, 'responded' to Pomerantsev's article – with a torrent of abuse.

The characteristic feature of the first period of the history of the post-Stalin *Novy Mir*, as of the intelligentsia as a whole, was a fight on a broad front against literary stereotypes, against socialist-realist clichés and routine. The essence of this fight was the liberation of art forms from the fetters of dogma, a return to artistic quality. In itself this programme had nothing political about it; naturally, however, it met a hostile reception from the Stalinists. The ruling body of the Writers' Union adopted a resolution 'On the Mistakes of the Journal *Novy Mir*'. Pomerantsev was accused of all the mortal sins. Tvardovsky was charged with printing 'incorrect and harmful articles'[50] and removed from his post. It was declared that Pomerantsev had 'called for a one-sided portrayal and exaggeration of the negative phenomena of our reality.'[51] At the same time sentence was passed on F. Abramov's article 'People of the Collective-Farm Countryside in Postwar Prose' and Mikhail Lifshitz's mocking review of the book *The Diary of Marietta Shaginyan* in which he said, in particular, that 'the inflation of big words results in their losing all their value.'[52] Later, as we know, Lifshitz reformed and began to engage in the exposure of 'revisionism'. In those years, however, his article figured among the writings which censured the prevailing system of literary clichés and seemed incredibly bold.

Pomerantsev's article provoked a storm of indignation from the conservatives, who at that time received – quite deservedly – the nickname of 'right-wingers'. It was typical, though, that even A. Karaganov, while blaming Pomerantsev in the pages of *Novy Mir* on the grounds that his 'sincerity is at odds with, or does not coincide with, Communist principles', and his arguments about freedom were nothing but an expression of 'petty-bourgeois subjectivism',[53] at the same time took up arms against 'canons and clichés'. In the same article in which he said that 'true freedom for the artist is born of the sense of organic union with the Party'[54] – in other words, true freedom consists in voluntary slavery, in freedom *from* thought – the author called on his readers 'to see the limits to all laws and not to carry them beyond bounds, through canonizing settled habits and influences or methods which are fashionable and therefore seem universally recognized.'[55]

The process of liberalization marched on. Under the leadership of K. Simonov, who temporarily replaced Tvardovsky, *Novy Mir* held to the same course. Truth made its way increasingly into the pages of the press. Literature began more and more often to speak of the reality of life in our country. V. Ovechkin's sketches appeared, telling of the actual situation in the villages, of the causes of hardship, of the need for democracy. Today the sketches of Ovechkin, G. Troepol'sky and V. Tendryakov, which were published immediately after Stalin's death, do not make the same impression as they did earlier – they can occasionally be reproached for insufficient profundity – but in their day they brought about a real revolution, for in them, in the words of M. Shcheglov, a well-known critic of the period, 'the countryside of our time stood before the reader as it really was',[56] instead of the popular-print 'pictures from an exhibition' to which Stalin's publicity machine had accustomed the public. These reflections might often seem muddled and imprecise, but they disturbed people's ideas and compelled them to look for answers.

The Impact of the Twentieth Party Congress

The critical tendency strengthened and was reinforced after the exposures carried out at the Twentieth Party Congress, the condemnation of the Stalinist practices which were delicately referred

to as 'the cult of personality'. In his secret report to the Congress
Khrushchev talked about many of Stalin's crimes, but he ascribed them
exclusively to subjective causes. This version went into all subsequent
textbooks, which repeated that the whole trouble was due to the fact
that 'Stalin believed in his own infallibility, began to abuse the Party's
trust, to violate the Leninist principles and norms of Party life, and to
allow unlawful actions.'[57] Consequently, the effect of the Congress
exposures on the public – and especially on the intelligentsia – was
twofold. On the one hand it was a gigantic step forward: 'Whatever
may have been N. Khrushchev's aims when he made his report, that
report will remain in the memory of descendants as his greatest service,
and one that indisputably belongs to him alone,' wrote Roy Medvedev
in his *Political Diary*.[58]

On the other hand, however, Khrushchev's report produced
bewilderment and a demand for deeper analysis. Explanation in terms
of 'the cult of personality', not relating the tragic events of the Stalin
era to social processes in the country and its political institutions,
sounded 'like mockery of any Marxist analysis of history'.[59] This was
immediately remarked upon by many people, both in the USSR and
also – especially – in the West. The very expression 'cult of personality'
could not but cause bewilderment. 'If all the unappealing aspects of
Stalin's rule had been limited to the cult of his "personality",' an
American scholar observes, 'there would have been no need for de-
Stalinization.'[60] The restoration of the truth about many Party leaders
who had been executed by Stalin was not accompanied by the
rehabilitation of such major leaders of Bolshevism as Trotsky,
Bukharin, Rykov, Kamenev and Zinoviev, which in itself signified, in
Tucker's words, a 're-falsification of Soviet history'.[61] The state's policy
changed, but the structure of the state and the Party remained, on the
whole, what it had been under Stalin. 'To bring back old Bolsheviks
and others from Siberian exile', writes Tucker, 'does not restore the
Party as they once knew it.'[62] But the people who returned from the
camps and from exile brought the truth about the past with them, and
thereby raised new questions in people's minds.

The freeing of Stalin's prisoners, writes Boffa,

> had psychological and political repercussions throughout the country. By how
> many the population of the prisons and camps was reduced in 1956 and, in
> general, after Stalin's death, is not known. But it is clear that the Twentieth
> Congress lightened the lot of many millions of people. Under Stalin it was
> impossible even to mention the concentration camps and exile; not only in
> the press but in private conversation, too, it was preferable to say nothing
> about them. Now the sufferers were returning *en masse* to civil life, and could
> talk freely about their past. Some were broken, physically and morally, but

others, on the contrary, felt ready to engage in fresh activity, fearing nothing any more, and demanded justice.'[63]

Among the latter were Kopelev, Gnedin, Solzhenitsyn, Shalamov and many others.

It was not possible to organize discussion of Stalinism within the CPSU. 'Attempts by individual Communists to continue discussion of the problem of the "cult of personality" were cut off', writes Roy Medvedev.[64] But the questions did not go away, and even if the fact that, as Shatz puts it, Khrushchev had 'offered a most "un-Marxist" interpretation of a quarter-century of Soviet history'[65] might remain unappreciated among the intelligentsia, nevertheless the incompleteness of Khrushchev's explanations and interpretations was obvious. Bukovsky wrote:

> Khrushchev seemed to think that he had explained everything, that he had given answers to all the questions. According to Khrushchev, they had got to the bottom of it, released the innocent, spoken well of the dead, and life could go on. But for us, and especially for my generation, the questions were only just beginning.[66]

The spring of 1956 – when, throughout the country, Khrushchev's 'secret' report was being read to hundreds of thousands of listeners – was a time of questions, hopes and illusions. Hopes rose sharply and the public's expectations quickly clashed with the plans of the leadership. For Khrushchev's group at the top, the Twentieth Congress marked the conclusion, as it seemed to them, of the necessary process of liberalization. For those who heard the 'secret' report it marked the beginning of that process. The hopes and expectations of the intellectuals could not be approved and they consequently became undesirable in the eyes of the statocracy, for there was danger that further demands would be put forward. And that was what happened. During the stormy discussion of Khrushchev's report in the Writers' Union such proposals were advanced as a freer system of election, a public investigation of Stalin's doings, and so on. As before, the left-wing intellectuals looked for fresh steps towards liberalization to be taken by the ruling statocracy themselves, but even so they did not want to linger and stand still. R. Orlova said:

> The days we are now living through remind me of the days right after October – there is the same mass-meeting type of democracy. Everybody wants to speak. Those who have long held their tongues. And those who long spoke nothing but lies. And those who sincerely believed and who are now being told they believed in lies. People are coming to an accounting with their

own consciences. .... But we can't allow ourselves the luxury of resting at this stage.[67]

The criticism of the past – begun very cautiously and inconsistently at the top, as Pomerantsev also thought – met with active support from below which was not welcomed by the men at the top. The 'Movement of Solidarity' with the Twentieth Congress, the appearance of the writings of Pomerantsev and Dudintsev, the verses of Yevtushenko, Okudzhava and others, came as a surprise – an unpleasant one – to Khrushchev. As Roy Medvedev writes, he 'was not yet ready to lend his active support to the thaw.'[68]

The Youth Movement

A feeling of rejection determined the mood of the intelligentsia. 'Rejection of what has been or is being outlived', wrote the critic V. Kardin, 'is natural, healthy and, above all, necessary. It frightens only those who are being rejected.'[69] The rebellious youths in Viktor Rozov's plays really were 'typical representatives' of a new generation and a new epoch. These 'rebellious youths' soon became a serious political problem. In 1956 an oppositionist student movement began to take shape which could no longer express itself within the bounds of 'permitted criticism'. The exposures at the Twentieth Congress produced in wide circles of the population, as Roy Medvedev acknowledges, 'confusion, bewilderment and disillusionment'.[70] For those who had known at least part of the hidden truth, the Congress was proof that the ruling group might give up lying and become sincere, while for those who had known nothing previously the Congress revealed, on the contrary, that the rulers were dishonourable and capable of lying. This resulted in distrust of the upper circles by the lower orders, a feeling which found expression mainly in political apathy. Whereas for the intelligentsia the 'secret report' signified hope for change, for millions of workers and peasants who, earlier, had blindly believed the official propaganda, it was a shock. The students, being an intermediate stratum between the intellectual 'elite' and the working masses, were gripped by the intelligentsia's enthusiasm, yet at the same time, like the lower orders, felt acute disappointment with the system that had deceived them. Consequently, they set about forming oppositionist organizations with a revolutionary tendency. David Burg writes:

In 1956–1957, after the XX Congress, opposition elements within the institutes and universities began to wage an open battle against Komsomol leadership. They sought, first of all, to gain freedom of criticism and expression and second to introduce a degree of intra-Komsomol democracy that would make the Komsomol a truly representative organization with an honestly elected leadership. Freedom of expression was in fact gradually achieved at that period by a kind of procedure of protestation, and extraordinarily sharp critical comments were heard more and more commonly at meetings.[71]

On 9 August 1956 *Komsomolskaya Pravda* reported what had happened at a seminar on the documents of the Twentieth Congress held in Taganrog Radio Engineering Institute. Two students were expelled for asking what the teachers considered 'improper' questions. In August 1956 the momentum of the Congress was still strong, and the fears aroused by the 'Polish October' and the Hungarian Revolution were yet to come. The wave of de-Stalinization had still not abated. The expelled students were readmitted, and the newspaper defended them. True learning, said *Komsomolskaya Pravda*, cannot progress 'without disputes, without thought'; it is not possible to 'protect' Marxism from questions and suppose that it can be studied like 'God's laws'.[72] Such statements in newspapers merely poured oil on the fire of opposition. The first unofficial publications appeared, with 'odd names' like *Heresy, Fresh Voices, Phoenix, Boomerang* and *Cocktail.* In Leningrad a group of students launched a journal called *Kolokol* [The Bell]: it is interesting that towards the end of the Khrushchev era another attempt to establish a journal with this historic name was made in Leningrad, under the editorship of V. Ronkin and S. Khakhaev. At this time, however, the students tried to make use of legal forms of work: 'They ... made a point', Bukovsky recalls, 'of attending official Soviet lectures and discussions, where they would speak up, ask questions and start genuine arguments on real issues.'[73]

Besides unofficial *samizdat* there appeared what might be called 'official' or, more precisely, 'institutionalized' *samizdat*: 'Wall newspapers began to print "undesirable" articles,' writes Burg. 'In official literary conferences literary enthusiasts began to raise subjects formerly discussed only among intimate friends – for example, the question as to whether Soviet literature was basically truthful.'[74] But the students became especially agitated during the revolution in Hungary. A Komsomol meeting in Moscow University was turned into a meeting of solidarity with the government of Imre Nagy. Leaflets appeared, and groups began to be formed with organizers like Pimenov and Krasnopevtsev and theoreticians like Krylov, Cheshkov and Sheynis.

Among the activists in the student opposition there was a small group of religious youngsters and pro-Western liberals, but at that time they constituted no very important part of the movement, either in numbers or in their role in its activities. Groups of socialists also appeared, who considered that

> a pluralist socialist society must be established, in which industry would be placed under the direct control of labour, and agriculture under the direction of free co-operatives, and political power would be transferred to democratically elected soviets or other representative institutions. The dispersion of power would guarantee the free play of social forces, which in turn would assure personal freedom.[75]

The predominant force in the student movement, however, was not the socialists but the neo-Bolsheviks. Burg, although very displeased with the fact, acknowledges that 'the leaflets issued by clandestine groups generally expound the neo-Bolshevik line.'[76] Even Bukovsky wrote later, with irritation, that among those who took part in the student movement at that time 'were a lot of neo-Marxists and neo-Communists of various kinds.'[77] The activist in the youth opposition, Volodya Bukovsky, easily found a common language with them and they even thought him one of themselves. The present *émigré* Bukovsky, of course, disowns such acquaintances in every way and tries to depreciate the part played by 'those people'. Nevertheless, all participants in the movement recognize that the neo-Bolsheviks predominated in it during the 1950s. That was to be expected. The Twentieth Congress had revealed Stalin's distortion of Lenin's line, and it was precisely Lenin's line that was counterposed to Stalinism. Lenin's ideas were well known and his writings accessible. Clearly, it was to him that the anti-Stalinist rebels turned in the first place. Paradoxically, both the rulers and the opposition were appealing to the same ideas and values.

Another source of new ideas was the Yugoslav experiment, which had shown that workers' self-management in production was a possibility. This experiment also remained within the limits of Communist ideology, while at the same time widening those limits. Both the neo-Bolsheviks and the socialists looked towards Yugoslavia, although what interested the former was the system of self-management, whereas the latter focused their attention on the market mechanism and competition between nationalized enterprises. But, as Burg notes, 'the liberal socialists differ little from the neo-Bolsheviks on overtly political questions.'[78] However, the neo-Bolsheviks were still disposed to support a one-party system of the Yugoslav type, supplemented by self-management in the economy. On the whole they maintained the positions of the official ideology, although representing a 'purer' variant of it.

That was dangerous enough. In 1957 the tone of the official newspapers changed. *Trud* published an article by M. Tsutskov which attacked the student youth. The author complained that in the Komsomol *aktiv* at the Leningrad Institute of Precision Engineering and Optics, the student Gorelik 'spoke of suppression of the students' creative initiative'; in Moscow University the wall-newspaper *Tribuna* contained 'slanderous attacks on the Soviet press'; in Uralsk Political Institute, 'under the flag of criticism and development of democracy, certain students made demagogic statements counterposing the Komsomol to the Party.'[79] The newspaper called for 'a resolute rebuff' to be given to the student movement, and naturally, such a rebuff was given. Some activists (for example Sheynis and Krylov, who later became well-known Soviet political scientists) were expelled from their institutes and universities, while others were arrested. 'These arrests', writes Zhores Medvedev, 'are not well known, because the rehabilitation of millions of victims of the Stalin terror was under way at the same time. When millions were being released, the hundreds of new arrests could easily pass unnoticed.'[80]

The suppression of the political groups did not eradicate the opposition, but gave it a new cultural form. Thenceforth the illegal organs of the cultural opposition were 'the Ryleyev Club' and other such youth centres, which ceased to be political organizations. The club published a journal, *Russkoye Slovo*, and along with this one of its leaders, Kushev, published *Tetradi Sotsial-Demokratii*. But this activity was of secondary importance. The most important role was played by the famous 'Mayak'. Bukovsky recalls:

In the summer of 1958 a statue of Mayakovsky was unveiled. At the official opening ceremony a number of official Soviet poets read their poems, and when the ceremony was over, volunteers from the crowd started reading theirs as well. Such an unexpected and unplanned turn of events pleased everybody, and it was agreed that the poets would meet here regularly. At first the authorities saw no particular danger in this, and one Moscow paper even published an article about the gatherings, giving the time when they took place and inviting all poetry lovers to come along. Young people, mostly students, assembled almost every evening to read the poems of forgotten or repressed writers, and also their own work, and sometimes there were discussions of art and literature. A kind of open-air club came into being. But the authorities could not tolerate the danger of these spontaneous performances for long, and eventually stopped the gatherings.[81]

However, in 1960 Bukovsky and his friends managed to revive the 'readings at Mayakovsky's statue', giving them an even more openly political character.

The youth movement was still very broad. Even among Komsomol functionaries, Bukovsky recalls, 'we had a lot of sympathizers'.[82] In April 1961 a real battle with the militia took place in Mayakovsky Square. In October of that year, however, on the eve of the Twenty-Second Party Congress, the authorities finally succeeded in suppressing open youth demonstrations. It is noteworthy that this task had taken five years to accomplish.

The Limits of Liberalization

The defeat suffered by the student opposition and its disappearance from the scene on the eve of the Twenty-Second Congress explains the fact that for some time thereafter the legal opposition within the system, the mouthpiece of which was *Novy Mir*, remained predominant despite the exposures made at the Congress, which went even further than those at the Twentieth. A feeling was created that the Communist radicals – the students, who set themselves against the system – were on the wrong track, were suffering to no purpose; whereas the Communist liberals – the writers connected with *Novy Mir*, who placed their hopes on an evolution of the system itself – were much wiser. The very fact that despite periodical frosts and arrests of neo-Bolsheviks, the 'thaw' was still going on inevitably strengthened the liberals' illusions, convincing the intelligentsia that the system was evolving in the required direction and any attempts at direct action against it could only be harmful, because they would play into the hands of the neo-Stalinists.

At the same time it must be borne in mind that it was precisely the radical youth who made up the bulk of the audience of the critical writers. There were no frontiers between radicalism and liberalism. Broadly speaking, the differences between them were not so much in ideology as in mood. Members of the 'liberal' intelligentsia of the fifties and sixties were not at all disposed to wait passively for democratization to occur. They strove to promote it and clashed with the authorities, even though they did not regard the latter as fundamentally vicious. All the same, their protest was not political but cultural and moral. The journal *Der Spiegel* wrote that 'the revolt of the writers, especially the Russians among them, is philosophical rather than political.'[83] The same logic of ideological development which impelled the students to form secret societies impelled them to struggle openly for *purity of ideas*. Roy Medvedev wrote:

In those years, the literature on Stalinism never posed the problem of the regime's power in direct terms; indirectly, however, it brought up questions in people's minds: How could such things have happened? Was the system somehow defective?[84]

But primarily – and this was natural for writers – they exposed not the organizational but the moral and psychological defects of the system, while trying to counterpose to it their own moral ideal, their own beliefs.

Of greatest interest for an analysis of the Khrushchev era is, perhaps, the figure of Yevtushenko. The period of the Twentieth Congress engendered a new poetry and new poets. 'This "public" poet *par excellence*', an American observer remarked later, 'symbolized the anti-Stalinist rebellion of the 1950s and early 1960s.'[85] Yevtushenko symbolized the new poetry. In his *Political Diary* for 1966 Medvedev wrote that he embodied 'all the merits and all the shortcomings' of the new poets who became the idols of youth after 1956.[86] 'His popularity', said an American writer, with surprise, 'is comparable to that of a movie star in the West.'[87]

Yevtushenko's attitude to the system is a mixture of protest with admiration for leaders who made up their minds to expose Stalin. 'Criticising', he said in those days, 'does not mean getting angry, it means loving ardently. And how can I repudiate Soviet reality? Soviet life is my life!'[88] Like the rebels of the fifties, he came to the conclusion that 'we must fight to the death against those who preach Communism in theory while in practice discrediting it. I guessed', he emphasized, 'that this fight would be protracted and complex. Persons who look on Communism as almost their monopoly, usually say that anyone who attacks the distortion of Lenin's ideas is attacking the fundamentals of Leninism.'[89] On their part, the Left radicals and liberals of the sixties considered themselves the true bearers of Lenin's ideas. The intellectuals were convinced that they, and not the ruling bureaucracy, gave authentic expression to Communist principles, and this was partly true. Doubt was not cast upon the actual principles of Bolshevism. Furthermore, the opposition did not yet perceive the fundamental contradiction between its principles and aims and those of the government. After the Twentieth Congress illusions and hopes were so strong that neither Khrushchev's waverings nor the suppression of the 1956 revolution in Hungary could shake them. De-Stalinization seemed not only irreversible but also irrepressible. Yevtushenko wrote:

I don't agree with the use of the word 'thaw' taken over from Ehrenburg to describe this process. I have objected to it several times in the press and should like to object again. There can be a thaw in winter, but the present season is the spring – a difficult spring with late frosts and cold winds; a spring which takes a step to the left, a step to the right and a step back, but which then takes two or three steps forward all the same.[90]

Yevtushenko's autobiography, in which he tried to formulate his views, was published in the West, where it struck many readers as extremely naïve, although Deutscher, for example, stressed that, from a man brought up in Stalinist society 'his occasional *naïvetés* are hardly surprising.'[91] It is important to realize, though, that in this respect Yevtushenko was not alone. Others thought just as he did. Nevertheless, the democratic intelligentsia discovered very soon that liberalization had limits that were sharply drawn by the rulers. True, as we shall see later, these limits shifted, albeit not without pressure from the opposition. All the same, limits there were, and that was a reality one had to reckon with. One of the questions where these limits made themselves apparent was anti-Semitism.

On 19 September 1961 *Literaturnaya Gazeta* published Yevtushenko's poem *Babi Yar*, devoted to the massacre of Kiev's Jews by the Hitlerites. It might seem that there was nothing reprehensible in that, but Yevtushenko had 'dared' to mention our own home-grown anti-Semites as well. Their response was not long in coming. The editors of *Literaturnaya Gazeta* had decided to publish this poem only after some hesitation, expecting some unpleasantness. Their fear was justified, as often happens in such cases. *Babi Yar* produced a storm of indignation in the ruling class, and among those who took offence was Khrushchev himself. 'There is no Jewish question in our country,' he declared, 'and those who invent it are slavishly repeating what other people say.'[92] According to Khrushchev, 'the poem reveals that its author ... was ignorant of historical facts.'[93] In reality, of course, it was Khrushchev who showed himself to be 'ignorant of historical facts' when he alleged that even in Tsarist Russia there had been no discrimination against the Jews, and the Jewish poor simply 'shared the plight of the Russian, Ukrainian and other workers.'[94] He even tried to avoid recalling the policy of complete extermination of the Jews which the Hitlerites had carried out in the occupied territories. His line enabled the anti-Semites to lift their heads. *Literaturnaya Zhizn'* wrote, ironically:

Standing on the brink of Babi Yar a young Soviet writer found there only a subject for verses about anti-Semitism! And, thinking today about the people who were killed – 'the old man shot', 'the child shot' – he could think only about the fact that they were Jews. That was what seemed to him most important, the main thing, the most stirring aspect! ...[95]

The newspaper omitted to mention, of course, that these old men and children were shot precisely *because* they had the misfortune to be born Jewish. It is important that Yevtushenko did not write about *Soviet* anti-Semites but merely referred to the pre-revolutionary Black Hundreds. However, as they say, an uneasy conscience betrays itself. Those who launched the campaign against Yevtushenko gave their own game away.

Although the moral victory fell to the Lefts, the *Babi Yar* affair showed that there were definite limits beyond which the liberalism of the rulers would not go. In general the question of anti-Semitism is not in itself of central importance either ideologically or politically, especially since the official line of the authorities repudiates the anti-Semites. But Yevtushenko had trodden on the prejudices of the ruling class and had 'received the rebuff he deserved', even though he had not attacked the foundations of the system.[96] At times the limits of liberalization proved extremely narrow.

These limits were also seen in the matter of Stalin's role in the history of the USSR. A Western scholar has written that Khrushchev was a 'reforming despot' of the sort encountered only in Russia.[97] Perhaps he was even a liberator-despot. His entire activity, together with his contradictions, can be expressed in that contradictory definition. His policy imposed new rules of the game upon the intelligentsia: 'Thus it was the state which not only initiated dissent but established the framework within which, at least at the beginning, that dissent was to find expression.'[98] Moreover, Shatz continues,

> by and large, unofficial criticism of Stalin accepted the limits Khrushchev had imposed on the subject. For the next ten years, until the Sinyavsky-Daniel trial of 1966, the voices of dissent evoked by Khrushchev's speech confined themselves largely to the moral plane, calling for a change in the character and attitudes of the people running the Soviet system while exempting the system itself from direct criticism or serious analysis.[99]

On the other hand, in the beginning, the inner logic of the development of dissent itself dictated this approach. The whole history of social thought confirms that people moralize before they start analysing. It is said that Khrushchev was inconsistent. That is undoubtedly true; but it would be wrong to see his waverings as mere concessions to external pressure from right-wing dogmatists. His policy fully corresponded to his own notion of what de-Stalinization ought to mean. From the outset he understood very well that its scope must be limited, and he defined the limits clearly enough. He drew near to those limits or else withdrew from them, depending on circumstances, but he could not and did not want to step over them. It was impossible to cast doubt on the basic institutions and principles of the state which had been inherited from Stalin – all that ensured the dominant position of the statocracy in society. Even after the Twentieth Congress he spoke out against 'a sweeping denial of Stalin's positive role',[100] and even after the Twenty-Second Congress he continued to say that 'the Party pays credit to Stalin's services'[101] while periodically he reminded people that Stalin 'did much that was beneficial for our country.'[102] Although condemning the terrorist methods of the 'leader and teacher', he did not choose to condemn his actual policy.

The Literary Renaissance

The longer the period of reform went on, the clearer it became that what was being undertaken was no radical transformation but a 'controlled modernization, reflected also in ideology'.[103] At the beginning, however, the limits to liberalization were not yet obvious to the Lefts, if only because their attention was centred not so much on political as on artistic questions. It was necessary to 'clear up the mess in our own home', getting rid of the Stalinist stereotypes of pseudo-artistic thinking. Until he had shaken *them* off a writer would be simply unable to tell the truth, even if he wanted to. As Solzhenitsyn said, the socialist-realist dogma bound writers like a collective 'solemn pledge to abstain from truth'.[104] Consequently, a struggle was waged in the sphere of art for a new form, for a break in practice with the dogmas of 'socialist realism'. But a new form implied also a new world-view. The place of dogmatic pseudo-realism had to be taken by truly realistic art. The principles of the new artistic creativity must be sincerity, actuality, return to the sources. The first two principles had already surfaced in Pomerantsev's article, while the third began to play a special role after the Twentieth Congress.

The rehabilitation campaign that then began forced people to look at the past in a new light – to rethink it. It was in this period that the foundations of present-day Soviet literary criticism were laid. One of the first literary critics to proclaim the new principles guiding attitudes to art and reality, as early as the fifties, was Mark Shcheglov. Although he died young, he succeeded in seriously influencing many of his own generation (for example V. Lakshin, who later did much to ensure that Shcheglov was not unjustly forgotten). Shcheglov cast doubt upon authorities and principles which had until then been unshakeable. He subjected to critical examination the novel *The Russian Forest*, a 'classic' of 'socialist realism', by L. Leonov and revealed the mass of defects, the artificiality, the striving for effect and the lack of warmth in this work. Shcheglov wrote also about the 'conflictlessness' of the literary sketch in the Stalin period:

> From writings like these, especially sketches (which allegedly 'photograph' real life) the ordinary reader could become accustomed only to reading one thing while seeing something different in reality.[105]

He noted the spiritual degeneration suffered under Stalinism by the reader and by the writer, whose mind gradually 'got used to seeing in life only comforting phenomena',[106] which enabled him quite sincerely to write lying sketches about nonexistent successes and dubious achievements, to describe the hungry countryside like a 'happy Arcadia', where, 'under the influence of sky-blue fences, rose-coloured cottages and the heartfelt words of good leaders, the countryside is undergoing moral rebirth and even the eradication of alcoholism.'[107] Arguing against Lunacharsky's idea of the 'higher' truth of the future, which had hitherto been the foundation of 'socialist realism', Shcheglov wrote: 'Ignoring the everyday "arithmetic" of facts in the name of some "higher algebra" can lead to no good.'[108] He was able to quote in support more than enough examples which had accumulated in the Stalin era. One had only to look back over the Soviet theatre in the previous twelve years to be convinced. Shcheglov observed that the theatres preferred to put on classics because the Soviet repertory contained no real 'plays from life':

> In our plays the power of art receives so little generalization, there are so few symbols and types and so many particular cases, there is so little high theatricality, so little spectacle, and, on the contrary, in everything we see an element of barren dramatization, of naturalism; hence also our extreme poverty of genres and fear of rising to the heights of tragedy and revolutionary romanticism.[109]

Liberalization facilitated access to foreign culture, and many people encountered Western literature for the first time. (A journal entitled *Inostrannaya Literatura* – 'Foreign Literature' – even began to appear, something without precedent in Stalin's last years.) 'The vigorous curiosity' of educated Russians who contrived – heaven knows how – to become aware of the latest plays in the London theatres and the latest books in the bookshops of Paris, it was admitted by many Western observers, 'cannot fail to surprise and astonish the visitor from abroad.'[110] The rehabilitation of writers put to death under Stalin confronted the history of literature with complex problems. It was necessary, as an American journalist said, 'to see beyond the wreckage of the thirties and forties back to the cultural world of the twenties.'[111]

Novy Mir printed articles in which the authors sought to take a fresh look at literary history. S. Shtut wrote:

> Our debts are heavy, and to pay them it is not sufficient to 'insert' some previously unmentioned names in a chart long since delineated. We need to change the chart itself in many ways. We must say frankly that Soviet literature was, in reality, worse than it appeared in our idealized notions.[112]

At the same time, despite the general critical re-evaluation, there was an effort to find in the past something beyond question – an authority, a principle, a direction on which one could rely in the struggle against Stalinism and for the renewal of spiritual life. The intelligentsia saw the exposures at the Twentieth Congress as proof that there were healthy forces in the system; that it was not in itself to be blamed; that its primordial basis was sound. The task was to get back from the Stalinist *distortion* of principles to the principles themselves. The decisions of the Congress constituted a return to Lenin, and a similar rebirth of principles could be observed in the sphere of art. Moreover this was conceived, by those who participated in it, as a single process. 'Such was the time, the time of the Twentieth Congress. ...' O. Yefremov, the founder of the Contemporary Theatre, recalled later. 'It could not fail to affect art.'[113] And so a discussion began in the theatrical world concerning Stanislavsky's system, which until then had been regarded as obligatory upon everyone. Stanislavsky's pupil M.O. Knebel' wrote in those days:

> they inculcated Stanislavsky's ideas in mechanical fashion, using his prestige to suppress dissident artists who were trying to go their own way. ... At that time the name of Stanislavsky served as the only password for admission to the camp of the 'orthodox' realists, and so everybody without exception swore by that name, including those who in their hearts had no faith in it.[114]

And now, after the Twentieth Congress, actors, producers and especially theoreticians saw their task as returning from the dogmatic, scholastic 'Stanislavsky' to the real Stanislavsky. Knebel' wrote:

> The shadow of one phenomenon fell upon another, and at once amateurs were found who put the blame for everything on Stanislavsky. But, of course, the founders of the Moscow Art Theatre were in no way responsible for the fact that, in later years, dramatic art developed on worse lines than we should have wished. There were other reasons for that – they were recorded in the decisions of the Twentieth Congress, we know them, and we are fighting against everything that hinders our art from developing and growing. Can it

be said that Stanislavsky was responsible for 'conflictlessness' in art, the prettifying of reality, the reign of half-truth? Can we blame Stanislavsky for our timidity, for the fact that, for a time, we lost the spirit of discovery and ceased to approach his system in a creative way? No, in my view neither Stanislavsky nor Nemirovich-Danchenko has anything whatsoever to do with that![115]

N. Krymova, who quickly became one of the theoreticians of the new generation of the intelligentsia, called upon them, in her dissertation, not to rest content with 'using the terms of the system and making general appeals to truth and experience'.[116]

An endeavour to get back to genuine realism was the basic programme of the Contemporary Theatre, and these ideas also inspired A. Efros. In its turn, V. Yu. Lyubimov's theatre attempted to 'throw a bridge across' to Brecht and the dramatic ideas of the twenties, which had been hushed up in the period of Stalin's 'socialist realism'. But this was not just a renewal of art, it was also a political struggle, and people wrote and spoke of that fact almost openly. 'The Contemporary Theatre', wrote Kardin, 'was born in the year of the Twentieth Party Congress, and, in their avoidance of the high-flown, its actors called themselves "children of '56".'[117] The young Contemporary Theatre, and, later, Lyubimov's theatre on the Taganka carried out a real revolution in the field of drama, and this revolution in artistic form would have been impossible if the artists of the new generation had not based themselves also on new social ideas, a new world-view. The famous Leningrad producer G. Tovstonogov, who emerged in this period, emphasized that

> the ideological content of a work, its civic spirit, cannot be 'one problem among others' for the artist. It is the basis, the premiss – here the work of art either begins or does not begin. One can possess refined technique and even talent and yet not be an artist, for if a person is not sensitive, with the keenness of a perfect barometer, to the pulse of life, the breathing of the age, his creation will be, all in all, an intellectual trick, a game of fantasy and nothing more.[118]

The renewal of social ideas and the renewal of artistic forms have always been closely connected, and the 'children of '56' understood that connection.

Desire to tell the truth implies hatred of those who defend lying. For people who think like this, moral and political principles are inseparable. The one implies the other – more: each *is* the other. There is political significance in the fight for the artist's creative individuality, his right to speak for himself. These elementary truths were struggling to break through. When B. Runin said that 'self-expression by the artist is the necessary precondition for any creative work',[119] the right-wingers responded by practically accusing him of an attempt to subvert the Soviet order. Since he had referred to the views of Marx and Lenin, they charged him with distorting those views. So the battle went. However, the Left conquered one position after another.

As a result, the change effected in the type of thinking on artistic questions led to political conclusions and compelled people to take up the position which later, in the seventies, came to be called 'dissidence'. The counterposing of 'idea' and 'reality' was only the first step. It was not hard to see that the bureaucracy's practice contradicted the theory which they claimed to be correct (whether Marx's or Stanislavsky's), but it still had to be understood why and how this 'false practice' had developed, what its sources and laws were, and what was the nature of those who carried it out. So it could be said that thinking Russia passed from an attitude of rejection, albeit by a long and difficult process, to analytical criticism.

In December 1956 K. Simonov, who took over the editorship of *Novy Mir* after Tvardovsky's dismissal, published 'Literary Notes', in which he called for an investigation of the nature of Stalinism:

> We cannot define all the influence that the cult of personality exercised upon literature by means of a formula that fits into a single phrase. We need to examine, by joint effort, just how the cult of personality affected literature and, concretely, how that effect was expressed. Unless mistakes are analysed it is hard to correct them.
>
> It is not a matter of repentance, of purging oneself of 'sins', or of casting blame off one's own back on to others. The point is that, without such analysis, all our future work will be made difficult. Without it we cannot write a truthful history of literature, nor is genuine literary criticism conceivable. Such analysis is needed by all writers. Every one of them, when working on new books and remembering the past of literature, evaluating his own former work, is undertaking analysis of this sort on his own account. But would it not be more useful to carry out this analysis, which is going on anyway, not separately but collectively?[120]

Analysis of literature is only part of an analysis of society. It is, of course, good to criticize outlived aesthetic norms: 'But, we ask ourselves, what can be changed in reality, and not just in words, unless we have clarified the real situation in which these necessary changes have to be made?' Finally, our analysis of society must be objective and truthful, otherwise the new art will create nothing of value: 'when talent becomes entangled with falsehood, it is impoverished.'[122] Simonov himself tried to appraise Stalinism in his work *The Lessons of History and the Writer's Duty*, but this was not published. Thus the need for collective endeavour was thrust upon the writers by the censorship: where one had not succeeded in 'breaking through', perhaps others might. To oppose the censorship apparatus a unified centre of literary endeavour was required.

Actually, the chief problem in this period was not the omnipotence of the censorship but, on the contrary, its lack of independence, the censors' diffidence. An American observer wrote later:

> the censors, be they editors in publishing houses or officials of the central censorship organ, tend to act less out of conviction than from fear – that ever-present element in Soviet society. Page after page is cut and passages sacrificed because 'they' (the Party authorities) would not want them to appear.[123]

It was impossible to negotiate as an individual with the Party bureaucracy. There had to be a writers' society. The official Writers' Union would not do. *Novy Mir* became, at the end of the fifties and in the sixties, the centre for studying Stalinism through literature. In this sense its role was unique. Under the leadership of Tvardovsky – and, to some extent, of Simonov – *Novy Mir* revived the tradition of the 'thick journals' of the nineteenth-century literary opposition – *Sovremennik* and *Otechestvennye Zapiski*. In a society where features of Stalinist totalitarianism were still present, the journal managed to defend its editorial independence. '*Novy Mir*', writes Roy Medvedev, 'never "fell on its knees", but pursued its own line under extremely difficult conditions.'[124] The first step on this plane, which was taken after the Twentieth Congress, was probably the publication in *Novy Mir* of V. Dudintsev's novel *Not By Bread Alone* (even before the appearance of Simonov's 'Literary Notes'). In its day this novel enjoyed immense fame. The discussion of it held at Leningrad University resembled an anti-government meeting.[125] The debate on the novel in the Writers' Union also produced some highly instructive scenes. K. Paustovsky made a sharply anti-bureaucratic speech.[126]

In the same issue of *Novy Mir* in which the first part of Dudintsev's novel appeared was also published D. Granin's story 'Private Opinion', and in 1958 the journal carried G. Troepol'sky's *Kandidat nauk*. All these works, though written very differently, were devoted to a single theme: the bureaucratization of science. But that was not all they had in common. They focused on 'the new man' engendered by the statocratic regime and its pseudo-communist ideology, studying and anatomizing him from every angle. The essence of these works was not the conflict between bureaucrats of science and scientists by vocation, as might seem at first glance, but the conflict between bureaucracy and science itself, their incompatibility.

M. Voslensky observes wittily about Dudintsev's book:

> From the Western point of view, the plot of the novel sounds like a farce: the *nomenklaturist* Drozdov, a factory manager, engages in vigorous intrigue to prevent the introduction of new machinery that will increase his output.[127]

In reality such a situation is very familiar to us and quite normal even now, a quarter of a century after Dudintsev's novel. It was precisely the typicality of the conflict, the familiarity of the situation that enraged bureaucratic circles. Many people recognized themselves in Drozdov.

'Bureaucratic man' appears in a variety of avatars. Before us is a whole gallery of bureaucrats, 'soft' and 'hard', military and civil, but gradually the features they have in common become apparent: above all what Troepol'sky calls their 'weather-vane quality', when a change of purpose entails a change of principles. Troepol'sky's hero first

> cut his hair 'like Mendel', then combed it 'like Lysenko', and now he would very much like to have a hairdo 'like Mal'tsev', but ... he was already balding, with only a few strands of hair left. Still, that wasn't important. What mattered was inner conviction.[128]

The result is incompetence and putting the interests of one's career or of 'one's own' clique before the interests of the task in hand. A character in Dudintsev's novel formulates, before Parkinson, the principle of incompetence, and adheres to it in his life:

> A man's job should always be a little beyond his powers ... And as soon as one began to be equal to the job, as soon as one had been praised once or twice – the thing to do was to move up into a region of fresh difficulties. ...[129]

Bureaucratic man's lack of principle does not mean in the least that he is tolerant of other people's ideas – quite the reverse. People with staunch principles scandalously obstruct the working of the bureaucratic machine; they hinder its 'mobility'. Hence the bureaucrats' hatred for all dissidents, a hatred which is essentially antisocial and antipopular. 'It is impossible', wrote Dudintsev, 'to destroy those who think differently – they are needed, just as a conscience is needed.'[130] The bureaucracy is hostile to all thought, to every idea, to any conscience:

> Their aim is to stay put in their easy chairs, and to go on getting richer. But a discoverer of new things is serving the people. A discoverer always thinks

differently, in any sphere of knowledge. Because he has found a new and shorter way, he rejects the old habitual one.[131]

Dudintsev's book aroused interest out of all proportion to its artistic merits. '*Not By Bread Alone*', writes the American scholar Joshua Rubenstein, 'is not an elegantly written novel. The characterizations are crude, and the story takes predictable and not wholly convincing turns.'[132] As regards the alleged 'unconvincingness' of the story one may disagree: the misadventures of the inventor who tries to overcome the bureaucratic barrier are described in a lifelike way. For the rest, however, Rubenstein is right: the book is far from perfect. From the artistic standpoint, the novel was, as Shatz puts it, 'a peculiar mixture of conventional socialist realism and relatively penetrating criticism'.[133] Dudintsev's success was a *succès de scandale*, a political success. The right-wingers cried panic, which only increased the interest taken by the youth and the intelligentsia in this novel.

In December 1958 *Literaturnaya Gazeta* quoted with approval some dramatic utterances by various neo-Stalinists, such as: 'The danger of revisionism ... has touched literature with its dark wing', or 'the nihilistic wind from the West has also enlivened our own nihilists. ... They are slandering our Soviet way of life, sometimes with subtlety and sometimes crudely.'[134] The 'revisionists' included Dudintsev, A. Yashin and others. The journal *Teatr* was also attacked. In that same year Pasternak published (abroad) his novel *Doctor Zhivago*. This was the first case of its kind for many years. There was reason to sound the alarm. Khrushchev himself showed irritation (as he often did) and spoke out against Dudintsev. 'His book *Not By Bread Alone*,' he said, 'which reactionary forces abroad are now trying to use against us, contains tendentiously selected negative facts interpreted with an approach that is biased and unfriendly.' That almost amounted to subverting the system. 'This approach to the presentation of reality in works of literature and art is nothing short of a craving to misrepresent reality, as it were through a distorting mirror.'[135]

In Stalin's day a writer would immediately have been put down for such 'sins'. But times had changed. The fact that an open conflict between a number of writers and the authorities led to a polemic and not to the taking of repressive measures had, in itself, a positive influence on the social climate. 'Warm spells' alternated with 'frosts', but on the whole it was clear that the 'thaw' was continuing. Simonov, in charge of *Novy Mir*, came under sharp criticism, but in the end the only result was that Tvardovsky resumed the editorship. The journal *Teatr* and some other publications joined *Novy Mir* in its campaign.

It was then, at the end of the fifties, that V. Kardin's famous review of Shtein's play *Hotel Astoria* was published, putting a question mark over the very foundations of Communist ideology. The article began by discussing the change in artistic taste and the collapse of Stalinist stereotyped thinking. The first signs of this were 'negative':

> We are already incapable, not just aesthetically but also, I would say, physically, of accepting certain theatrical contributions of the late forties which, in their time, were presented as great achievements in drama.[136]

Whereas, previously, exact following of 'the rules' had been valued, today what is valued is 'the new word', fresh thought, the topical problem. And Kardin put this question: Is Marxism a science or an atheistic religion? Depending on how he answered that question a person was in the camp of the reformers or in that of the conservatives, either with the Lefts or with the Rights, either on the side of the progressive intelligentsia or on the side of the narrow-minded dogmatists. Kardin raised the central question of the fifties and drew the line of demarcation, and the ideas he formulated have not lost their value even for the seventies and eighties.

The dogmatists sought to praise 'soldierly faith' and 'devotion to the Party', 'optimistic fatalism',

> as if the power of our faith consists in blindness, in unthinking obedience, as though faith is the enemy of reason and is afraid of facts, as if it comes not from real understanding of everyday life and its processes but from revelations sent down from on high.[137]

The left-wing intelligentsia opposed such dogmatism. 'For an artist,' wrote Kardin, 'an altar, even a renovated one, is a poor observation point. Ideas are displaced and real connections disrupted. And fear arises – fear of thought and of reality.[138] A state of mind like that is impotent to create: 'Once blind faith becomes the supreme ideal, what is most appropriate is holy mindlessness, setting one's hopes on the higher powers. Nothing happens without God's will.'[139] In just this way the petty bureaucrat in Tendryakov's writings, although he is constantly quoting Marx and Lenin, firmly believes 'that the great doctrine is fully accessible only to those who are high above us, at the helm of state.'[140] It is not given to those down below to think about it and understand it.

For his part, Kardin, referring to the experience of the Twentieth Congress, declared that 'it is precisely knowledge, culture, that gives true Communist conviction, inflexible faith in radiant ideals.'[141] Basically antipopular were the attempts of the official ideologues to counterpose 'intellectual theorizing' to the unthinking faith of 'the simple man'. Such attempts revealed the desire of those in power to keep the masses in ignorance, to isolate them from culture and crush their minds. Their tenderness before 'the simple Soviet man' was false through and through: it concealed contempt for him – a conception of him as 'cattle', a beast of burden, or cannon-fodder.

The Social Role of the Intelligentsia

In this way there began in Russian literature the trial of Stalinism, in which the weightiest argument became not Khrushchev's reports at the Twentieth or Twenty-Second Party Congresses, but Solzhenitsyn's novella *One Day in the Life of Ivan Denisovich*. A new system of positive values took shape. Literature and criticism in 'the great decade' which followed Stalin's death were, in the words of V. Lakshin, one of the leading theoreticians of *Novy Mir*, 'imbued with that vivid organic humanism which is nowhere equivalent to pleasing everybody and pardoning everything.'[142] Stalin had been a god, but the god was dead. Henceforth everyone bore responsibility for himself, and not only for himself but for society as a whole.

> In those memorable moments
> At the grave of the dread father
> We became fully answerable
> For everything in the world,
> To the end.

So wrote Tvardovsky in 1960.[143] Everyone thought about that, and everyone understood.

None the less, a particularly heavy responsibility lay on the shoulders of the intelligentsia. Stalin's policy had dispersed and declassed the proletariat. In the society which emerged from the crisis of 1953 there was no hereditary working class, and there were no democratic parties or even fully formed tendencies. The great mass of the people were not united in any way, and were therefore helpless. In 1960 more than half the engineering workers – traditionally the most conscious section of the workers – had been in industry for less than ten years. There was no real political and class alternative to the bureaucracy in the country, but a cultural and moral alternative to Stalinism did exist. Its bearer was the intelligentsia, the only subordinate social stratum which had at that time attained a certain social maturity. It was in this stratum that the new consciousness developed most rapidly, due to the very nature of the intellectuals' professional work (the development of new ideas, and so on). The intelligentsia spoke not only for itself but also for the entire oppressed mass which was as yet incapable of becoming 'a class for itself'. Here we hit upon a very important theoretical question: Why, all the same, did social consciousness awaken in the intelligentsia earlier than in the working class, if the intelligentsia was also dispersed and intimidated in the Stalin era? The working class, having lost its internal structure, had been temporarily transformed into a declassed marginal mass, but the intelligentsia, too, had to a large extent lost its traditional structure and a new structure was only in process of formation. This problem has been examined with particular attention by some Hungarian Marxists, who have reached useful conclusions.

The experiences of Stalinism laid a tremendous moral responsibility on the intelligentsia and on every thinking person. Whoever approved of the system bore moral responsibility for the crimes by which it had been created. By virtue of their position in society members of the intelligentsia knew more, and so they bore greater responsibility. 'The tragic thing about this situation', writes Rakovski, 'was that it had something inevitable about it: one could not decline the choice.'[144] Choice, of course, is not a privilege of intellectuals, but it was not only that. 'One could ask', he goes on,

> why the Soviet intelligentsia has not made contact with the working class, but that is not the right question. The question which in fact corresponds to the situation in Soviet-type societies is as follows: why is the intelligentsia – which does not constitute an autonomous class – able to create its own ideology and its own culture, and even its own counter-culture and embryonic counter-institutions, while the basic classes are unable even in this very restricted sense to form themselves into a class as a practical entity?[145]

This can be explained, to some extent, by the fact that

> the intelligentsia is in a privileged position compared with the basic classes. Because of the irreducible prerequisites of mental labour in the humanities and the sciences, the intelligentsia has, if not independent political organizations, then at least a functional equivalent to them. The relatively broad extent of academic communication (which certainly surpasses that of the basic groups) enables ideological and political allusions within the limits of the regime's ideological tolerance to be encoded and decoded regularly.[146]

One can mention some further advantages enjoyed by the intelligentsia. Being the group that elaborates society's ideology (Pokrovsky liked to recall that 'it is the intelligentsia who elaborate it, and nobody else,'[147]) it arrives sooner than any other at awareness of its own interests. At the same time we must remember that political liberties, which are unquestionably needed by *all* the working classes, are *also* a professional necessity for the intelligentsia – their *specific* interest. Hegedüs writes:

the interest of the members of the intelligentsia – to the extent that they really identify with their function – is related not to any particular institution but to the special field of the creation, application and communication of intellectual values. In this way the particular interest of the intelligentsia is more easily raised to the level of the general interest. This, of course, does not rule out the possibility of particular individuals turning the general interest of the intelligentsia into a special aim of their own, one which would then come into conflict with the general interest. We could instance innumerable examples to prove this, from every field of science, art and education.[148]

In one way or another the intellectuals, by virtue of their position, become aware more quickly of their common interests, and this in turn promotes their rapid social consolidation.

The fact that the intellectual traditions were preserved was of very great importance, for 'newcomers' assimilated them along with the elementary habits of brainwork, whereas the newcomer from the village to the factory bench did not absorb the traditions of the proletariat, since these are not lodged in the *technology* of production. People who are either incapable or unwilling to assimilate the traditions of the intelligentsia do not remain long in their ranks, but look upon education as a springboard to a bureaucratic career (including one in the bureaucracy of literature). The traditions of the Russian intelligentsia possess distinctive features, and it must be said that the Hungarian sociologists have overlooked that aspect of the matter (unlike British and American scholars, who have seen nothing else). Democratism and criticism have become intrinsic elements of Russian literary thought. Consequently, in our country, as Shatz very rightly observes, 'literature does not merely attract dissidents, it generates them.'[149]

We must mention also that despite all the upheavals, the proportion of hereditary intellectuals in 1953–56 and in the sixties was incomparably larger than the proportion of hereditary workers.[150] At the same time, the 'new generations' came, as a rule, from a semi-intellectual milieu. These people, while not actual bearers of the intellectual traditions, did at least share them. This enabled the intelligentsia to accept 'newcomers' in large numbers without losing the orderliness of its social structure and its psychological unity.

But as I have said, once it was in the vanguard of the social movement the intelligentsia had to speak for society as a whole, for the strata that were not yet ready to put forward their own demands, and this meant that the position of the nineteenth-century Russian intelligentsia and that of the Soviet intellectuals of the Khrushchev era – and, to a considerable extent, of the Brezhnev era as well – were similar. The intelligentsia found itself once more in a tragic situation: waging a struggle for the people's rights while not being understood by the people itself. 'In such a critical situation,' wrote Ernst Fischer in 1966, 'it is the duty of intellectuals to confront the people, because that is what will help the people to go forward tomorrow.'[151] This 'running ahead' created a very difficult psychological situation, which later gave rise to a real spiritual crisis and even loss of belief in change – a conviction that the Soviet working class was incapable of decisive actions which, by an irony of history, became most widespread just at the time when there appeared the first, still feeble signs of an awakening of the workers. However, in Khrushchev's time the intellectuals were still full of hope and also, alas, of illusions.

The literature of the sixties turned, as it were, towards the past. Its task was to recall and tell about that which it had not been possible to record of its own time. ... There was a sharp increase in interest in reminiscences and authentic 'documents of the epoch'. *Novy Mir* published 'The Diary of Nina Kosterina', a young woman who was killed at the Front during the war. Of this the critic I. Solovyova wrote: 'here we have the *whole* of that period ...'.[152] Yu. Trifonov published in *Znamya* a documentary story about his father, a Bolshevik shot by Stalin, in which the writer did not hesitate to include entire pages from letters and documents. What was important to him was to tell truthfully and objectively about the heroes of the civil war. The author held himself back, so to speak, refraining from giving his own view on the disputes of those years out of concern lest he insult the memory of the revolutionaries, who had 'now all been made equal, as it were, by their fate, in that they were all destroyed by Stalin.'[153]

Ilya Ehrenburg published in *Novy Mir*, year after year, his memoirs *People, Years, Life*. These were not the mere memoirs of a writer. They were also the history of an epoch, seen through the fate of a Russian Jewish intellectual – a book which astonished not only Soviet but also Western readers by its truthfulness and objectivity. 'One might venture to say that *People, Years, Life* will prove to be the most important book to be published during this decade in the USSR,' an American writer has said. 'Ehrenburg is the first writer in Russia to have described the past in a tone relaxed and yet so incisive.'[154] Here we find Stalin's repressive measures, and the destruction of churches, and the hopes or illusions of that time – real life described honestly and simply. Everything was said that could be said, and a great deal could be said at that time – at least about the past. True, we find Ehrenburg himself writing in a letter about the publication of the sixth part of his memoirs: 'We'll talk about the cuts when we meet.'[155] The seventh part of the memoirs was not published, but came out in *samizdat*. On the whole, though, the sixties can be described as a time of relative liberalism on the part of the censors. This general liberal tendency survived the fall of Khrushchev in 1964, lasting until the collapse of the economic reform and the Moscow bureaucrats' intervention in Czechoslovakia.

The Erosion of 'Socialist Realism'

The literary criticism, writing on current affairs and theoretical investigations of those years were so variegated that they deserve special study. Here we can look at only a few of what seem to me the most interesting questions. Above all, what happened in the sixties was a marked erosion of 'socialist realism'. On the one hand both the Left and the official theoreticians of the time sought more flexible and, consequently, vaguer definitions of the doctrine. People wrote of 'socialist realism' as an open, developing system, of its links with other tendencies, of the fact that adherence to 'socialist realism' was determined primarily by the artist's world-view and not by the form assumed by his work, and so on. But the liberals, as a rule, invested this concept with a content quite different from that given it by the Stalinists. Essentially, this meant a form that washed away the firm and *unambiguous* canons of 'socialist realism'. Attempts like this were made also in the official press and, still more frankly, in the *samizdat* publications which had begun to circulate. Medvedev's *Political Diary* belatedly summed up these ideas in October 1966: 'What is now especially important is somehow to shake people up and show them reality not as they would like to see it but as it really is.'[156] That was the task of 'socialist realism' as Roy Medvedev presented it. But his *Political Diary* attributed to 'socialist realism' a task which was *directly opposite* to the one assigned to it in the thirties by its founders and inventors – Stalin, Gorky, Lunacharsky.

Clearly, nothing of 'socialist realism' remained but the name, yet the fact that people did not want to reject that odious name is significant. Even in the ideological sphere the intellectuals of the sixties always fought not against the official principles but only against distortion of these principles. The ideology of 'true Communism' was not in the least a concession to pressure from without, it was at that time absolutely organic for the left-wing intelligentsia. Solzhenitsyn, who continually abuses 'those who submit to the censorship', has to acknowledge that 'to *Novy Mir*, Marxism was not compulsory ballast required by the censors.'[157] Of course, this seems to him unnatural. In another place he writes, maliciously, that the *Novy Mir* group were Octobrists 'in pre-revolutionary terminology: like the pre-revolutionary *Oktyabristy*, they wanted the existing regime to continue but to observe its own constitution.'[158] The Lefts saw their task as criticizing the rulers in their own language. Solzhenitsyn thought otherwise, but in those years he was obviously in a minority and even adapted himself to the prevailing mood.

'Of course,' V. Lakshin recalls,

> *Novy Mir* agreed with Solzhenitsyn on this point. We too disliked state-bureaucratic socialism, we defended human rights against their merely formal recognition, we shuddered at the horrors of Stalin's camps and protested wherever we could against the subtle forms of social hypocrisy. But we believed in socialism with a human heart and not only a human face. For us the democratic rights of the individual were beyond question.[159]

The ideology of *Novy Mir* and of Yevtushenko's *Autobiography* was widely accepted. 'We need to remember', writes Roy Medvedev,

> that in the sixties the main line of political and ideological struggle in our country ran between different tendencies in *socialist* thought and between different currents within the Party itself – to put it crudely, between Stalinists and anti-Stalinists. In the first half of the sixties there were practically no other tendencies: others began to find expression only at the end of that decade.[160]

Later, people saw this as the weakness of the opposition in Khrushchev's time, but its weakness did not in fact lie there. The serious problem for the dissidents of that period was that they did not understand the fundamental contradiction: the incompatibility between their democratic-socialist *ideal* and the pseudo-socialist *phraseology* of the statocracy. On the contrary, they set great hopes on the statocracy and even imitated its language.

'In the first years after the Twentieth Congress it seemed (perhaps for longer than it should)', writes E. Gnedin,

> that it was possible, by means of public statements in written appeals to the government, to hasten the process of renewal, to make it possible, by indirect action, for society and the right-thinking section of the state and Party apparatus to see that the country needed complete restructuring. It seemed that one could establish historical truth, and also prevent lawlessness (especially through the use of judicial procedure for repressive purposes), that one could prompt those in power to promote the establishment of truth

and justice by addressing them in the language they were used to, not shrinking from use of their own stereotyped expressions.[161]

Despite the obvious limitations of such thinking, much was achieved, especially in the sphere of art and aesthetic theory. There was a systematic critique of aesthetic dogmatism, under whose influence of the official theoreticians did renounce – even if only in words – the normative approach to art. Setting out the views of the Lefts, Lakshin wrote:

> Any normative conception is hostile to what it regards as unnecessary questions. It is strong in its self-importance and blindness to everything around it. It is rounded and smooth, and not even grass grows there. When a writer depicts real life the very text of the work is felt as an obstacle.[162]

On the other hand, modern art was explicitly rehabilitated, as it was found to be compatible with 'socialist realism'. On this plane the memoirs of Ehrenburg, mentioned above, were important. The author of *People, Years, Life* strove to give the so-called modernists their due – to show their importance for the development of European art in the twentieth century:

> The Futurists were accused of disrespecting the past, but the Futurists' weapons were pens, not picks and shovels. When forests were cut down in the thirties it was not only chips that flew but sometimes age-old stones. In Archangel in 1934 I saw them blow up the customs house built in the time of Peter the Great; when I asked why, I was told: 'It interferes with the traffic'; yet in those days you could count the cars in Archangel on the fingers of two hands.[163]

While proclaiming respect for tradition, for popular creativity and for the classics, the Stalinists in reality did not hesitate to destroy historical monuments. Epigonism announced as a virtue had nothing in common with respect for tradition, or with art in any way at all. 'The age of idols is past,' wrote Ehrenburg,

> not only in religion, but also in art. Iconoclasm died with the worship of icons. But does this mean that the desire to say new things in a new way has disappeared? Recently I read in a certain journal the words 'modest pioneering'. At first they made me laugh, then they made me very sad. An artist must be modest in his behaviour, but never moderate, lukewarm, limited in his creative ambitions. I am sure that it is more worthwhile to scrawl something that is one's own, in one's own way, than to write out old adages in a copperplate hand. I do not believe that collective farmers painted in the manner of the academic (Bolognese) school can give many people

pleasure, nor that it is possible to convey the rhythm of the second half of the twentieth century by that profusion of subsidiary clauses which Leo Tolstoy used so brilliantly.[164]

As the sixties advanced, however, the orthodox socialist realists tried to launch a counter-offensive. But they failed to receive the support from above which they had counted on: the ruling class was, for the time being, trying to avoid unnecessary conflicts and displayed a certain liberalism. This can be explained, above all, by the unwillingness of the rulers to return to the use of Stalin's methods, which had often meant 'firing on their own people'. Consequently, in the literary disputes of those years the authorities often preferred the role of arbiter between Rights and Lefts, while leaning, naturally, towards the former rather than the latter. For example, Khrushchev did not like Ehrenburg's memoirs: 'It appears that the author of the memoirs has great sympathy for the representatives of the so-called "left" art, and assumes the task of defending this art.' Khrushchev did not share this sympathy, and concluded: 'Comrade Ehrenburg is making a gross ideological mistake, and it is our duty to help him to realize this.'[165] He did not like, either, the pronouncements made by the young poets, *cinéastes* and artists, which he saw as an attempt 'to set youth against the older generations'.[166] He himself was firmly convinced that in our society there are 'no contradictions between generations. There is no "father and son" problem in its old sense. It has been invented. . . .'[167]

What the Rights needed above all, however, was administrative support in the form of bans, exilings and arrests. But for the time being that support was not to be had. Although the Stalinist journal *Oktyabr'* printed, in issue after issue, spiteful anti-intellectual novels and denunciatory articles, it achieved nothing by these methods, and the critics writing in *Novy Mir* were merely supplied with fuel for their witticisms.

The most interesting attack on the left-wing intelligentsia was I. Shevtsov's novel *The Louse*. Its preface was contributed by A. Laktionov, a member of the Academy of Art. Quite a large number of copies were printed. In this novel the author, a well-known reactionary and anti-Semite, wrote that in the world of art were operating 'the elusive forces of an obscure but well-knit, single-minded group' – 'not numerous but amazingly active', 'fanatics of modernism', 'cosmopolitans', 'incendiaries'(!), 'aesthetes and formalists of every stripe'. They 'sneer with impunity' at honest artists and give them advice in which 'there is something diabolically seductive, or, rather, scheming'; they 'bring in devil-worship'; they try to 'insinuate their own people' everywhere; they propagate 'sedition'.[168] Shevtsov was answered in *Novy Mir* by Sinyavsky who, as 'A. Tertz', was the author of an essay published in the West under the title *What is Socialist Realism?*:

> Although 'war is war', there are, obviously, different forms and methods in the waging of it. The war that Ivan Shevtsov wages in his book verges, in my view, on such non-literary forms as street brawling, squabbles in trams, rows in flats. ... To join in this polemic under the conditions offered would be shameful, degrading, and to answer his arguments with passion would be a joke.[169]

Actually, Sinyavsky did not need to argue with Shevtsov. He merely paraphrased – and sometimes quoted – some passages from the novel which betrayed the author's utter ignorance in matters of art:

> Puzzling, too, is Shevtsov's interpretation of realism. In realism particular importance is ascribed to the painstaking depiction of details, even to the extent that, in the genre painting 'At the Registry Office', which is presented here as a masterpiece, the feelings of the bridegroom 'can be read in the quivering of his long eyelashes', and on the desk we see 'a blank form' on which 'lay a pen', ready to register the marriage. If we consider that all this, with a mass of other details, 'is shown on a small canvas', it becomes clear how laboriously the artist has toiled at giving the finishing touches to trifles, seeing in this the true triumph of realism.[170]

Uproar ensued. *The Louse* was condemned by all the publications, the right-wing ones included – by *Ogonyok*, *Komsomolskaya Pravda*, *Literaturnaya Gazeta*. Of no little importance here was the fact that Shevtsov had naïvely 'blown' his own side, exposing the mode of thought of the orthodox 'socialist realists', the hostility of their system to art. Unintentionally, he had let his friends down. Laktionov repudiated his own preface, saying that he had neither read the novel nor written the article. Thus Shevtsov found himself under fire from all sides. 'Such unanimity is a matter for rejoicing,' wrote Sinyavsky,

> although it seems to me that sometimes criticism of *The Louse* such as appeared in *Ogonyok* descends, in its tone, to the level of the novel under discussion, and offers the author a testimonial by reminding us of his sort of art.[171]

In the course of the sixties traditional 'socialist realism' was completely discredited. On the one hand it had virtually ceased to exist; while on the other, it was impossible for some time to give up using the obsolete and empty expression. This paradoxical situation in which 'socialist realism' was being eroded was described by G. Nedoshivin in an article in 1969 which tried to present the balance sheet of a decade of struggle. Examining one after the other the principles of socialist-realist aesthetics, he showed their inapplicability to the art of the sixties. 'What is a landscape painting according to socialist realism?' he asked,

> Formerly, acting on the thesis that the distinctive method of socialist realism is the ability 'to see what is new', people were inclined to consider that what was typical of a Soviet landscape painting was the depiction of nature 'transformed by man's hand'. However, even the most hopeless dogmatists of the forties did not assert that any depiction of nature which failed to include high-voltage transmission lines or something of that sort was *thereby* outside the limits of socialist realism.[172]

Nedoshivin also rejected the official-traditional interpretation of 'partisanship', showing that it had nothing in common with Lenin's views. Here the Soviet aestheticist was essentially repeating what E. Fischer and F. Marek had said in their book *What Lenin Really Said*. That book had been condemned in the USSR, yet Nedoshivin's article was published. Truly, the ways of the censor are inscrutable!

Nedoshivin wrote quite correctly, about Lenin's article, that

> 'Party Organization and Party Literature' never had or could have any restricting, let alone 'prohibiting', significance. Lenin was less concerned than anyone else to lay down what an artist 'must not do', and did not in the least seek to set any barriers before creative freedom. Moreover, the sense of Vladimir Ilyich's article is consistently for freedom in art, real freedom, which includes the *freedom* of the artist to be a partisan.[173]

Comparing some 'socialist-realist' works with works by Western artists who were far from being Communists, Nedoshivin showed that there were no *artistic*, stylistic differences between them. He came to the conclusion 'that the futility of an attempt to draw up a precise *list of distinctive features* of socialist realism is rooted in its very nature.'[174] Thereby he recognized the aesthetic emptiness of the expression 'socialist realism'. In its place a new conception of socialist art was set up. These two terms were at first used in the article as synonyms, but the former was later ousted by the latter. Of the old aesthetics only meaningless words remained. Subsequently, in the seventies, the problem of 'socialist realism' simply vanished. The expression 'socialist realism' is recalled two or three times a year in editorials on the eve of national holidays, but for the rest of the time it is happily forgotten. 'We find ourselves', wrote Nedoshivin, 'at some kind of serious turning point, and perhaps, both for theory and for art itself, "the spirit of inquiry" is what we need today more than − please forgive the *jeu de mots* – irresponsible responses.'[175]

The expression 'spirit of inquiry' was a good one. The collapse of the old aesthetic theory meant that a search for a new conception of art had begun. At first, however, this did not develop around aesthetic problems as such. What was studied was the question of art and society, of art and 'us'. Culture was becoming more and more a field of social and political conflict. The new theory was, naturally, elaborated most properly (from all points of view) on the basis of new forms of art. No heap of theoretical dogmas had yet been accumulated in this field and it was possible, skipping a phase of 'exposure', to proceed to examine the laws of the genre. For this reason one of the best theoretical works on art in the sixties was devoted to television. This was V. Sappak's book *Television and Us.*

In 1960 Sappak wrote a long article for *Novy Mir* and in 1963, after his premature death, his book appeared. The main thing in it was 'the idea of truth as the only language that television could speak, the idea, so to say, of steady, natural *self-turning to truth* ...'[176] Sappak's approach, from the purely methodological standpoint, is as unusual as it is fruitful. He looks at television as a whole and tries to create a *general* theory of it. Consequently, for him, 'the latest news' or some reportage from a factory is of no less importance as an *aesthetic* event than a play or film series. This approach is perfectly well founded since television, unlike the cinema or the theatre, broadcasts continuously throughout the day, and the 'ideal' viewer should watch everything in succession and receive some sort of integral impression.

Sappak did not take sides in the argument between the advocates of television and its opponents. As he saw it, the trouble is not television itself – what matters is who is in charge of it. The possibilities of the new art are immense: a news programme, let us remember, is here also regarded as an artistic phenomenon; it too has to be presented, the announcers and the material have to be selected and the right way found for putting it across. But in the wrong hands television's virtue turns into vice. Soviet television is a grand piano being played by a Neanderthal man. The instrument is too perfect – it is not suitable for the aims pursued, and merely betrays the nature of the barbarian who is using it. Analysing propaganda broadcasts, Sappak shows their ineffectiveness and even their capacity to produce the opposite effect to what was intended. Propaganda on television is self-exposing; it sobers people up. When an orator holds forth from the platform it is easy for him to play the demagogue. But when he comes, with the help of the sky-blue screen, into your home – when he has to talk to you as man to man, intimately – he proves helpless. It is harder to deceive someone when you look him in the eye. False intonations give you away:

We do not experience reciprocal feelings when, addressing us viewers, they repeat, pressing down the pedal, in moving tones: 'Dear friends!', 'Dear friends!' ... In general, we do not issue advances and guarantees of emotion. And when they say to us 'Rejoice!' we reply: 'Somehow I don't feel like rejoicing. ...'[177]

The result of a broadcast is very often the opposite of its aim, but that result corresponds to its essence. Sappak concludes:

> The TV screen unmasks a lie. However it tries to hide, it will stand out, it makes itself quite clear, it swells up, forcing us viewers to curse the evil thing and switch off the set. A demand for truth and honesty is the first article in television's code of morality.[178]

Sappak's theoretical views differ markedly from many Western conceptions of television and in my opinion are much less speculative and more original. But that is not the point. Ten years after Pomerantsev the talk was still of truth and sincerity. But of what, in essence, had all the critical and literary activity of that generation consisted of, if not of a struggle for truth!

De-Stalinization: The Literary Mirror

The Twenty-Second Party Congress gave a fresh powerful stimulus to de-Stalinization. The criticism of Stalin was now not 'secret', but rang out in open session. The struggle against Khrushchev begun in 1957 by Stalin's former henchmen – Molotov, Kaganovich and Malenkov – who quickly lost influence, merely intensified the anti-Stalinist tendencies in the new leadership. Criticism of the 'cult of personality' remained a mighty weapon for Khrushchev in his struggle for power. At the Twenty-Second Congress he dealt his opponents a powerful blow. 'After the drab Twenty-First Congress,' wrote Solzhenitsyn,

> which damped and muted the splendid promise of the Twentieth, there was no way of foreseeing the sudden fury, the reckless eloquence of the attack on Stalin which Khrushchev would decide upon for the Twenty-Second! Nor, try as we might, could we, the uninitiated, ever explain it! But there it was – and not even a secret attack, as at the Twentieth Congress, but a public one! I could not remember when I had read anything as interesting as the speeches at the Twenty-Second Congress.[179]

In connection with the Twenty-Second Congress, Giuseppe Boffa writes:

whatever Khrushchev's intentions may have been when he organized the anti-Stalin polemic, its influence in the country was even greater than at the time of the Twentieth Congress. While the limits of criticism stayed as before, this criticism now came not only from above, it corresponded to a new mood which had developed among the intelligentsia, the youth, the former inmates of the camps and prisons: society was better prepared to assimilate its conclusions. The official ideology was momentarily thrown on to the defensive.[180]

In his report Khrushchev frankly recognized that there were in the Party 'forces which clung to the old and resisted all that was new and creative.'[181] Although he was talking about the period of the Twentieth Congress it was clear that those forces had not disappeared, even if Khrushchev did not say that. At the Twenty-Second Congress Stalinism was no longer reduced to one man's mistakes, to the personality of Stalin. Some of the accomplices of the 'leader and teacher' were mentioned by name. In his address Shvernik spoke directly about the doings of 'the dogmatists and splitters Molotov, Kaganovich, Malenkov, Voroshilov, Bulganin, Pervukhin, Saburov and Shepilov'.[182] He spoke, too, about the role that Malenkov, Molotov and Kaganovich had played in the repressions. For the first time such exposures as these were uttered openly and published in many copies. The facts of Stalin's crimes were given documentary confirmation by the Party leadership itself.

Although Khrushchev realized that the exposures 'might arouse a certain bitterness and even discontent ... among the people',[183] and in spite of the obvious crisis in the confidence felt by 'those below' in 'those above', he stressed the need to continue along the road of de-Stalinization. Stalin's corpse was removed from the Lenin Mausoleum and the monuments to him which still stood in some places even after the Twentieth Congress were taken down. *Pravda* published Yevtushenko's poem *The Heirs of Stalin*, and *Novy Mir* published Solzhenitsyn's *One Day in the Life of Ivan Denisovich*. The appearance of this novella in 1962 produced a lively discussion. 'It is hard to realize that only a year ago the name of Solzhenitsyn was unknown to us,' wrote Lakshin.

It seems now that he had long been there in our literature, and without him it would emphatically have been incomplete. Each new story of his, whether praised or abused by the critics, leaves no reader unmoved. People talk about him, quote him, judge him with a sort of special exactingness which is unusual for our literature and is the first sign that we have really been moved and disturbed.[184]

Publication of the novella coincided with a new wave of de-Stalinization

– otherwise, indeed, it would hardly have been published. Khrushchev liked it, and *Pravda*, *Izvestiya* and *Literaturnaya Gazeta* rallied to its support. *One Day* was put forward for a Lenin Prize. Nor was this novella of Solzhenitsyn's the only work on a 'labour-camp' subject. For example, in 1964 *Zvezda* published G. Shelest's *Kolyma Notes*, which had much in common with *One Day*, although it was written from the standpoint of a Communist soldier who looked on what had happened with different eyes, trying to remain a Communist even in the camp. What was distinctive about Solzhenitsyn's novella was not only that it dealt with life in a labour camp but also – and above all – its literary qualities. There is no time to discuss the book here in detail: what concerns us is something else.

The consequences of the publication of *One Day* were many-sided. It was truly an event *of historical importance*. Perhaps one of the most important results was the development of *samizdat*. The novella evoked a great number of replies, imitations and reflections. A flood of 'camp writing' poured into editorial offices, as though a dam had broken. Soon, however, an instruction came down from 'on high' that this sort of material was not to be published any more. But people went on writing and reproducing what they had written; the flood merely took a different direction. Whatever the state publishing houses did not accept was circulated in *samizdat*. At this time, the circulation of *samizdat* material was not regarded as being anti-government – at least, in the minds of the intellectuals who engaged in it. Their activity was no direct challenge to the statocracy. 'The circulation of typewritten copies was seen', writes Rakovski, 'as a kind of pre-publication which would be followed by their being brought out by state publishing houses or in journals.'[185] There actually were instances when material which had first been passed around in manuscript was eventually published, albeit with cuts by the censor. The editors of *Novy Mir* took care not to let the manuscripts they received go into *samizdat*, as this might make publication difficult: at that time there was no clear-cut dividing line between what was 'permissible' in literature and what was not; it was defined afresh in each concrete instance. But this situation did not last long.

'The publication of *Ivan Denisovich* and *The Heirs of Stalin* seemed to be a prelude', writes Shatz, 'to a new wave of de-Stalinization and a new attack on the conservative diehards. That wave never broke.'[186] In December 1962 Khrushchev visited an exhibition by young artists of the 'modernist' school, at the Manège and went into a frenzy. Nobody was in any doubt that the whole business of his visit to the exhibition had been set up by conservative elements in the leadership who were trying to put an end to the prolonged 'romance' between Khrushchev and the Left intelligentsia.

It is important to note that the summer of 1962 had seen a mighty wave of strikes, caused by increases in the cost of food and by bad housing conditions. The position of the workers was indeed frightful. 'For example,' some American Sovietologists wrote at that time, 'by 1961, after an intensive housing-construction drive, the average living-space per Soviet inhabitant was approximately 8 square metres. (The minimum sanitary standard recommended by the United States Bureau of Prisons is 9 square metres.)'[187] Later, in 1964–70, thanks to the economic reforms (which will be discussed below) the workers' standard of living improved considerably. We even attained that American prison minimum.

It would be interesting to know what influence the strikes had on the balance of forces within the statocracy. In any case, they could not have passed unnoticed. The well-known strike at Novacherkassk, which ended with firing on a workers' demonstration – comparable only with the Tsarist shooting-down of the workers in St Petersburg on 9 January 1905 or the Lena massacre of 1912 – was far from being the only initiative taken by the lower orders. Strikes spread all across the country.[188] Most probably these events, by intensifying the nervousness of the bureaucracy, facilitated the progress of intrigues by Suslov and other conservatives. This question we must leave to future historians who will be able to work in the Kremlin archives.

In any case, Khrushchev yielded to the provocation. He came down on the 'modernists' with all the violence of his temperament, declaring that 'formalist and abstractionist vagaries are alien to and not understood by the people'.[189] For some reason he was particularly shaken by B. Zhutovsky's self-portrait. 'But whom has B. Zhutovsky portrayed?' exclaimed 'our Nikita'.

A freak! Looking at his self-portrait, you could be frightened. Shouldn't anyone be ashamed of wasting his efforts on such a disgraceful object! How can it be that he has studied at a secondary school and a higher educational institution, that the people's money has been spent on him, and he eats the bread provided by the people? And how has he repaid the people, the workers and peasants, for the money they have spent on his education, for the benefits they are giving him now? With this self-portrait – this abomination and monstrosity.[190]

Zhutovsky had depicted himself, and the people had nothing to do with it. But Khrushchev sometimes reacted like an offended property-owner (a lot of money has been spent) and sometimes like a man who is going to buy a machine for making tarpaulin boots and at the last moment discovers that what it actually turns out is steel tubing (even of the finest quality) – that is, like an offended customer.

Brzezinski and Huntington say that 'Khrushchev's remarks, crude and often vulgar, were also designed to stir up the anti-intellectual prejudices of the masses.'[191] That is unlikely. What is more likely is that Khrushchev was giving free rein to his own prejudices. At that moment he spoke as a typical man of the Stalin era, antagonistic towards new ways. 'But the so-called fashionable modern dances', he said with indignation,

> are simply something unseemly, mad and the devil knows what! They say that one can see such unseemly things only in the religious sect of the *Triasuny* [Shakers]. I don't know whether that is actually so, because I have never attended any of their meetings.[192]

Ortega y Gasset once wrote that, when a man cannot understand a work of art, 'he feels vaguely humiliated and this rankling sense of inferiority must be counterbalanced by indignant self-assertion.'[193] That was exactly what happened with Khrushchev. True, while going for the 'modernists' he also mentioned that 'works in which Soviet reality during those years is truthfully depicted from Party positions have appeared' – such as Solzhenitsyn's *One Day in the Life of Ivan Denisovich.*[194]

In 1963 policy towards the intelligentsia changed again, and a struggle was waged for Solzhenitsyn to be awarded a Lenin Prize: it did not succeed, but was significant nevertheless. However, liberalization was on the ebb. This was not due to a weakening in Khrushchev's position but because he had already reached the limits of toleration by the ruling statocracy, which increasingly saw in his reforms a threat to *their* corporate interests. The 'thaw' was ending, and a time beginning for its first results to be summed up.

After Solzhenitsyn's novella had been published in *Novy Mir*, and later as a separate work, the one and only possibility was created for discussing the essence of Stalinism in a legal periodical. Of course, the question of its class character – the principal historical question – could not be raised. Moreover, at the beginning the social thought of the intelligentsia's members, who had been taught to think in pseudo-Marxist categories but were poorly acquainted with Marxist method, was simply incapable of conceiving such a question. The left-wing intelligentsia still saw the resolutions of the Twentieth and Twenty-Second Party Congresses as models of critical analysis, and its illusions connected therewith had not been outgrown. Yet the official explanation of the 'cult of personality' was utterly idealistic, reducing everything to Stalin's psychology, to his incorrect theoretical views, and so on. In this sense, the articles in *Novy Mir* and *Problemy mira i sotsializma* were very much more profound than the official conceptions. The discussion around *One Day in the Life of Ivan Denisovich* made possible an extension of the critique of Stalinism, touching on political questions and, as we shall see, really getting close to social questions. 'The logic of real life,' noted Yu. Karyakin, 'the logic of class struggle shows that the novella is hated and feared more and more as one hates and fears a living and powerful enemy, and the author can only rejoice in such hatred directed at him.'[195]

'*One Day in the Life of Ivan Denisovich*', wrote Lakshin,

> was read even by people who do not usually read novellas and novels. One such 'irregular' reader said to me: 'I don't know whether it is written well or badly. It seems to me it couldn't be written in any other way.'[196]

It is curious that this little novella had more influence on public opinion than Solzhenitsyn's later work on *The Gulag Archipelago*. That was not only because *One Day* was printed in many thousands of copies, whereas the *Archipelago* was an 'underground' publication (on a relatively large scale, to be sure). The simple denunciatory force of this remarkable work was extremely great – greater even than that of articles specially devoted to the subject. Lakshin wrote rightly: 'Solzhenitsyn disappointed those who had expected from him a story of crimes, tortures, bloody torments and excesses of inhumanity in the camp, a story of martyrs and heroes of penal servitude.'[197] That would come. But for the time being he had written an artless tale of camp life, of one happy(!) day in a prisoner's life. It had a very powerful impact.

The main thing in Solzhenitsyn's book that struck Lakshin, Karyakin and other left-wing theoreticians of the sixties intelligentsia was its conclusion concerning the antipopular essence of Stalinism. 'The word "people"', wrote Lakshin, 'was transformed in Stalin's mouth into an empty abstraction. It was as if there existed something called "the people" and yet no single individual belonged to the people.'[198] But the antipopular character of the regime does not only arouse anger. Understanding it enables us to perceive in the people that force which, sooner or later, will put an end to tyranny – we see in the people our grounds for hope. 'Consequently,' wrote Karyakin,

> it is not just a matter of the tragic fate of some individuals but also, and this is what is most important, of the forces which make it possible to overcome that tragedy, of the elimination of the illusions of the 'cult', and of the maturing of the people's verdict on arbitrary and lawless rule. And all that, of course, refers not just to the past.[199]

Karyakin aimed the point of his criticism at Stalin's heirs. First and

foremost he had in mind the Maoists in China, but his general
theoretical conclusions were of a rather wider application. *One Day in
the Life of Ivan Denisovich* made him remember what Marx wrote
about barracks-Communism. In those words he saw the theoretical key
to the understanding of the Stalinist phenomenon. Marx did not live to
see his opponents in power, but what had happened in Russia proved
once again the rightness of his humanist and democratic approach to
socialism, and the justification of his fears. 'In their pretensions,' wrote
Karyakin,

> the supporters of barracks-Communism are comic, but once they have
> obtained even a little power, let alone all power, they become terrible: their
> farce is fraught with tragedy for the people. ... And if you scratch a man
> who, 'in the name of Communism', employs Jesuitical means, you will find
> that he conceives the aims of Communism in a perverted way.[200]

The formula for the political practice of barracks-Communism,
according to Karyakin, is given in *One Day*. The camp is the Stalinists'
ideal of the new society: 'A step to right or left is considered an attempt
to escape and the escort has orders to shoot without warning.'[201] That is
the first and fundamental principle. Under Stalinism the people do not
exist; there are only *zeki* [prisoners] – some in camps, others 'in
freedom'. Stalinism can be explained, wrote Karyakin, 'but it cannot be
justified, we must not accept its *victory* as fatally inevitable, nor must
we *reduce* to this the complex history of a whole people over many
years.'[202] There had been many different experiences in that life,
including successes, but the victories won were won not thanks to
Stalinism but in spite of it.

The defenders of Stalinism are spiritually sterile. They can only
suppress ideas; they cannot create them. In place of the social sciences
they engage in demagogy, whereby 'to conceal their striving to usurp
power over the Party and the people'.[203] Their mentality is 'a secular
variant of the religious mentality'. 'Lack of confidence in the masses,'
Lakshin wrote in this connection,

> self-satisfaction and boasting, if allowed free exercise, lead to self-deception,
> to the formation of an illusory, invented picture of life. What is desired is first
> presented as really existing, and then taken to be real by the phrasemongers
> themselves. A vicious circle is formed.[204]

The best description of the situation is the biblical phrase about 'the
blind leading the blind'. 'The worst enemy', wrote Karyakin,

> cannot do as much harm to the ideas of Communism as is done by those who

transform these ideas into a variety of religious dogma (nourishing thereby the arguments of many anti-Communists). What can be more contrary to nature than a blindly believing Communist and a Marxist who bows down before an idol?[205]

The anti-Stalinists sought, above all, to draw support from Lenin's criticisms of bureaucracy and dogmatism. 'As a writer,' wrote Lakshin,

> Lenin was hostile to the evasiveness of platitudes, cautious reservations and the abstract treatment of subjects. ... Lenin's articles, by their method of analysis and their freedom from clichés, wage war in their very form against what they attack in substance – against narrow-minded dogmatism, against thought which had gone to sleep, against sectarian deification of formulas.[206]

Lenin said that our country's destiny depends on 'the really enlightened elements for whom we can vouch that they will not take the word for the deed, and will not utter a single word that goes against their conscience.'[207] It was to that appeal of Lenin's that the anti-Stalinist intellectuals sought to respond. They felt a new sense of responsibility. Karyakin considered, however, that it was necessary to go further:

> Too high a price has been paid for us to restrict ourselves, in the end, *merely* to the safeguarding of those convictions with which the Communists began the hard task of building a new world. That is necessary but insufficient. And if such a price has been paid, we must extract everything we can from the experience we have undergone.[208]

Although Karyakin called for deeper analysis, in his own writings there is nothing but criticism of ideology. Nevertheless, Solzhenitsyn had raised questions which could be answered only on the social plane. What was at issue here?

When Karyakin sees Stalinism as merely an obstacle on the road to socialism, he is right, in the last analysis. But it is not difficult to suggest that this obstacle was, in its own way, logical and inevitable – that Stalinism did not come from nowhere, without any roots, and that it played a certain role in our country's modernization. All of which needs to be looked into. And then, when we have understood the roots of Stalinism – its essential nature – we must investigate how to overcome it. Characteristic of the first post-Stalin decade was a striving to tell the truth, to expose, to reveal the reality of society. Now a new need was arising – to go into the inner mechanism of things and analyse it.

The Limits of Moral Criticism

The change in the problem to be tackled and the change in the nature of the left-wing intelligentsia's thinking brought on a crisis. The Twentieth Congress had given hope, but it had also proved a source of illusions. It had prevented us from perceiving the main thing – the class nature of the regime. The liberals of the sixties believed that society as a whole, the system as a whole, was moving towards the elimination of Stalinism, yet what happened was merely its updating. They saw in the Twentieth and then in the Twenty-Second Congresses the beginning of a new course but in fact that was, in both cases, the end of it. They did not realize that everything that had happened was closely connected with the class struggle. Oddly, people who were Marxists when they analysed the West seemed to forget class analysis when they turned to their own country. In 1965 M. Gefter, Ya. Drabkin and V. Mal′kov published in *Novy Mir* an article entitled 'The World During Twenty Years' which was a real manifesto of Soviet liberalism; in it they called for 'the creation of political, ideological and moral guarantees to make impossible any revival of the cult of personality'.[209] Note that they spoke of moral problems, yet said nothing about social problems – this was due not to censorship but to the writers' way of thinking. One can distinguish two weak aspects of the ideology of the Lefts in Khrushchev's 'great decade'. On the one hand there was their naïve belief in 'true Communism'; on the other their moralism. They tried to think about political questions exclusively in cultural categories and, though sincere supporters of Marxism, they had not mastered the Marxist method of social criticism. 'Of course,' writes Rakovski,

> the critique of theoretical 'dogmatism' went hand in hand with the denunciation of political and sometimes institutional 'distortions'. But the unofficial Marxists of this period never used the argument that in Soviet-type societies it is only the vocabulary of the official ideology that is socialist.[210]

Stalin's crimes were not 'mistakes' and 'deviations' from 'the correct line'; they were themselves 'the correct line' *of the statocracy* at a certain stage of its struggle against the working classes and against socialism. Legal Marxism was censored, and in this case it is clear that such an idea could be voiced only in *samizdat*: but up to that time it had not been heard in *samizdat* publications.[211] This resulted from the willingness of the 'true Communists' to remain within the limits set by official dogmatics. It is important to remember that even in the best period of Khrushchev's 'thaw', the left-wing intelligentsia was unable to break away from the 'Procrustes' bed' of the Stalinist schemas, and thought in terms of the old categories. Subsequently a long (and still uncompleted) struggle took place against the schematism of 'Communist' dogma and for dialectical thinking. Getting rid of schemas and starting to think about the world freely and critically proved, as we shall see later, extremely difficult. In the sixties 'critical' thinking still confined itself to correcting dogma in accordance with a commonly accepted schema, finding internal contradictions in the dogma and studying them, squeezing into the 'ideological fissures' of Stalinism.

Such 'fissures' existed in the sixties and were constantly being widened owing to the political conflicts within the statocracy itself. Certain groups in it were disposed to support the Lefts, and so we had the publication of *One Day in the Life of Ivan Denisovich*. After Khrushchev's fall the statocracy closed its ranks. Attempts by oppositionists to squeeze into the 'political fissures' between its different groups proved less and less successful, and the 'fissures' themselves became narrower. Under Brezhnev the statocracy achieved an ideal equilibrium such as it had not possessed either under Stalin or under Khrushchev. True, this did not rule out the appearance of new groupings and new 'fissures' after Brezhnev, but that is another question. What matters is that in the seventies the ideology of 'true Communism' ceased to be 'operative'.

Moralism had a rather different significance. We must remember that the movement of the sixties was *necessarily*, at first, not a political but a literary and cultural movement, subject to the laws of literature's development and Russia's cultural traditions. Given the existence of censorship, literature had to bear an additional political workload, but politics itself became 'literary'. Russian literature is in no danger of being 'over-politicized', for in order to continue as art it rethinks politics in philosophical and – especially – in moral categories (one has only to remember Dostoevsky, Tolstoy, and Solzhenitsyn's best works). It exercises moral judgement over politicians. But here a danger of a different order arises. Shatz writes:

> As Solzhenitsyn noted in his Nobel speech, literature by its very nature deals with the problems of mankind in moral terms, that is, in terms of the clash between good and evil. Indeed, it is the great tradition of moral seeking that has given Russian literature so much of its universal appeal and intensity.

However, he observes, 'not all political and social issues are moral issues ... nor are they always susceptible to moral solutions.'[212] Another unfortunate circumstance is that in history such moralists as Saint-Just,

Robespierre and their like have showed themselves bloodthirsty enough in their striving to 'punish the wicked'.

Political activity must be based (despite the hypocritical chatter of the Philistines to the effect that politics 'in general' is amoral) upon definite moral principles, but it cannot be reduced to those principles. Moral indignation and a thirst for justice do not, by themselves, help to revive an economy. 'Russian literature', writes Shatz,

> has a long and honourable history as an opponent of political oppression and social injustice. But it is a form of opposition with inherent limitations, limitations that the pre-revolutionary intelligentsia frequently displayed and that have left their mark on Soviet dissent.[213]

It is impossible not to agree with this judgement. Oppositional moralism and official schematism, as we shall see later, dominated the consciousness of the intelligentsia even during the seventies, but already in a *new* form.

Notes

1. *Novy Mir*, no. 9, 1966, p. 193
2. R.A. Medvedev, *On Stalin and Stalinism*, Oxford 1979, p. 148.
3. Loren R. Graham, *Science and Philosophy in the Soviet Union*, 1973, p. 18.
4. Boffa, *Storia dell'Unione Sovietica*, Milan 1976, vol. 2, p. 381.
5. Ibid.
6. R.A. Medvedev, *Let History Judge*, 1971, p. 483.
7. See A. Maksimov, 'Protiv reaktsionnogo einshteinianstva v fizike', *Krasnyi Flot*, 23 June 1952; and 'Teoriya otnositel'nosti i materializm', *Pod znamenem marksizma*, no. 4–5, 1923. Also *Filosofskie voprosy Sovremennoi fiziki*, Moscow 1952, p. 47.
8. See G. Naan, 'Sovremennyi fizicheskii idealizm v S Sh A i Anglii na sluzhbe popovshchiny i reaktsii', *Voprosy filosofii*, no. 2, 1948.
9. Graham, p. 120.
10. Stalin, *Concerning Marxism in Linguistics*, 1950 ('Soviet News' pamphlet, p.21).
11. Ibid. Significantly, an intense Russification of the national regions was being carried on at this time. In Moldavia the Latin and in Central Asia the Arabic alphabets were replaced by the Russian alphabet. (After the revolution the Bolsheviks had imposed the Latin alphabet on the Muslim peoples of the USSR, in the name of Europeanization, but Stalin put this down to 'bourgeois influence'.)
12. W. Scharndorf, *Istoriya KPPS*, Moscow 1962, p. 70.
13. Boffa, p. 384.
14. *Bol'shaya Sovetskaya Entsiklopediya*, 2nd edn, Moscow 1953, Vol. 23, p. 567.
15. *Voprosy Literatury*, no. 8, 1981, p. 212.
16. Interestingly, this 'staggering' story about Kryakutnoy is still repeated nowadays by Russian chauvinists. See V. Pikul, *Slovo i delo*, Leningrad 1974, p. 250.
17. See *Kommunist Tadzhikistana*, 14 January 1954; 8 January 1955, etc.
18. On Marxist and Stalinist interpretations of morality in history, see L. Kolakowski, *Elogio dell'incoerenza*, Florence 1974 (Milan 1982).

19. See N. Yakovlev, 'O prepodavanii otechestvennoy istorii', *Bol'shevik*, no. 22, 1947, pp. 22–9.

20. See B. Gafurov, *Istoriya Tadzhikskogo naroda v kratkom izlozhenii*, Moscow, 1955, vol. 1; also 'O nekotorykh voprosakh istorii narodov Sredney Azii, *Voprosy Istorii*, no. 4, 1951.

21. *Pravda*, 28 January 1949.

22. Ibid.

23. Ibid.

24. *Pravda*, 10 February 1949.

25. Ibid.

26. Ibid.

27. *Politichesky dnevnik*, vol. 1, p. 224.

28. Ibid.

29. Boffa, vol. 2, p. 394.

30. Emmanuel Mounier, *Oeuvres*, Paris 1961, vol. 1, p. 524.

31. Hingley, p. 45.

32. *Pravda*, 13 January 1953.

33. *Novy Mir*, no. 4, 1953, p. 170.

34. V. Bukovsky, *To Build A Castle*, 1978, p. 81.

35. Marcuse suggested that the course towards liberalization was already latent while Stalin was still alive, but 'the leader and teacher' could not 'personally' set it going. Whether that is true or not, an economic and scientific need for liberalization existed, owing to the pressure of rivalry on the world scale.

36. R.C. Tucker, *The Soviet Political Mind*, p. 141.

37. *Novy Mir*, no. 12, 1953, p. 218.

38. Ibid., p. 219.

39. Ibid.

40. Ibid, p. 229.

41. Ibid., p. 232.

42. Ibid., p. 233.

43. Ibid., p. 234.

44. Ibid., p. 237.

45. Ibid., p. 234.

46. Ibid., p. 238.

47. Ibid., p. 241.

48. Mark Perakh, 'Contemporary Dissent in Russia', *Partisan Review*, no. 2, 1978, pp. 249–51.

49. E. Yevtushenko, interview given to the Sofia newspaper *Narodna mladezh*.

50. *Novy Mir*, no. 9, 1954, p. 5.

51. Ibid., p. 3.

52. *Novy Mir*, no, 2, 1954, p. 219.

53. *Novy Mir*, no. 1, 1955, p. 236.

54. Ibid.

55. Ibid.

56. M. Shcheglov, *Literaturnaya kritika*, Moscow 1971, p. 175.

57. *Istoriya KPSS*, p. 577.

58. *Politichesky dnevnik*, vol. 2, p. 68.

59. W. Scharndorf, p. 84.

60. P. Hollander, *Soviet and American Societies: A Comparison*, New York 1973, p. 57.

61. Tucker, p. 194.

62. Ibid., p. 195.

63. Boffa, vol. 2, pp. 511–12.

64. R.A. Medvedev, *On Stalin and Stalinism*, p. 168.

65. Shatz, p. 99.

66. Bukovsky, p. 84.

67. *An End To Silence*, p. 112.

68. R.A. Medvedev, *Khrushchev*, 1982, p. 101.

69. *Teatr*, no. 1, 1963, p. 45.

70. *Let History Judge*, p. xxviii.

71. David Burg, 'Observations on Soviet University Students', in Pipes, ed., *The Russian Intelligentsia*, p. 90.

72 *Komosomolskaya Pravda*, 9 August 1956.

73. Bukovsky, p. 117.

74. *The Russian Intelligentsia*, p. 90.

75. Ibid., p. 96.

76. Ibid., p. 95.

77. Bukovsky, p. 118.

78. *The Russian Intelligentsia*, p. 96.

79. *Trud*, 8 January 1957.

80. Zh. Medvedev, p. 101.

81. Bukovsky, p. 116.

82. Ibid., p. 122.

83. *Der Spiegel*, no. 18, 1968, p. 93.

84. R.A. Medvedev, *Intervista sul dissenso in USSR* [On Soviet Dissent], New York 1980, p. 63.

85. *Problems of Communism*, no. 3, 1980, p. 58.

86. *Politichesky dnevnik*, vol. 1, p. 174.

87. O. Andreyev Carlisle, *Voices in the Snow: Encounters With Russian Writers*, 1963, p. 81.

88. Yevtushenko, interview with the newspaper *Narodna Mladezh*.

89. Yevtushenko, *Autobiography* (*samizdat* version), p. 41.

90. Yevtushenko, *A Precocious Autobiography*, 1963, p. 104.

91. I. Deutscher, *Ironies of History*, 1966, p. 275.

92. *Khrushchev on Culture*, *Encounter* pamphlet 9, 1963, p. 38.

93. Ibid.

94. Ibid.

95. *Literaturnaya Zhizn'*, 27 September 1961, p. 3 (D. Starikov, 'Ob odnom stikhotvorenii').

96. It deserves to be mentioned, though, that the discussion around *Babi Yar* was, essentially, the only public discussion of anti-Semitism to take place in the postwar period, and the poet's adversaries did not stress their anti-Semitism. On the contrary, they said that they were not, 'in general', hostile to the Jews, but were merely protesting against 'excessive' interest in the Jewish question. Under Brezhnev the anti-Semites began to voice their views more openly, under the flag of 'anti-Zionism', both in the official press and in *samizdat*. We need merely recall the statements by Messrs Yevseyev, Begun, Yemel'yanov, Boroday and others (see later chapters).

97. Shatz, p. 96.

98. Ibid.

99. Ibid., p. 100.

100. N.S. Khrushchev, *Literature, the Arts and the Life of the People*, 1957, p. 16.

101. *Khrushchev on Culture*, p. 17.

102. Khrushchev, *Literature . . .*, p. 16.

103. Wolfgang Leonhard, *Was ist Kommunismus?*, Munich 1976, p. 58.

104. Solzhenitsyn, *The Oak and the Calf*, 1980, p. 8.

105. Shcheglov, p. 173.

106. Ibid.

107. Ibid.

108. Ibid., p. 177.

109. Ibid., p. 225.

110. *Midway*, Winter 1978, p. 21.

111. Ibid., p. 24.

112. *Novy Mir*, no. 9, 1956, p. 245.

113. *Govorit i pokazyvaet Moskva*, no. 16, 1981, p. 6.

114. *Teatr*, no. 6, 1957, pp. 11–12.
115. Ibid., p. 11.
116. *Teatr*, no. 8, 1957, p. 104.
117. *Teatr*, no. 1, 1963, p. 44.
118. G. Tovstonogov, *Zerkalo stseny*, Leningrad 1980, vol. 1. p. 44.
119. *Novy Mir*, no. 11, 1960, p. 199.
120. *Novy Mir*, no. 12, p. 239.
121. Ibid., p. 241.
122. Ibid.
123. Sergius Yakobson, 'The State of the Word', in *Problems of Communism*, no. 6, November–December, 1974, p. 49.
124. R.A. Medvedev, *Tvardovsky i Solzhenitsyn* (*samizdat*), p. 7.
125. See *Pamyat'*, no. 2: 'Vospominaniya', by R. Pimenov.
126. *Let History Judge*, p. 543.
127. M. Voslensky, p. 135.
128. *Novy Mir*, no. 12, 1958, p. 87.
129. Dudintsev, *Not By Bread Alone* (trans. Edith Bone), 1957, p. 4.
130. Ibid., p. 216.
131. Ibid., p. 217.
132. J.R. Rubenstein, *Soviet Dissidents: Their Struggle For Human Rights*, Boston 1980, p. 9.
133. Shatz, p. 104.
134. *Literaturnaya Gazeta*, 28 December 1958.
135. Khrushchev, *Literature...*, pp. 22–3.
136. *Teatr*, no. 5, 1957, p. 47.
137. Ibid., p. 49.
138. Ibid.
139. Ibid., p. 50.
140. *Novy Mir*, no. 2, 1954, p. 79.
141. *Teatr*, no. 5, 1957, p. 51.
142. *Novy Mir*, no. 10, 1958, p. 243.
143. A.T. Tvardovsky, *Izbrannye sochineniya*, Moscow 1981, pp. 601–02.
144. Rakovski, p. 39.
145. Ibid., pp. 42–3.
146. Ibid., p. 48.
147. M.N. Pokrovsky, *Ocherki po istorii revolyutsionnogo dvizheniya v Rossii*, p. 107.
148. Hegedüs, p. 186.
149. Shatz, p. 141.
150. Essentially, among all the countries of the Eastern bloc, only Poland, where no collectivization of agriculture took place, retained a hereditary working class, and this led to the rapid growth of the working-class movement expressed in the mass strikes of 1956, 1970, 1976 and 1980–81. In the other countries a hereditary working class was being formed afresh between 1960 and 1980.
151. Ernst Fischer, *Kunst und Koexistenz, Beitrag zu eines modernen marxistischen 'Aesthetik'*, Reinbek bei Hamburg 1966, p. 63.
152. *Novy Mir*, no. 1, 1965, p. 253.
153. *Znamya*, no. 2, 1965, p. 157.
154. Carlisle, p. 139.
155. *Voprosy literatury*, no. 2, 1981, p. 245.
156. *Politichesky dnevnik*, vol. 1, p. 174.
157. Solzhenitsyn, *The Oak and the Calf*, p. 248.
158. Ibid., p. 274n.
159. V. Lakshin, 'Solzhenitsyn, Tvardovsky i "Novy Mir"', *Dvadtsatyi vek*, London 1977, vol. 2, pp. 200–01.
160. R.A. Medvedev, *Tvardovsky i Solzhenitsyn*, pp. 7–8.
161. E. Gnedin, *Iz istorii otnoshenii mezhdu SSS i fashistskoy Germaniei*, New York

1977, pp. 5–6.
162. *Novy Mir*, no. 4, 1965, p. 234.
163. *People, Years, Life*, vol 2, 1962, p. 73.
164. Ibid., p. 61.
165. *Khrushchev on Culture*, p. 24.
166. Ibid., p. 12.
167. Ibid.
168. *Novy Mir*, no. 12, 1964, p. 228.
169. Ibid.
170. Ibid., p. 232.
171. Ibid.
172. *Realizm i khudozhestvennye iskaniya XX veka*, Moscow 1969, p. 9.
173. Ibid., p. 31.
174. Ibid., p. 7.
175. Ibid., p. 42.
176. V. Sappak, *Televidenie i my*, Moscow 1963, p. 117.
177. Ibid., p. 110.
178. Ibid., p. 117.
179. Solzhenitsyn, *The Oak and the Calf*, p. 14.
180. Boffa, vol. 2, p. 599. The chapter heading reads, instead of 'The anti-Stalinist offensive of the Twenty-Second Congress', 'The anti-Fascist offensive ...' (p. 813). A significant misprint!
181. Khrushchev, *Report to the Twenty-Second Congress of the CPSU*, Soviet Booklet no. 80, 1961, p. 74.
182. N.M. Shvernik, *Rech' na XXII s'ezde KPSS*, Moscow 1961, p. 5.
183. Khrushchev, *Report...*, p. 76.
184. *Novy Mir*, no. 1, 1964, p. 223.
185. Rakovski, p. 53.
186. Shatz, p. 111.
187. Z. Brzezinski and S.P. Huntingdon, *Political Power: USA/USSR*, London 1964, p. 272.
188. The actual scale of the movement became known only later. See *Workers Against Gulag*, Indiana 1979; *Arbeiter-Opposition in der Sowjetunion*, Reinbek bei Hamburg 1980.
189. *Khrushchev on Culture*, p. 28.
190. Ibid., pp. 28-29.
191. Brzezinski and Huntingdon, p. 113.
192. *Khrushchev on Culture*, p. 30.
193. J. Ortega y Gasset, 'The Dehumanisation of Art' (1925), in Bernard F. Dukore, ed., *Dramatic Theory and Criticism: Greeks to Grotowski*, New York 1974, p. 757.
194. *Khrushchev on Culture*, p. 12.
195. *Novy Mir*, no. 9, 1964, p. 239.
196. *Novy Mir*, no. 1, 1964, p. 223.
197. Ibid., p. 224.
198. Ibid., p. 245.
199. Ibid., p. 232.
200. *Problemy mira i sotsializma*, no. 5, 1963, p. 36.
201. Solzhenitsyn, *One Day in the Life of Ivan Denisovich*, 1963, p. 46.
202. *Novy Mir*, no. 9, 1964, p. 235.
203. Ibid., p. 236.
204. *Novy Mir*, no. 5, 1965, pp.266–7.
205. *Novy Mir*, no. 9, 1964, p. 237.
206. *Novy Mir*, no. 5, 1965, p. 264.
207. Lenin, *Collected Works*, 4th edn, English Version, vol. 33, p. 489.
208. *Novy Mir*, no. 9, 1964, p. 238.
209. *Novy Mir*, no. 6, 1965, p. 221.
210. Rakovski, p. 11.

211. R. Pimenov says in his 'reminiscences' that Sheynis expressed this view as early as 1956, but could not bring himself to put it on paper *even in samizdat*. Roy Medvedev refers to early underground studies in which this question was raised, but he himself rejects such an approach in the name of the ideas of the sixties.

212. Shatz, p. 115.

213. Ibid., p. 116.

5

The Turning Point, or The Crisis of Dissent

The Political Background to Economic Reform

The year 1965 was the time of the second liberalization which followed the fall of Khrushchev. The statocracy again introduced reforms, but this time on the economic front. As was to be expected, though, acute conflict immediately broke out around these reforms. To understand the polemic to which the economic reforms gave rise, we need to analyse more closely the general political situation in the country after Khrushchev's removal. This situation was extremely contradictory.

After Khrushchev's departure some of the intellectuals were, for a time, afraid that the changes at the top might lead to a return of mass terror. That did not happen, and could not have happened in the new economic and social conditions. At first, though, until 1968, the rulers' policy seemed very difficult to understand. On the one hand, Lysenko suffered final defeat and economic reforms were introduced; but on the other, Sinyavsky and Daniel were brought to trial and preparations were made to rehabilitate Stalin. The rulers themselves had not yet finally decided on their policy: a new line had not been formulated.

The fall of Lysenko took place immediately after Khrushchev's removal and was an important stage in the fight against Stalinism in the scientific sphere. It was at last possible to criticize Lysenko. *Novy Mir* published articles by anti-Lysenko writers who had previously been denied access to the press. True, already at the beginning of Khrushchev's 'thaw', Troepol'sky – an agronomist by profession – showed what he thought of Lysenkoism in his novella *Kandidat nauk*; but this was only a story, and besides, far from everything could be said in it. Now, however, polemical and scientific articles directed against Lysenko appeared in *Novy Mir* – in particular, Zhores Medvedev's.[1] It was typical of the period that Medvedev was recommended to the editors by Solzhenitsyn. The united front had not yet been broken.

Materials on Lysenkoism appeared also in more official publications, such as *Komsomolskaya Pravda*. It might seem that the Lefts had cause to rejoice. But at this very time A. Sinyavsky and Yu. Daniel were arrested and their trial prepared. The authorities had not decided on taking this line in a hurry. The government even sought beforehand the opinion of the leaders of the Writers' Union – but, as was to be expected, these officials of the world of literature readily sacrificed their brothers of the pen.

The trial of Sinyavsky and Daniel served a quite definite purpose. 'It might well be asked', writes Shatz,

> why the Soviet government bothered in the first place to prosecute two fiction writers for a few short stories that were not even available to the Soviet public. The question can be answered, and the trial itself comprehended, only in the light of Russian literature's traditional role as a vehicle of social and political protest.[2]

The trial was a trial not of Sinyavsky and Daniel but also of all uncensored literature. The state was laying down the limits of the permissible. 'The trial of Sinyavsky and Daniel', writes Rubenstein, 'was meant to intimidate the intellectual community, but the government miscalculated. Since the death of Stalin, Soviet society had changed.'[3] The trial stirred up a wave of protest and caused the opposition to become livelier.

It must be mentioned that the conduct of Sinyavsky and Daniel in publishing books in the West under pseudonyms was far from meeting with approval even among the Lefts. Many regarded it with bewilderment. Hardly anybody read the books themselves. It was announced that whoever wished might see them at the Writers' Union, but for some reason nobody took up the offer. But they knew of some observations by Sinyavsky about 'socialist realism' which did not tally with the denunciatory ideas of his publications abroad. That put people on their guard.

The action of the government, which spent a great deal on discovering the real names of the authors (a real espionage operation was carried out abroad) seemed simply ridiculous. If the authorities had not gone so far as to stage a trial but had confined themselves, as in Pasternak's case, to the 'usual' hounding of the authors in the press, many would have concluded that nothing out of the ordinary was happening. But a trial – that was too much. The authorities had obviously gone too far. The intelligentsia became agitated. On 5

December 1965 Bukovsky and his friends succeeded in assembling about 200 people in Pushkin Square for a protest demonstration, against the judicial onslaught that was being prepared against the writers. (To this day Pushkin Square has remained the favourite place for dissident demonstrations.) On 16 February 1966 – two days after Sinyavsky and Daniel had been sentenced – a stormy meeting took place at the Institute of Marxism–Leninism, to discuss Nekrich's book *22 June 1941*, which exposed Stalin's mistakes on the eve of the war. The Stalinist Deborin had been appointed *rapporteur*, and that immediately aroused in those present, as Gnedin later recalled, the suspicion that they 'were to witness an attempt to prepare public opinion for an open departure from the policy of the Twentieth Congress and for a rehabilitation of Stalin's baneful policy.'[4] The anti-Stalinists spoke up, sharply and unanimously. Gnedin even ended his speech with these words: 'The question of the accuracy and truth of information is still today a burning question',[25] thereby obviously alluding to the policy of the new rulers. Rubenstein writes that 'the meeting turned into a raucous denunciation of Stalin'.[6] The dissenters were openly taking revenge for what had been done to Sinyavsky and Daniel. Their success was relative. In the end Nekrich's book was banned and he himself was expelled from the Party, while Gnedin received a Party reprimand. All the same, they had scored a moral victory.

The struggle around the rehabilitation of Stalin was still only warming up. As early as the beginning of 1965 some extreme Stalinists among the statocrats (Trapeznikov, Yepishev, Pospelov) started to campaign for the rehabilitation of their 'friend and teacher'. The intelligentsia answered with such means as were available to them – *samizdat*. 'It was precisely in these months', Roy Medvedev recalls,

> that a whole variety of manuscripts and materials began to circulate among the intelligentsia, protesting in one form or another against the rehabilitation of Stalin (e.g., the letter of Ernst Henri to Ilya Ehrenburg, a pamphlet by Gregory Pomerants, etc.).[7]

When rumours got around that the Stalinists might win the day at the Twenty-Third Party Congress the intelligentsia began to write collective letters:

> One letter in particular made a major impression – it was signed by twenty-five leading members of the Soviet intelligentsia, including Academicians Peter Kapitsa, Leonty Artsimovich, Mikhail Leontovich, Andrei Sakharov, Igor Tamm, Ivan Maisky; the writers Valentin Katayev, Viktor Nekrasov, Konstantin Paustovsky, Kornei Chukovsky, Vladimir Tendryakov; the theatre

people Maya Plisetskaya, Oleg Yefremov, P.D. Korin, V.N. Nemensky, Mikhail Romm, Innokenty Smoktunovsky and A.G. Tovstonogov. The first twenty-five signatories were soon joined by others, including Academicians A. Khlmogorov, A. Alikhanov, Mikhail Knunyants, Boris Astaurov, P. Zdradovsky; the writers Ilya Ehrenburg, Vladimir Dudintsev; the artists G. Chukhrai, Vanno Muradeli, Igor Ilinsky.[8]

Neither at the Twenty-Third Congress nor subsequently was Stalin rehabilitated, although in 1969 everything was made ready for this to happen. The Stalinists' failure can be explained by a number of factors, among which not the least must be considered the interests of the statocracy themselves, for whom Brezhnev's regime, with its conservative stability, was very much more convenient than direct reaction in the form of a return to Stalinism – that is, to a time when even members of the ruling class did not feel safe. But the intelligentsia, too, made a definite contribution to the victory over the Stalinists in the 1960s. Their letter left an impression.

The Economic Reform Discussion

In this uncertain situation a polemic flared up about the economic reforms. A group of progressive economists backed these measures, which were attempts to effect a definite change in the economic structure and thereby to democratize the economy. It was now that economic questions entered the realm of public opinion for the first time and became a subject for reflection by the intelligentsia: not only economists and sociologists but the intelligentsia as a whole. N. Petrakov, one of the participants in the discussion, wrote later that at the end of the 1960s interest in economic problems markedly increased. The economist, as such, somehow imperceptibly 'acquired an importance which the physicist and the lyric poet might envy.'[9]

The new economists and writers about economics – Liberman, Birman, Volin, Lisichkin, Kantorovich, Latsis, Petrakov, Volkov and many others – were working in the same direction as O. Šik in Czechoslovakia, R. Nyers and J. Kornai in Hungary, or W. Brus in Poland. It was really a case of the appearance of a single East European school of Marxist economics, on the theory of the planned market.[10] *Novy Mir* opened its pages to the new theoreticians. Its economic articles were for several years the most interesting things being printed.

The economists around *Novy Mir* even worked out a sort of division of labour among themselves. A. Birman spoke as a theoretician, providing a very general foundation for the theory of the socialist market and defending the reforms introduced after 1965. 'The objective possibility of voluntarism is inherent in the system itself,' he wrote, 'in the very process of planning, we must not fear to say that.'[11] It was therefore necessary to make use of market relations, creating a real, *objective* basis for planning. The remedy for bureaucratic voluntarism was democratization, control from below, the ending of overcentralized authority, and the granting of extensive rights to the enterprises. And finally, freedom of thought on economic matters must be allowed.[12]

P. Volin and O. Latsis spoke as propagandists for the market economy. Coming down from the height of pure theory, they directed the reader's attention to concrete facts, speaking in a lively and interesting way about new ideas and the absurdity of the existing economic system. Malicious mockery of the system of 'indices' employed for the guidance of production became the theme of many articles:

> It costs a lot – never mind, so long as the quantity is increased. ... It's worse in quality – no worries, so long as it [i.e. production] is greater. The consumers don't need all this – that doesn't matter, the main thing is to manufacture the stuff and send it off, what happens after that is no concern of yours. They want different goods, not the old sort – shut your eyes to that, the old ones are quicker and easier to make.[13]

But the central figure among them was undoubtedly G. Lisichkin. We are not concerned here with how original his ideas were, but with something else. In the sixties he probably did more than anyone else to spread the new economic theory. In particular, his articles in *Novy Mir* were devoted to agriculture, the sickest branch of the Soviet economy. He not only criticized the situation which had been created and showed the causes of the trouble; he put forward concrete solutions. Above all, it was necessary to reject excessive centralization and directive planning. All that had nothing to do with socialist economics. Directive planning, wrote Lisichkin, had been 'invented' long before its present furious defenders were born. In Russia in 1914–16 plans had also been sent down to *uyezd* level for the production and sale of corn at prices fixed by the state.[14] In fact, by laying down fixed purchase prices for the various products of agriculture, the state was already planning production. Besides this, the state exerted planning influence on enterprises by means of taxes. Any planning that went further than that could only do harm. Directive planning hindered economic development.

The salvation of agriculture required organizational reform.

Increased capital investment was 'not the decisive condition for increasing agricultural production'.[15] Retention of the existing system of capital investment resulted in losses rather than profits, and investments were distributed inefficiently. The way forward lay through increased autonomy for enterprises and self-management by labour-collectives. 'The mechanism of self-management', Latsis declared, summing up the results of experiments carried out during the period of reform, 'will work without a hitch.'[16] In the seventies this formula became almost a commonplace with East European socialists, but it was first uttered at this time. For Lisichkin the collective farm was a higher form of organization than the state farm, because it retained elements of independence and self-management and production was more closely related to the market. Lisichkin set out his views systematically in two books – *Plan i rynok* [Plan and Market], 1966, and *Chto cheloveku nado?* [What Does a Man Need?], 1974. It is significant that his articles for *Novy Mir* were bolder and livelier than his books. Nevertheless, the books had the advantage of enabling the theoretician to expound his ideas in greater detail.

Economic thought now developed dynamically in the Soviet Union and – most importantly – became for the first time for many years part of worldwide economic thought. It was not accidental that Lisichkin's book *Plan i rynok* – which was not without defects and also included many 'reticences' due to the censors – was published in Prague, in Czech, on the eve of the 'Prague spring'. An American economist who studied the problems of Soviet-type economies wrote later that in the USSR in the sixties 'a real revolution in economics as a science had taken place.'[17]

The new economists came to the common conclusion that the chronic misfortunes of the Soviet economy – production of goods which found no buyers, shortages of many other goods, low quality, inefficiency of agriculture, and so on – prevented a move towards an intensive model of economic development and made the whole system rickety. All these shortcomings could be laid at the door of bureaucratic centralism. It was necessary to devise a programme for transforming this, because the difficulties that arose in the Soviet economy were due to the existing type of organization and could not be eliminated so long as that obtained. In its turn, the reform programme presupposed the granting to different groups in society of a high degree of social autonomy in relation to the ruling statocracy, and so – democratization. The reforms certainly affected people's attitude to work, and even their psychology. Lisichkin referred to the celebrated 'Shchekino experiment', when an enterprise was given greater independence than usual in the sphere of wages policy, and so on. This decision 'radically altered the logic of the conduct of the leaders of the enterprise and also the logic of the interest in their work taken by the whole production-collective.'[18] Finally, consistent implementation of these reforms would have meant, sooner or later, the social decomposition of the statocracy itself and its elimination as a special corporation of the class type. The experience of the 1968 reforms in Czechoslovakia, where a similar programme was openly formulated and partly carried out, leaves no doubt of that.

The central point of the reformers' programme was therefore that no improvement in the economic situation was possible without democratization. This idea was later formulated thus by Euro–communists: 'The maximum development of the personality and abilities of man are becoming a necessity of production, an economic necessity.'[19]

In the sixties the first symptoms were noticed of the general economic crisis which was to strike Eastern Europe in the eighties: a fall in the growth rate of production and inability by the state to overcome disproportions between branches of production. 'It would be harmful complacency', wrote Lisichkin,

> to explain the falling-off in the rates of growth of our economy merely by saying that the way is easier from the lowest level to the highest, that every percentage increase now means a bigger mass of income than before. All that is true, but disproportionality in the development of the separate branches of the economy is hindering the general progress of development. Each time that some rupture becomes particularly obvious, this is usually levelled out by adoption of the appropriate emergency measures. But frequently, this happens after the event, that is, when the economy has already suffered enormous damage.[20]

All the new economists concurred in the view that the centralized system of management of the economy was not capable of 'improvement'. Through the reforms they advocated it would be possible to replace this system by 'market socialism'. Lenin's New Economic Policy of 1921 could serve as prototype, provided it was interpreted quite differently from the version given in the official textbooks. Lisichkin said that Soviet industry in the NEP period 'consisted already for the most part of socialist state enterprises.'[21] NEP proved, above all, the need for market relations in the course of socialist construction or, more precisely, it proved that state enterprises need the market. That experience was valuable for the sixties as well. Planning could be based on the market and state enterprises could compete among themselves within certain limits, working efficiently in the setting of a market economy.

But a still greater influence on our theoreticians was the experience of self-management and market economy in Yugoslavia. The NEP experience was reappraised in the light of the Yugoslav experiment. This, however, could not be said openly, so an idealized picture of NEP had to be presented as the sole practical experience, to date, of market socialism. Nevertheless, the story of NEP could display the necessary elements: independence of state enterprises, use of the market as checking device, and so on. After 1928 the Stalinist bureaucracy rejected Lenin's economic principles: 'economic methods were gradually ousted by administrative regulation and the market mechanism was increasingly switched off.' Later, Stalin 'provided a theoretical basis' for this practice.[22] These theoretical constructions by the Stalinists had to be criticized and their unsoundness demonstrated.

Lisichkin directed his readers' attention to the fact that official theory and practice ignored an elementary truth of Marxism: the law of value. The experience of the Soviet economy showed

the bankruptcy, the lack of economic sense, of any principle of distribution other than one based on commensurability of what is contributed to society and what is received from it, that is, on buying and selling. This basic feature of the law of value is ignored, and it takes its revenge in the low level of efficiency in our use of technology and the high cost of what we produce.[23]

Lisichkin gave a deadly definition of the theorizing of the creators of the so-called 'political economy of socialism' as

lofty forms of abstract thought, of which are capable only men who stand in devastated places that have just been cleared of floods and who are discussing sagely: is it or is it not possible to assume, from theoretical starting points, that there could be cases of flooding in this place? It will be bad for the inhabitants of the place in question if it turns out that, theoretically, operations by the elements cannot happen there. As for the facts, meaning the broken branches of trees scattered here and there, the ruined crops, the demolished houses, and so on, well, what of it, this sort of theoretician replies, so much the worse for the facts.[24]

In opposition to the abstractions of the official political economy the new economists created their theory on the basis of reality, using the experience of NEP, of Yugoslavia and of the West and interpreting critically the experience of their own country. Their general conclusions can be summarized as: socialist enterprises can function successfully in a market-economy setting;[25] effective planning is impossible in the absence of such a checking and regulating device as the market; the action of elemental market forces can be kept under control by the framework of the plan; transition to market socialism necessitates rejection of directive planning by means of indices and enlargement of the independence of enterprises – new methods of planning are needed: through taxes, price control, investment policy, defining the 'macroeconomic limits' of the development of an enterprise, and so forth. By decentralizing the management of the individual enterprises, 'the central organizations would be able to concentrate on the overall problems which are really theirs. ...'[26] Only given these conditions can a plan's influence 'become real and not imaginary'.[27]

Transformations like these would have brought about marked changes in the social situation, but it must be admitted that Soviet dissidents underestimated the importance of the struggle being waged, and often failed to understand it. Bukovsky, for example, admits: 'we didn't notice' the polemics around the reforms, and writes with disdain of 'the so-called economists', adding that 'they had no special theories.'[28] The fighters for 'intellectual independence' did not appreciate the anti-bureaucratic implications of the idea of market socialism and did not realize that without economic reforms they would not 'see the age of freedom', for these reforms aimed at a democratic transformation of society. The new economic ideas won more and more supporters, but this happened more slowly than their authors would have wished. At the same time it became clear that apart from the idea of economic reforms, the oppositionists had no constructive *social* ideas. But it is impossible not only to build but also to destroy anything in society unless one has a positive programme. On the whole, the true significance of the new economic theory was understood only later. Meanwhile, the ruling statocracy very quickly understood how the proposed changes threatened it.

The statocracy was not, of course, united and there were groups in it which advocated reform. But these were mainly 'underprivileged' groups, with insufficient powers and rights. It was for this very reason that they supported reform, hoping thereby to win more power, but they could not get the better of their more conservative 'class brothers'. Those who wanted changes lacked sufficient power (which was why they wanted them), while those who did not want changes had power (which was why they did not want them). Those with more power had more chances of success. This situation could change only in circumstances of crisis, when the usual bureaucratic game was no longer capable of settling anything. Such a crisis occurred in 1968 in Czechoslovakia, but not in the USSR.

The necessary changes were not made. Reform got bogged down in the initial phase, blocked by the bureaucratic apparatus. As the reforming tendencies failed, so the technocratic tendencies gained strength. The technocrats' illusion that the existing system could be rationalized, without any changes in principle, was closely connected with hopes set upon cybernetic methods of management.

Cybernetics was rehabilitated at the end of the fifties, and very soon the ruling circles came to swear by it. Alongside the oppositionist idea of market socialism, elements of a new idea appeared – cybernetic socialism. 'Cybernetics', writes Graham,

> revitalized, at least temporarily, the Soviet leaders' confidence that the Soviet system could control the economy rationally. This renewal came exactly at the moment when the possibility seemed to be irretrievably vanishing. This rebirth of hope was the explanation of the intoxication with cybernetics in the Soviet Union in the late fifties; in the period after 1958 thousands of articles, pamphlets and books on cybernetics appeared in the Soviet press. In the more popular articles the full utilization of cybernetics was equated with the advent of Communism and the fulfilment of the Revolution. If the curious mixture of ideology and politics in the Soviet Union can upon occasion affect certain sciences adversely – as it did at one time with genetics – it can also catapult others to unusual prominence.[29]

The idea that the economy could be roused by adopting advanced methods of management, without changing the organization, was utopian and absurd. It failed at once when put into practice, because owing to the outdated relations of production the introduction of any new achievements of science and technology – in particular the use of computers – came up against many difficulties and proved ineffective. Soviet experience in the sixties and seventies brilliantly confirmed Šik's conjecture: that unless organization was reformed,

> the new computer technology not only will not secure ideal economic development, but may even serve to justify absolutely one-sided development, aimed at the solution of simplified tasks which do not correspond to the public interest.[30]

This became clear pretty soon. For this reason, evidently, technocratic tendencies (in the form of pan-cyberneticism or any other) turned out not to be so strong here as could have been expected at first. Nevertheless, they did affect the ideology of the government, the opposition's ideas, and even – as we shall see – literature as well. Technocratic illusions can be perceived in the views of Khrushchev and Brezhnev no less than in the ideas of Sakharov and Turchin, and they are apparent in the plays of Dvoretsky and Shatrov. On the whole, though, no special ideology of 'technocracy' arose in the USSR as it did in the USA in the sixties. True, the incapacity of the statocratic system to 'get rationalized', which dismayed experts of the Western type, gave rise at the end of the sixties and in the seventies to such strange phenomena as 'the disappointed technocrat' and even 'the enraged technocrat' – of whom more later.

As regards the years 1965 to 1968, when bureaucratic sabotage was obviously dooming to frustration all hopes for successful practical measures to introduce reforms, the struggle moved on to the theoretical plane. The left-wing economists continued to pay attention to the grave economic situation and to uphold their views, while hoping to find supporters in the future rather than counting on being able to influence the fate of reform in the present. Every serious statement on their part met a rowdy response in the official press, which began to 'unmask' the new theoreticians. In reply, the latter set out their views again and again in *Novy Mir*, deepening and sharpening the argument. In 1967 V. Kantorovich published an article, 'Sociology and Literature', in which he tried to break out of the limits of a purely economic discussion. The problems raised by reform on the economic plane were transferred to the social plane, and from there to the cultural plane. The discussion revealed the need for a new approach to Western sociology and philosophy, especially to the Frankfurt School, which had elaborated the scientific instrument so badly needed by the new economists. The reform also showed the bankruptcy of the existing organization of education and culture, the contradiction between the rising intellectual level of the working people and the prevailing forms of work organization. Art had already done quite a lot to concretize these problems and attract public interest to them. Another important point of contact between the new economists and the creative intelligentsia was that both swept aside all vulgar-sociological stereotypes and mechanical schemas and tried to see life in its many-sidedness, complexity and dynamism. It was not by chance that A. Birman advised those educated in the humanities to study economics, hoping that they would see reality 'in a more three-dimensional way'. Kantorovich, too, summoned the creative intelligentsia to the aid of the ideologues of reform. In so doing he referred to the 'Prague spring' activist Z. Mlynař. Alas, this association was not accidental.

As fewer and fewer hopes survived in Soviet society for rapid changes for the better, attention became more and more focused on Prague. The hopes of the left-wing intelligentsia was concentrated on Czechoslovakia. Prague became the Mecca of the Soviet opposition. The Medvedevs' *Political Diary* regularly published translations and abstracts of Czechoslovak writings from 1965 onwards. In 1966–68 much material came out in *samizdat*. A great deal arrived, too, through official channels.[31] Despite the fact that the Soviet reader was allowed to see an abridged version of the action programme of the Central Committee of the Czechoslovak Communist Party, adopted in April 1968, a complete translation of it was passed around in Moscow. *The Political Diary* recorded at the time that 'some Muscovites who know Czech are translating ... material from *Rude Pravo* and circulating it among their friends.'[32] The official leadership in the Kremlin showed a certain tolerance at the beginning of the 'Prague spring', hoping that the process of change in Czechoslovakia would not go too far. Kalvoda writes that Dubček even enjoyed at first the confidence of the Soviet leaders: 'Brezhnev called him "our Sasha".'[33]

The invasion of Czechoslovakia and the restoration there of the old political and economic system meant the end of the Soviet economic reform and also of hopes for a new wave of liberalization. Until 1968, to be sure, the new economists carried on a sort of 'rearguard battle' for economic modernization. Two articles in *Novy Mir* by N. Petrakov served as requiem for reform and warning for the future. He reminded readers that the country was living beyond its means, that having money did not ensure acquisition of goods and, finally, that it would be necessary, sooner or later, to pay for the protracted refusal to recognize the laws of the market. These warnings, though, were sounded either too soon or much too late. Reform had been frustrated, but the crisis of the economic mechanism had not as yet reached the point where it could stimulate a serious revolutionary ferment. 'By the end of the 1960s at the latest,' writes Rakovski,

> the ideology of 'market socialism' had undergone a total defeat everywhere. But the defeat of the ideology only moderated the amplitude of oscillations round a general tendency, and has in no way changed the tendency itself.[34]

Market socialism had not suffered an economic defeat, only a political one. Where the economic experiments were continued for a fairly long time they produced, on the whole, some positive results – although new problems were also revealed. The classic examples of experiments more or less consistently pursued were Hungary and Yugoslavia. These countries achieved the biggest successes in Eastern Europe. Experiments in a number of factories in the USSR gave excellent results, but the ideology of 'market socialism', in its original form, was closely bound up with Communist reformism and a naïve belief in the pragmatism of the ruling statocracy and the socialist nature of the existing system. The hope that market socialism might be introduced from above proved illusory, and that predetermined its defeat.

It was significant that the greatest successes were achieved in Hungary and Yugoslavia, countries which had experienced popular revolutions. The reforming section of the ruling circles would never have realized their aims *by themselves*, without pressure from below. The exception here was Czechoslovakia, but ultimately this exception proved the rule: the reformers failed. Consequently the idea of market socialism underwent a crisis, to rise again later in the programme of forces which were not so much intrasystemic as openly oppositional, extrasystemic. The words 'socialist market economy' were banned from the official press. After 1971–74 it was possible to defend those ideas only in *samizdat* and foreign publications. True, in the legal press too, many economists wrote in favour of a market-socialist economy,[35] but the actual expression had to be replaced by something else, and hints resorted to. One could be frank where partial questions were concerned, but no developed theoretical programme could be advanced, as Birman, Lisichkin and others had done in the sixties. The economists themselves began increasingly to feel that they were outsiders, and to compare themselves to a doctor whom a patient asks for prescriptions, only to throw them away in the nearest rubbish bin.

The defeat of market socialism was not final. It would be revived in a fresh political form: the future of the socialist opposition was bound up with the solving of the problems it posed. But before new democratic ideas began to spread there was disappointment at the fate of the reforms, loss of confidence in Leninism, Communism, socialism – everything one had so naïvely believed in during the sixties. As usually happens, the baby was chucked out with the bath water. Still, in history things never happen in any other way.

There was a pause in the social struggle. A great deal had to be thought about and understood. On the morning of 21 August 1968 the entire ideology of Soviet liberalism collapsed in a few minutes, and all the hopes aroused by the Twentieth Congress fell to the ground. Whereas previously liberal intellectuals had comforted themselves with the thought that, on the whole, our society has a sound foundation, that it has not lost its socialist character, that – as Yevtushenko wrote in his *Autobiography* – the revolution was sick but not dead, the events of 1968 scattered those illusions. It was not a matter of 'the excesses of Stalinism' but of the system itself. For many, recognition of this fact meant spiritual and ideological collapse. Understanding of the new truths did not, of course, come to everyone at once, but an obvious re-examination of values began. Rakovski wrote that 'it would be unhistorical not to see the real heroism' in the Communist liberals of the 'thaw' period,[36] despite their naïvety. But 1968 put an end to their hopes, and along with them their ideology, in the form it then bore. It had proved helpless to withstand the tank armies of the neo-Stalinist state upholding its monopoly of 'Communism'.

It was almost like Mayakovsky's verses:

Communism from books
　　　　　is easy belief.
(To serve it up in books
　　　　　is fashionable)
But this –
　　　brings 'rigmarole' to life,
and shows Communism
　　　　　in flesh and blood.[37]

1968 and the Crisis of Reform Ideology

Political experience affects social consciousness much more strongly than any theories, even the most sophisticated. If social experience does not favour them, ideas cannot be assimilated by a sufficiently large number of people. In 1969–78 the overall situation was unfavourable to the spreading of reformist-Communist theories. The illusions of the sixties had become patent. It was clear that if socialist ideology was to revive at all, it must be in some new – and certainly non-Communist – form. Even some prominent figures of the 'Prague spring' said so. J. Pelikan wrote, after 1968:

> First and foremost it must be realized that the very term 'Communism' has been discredited among the peoples of Eastern Europe. They associate it with the ideas of one-party rule and dictatorship of the apparatus, relying on the hegemony of the Soviet Union in a particular geographical region.[38]

However, disappointment has its logic no less than hope, and it is the logic of inertia. Rejection of Communist reformism led many unofficial intellectuals into hostility towards Marxism and socialism – still further: to denial of progress, revolution, democracy even (for all these values were proclaimed by the left-wing ideologues, including the Communists). Pelikan wrote that the majority of active opponents of the regime in the USSR

> identify socialism with Stalinism (they have seen nothing else), and so they reject socialism in general, as though it cannot be reformed or modified. Personally I do not agree with such views, although I can understand them as an emotional and moral reaction to the situation that exists in the USSR.[39]

It was important, though, that the countries of Eastern Europe had practical experience of Communism reformism, which produced real successes. The theories of Pelikan, Šik, Lukács and Kardelj were for these peoples not just 'fantasies' but definite practices, even if they had not been carried to completion. The Soviet intelligentsia lacked such experience: instead we had suffered, along with the Hungarians, the intervention of 1956 and, along with the Czechs, the invasion of 1968. These were events in *our* history; they were *our* experience, which was, in the upshot, as negative as could be. The tragedy of the Russian intelligentsia of the seventies was that without having directly witnessed the victories of reformism, it was present at its collapse. The defeat suffered by the ideology of 'the liberal decade' in Russia was therefore complete and crushing. It was no accident that Solzhenitsyn, who after 1968 took up more frankly some extreme right-wing positions, wrote: 'Those days, 21 and 22 August, were of crucial importance to me.'[40] If until then the intelligentsia had retained some sympathy with socialism, in 1967–68 it disappeared. A frenzied quest began for new values to counterpose against the old. They wanted not only to burn what they had worshipped but also to worship what they had burned – although, in fact, what they worshipped and burned were often the same thing under different names.

Disappointment had already begun to take possession of the public consciousness after Khrushchev's fall. In the *Political Diary* for October 1965, V. K——v wrote:

> A substantial section of the youth cannot believe in the truths that we believed in, and this loss of faith in the spiritual values of the past allows the attitudes of despair and disenchantment, now fashionable in the West, to penetrate into the ranks of our young people by the most varied channels.[41]

The crisis of ideology in the sixties is very well illustrated in the evolution of Yevtushenko, the poet who was at one time seen as the spokesman for the new ideas. A civic position of the old type (as shown in *Bratsk Power Generating Station* and *Babi Yar*) was no longer possible after 1968 – not so much because of the censorship as because the very notion of renewing the system and getting back to 'true Leninism' and so on had been discredited. In the new state of affairs one's civic position had to be 'extrasystemic', and so the poetry came out in *samizdat*. It also appeared in the form of the 'guitar songs' so despised by Solzhenitsyn,[42] which were disseminated about the country in millions of tape-recordings. This democratic poetry proved really popular because its authors openly challenged the system (like A. Galich) or else (like V. Vysotsky) simply turned their back on it. The latter type of poetry corresponded to the feeling of the broadest masses of the working people in the seventies. But it called for thinking – not only political but, *above all*, poetic – of a kind quite different from Yevtushenko's. Finally some, especially B. Okudzhava, turned to history and the experience of the war, seeing in this the last refuge for civic poetry.

Yevtushenko did not try to carry on in his old way, and this was sometimes sad and sometimes funny. He got lost. Tactics degenerated into politicking. Yevtushenko's misfortune was not that he hoped simply to reform the system but that he could not make up his mind to break the official rules of the game, which no longer gave him scope to continue as a civic poet. After 1968 intrasystemic reformism assumed extrasystemic form, being obliged to proclaim its ideas in *samizdat*, to lead an underground existence or to function within the dissident movement. At the beginning of the 1980s Roy Medvedev still defended the reformist ideas of the Khrushchev epoch, but he was able to do so successfully only as a dissident.

On the other hand reformist ideas are better expressed, after all, in articles than in verses. In 1960 the reformists were the extreme left wing of the official Party, but in the 1970s they became the moderate wing of the opposition. And while moderation is good and helpful in politics (especially when there is no revolutionary situation), it is out of place in poetry. Poetry is not at all the domain of moderation. The poet who is a revolutionary is a combination encountered quite frequently, but a poet who is a reformist is absolutely unthinkable. Of course, among poets, there have always been people who held reformist views. But can one recall even one good poem in praise of moderate reformism? 'It is impossible to be oneself if one is not constantly in quest of oneself,' wrote Yevtushenko.[43] His misfortune was that he lost himself in the sixties, and did not manage to find a new 'self' in the seventies. And that was not his fate alone.

The political turn was sharp, and many were taken by surprise. Many lost their heads. Many others tried to save what could still be saved. At that time Solzhenitsyn and the writers who supported him waged such a struggle. Reformist ideas did not yet go further than abolition of the censorship restrictions on art. Essentially, this was a campaign of self-defence for literature. Its programme was formulated before the invasion of Czechoslovakia, in Solzhenitsyn's letter to the Fourth Congress of the Writers' Union, in May 1967. A number of writers expressed support for the letter: P. Antopolsky, G. Vladimov, V. Sosnora, V. Konetsky. The last-mentioned wrote that the questions raised by Solzhenitsyn were 'the fundamental questions for our literature'.[44] The oppositionist writers rallied round Solzhenitsyn at that time, 'in battle order', but already not for offence, only for defence.

Novy Mir

The last line held by open oppositionists within the limits of censored literature was the journal *Novy Mir*. In spring 1968 its editorial board suffered a blow. Zaks and Dement'ev were removed, but this only facilitated the editors' movement to the left. Owing to bureaucratic slovenliness the authorities had got rid of the very members who were most moderate and timid. The journal became more militant. As often happens, bureaucratic decisions had the opposite effect to the one intended. At the same time the authorities could not make up their minds to suppress the journal. The conviction prevailed for a long time in Stalinist circles that *Novy Mir* 'ought not to be suppressed', that it was the journal for 'a certain section of the Soviet intelligentsia which includes writers who, if there were no *Novy Mir*, would send their work abroad, like Sinyavsky.'[45] This view, experience showed, was quite sensible. Nevertheless, the editors themselves knew that the destruction of *Novy Mir* was only a question of time. Not a single number came out without a struggle. It was not only the political censorship that had to be fought. Getting Bulgakov's *Teatral'nyi roman* 'through' proved very difficult, although there was no politics in it. The bureaucratic leaders of culture considered that to cast doubt on the authority of K.S. Stanislavsky in theatrical matters, as Bulgakov did, was like criticizing Lenin in politics. There must be no encroachment on sacred ground. After 1963 the editors of *Novy Mir* were guided by the principle: 'Treat every issue as though it were the last.' They had to work in inconceivably difficult circumstances. For example, a special personal censorship was introduced for the articles of V. Lakshin, who was regarded as the chief ideologue of the tendency. However, the authority of Tvardovsky (and other factors too, perhaps) put off the dispersal of the editorial board for at least eighteen months, and that interval was well employed. The journal continued to publish very interesting works by Kolman, Kon and others. This was its 'swan song'. Although *Novy Mir* was obviously doomed, it kept up its resistance.

Le Monde wrote later:

> Despite the change of façade, Tvardovsky's group (those of them who remained in 1969) and a new group of polemicists published some pointed articles. Even though the official press criticized them and raised various objections, they managed, as before, to get round the censorship which, in 1968–73, was more vigilant than usual. Undoubtedly these articles had to be read with attention, one needed to be able to read between the lines, but, then, that method of analogies and parallels was traditional in Russian literature: Pushkin, Saltykov-Shchedrin and Dostoevsky had all resorted to it. To judge by the use of allusions, and the nuances of the text, we may conclude that *Novy Mir*'s traditional nonconformism had given place to scarcely restrained fury, bitter reflections and murderous satire.[46]

It is important to make clear that it was not only a question of allusions.

I have already said that the view – widely held in the West, and even in some circles at home – that liberal scholars use material from the history of other societies merely as a pretext for throwing light on our own is quite mistaken. Serious research is not done like that, although a method of the sort may sometimes be employed in artistic creativity. When Tovstonogov put on a dramatization of Saltykov-Shchedrin's *A Present-Day Idyll* at the Contemporary Theatre, it was clear that the satire was aimed not at nineteenth-century bureaucrats and deserters from the opposition camp of those days, but at their present-day successors. Similarly, *Mother* at the Theatre on the Taganka was essentially concerned not with a past revolutionary crisis but with one in the future. On the whole, though, as I have said, the true method of culture – especially theoretical culture – is not the 'allusion' or the 'hint', but broad philosophical generalization. Every genuine work of culture oversteps the bounds of its original task. Analogies and parallels are not only 'read off' by readers of philosophical works but also 'read into' them. Everyone finds there what he is looking for. On the other hand, the writer's desire to speak about what concerns him obliges him to speak generally.

The theme of the publicists and theoreticians of *Novy Mir* in the period 1968 to 1971 can be called 'the intelligentsia and the reaction'. This theme was pursued on the basis of various materials and by a variety of methods, but in the last analysis we arrive at a single system of conclusions. It may be that it is only at the beginning of the 1980s, ten years later, that we can evaluate fully the prophetic significance of those thoughts.

From the chronological standpoint, Granin's article 'A Sacred Gift' closed the discussion, but for several reasons it would be best to start with this. Here the theme was presented sharply, Russian material used, and the general philosophical significance of the question clearly emphasized. What made this writer, the author of novellas and tales, appear in the role of historian? The article deals with something that happened in the nineteenth century. Most probably it was the need – the painfully acute need – to draw some preliminary conclusions from the spiritual history of post-Stalinist Russia. 'A Sacred Gift' is the story of Pushkin and Bulgarin, the Mozart and Salieri of Russian literature. It is both an article and a story. Granin appears here not only as a historian and a writer, but also as a biographer in the manner of Plutarch; this is a kind of 'comparative biography'. In the foreground, however, we perceive not the concrete facts but the symbolic meaning of the relations between these two men. And, as might be expected, it is not Pushkin who interests Granin – we know a great deal about him – but Bulgarin, the informer and reactionary.

'The history of Russian reaction is rich and instructive,' observes Granin. 'It had its own traditions, its own attempt at theory, its own heroes, from the time of Malyuta Skuratov right down to Katkov and Shul'gin.'[47] The author traces, step by step, the path of development followed by culture and science in Russia, so as to establish the fact that in our country, spiritual life always took hold in spite of and in conflict with the state. The reader is horrified to find that *that* old society was so much like *our* new society: identical in many ways. But should he be surprised? Reaction is always and everywhere like itself. All that matters is to show its common historical features, to reveal the archetype of the reactionary and understand his logic.

In art, Granin says, the real struggle goes on not between tendencies but between talent and mediocrity: 'Talent and mediocrity pursue different aims in art.'[48] Mediocrities cluster round authority, making up for their lack of talent with an excess of trustworthiness. Reaction constantly replenishes the ranks of its defenders from among the intelligentsia. Mediocrities systematically betray their own people: 'The former liberal easily turns into an extreme obscurantist.'[49] So it was with Pushkin and Bulgarin; so it was, at the turn of the century, with Suvorin[50] – and so it was with many who began in the 1950s by riding the wave of de-Stalinization.

The conservative official pseudoculture has many tasks, but one of the most important is constantly to neutralize true culture and render it harmless. It tries to depict every opponent, once he is dead, as its own precursor. Pushkin, Gogol, Pasternak, Tvardovsky, Vampilov – all, despite the persecution they suffered in their lifetime, became classics after their death. The same thing seems now to be happening with V. Vysotsky. When he was alive not one line of his was ever printed – except in the collection entitled *Metropol'*, published abroad – but as soon as he died the authorities' attitude towards him improved. True, this change was facilitated by the way his funeral turned into a mighty popular demonstration. Vysotsky had to be transformed without delay from a bard of the opposition into a 'popular Soviet poet and songwriter'. Reaction needs geniuses, but only dead ones. Reactionaries feel easier, more comfortable with them. Where the dead are concerned, there can be no inferiority complex. Dead men do not give interviews to the foreign press or get mixed up in current political life. The Bulgarins claim the role of executors to the Pushkins:

What force is it that draws them irresistibly towards those they have killed? They take their stand in the guard of honour, their faces pious and sorrowful, their eyes bright and clear. They are sure nobody will dare to drive them away. They make better use of this death than anyone else. They get to work at once after the funeral is over. The deceased genius has to be adapted, given the required appearance. Pleasant portraits are produced, together with moving and instructive biographies. Whatever is not needed and out of place is deleted. From selected quotations, canons and dogmas are built which are as solid as prison walls.[51]

But on one plane they are mistaken. The essential characteristic of a genius is that he remains spiritually alive for us even after his physical death – whereas a reactionary mediocrity falls victim to oblivion while still with us. In this sense Bulgarin's fate was tragic: he fought a notoriously hopeless battle with Pushkin, and even the genius's death left him no choice of victory. Bulgarin was doomed: in the twentieth century who will ever read his book about Vyzhigin? But others come to take Bulgarin's place: mediocrities just like him, while nobody has replaced Pushkin.

Is there a solution to this tragic collision? And does not history, in the end, ensure the triumph of Pushkin over Bulgarin? Granin does not put this question to us, but nobody is left with any doubt as to whose side he is on. Reaction, though, does not come from nowhere. It is based upon certain classes, on state institutions, on the bureaucracy. Consequently progress, too, can base itself not only on the abstract power of reason but also on quite real social forces. The victory of reason, said Brecht, is possible only as the victory of the rational – as the victory of the advanced classes and parties which can smash reaction.

This revolutionary force is the working masses, including the intelligentsia – masses which have acquired political (class) self-awareness. But is the intelligentsia a real force? Igor Kon, in 'Reflections on the American Intelligentsia', came to this conclusion, from the sociological standpoint. Kon's article, which belongs in the context of the general theories of the Frankfurt School (he refers directly, for example, to 'the remarkable book by Robert Wolff, Barrington Moore and Herbert Marcuse, *A Critique of Pure Tolerance*'[52]), is undoubtedly related to the most interesting researches of the New Left movement. According to the German political scientist Mehnert, 'Kon's work is also of interest to the Western reader.'[53] Such profound penetration into the heart of the problem was possible because, to a certain extent, Soviet oppositionists at the end of the 1960s were able to identify completely with the movement of the new intellectuals in the West.

Kon examines the making of a mass intelligentsia, its transformation into a 'new working class', and so into a mighty economic and political force:

The intelligentsia has ceased to be a superior elite standing somewhere on the periphery of society and, as a result, relatively autonomous in relation to it and engaged in seeking to look at society 'from without', so to speak. It has become a very important component of society, inside the basic social classes and along with them.[54]

Following Gnedin and, like him, drawing upon the young Marx, Kon criticizes the bureaucratic hierarchy and shows how it stands in opposition to the intelligentsia and to intellect in general. The bureaucracy sees the work of the intelligentsia as merely a means to the attainment of *its own* aims. Consequently it tries to subordinate to itself other people's minds, other people's knowledge, imposing extraneous tasks upon them. The intelligentsia's reply to the bureaucrats' policy takes the form of outbreaks of student rioting and the growth of the New Left (France and Poland both provide examples). Protest against alienation leads to revolutionary action.

Of course, the revolt of the New Left in the West took place in quite different conditions from those in the USSR. The Western intellectuals rebelled against 'repressive tolerance', whereas the Russians suffered from a much more repressive intolerance. 'Paradoxically, these differing conditions tend to have a similar effect on the political attitudes of the intellectuals of the two countries,' write Brzezinski and Huntington, comparing the intelligentsias of the USSR and the USA. 'In both cases they stimulate the sense of political frustration or even alienation.'[55] However, the American scholars also mentioned what seemed to them another paradox. The American intellectual protests against the alienation, the counterposing of people to one another in bourgeois industrial society, whereas the Soviet intellectual is revolted by official collectivism: 'The alienated American attempts to escape *into* just exactly what the alienated Soviet citizen attempts to escape *from*.'[56] But this contradiction is only apparent. Soviet official collectivism does not really unite people: on the contrary, it alienates them to an even greater degree than 'the American way of life' or capitalist competition. It unites people with false, formal, obligatory bonds which are substituted for the natural ones and thereby prevents genuine informal human unity. It is no accident that horizontal bonds within all Soviet organizations (trade union, 'Party', and so on), between individual members or particular groups, are not only not provided for but are actually condemned. Under totalitarian collectivism every member of society is subject to 'the leadership' and counterposed to the other members. And nowhere is a person so lonely and isolated as in a collective where only *despite* official policy can informal bonds be established between individuals, as against those which are imposed upon them.[57] It was natural, therefore, that the Soviet intelligentsia's protest against alienation was in many ways similar to the protest of the Western New Left – not in form, but in content.

The experience of the New Left movement at the end of the sixties attracted much attention from Kon and Gnedin and other theoreticians of the *Novy Mir* circle (for example, L. Kopelev and R. Orlova). But in the West and in Poland in spring 1968 there was a political crisis. What was to be done, though, in a period of reaction, when the power of the ruling group was being consolidated and stabilized? What was to be done in a period of social stagnation? And that was what had arrived in the USSR, after the period of reform.

Political crisis activates the masses, but in a period of social stagnation, when there is no hope of political changes, the masses withdraw from politics:

> The atmosphere of intellectual terror and the absence of a new ideology led to the impoverishment of political life and the increase of civic apathy. Many, especially young people, ceased to interest themselves in politics and went off into the world of private interests and experiences.[58]

However, this de-ideologizing of the masses also meant a crisis of the official ideology. A period of apathy and stagnation is historically necessary: it precedes a fresh, authentic revolutionary upsurge:

> The propaganda machine continues and even intensifies its activity, people go on, from inertia, using the familiar ideological clichés ... without appreciating (for the time being) their intellectual bankruptcy, but these clichés have already lost their emotional appeal – they leave people indifferent, or even irritate them.
>
> Disappointment with the ruling ideology, the inflation of ideological values, is chiefly felt in a negative way, as a sense of devastation, lack of ideals, absence of prospects, ideological disorder. People who cannot think historically see nothing positive in this process of disintegration and look with yearning to the past. But this disintegration is a necessary precondition for the birth of new symbols of faith and action. Disappointment [the Russian word means, literally, 'taking away the cup'] is always agonizing, but it alone enables one to see the world as it really is, without any mythological bandages over our eyes.[59]

This process can last a long time, but this duration has its advantages. Gnedin wrote about that in his article with the symbolic title 'Lost Illusions and Discovered Hopes'.[60] The longer the calm and submissiveness of the working masses continues, the mightier and more deafening will be the eventual explosion. Where the philistine sees inactivity on the part of the people and omnipotence on that of the regime, in fact the revolutionary forces are accumulating. The situation is comparable to the compression of steam in a closed cylinder. Where there are no safety valves it is not apparent that pressure is increasing inside the cylinder. Outwardly all is calm, but the tension grows until the steam bursts the cylinder. A revolutionary crisis arrives. As they sense this, the rulers may intensify repression. In the new conditions, however, that has the opposite result to the one they expect: 'In relatively calm periods this can be advantageous to a reactionary government, but, at a time of political crisis, to intensify repression merely strengthens the forces of resistance.'[61] Thus a crisis of ideas and a period of stagnation should not be regarded as a catastrophe. On the contrary, society's spiritual crisis foreshadows renewal. The intelligentsia had to stand firm spiritually and be ready for the coming battles.

In a period of stagnation reason's chief weapon is irony. Kon calls for a distinction to be made between the 'wilful irony' of the middle strata 'who want, while doing nothing, to enjoy all the world's blessings and to feel that they are superior to everything around them – what Heinrich Böll aptly called "a drug for the privileged"' – and the tragic irony of the real intelligentsia. The nearer the crisis approaches, the quicker this demarcation becomes manifest. The irony of the left-wing intellectuals is constructive; it is ideological, akin to Hegel's negation, for it underlies every spiritual creation. The wilful irony of the middle strata expresses soullessness and ideological futility. The crisis of ideas is not a justification for lack of ideals. On the contrary, it obliges us to seek new positive values. Kon wrote:

> Today, the intelligentsia has become an organic component of society which penetrates into all parts of the social mechanism. And this means that its responsibility has immensely increased. Not seclusion in an ivory tower but active struggle for the realization of advanced ideas is the path to be taken by the best representative of today's intelligentsia. Freedom as merging with the progressive forces of society does not mean renouncing critical contemplation and self-analysis. The power of a philosopher, as such, does not consist in his knowing how to shoot. But when eighty-year-old Bertrand Russell joined in a sit-down demonstration, that was not only a political act but proof of the seriousness and sincerity of his beliefs. If intellectuals do not merely trade in ideas but live lives inspired by them, they cannot turn away from the struggle to realize these ideas.[62]

Kon's appeal was more than timely. The practical conditions of the creative work of the Soviet intelligentsia had become markedly more complex. In 1970 Tvardovsky was removed from the editorship of

Novy Mir. Under Kosolapov the journal soon began to lose its individual character, even though there was at first some attempt to retain it. After 1971 it could be said that *Novy Mir* had become a journal 'like the rest'. It kept a large number of its writers – Abramov, Aitmatov, Tendryakov, Trifonov and others belonged, as before, to 'the *Novy Mir* circle' – but on the whole it was no longer the tribune of the liberal intelligentsia. Moscow wits said that the title page ought to bear the words: 'Let us renounce *Novy Mir* [that is, the new world]!'

The Emergence of the Dissident Movement

The era of Brezhnev's 'historic compromise' began – a sociopolitical lull. A. Lim called the rulers' formula for this period 'the new social contract'.[63] The rulers guarantee the masses a certain degree of social stability while the masses, in return, are obliged to give up the struggle for their rights. The rulers guarantee that there will be no return to Stalinism, but do not carry out any further liberalization. The slogan of the era is 'neither reaction nor reform'. Its ideal is stability, understood as meaning immobility. Its policy is conservatism in the most precise sense of that word. Class and political struggles are temporarily frozen. True, in the economy mighty hidden processes of disintegration and breakdown are under way which cannot be halted without introducing reforms, and it becomes ever more difficult to keep to the terms of the new social contract. In the long run the prospective results of this course cannot fail to be catastrophic for the statocracy itself which has imposed this 'contract' on society. But at first it can feel satisfied with the situation.

On the whole the rulers maintained a passive role in the new conditions. Having, in the course of the 'preventive counter-revolution',[64] succeeded in crushing open opposition – in the legal press, at any rate – the statocracy went over to the defensive. 'The requirements of ideology', writes Rakovski, 'were now entirely negative: not to challenge the supremacy of the official ideology, or rather to celebrate ritually (on rare occasions only) a willingness to submit to that ideology.'[65] A Soviet culturologist called this 'ritual self-defilement'. But critical thinking – and consequently its bearer, the intellectual who disturbs calm and alarms the public conscience – had no place in Brezhnev's 'new order'. Lim writes:

> From the village teacher to the philosopher, the writer, the artist, all have been broken and torn to pieces, until nothing but the name remains. The instinct of self-preservation compels the intellectual to defend himself.

Conscience does not let him cease to be himself, and so society's observance of the contract presumes continual assaults on the intellectual, either literal or figurative, and he is forced to resist, to speak out, to reject, to refuse consent.[66]

The seventies brought into being new forms of cultural-political movement. Whereas in the sixties one could speak of a united anti-bureaucratic cultural front, a single stream in which the literary movement clearly played the leading role, in the seventies that unity no longer existed. This was not only because the common ideology of the 'children of '56' had already passed away. Culture itself had become more diverse, had split up into many different streams, running in different directions, clashing with each other. In the last analysis it was only in the seventies that one would say that a real cultural pluralism had come to birth. The crisis of the cultural movement of the sixties, its break-up, was in itself, perhaps, a step back in the political sense, but it also opened up new historical prospects before the Soviet intelligentsia.

The pressure from above – what Kon calls the intellectual terror – caused a blossoming of illegal literature. Besides *samizdat*, many Russian publications appeared abroad. Those who remained loyal to the hopes of 1956 and unwilling to adapt themselves to the new period were pushed aside, but at the same time they broke with the system. This was a tremendous step forward on the spiritual plane. Henceforth there began to take shape, alongside the opposition *within* the system which had predominated in the sixties, a new opposition *to* the system. The dissident movement emerged.

'Since the late sixties', write Bence and Kis (they also write under the pseudonym Rakovski),

> official culture has ceased to retain its monopoly in Eastern Europe. In some of these countries the non-official forms of communication have become customary, and in others, efforts have been made towards the same end. Works banned by the censor and works that had never been submitted to the state-controlled publishers began to circulate. This literature in some countries creates a whole system of non-official communication, a parallel culture; bulky volumes and periodicals appear, disputes flare up, different ideological tendencies become crystallized. Political ideologies, practical programmes and tactical conceptions are formulated and sometimes even political movements – though embryonic – are born.[67]

All this influences legal culture as well, for it cannot be separated from the illegal variety, if only because the same readers have access to both legal and illegal literature, and sometimes the same authors write for *samizdat* and for the official publications. It has been said that 'there is no going back' from *samizdat* to legal literature, but some writers (Iskander, Lakshin, Yevtushenko and others) have managed to demonstrate the unsoundness of this formulation. The degree of oppositionism among *samizdat* writers is no less variegated than the degree of loyalty among writers for the censored publications. In any case, there is no gulf between legal and illegal culture. The principal service rendered by *samizdat* is that it 'breaks the monopoly of the ruling ideology's patterns of thought, and introduces new concepts and alternative ideas into the social consciousness. Even the most ancient and reactionary myths', continues Rakovski, 'have a clearly positive role from this point of view, since they in fact multiply the number of patterns of thought which can be confronted with each other.'[68] Within the framework of *samizdat* the fundamental tendencies that exist in our thinking can formulate their principles more precisely, and this is very important.

Finally, *samizdat*, by virtue of its very existence, had a certain effect on the censorship, making it more liberal. P. Tamarin wrote in the uncensored Moscow journal *Poiski*:

> Without the free expression by Solzhenitsyn, Zinoviev, Vladimov, Kopelev, Voinovich, Kornilov and Chukovskaya, without the threat that many more writers would follow their example and independently publish their work abroad, quitting the supervision of the Writers' Union, would the authorities have allowed our publishing houses to bring out the writings of Okudzhava, Rasputin, Abramov, Trifonov, Aitmatov and others? ... Would they have let Karyakin publish a book on Dostoevsky which does not fit into the framework of the ruling ideology?[69]

The dissident movement is vitally necessary for the development of legal culture. This is one of its historical tasks and it is in this field that it has scored its greatest successes, even though the dissidents themselves say little about it.

The ranks of the dissidents included many *Novy Mir* writers. This transition did not take place at once, but painfully and over a long time. Nevertheless, one after the other, they took that road. It is now possible to draw up a sort of balance sheet. Kopelev, Orlova, Sinyavsky, Nekrasov, Solzhenitsyn, Voinovich, Popovsky, Zhores Medvedev, Nekrich, Aksyonov, Kol'man are all abroad. Tvardovsky, Simonov, Ehrenburg, Sappak, Trifonov have died. Gnedin, Kornilov, Iskander publish their works abroad while themselves remaining in the USSR. Only a few prominent writers – Lakshin, Karyakin, Volin, Kon – continue to publish in the USSR through legal channels. The list of names speaks for itself. An illegal culture has come into being alongside the legal one.

Originally, I intended to confine myself in this book to studying the legal culture, as I considered that *samizdat* and books published abroad, being accessible only to a minority, were, so to speak, on the periphery of our cultural life. But I gradually became convinced that it is not possible to talk about the legal culture without discussing *samizdat*. The same main tendencies are found in *samizdat* as in the legal culture, but are more frankly expressed. Therefore one can see the literature of the dissidents as part of a single cultural-political process. Two principal social groups have produced dissidents – the literary and scientific elites. The former were brought into the movement by the logic of the literary struggle which began in the sixties; the latter by the logic of scientific thinking. 'For true scientists,' writes Zhores Medvedev, 'the basic human rights are inseparable from their right of research. Violation of these rights only damages the creativity of work.'[70] Some of the highly placed scientists had great possessions, enjoyed considerable personal freedom and privileges, but such people speak out not only for themselves but for wider circles of the intelligentsia.[71] Naturally, therefore, members of the statocracy, who see gain as the only possible motive for people's conduct (everyone of limited outlook is inclined to attribute his own way of thinking to others) were taken aback by the initiative of the dissident scientists. No less unexpected for the rulers was the form assumed by the dissidents' activity, in defending Soviet laws against abuse by the authorities. Since the laws and public statements of the statocracy are contradicted by its practice (this is natural when a society is called socialist yet is not so in reality) such actions prove extremely hurtful for the ruling class corporation. 'The governments', wrote the Vienna journal *Neues Forum*, 'act illegally, the opposition upholds the laws.'[72]

The dissident movement as a whole remains a cultural movement, although its members sometimes think they are engaged in politics. But they do not confront the system with any programme for change or any new conception of society, or even any new ideology. The dissidents really have created an alternative, but only a *moral* alternative. Their actions were calls for individual honesty. They developed a certain model of personal conduct, but gave no answer to the question posed by society. Most of the political books they have published abroad are theoretically feeble.[73] Jean Elleinstein is obviously exaggerating when he writes that the books of the dissidents published in the West 'are undoubtedly no less dangerous to the *nomenklatura* than were the philosophical works of Voltaire, Diderot and Rousseau to the *Ancien Régime* in France.'[74] The theories of Sakharov and Amalrik are hardly to be taken seriously, for they consist of combinations of commonplaces with personal notions that are not based on study of factual material.

The most successful works by dissidents were those devoted to literature, especially works of fiction that made no claim to scientific sociological analysis.

One cannot really blame the dissidents for their lack of political thinking: it is not their fault but their misfortune. In a period when there is no mass-scale 'practical movement' for democracy in a country, conditions for the elaboration of political programmes are not very favourable. In the period of stagnation which began after 1968 a search for a global alternative might well seem an idle and needless occupation – besides which, the dissidents inherited all the shortcomings of the sixties intelligentsia. The dominance of art in spiritual life and the subordinate role played by philosophy were to be expected in a society which had only just emerged from Stalin's terror. Art could begin to flourish much more rapidly than the social sciences, which require for their development time and the accumulation of knowledge and experience. However, what was understandable in the sixties was perceived in the seventies as a weakness. The country felt acutely the shortage of theory, a sort of 'ideological hunger'. Everyone tried to satisfy this hunger to the best of his or her abilities. Under these conditions, writers, biologists and mathematicians came forward unexpectedly as social theoreticians, though their interventions were sometimes far from successful.

The elaboration of qualitatively new ideas and emancipation from the dogmas of the past is a process more complicated than might appear at first glance. This process has its blind alleys, its temptations and its imaginary ways out. As Rakovski has written,

> the intellectual traditions are so poor that the nonconformist intellectuals are forced to draw from the official ideology from time to time: they try to make themselves an image of idealism on the basis of manuals on 'dialectical materialism', to work out the essence of Trotskyism or Populism on the basis of manuals on 'scientific socialism'. Instead of creating true conceptual alternatives, they thus simply give real life to the phantom enemies of the official manuals.[75]

This shrewd observation provides the best explanation of an ideological phenomenon which could be called 'anti-ideas'.

The expression may seem somewhat artificial, but in my view it defines precisely enough the essence of a whole series of ideological systems which arose in the dissident movement and which were openly proclaimed in *samizdat* while also influencing legal literature. What was common to them all was their close links with the official ideology, so that they appeared as its shadow, its counterpart and its 'reverse side', but in no case an alternative to it. This is most noticeable in the case of

Solzhenitsyn and the Russian nationalists who came to the front politically at the very end of the sixties and in the seventies.

Nationalist Currents

'The intelligentsia suddenly began taking their vacations in the village at the graves of ancestors instead of in the Crimea, the Caucasus or the Baltic,' Alexander Yanov recalls.

> Suddenly everyone noticed that the peasantry of north-western Russia – the cradle of the nation – was disappearing. Young people began to wander around the dying villages collecting icons, and soon there was almost no intellectual's home in Moscow which was not decorated with symbols of Russian Orthodoxy. The writer Vladimir Soloukhin appeared in the House of Writers wearing a signet ring which carried the image of Nicholas II. An insane demand arose on the black market for books by 'White Guardsmen' and 'counter-revolutionaries' who had died in emigration.[76]

The numerous nationalist manifestations of this order naturally shocked and frightened the democratically inclined intellectuals, all the more because the 'Neo-Slavophils' of the seventies behaved aggressively and enjoyed – at first – obvious tolerance by the authorities. This caused Yanov to fear that Russian nationalism was developing 'an *alternative strategy* which the autocratic regime could use for its survival under conditions of crisis.'[77] Unfortunately, the representatives of the traditional left-wing intelligentsia failed to note the important fact that the nationalists remained almost as much isolated from the masses as the 'Lefts' themselves. Whereas the drama of *Novy Mir* had been played out before millions of people, the 'thaw' had affected the country's entire population in one way or another, and tens of thousands of workers took part in the strikes of the sixties and seventies, the comedy of the 'Slavophil Renaissance' was performed within a relatively narrow circle of the intellectual elite and part of the middle strata.

Yanov's book reflected very well the panic that seized the liberal intellectuals when the nationalists came on the scene. This was primarily an *ideological* panic, due to the helplessness of the ideas of 1956 in the face of a new situation and a new danger. The fear of the Neo-Slavophils felt by some left-wingers, though well founded, was greatly exaggerated. It is typical that Yanov is disposed to see the incident in the restaurant of the Central Writers' Club and Soloukhin's escapade, or statements made by the mediocre artist Ilya Glazunov, as events of almost planetary or at least national significance. Highly unconvincing, too, are Yanov's arguments to the effect that Russia's entire history is cyclical and a period of mild rule, such as Khrushchev's or Brezhnev's, is bound to be followed by a terrorist reaction in the spirit of Stalin and using nationalist slogans. There are no *special* laws of Russian history, nor can there be. The causes of political 'thaws' and 'frosts' have to be sought in concrete social processes, in political and class struggle. Abstract speculations are jejune, for history cannot be explained by any general schemas assembled through arbitrary combinations of facts. In order to understand the past and conceive the possible variants of the future one has to think *concretely*, taking into account social, economic and political conditions, the level of technological development and actual class interests. Otherwise, the construction of general schemas remains a mere futile pastime.

Any arguments concerning the new danger from the right are senseless in so far as they ignore the qualitative difference between the present industrial and consumer society in the USSR and Stalin's totalitarianism, or such important economic factors as the Soviet economy's dependence on the world market (which was not at all the case in Stalin's time),[78] the specific features of present-day science and technology, and so on.

It must not be concluded from what has been said that the nationalists are not dangerous. They may enlist the support of the declassed section of the population, the numerous Soviet lumpenproletariat, but only if the masses are not mobilized behind a different banner. In the struggle for the masses, the tendency which offers the clearest social and economic alternative will triumph. And it is precisely an economic programme and social ideas capable of mobilizing the masses that the neo-Slavophils lack.

Nevertheless, the development of the ideology of the New Right and their popularity are symptomatic. The crisis of the official ideology after 1968 occurred, as I have said, simultaneously with a crisis of the opposition, which had come out precisely for the purity of this official ideology. For intellectuals who had experienced 1956, 1966 and 1968, the crisis of ideas was extremely serious. The growth in the popularity of the New Right was evidence that the Russian intelligentsia was undergoing, in the seventies, the most profound spiritual crisis in its history. The situation that arose after the crushing of the 'Prague spring' can be compared only to the spiritual crisis that followed the defeat of the 1905 Revolution. But the crisis of the seventies was deeper and more acute. The earlier crisis produced only *Vekhi*, but this one produced a whole number of similar tendencies: with this difference, that the *Vekhi* writers were very much more profound in their ideas than are the lost intellectuals of today.

The collapse of the liberal ideology of 'true Marxism-Leninism' led to a deep division among the intelligentsia. While one section gave up its mythological illusions of liberal pseudo-Marxism in favour of scientific Marxism – and, on the political plane, of a conception of class struggle quite alien to 'the children of '56', who had at first supposed that 'ideas rule the world' – the other section turned sharply to the right.

The strongest tendency 'to the right of the government' is indeed Russian nationalism. This, however, cannot be considered in purely political categories, for the nationalists, as a definite tendency, are also organized around problems of culture. At the centre of attention this time is the question of Russia's originality and its alleged *Sonderweg*.

It is well known that both the Marxists and the Westernist-minded liberal intellectuals reacted with great hostility to the upsurge of nationalism. This attitude was most sharply expressed by the brilliant polemicist and culturologist L. Batkin, when he remarked that 'some people feel a "nostalgia for the East" which, though worthy of respect, is reactionary and therefore doomed.'[79] Batkin reproached these people for fearing to assume responsibility for their own actions and choice of direction, preferring to rely on ready-made absolute 'truths' – that is, clichés. A quest for one's own path and spiritual freedom, he insisted, does not mean a fall from grace. Some Christians, too (for example L. Pinsky and G. Pomerants), reacted negatively to the new nationalism even though the nationalists usually claim to be religious. Before starting to criticize Russian nationalism, however, we must note its heterogeneous character. Among the representatives of the 'back-to-the-soil movement', as the nationalists like to call themselves, there are moderate, liberal-minded people like S. Likhachev, the author of *Zametki o russkom*. There is a whole group – among whom are numbered our 'village prose' writers V. Belov, V. Rasputin, G. Troepol'sky and V. Soloukhin – who are mostly connected with the journal *Nash Sovremennik*, which, in the words of W. Kasack, 'has gradually become the organ linking the Russophil authors with the countryside.'[80] They see in their link with tradition, with popular culture, an alternative to official pseudo-populism, and turn to the values of the past in order to counterpose them to contemporary 'consumer society'.

Mikhail Agursky describes the characteristics of the political philosophy of the 'village prose school' as isolationism, anti-militarism and disappointment with internationalism, which is especially marked in Abramov and Rasputin. The 'village prose' writers are the most peaceable group among the nationalists, but the more aggressive Neo-Slavophils are also inclined towards isolationism:

For some, Russia itself is the ideal, even without the Union Republics; for others it is a powerful Russian Empire which will make other countries tremble but will not attempt to seize them by force. Isolationism is sometimes linked with pacifism, while militarism, on the other hand, is seen by others as an important, even essential part of national life without which the nation is in danger of degeneration.[81]

It must be realized that people like Rasputin think quite differently from somebody like Ilya Glazunov.

In Rasputin's novella *Poslednyi srok* [The Last Term] both present-day language and the values of the new generation of consumers clash with traditional values and, at the same time, with eternity – with death. They do not stand up to this test. Putting the question like that does not and cannot have any deliberately reactionary and retrograde implications. It is natural that in a period when the future is uncertain it is precisely the past, tradition, history that prove to be the only generally accessible criteria for testing and evaluating the present. The 'back-to-the-soil' people have at least two important positive ideas – defence of architectural monuments and protection of the environment (for them, nature and the art of the past are embodiments of the eternal). Both these problems, however, can bring together people of varying political views.[82] As early as 1963 the journal *Oktyabr'*, unquestionably of the reactionary persuasion, campaigned in defence of Lake Baikal, which was threatened with ruin through the building of an industrial complex on its shore.[83] At that time the fight for Baikal united many, from extreme conservatives to extreme liberals. The movement had little success. Pollution of the lake still went on, merely not as fast as before, and discussion of the matter in the press was strictly forbidden. But the 'village prose' writers were concerned that the public should learn of the catastrophic state of the environment, despite the silence of the newspapers. The ecologist B. Komarov wrote that 'in certain works of documentary-fictional prose such as V. Astaf'ev's *Tsar'-ryba* or V. Rasputin's *Proshchanie s Materoy*, there is more of the tragic truth about the destruction of nature than in strictly scientific writings.'[84] To the barbarism of a soulless society, to alienation, they try to counterpose certain absolute values. 'In the face of growing barbarism,' writes Komarov, 'both the author of the outstanding novel *Proshchanie s Materoy*, V. Rasputin, and the author of the documentary tale *Operatsiya "Kotel"*, V. Sapozhnikov, turn to the concepts "God" and "the immortal soul". They can find no other absolute, non-transient values.'[85]

One can, of course, find in religion many sound and profound moral ideas, but it is no secret that religion *in itself* provides no answers to concrete sociopolitical economic, social and ecological questions.

Turning to God, as Komarov says, 'symbolizes one's despair'.[86] And a sense of social despair is what impels people towards religion, in which they hope to find spiritual escape, at least.

The increasing popularity of religion had to be acknowledged in the official press as well. 'Young people, too, are to be seen', wrote E. Filimonov in *Izvestiya*,

> at services in Orthodox and other churches, especially at the prayer-meetings of the Baptists, Seventh-Day Adventists and Pentecostals. It has become 'fashionable' to get married in church, to have one's children baptized, and to wear little crosses next to the skin.[87]

These moods became widespread first of all among the intellectuals.

> 'Do we not reject religion too sweepingly?' said a young scientist. 'Go to church, listen to Rakhmaninov's "All-Night Vigil" as it sounds within the walls of an ancient church, by the bright gleam of candles and the gilded settings of icons! Isn't that marvellous?

These remarks by 'a young scientist' are quoted in the newspaper *Sovetskaya Kultura*, which admits that such views are held not by him alone, but 'not uncommonly'.[88] The newspaper even mentions the connection between interest in religion and disillusionment with propaganda, because 'our demands and tastes often prove to be on a higher level than is supposed by some information media and cultural institutions.' It notes that religion has succeeded in 'extending the frontiers of its influence, spreading this even among the educated strata of the population, the artistic and technical intelligentsia'.[89] *Izvestiya* also admits that 'we really do come into conflict with an increase of interest in religion and the Church.'[90] This admission is all the more valuable because when something similar was said by a Western ecclesiastic who had visited the USSR, his words were declared to be 'lies bordering on provocation'.[91] To be sure, when it comes to explaining *why*, the Soviet papers put the whole blame on the 'village prose' writers and propagandists for church music. Against the religious revival the authors of these articles can oppose only lectures and talks. They do not, of course, want to discuss the social and ideological roots of religion (in official circles in the Soviet Union Marx has long been forgotten). Filimonov complains that 'grandmothers' lead young people astray. Yet here's a strange fact. Twenty years ago the churches were full of old people, and it is the same today. But those old worshippers of twenty years ago are long since dead! A new shift has come on, and what is interesting is that today's 'grandmothers' were Komsomol members in the 1920s. Previously, they never went to church. Amazing, too, is the charge of 'conformism' hurled by Filimonov at the religious youth, for in a country where atheism has been proclaimed the state ideology and religion – to put it mildly – is not approved of, it is not conformism that leads a person into church.

People hope to find in the Church liberation from the dogmas of official ideology, but Orthodoxy can offer them only illusory liberation. In Lithuania they may still put their hopes in some liberating power possessed by Catholicism, but would it be a great gain if the rigid dogmatism of Stalinism were to be replaced by the dogmatism – no less rigid – of Russian Orthodoxy? At best we should be merely replacing a poor copy by the original, but is the original any good?

American scholars say that Stalinist pseudo-Marxism is the 'secular religion of Soviet society'.[92] Here we find its trinity, its saints and apostles; here are 'the holy scriptures of the Soviet belief system: the writings of Marx, Engels and Lenin'.[93] Even such an Eastern rite is practised as the mummifying of the remains of saints – Lenin, then Stalin. 'The so-called Red Corners (displaying the pictures of leaders and founding fathers, slogans and banners) are reminiscent of small shrines,' writes Hollander. 'Masses of people assemble to listen to secular sermons (at speeches and rallies). All these are among the quasi-religious manifestations of the Soviet belief system.'[94] Recently the Red Corners received a series of pictures which tell the life story of Saint Brezhnev. A Soviet person can count thousands of examples of this sort of thing, and it was not accidental that even after the publication of *One Day in the Life of Ivan Denisovich*, Yu. Karyakin spoke of the link between Stalinism and religion.

That such critical thinkers as Marx, Engels and Lenin should have become objects of worship is one of history's many bad jokes. What matters more to us now is that a crude pseudo-religion cannot, of course, compete on equal terms with the centuries-old tradition of Christianity. But when he rejects Stalinism in the name of Orthodoxy, a dissident intellectual is not making such a decisive turn as he thinks. It was precisely Stalinist pseudo-religiosity that fostered his inclination towards the religiosity of Orthodoxy. The new ideas turn out to be suspiciously like the old. It is typical that many are drawn to religion not by moral preaching or Christian internationalism (in this respect people like G. Pomerants and L. Pinsky are rather exceptional) but by ceremonies, rituals and authority – in short, not by those features that contrast religion to Stalinism but those in which they are akin. This is particularly noticeable when we consider the Orthodox nationalists. Among them are very many notorious reactionaries like Glazunov, anti-Semites like Pikul, monarchists and Fascists. It is the very absence of a clear-cut demarcation between the different tendencies in the 'back-to-the-soil movement' – and their common orientation upon the past makes such a demarcation extremely difficult – that has transformed this movement, as a whole, into a dangerous reactionary phenomenon. The attractiveness and spirituality of the 'traditionalists' in the cultural sphere can be exploited in politics by ultra-reactionaries. One of the dissidents compared the country's rulers to 'satiated wolves' and the monarchists and nationalists to hungry ones: 'idealists can be such good terrorists. If these nationalists come to power, it would become very dangerous.'[95] Disquiet is caused, too, by the fact that extremist groups among the nationalists find support among certain strata of the ruling statocracy.

One of Batkin's comments is very much to the point here. In circumstances when the old ideology has outlived itself and no longer attracts anyone, when ideological hunger appears, the desire grows to 'lean against' something – to find justification for one's conduct, moral support, in some sort of absolute values. The national-religious idea may serve as such a support. It becomes all the more attractive because on the one hand it has its heroes and martyrs and is oppositional, while on the other the rulers look indulgently upon it and indirectly encourage the growth of Russian nationalism. It is symptomatic that for some time now attacks on Solzhenitsyn, who has become since his exile to the West the chief ideologist of the nationalist reaction, have practically disappeared from the official press.

All this, of course, does not exhaust the question. The polemic around the 'back-to-the-soil movement' in the USSR has revived the old debate between the Slavophils and the Westernists. The mere fact that after a hundred years the old problems again start to be discussed with the same fervour – and not at all as problems of the past, but as relevant to the present time – tells us that they have not yet found their solution in history. At the beginning of the 1980s Russia finds herself once more in an extremely uncertain situation. The question of her path in history has risen again.

The acuteness of the problem was already apparent during the 1969 discussion about the Slavophils in *Voprosy Literatury*. The discussion was opened with an appeal from the editors to 'look calmly and thoroughly' into the heart of the matter.[96] No calm debate took place, however, nor could such a thing have been managed. 'Ideological rather than literary issues come under discussion,' notes M. Chapman in the American journal *Studies on Soviet Thought*.[97] Opening the debate, A. Yanov, in a critique of the Slavophils' populism, said that this proceeded from the principle: 'before you know "the people" you must love them.' Otherwise, 'you may unexpectedly notice in them not at all what you need to find, you may insult their divine holiness and purity.'[98] On the whole, though, Yanov called for an objective approach to Slavophilism. It was, after all, an oppositionist movement, counterposing 'Russia' and 'the people' to 'authority', which it treated as essentially 'un-Russian'. (Soon Solzhenitsyn was to speak in the same way about the Soviet period, although the Petersburg period would seem to him perfectly national.)

> But, as has often happened in history, one religion called another into existence. Slavophilism, having joined battle with despotism under conditions when there was no strong political opposition, counterposed to it a utopia which consisted essentially of a deification of 'the simple people', a hypertrophied, distorted democratism, a cult of social idolatry. ... A false and impoverished sociological model of reality led to an enormous general mistake in estimation of the political situation and the relation of social forces. This also led to rupture with the real political opposition, inability to achieve unity with the progressive forces, that unity which Herzen strove for so unsuccessfully with the Slavophils. This sort of religion of 'the simple people' ruled out the intelligentsia as a positive force and fatally led its adherents into the ranks of the chief adversary of the intelligentsia – the Black Hundreds, who became, in the last analysis, the heirs of Slavophilism.[99]

Yanov was well aware that the questions being discussed were contemporary when he emphasized that it was because it underestimated democracy and European humanism that Slavophilism degenerated. Although it began as an oppositionist ideology it gradually acquired conservative, pro-status-quo characteristics.

The neo-Slavophils made their voice heard through the notorious critic V. Kozhanov. He began with the wonderful statement that even in olden times the supporters of the idea 'Moscow is the Third Rome', which gave ideological justification for the 'right' of the Russian state to world domination, were 'the most advanced people of their time'.[100] Russian 'originality' was 'not in the least identical with conservatism', Kozhanov affirmed, and one ought not to make nasty parallels with the Black Hundreds.[101]

> A. Yanov sees the main flaw in Slavophilism as the utopian character of their social programme. But was not the Westernists' idea of transplanting European ways on to Russian soil utopian? Or is A. Yanov saying that the revolution of 1905, and, still more, that of 1917, transformed Russia in the image of Western Europe?[102]

sneered Kozhanov, thinking that Yanov would be unable to answer him in the censored press. What was utopian, argued this champion of 'originality', was not the idea of a special Russian road but the hope of bringing European democracy and political freedom on to Russian soil.

Kozhanov lauded 'the thousand-years' tradition of Russian thought' whose exponents were the Slavophils, with their anti-individualism, their 'people's idea'. Western observers noted with interest that 'the religious aspects of Slavophilism were certainly not dismissed by the contributors to the symposium.'[103] It was typical that nobody here took it upon him- or herself to criticize the Slavophils on that account – so great was aversion to the official atheist propaganda.

Finally, Kozhanov drew the general conclusion that it is Western thought, which has given birth to existentialism, that is based on an 'irrationalist, anti-scientific disposition', whereas 'Slavophilism, in contrast to the existentialist philosophy, was imbued with the sense of historicism.'[104] Hitherto it had been supposed that the idea of a possible return to the past which was cultivated by the Slavophils was anti-historical, but for Kozhanov – fully in the spirit of Stalinism – it was the nationalist utopia that was to be declared the only scientific and historical one.

Nevertheless, Yanov contrived to answer Kozhanov's provocative questions by referring to Lenin, who considered the 1917 Revolution not at all a manifestation of Russian 'originality' but rather a product of very distinctive capitalist development, a retarded and uneven Europeanization. 'Lenin was right,' said Yanov categorically, and this time it was his opponents who had to refrain from comment. In the pages of *Voprosy Literatury,* at any rate ...

On the whole, it must be said that despite Yanov's subsequent complaints, the neo-Slavophils of 1969 were as yet too weak and too few to give battle to the left-wing intellectuals in the pages of *Voprosy Literatury,* and there is no reason to consider that Yanov suffered defeat. But the 'originalists' did not lay down their arms, and the social situation favoured them. At the end of the seventies and the beginning of the eighties neo-Slavophil ideas were being proclaimed by that same Kozhanov even more openly than during the discussion in 1969.

It is, in general, very easy to rethink the history of our literature so as to make it correspond better to 'the Russian idea'. All that is needed is 'slightly' to disregard obvious facts. Thus the pessimist Chaadaev, with his revolt against Russia's history, becomes for Kozhanov a crier of the 'supreme superiority of Russian culture over all [!] others'.[105] Arbitrarily plucked-out quotations, assembled without any respect for Chaadaev's spiritual path and ideological striving, are summoned to support this 'stunning' discovery. But the repainting of Chaadaev as a Slavophil is, so to speak, a private hobby of Kozhanov's. Much more interesting are his general theoretical statements. The Russian people – and here Kozhanov refers to Metropolitan Illarion – is the bearer not of 'law' but of 'grace'. Law, Kozhanov explains, means 'spiritual slavery', whereas grace 'is the embodiment of spiritual freedom'.[106] Here we see displayed the superiority of the Russians – free in the 'highest' sense – over the 'limited' Western Europeans. Lest any doubt remain, Kozhanov explains that 'it is not so much a question of Christian as of Russian consciousness.' Further: 'Illarion expressed not a strictly Christian idea, but a Russian one.'[107] He who possesses grace has, in essence, no need of law, so that there is nothing bad about the fact that *Russian history is for the most part a history of lawlessness* (Kozhanov says nothing about the fact that it is also a history of self-sacrificing *struggle for law*).

Kozhanov's arguments were not original. The idea that Russia has no need of laws because it possesses a higher freedom was familiar to the old Slavophils – to K. Aksakov, for instance. In this connection Berdyaev wrote that such a theory 'is blatantly incompatible with historical reality and reveals the unhistorical character of the fundamental ideas of the Slavophils about Russia and the West.'[108] True, this sort of contempt for law was propagated in Russia for centuries and entered into the ideology of official Orthodoxy and the Muscovite autocracy. Thus, for Ivan the Terrible legality was something base and secondary, and lawlessness was not to be reckoned among the worst of sins: 'For if my transgressions are more numerous than the sand of the sea, yet I trust in the grace of God's mercy: he can drown my transgressions with the depths of his mercy.'[109] Instead, revolt, dissidence, variance from the ideology of the Russian state was unpardonable and unjustifiable, and 'the dread Tsar', who believed in the impunity of his transgressions, warned Prince Kurbsky that in denouncing his sovereign's lawlessness he had surely 'destroyed [his] soul' and even 'risen against God'.[110] A similar contempt for law as something beneath consideration is characteristic also of Stalinism.

It has to be admitted that law-consciousness was not able to develop to the Western level in the Russian people, either. But it was precisely against this anti-humanist, anti-law thinking, implanted by the ruling class, that modern Russian democratic culture fought unremittingly. Kozhanov not only presents that barbarism to us as a model, but even depicts it as the overcoming of the 'narrowness' of Western humanism.

The theme of 'spiritual freedom', in contrast to 'law' and 'right' – in short, to civic freedom – is a favourite idea of the Russian 'back-to-the-soil' writers who, instead of combating slavery, seek freedom in it. In Kozhanov we find everything – eulogy of the 'living' Byzantine culture, abuse of 'cosmopolitanism' and Zionism. In general cosmopolitans are, theoretically, 'persons without a homeland', while Zionists are those who call on the Jews 'to find a homeland'. Kozhanov calls Zionism a form of cosmopolitanism. It is not hard to explain this strange use of words. 'Cosmopolitan' and 'Zionist' were both terms used under Stalin as synonyms for Jews ... Anti-Semitism was concealed under phrases about anti-Zionism and anti-cosmopolitanism.

Here we learn that Batu's empire, which destroyed great civilizations, was no worse than the empire of Charlemagne, which laid the foundations of modern Western civilization. According to Kozhanov there was 'no fundamental difference between them'.[111] Generally speaking, the Tatar yoke did no particular harm to Russia, but unfortunately 'the Tatars...fell under the influence of cosmopolitanism'! Consequently, it became necessary to fight against 'the cosmopolitan horde'.[112] Thus Kozhanov is able, with a clear conscience, to justify Russian nationalism, because it developed 'under the pressure of cosmopolitan tendencies'.[113] (The writer forgets to mention that for the last 400 years nationalism was the ruling ideology, and there was no 'pressure' on Russian thought except that of the nationalist state.) Later, Kozhanov makes two or three more historical 'discoveries' – that Russian history is less sanguinary than that of the West, that there was always more creative freedom here than in Western Europe, and so on. In general, as he sees it, Russians were more complete persons than Westerners. Over there were 'handicapped' people, whereas here we had 'personalities' ('blessed with grace'): 'It is impossible not to see that the fullest freedom enjoyed by a handicapped person has nothing to offer a personality whose aim is a way and meaning of life that lies beyond that freedom.'[114]

Kozhanov proved excessively frank, and provoked a sharp outcry. *Pravda* denounced him. Nearly all the serious statements by the New Right in the legal press came to much the same conclusion. But those in power never tried to stop these people's activity altogether, as they did with *Novy Mir*. It may be that *Pravda*'s pronouncement merely increased Kozhanov's prestige among opposition-minded intellectuals who were disenchanted with Marxism. However, it is not only in such skirmishes with the official ideologues that we must seek the reasons for the success of the 'back-to-the-soil' writers. As I have said already, the neo-nationalists raised some real questions which had been little discussed before they appeared.

Russia really is a country of unrealized possibilities. Although rich in resources and with an immense territory and a numerous population, it cannot be numbered among the prosperous countries. So, then, potentialities neglected in the past must be exploited in the future. The only question is – how? What road must we follow in order to make the dream come true? That problem was already there in Pushkin's polemic with Chaadaev. We see it running through the entire history of Russian culture, right down to Tarkovsky's films (his celebrated *Zerkalo* [A

Mirror] makes us all return to this historical riddle). 'The Russian thinkers of the nineteenth century,' wrote Berdyaev, 'pondering over the destinies of Russia and its vocation, continually draw attention to the fact that this potentiality, this lack of expression, this failure to actualize the strength of the Russian people, is a very pledge of the greatness of its future'.[115]

The socialist and Westernizer Herzen and the anti-socialist 'back-to-the-soil' thinker Dostoevsky were united on one point: Russia will bring renewal to Europe. Here their thinking coincides; but here, too, begins the sharp conflict between them. For Dostoevsky this renewal must be linked with a return to the roots, to Orthodoxy, to traditions, to Russia's originality. For Herzen, in order to renew Europe Russia herself must be renewed. Another coincidence of attitudes should be mentioned: Gogol and Dostoevsky are no less anti-bourgeois than Belinsky and Herzen – even more so. Only for them, 'bourgeois-ness' is not a social concept but a geographical, national one. For the later Gogol and for Dostoevsky Russia had become too European, and consequently too *embourgeoisé*. On this point the neo-Slavophils are wholly in agreement with them: for example M. Lobanov, the author of a book about Ostrovsky. He 'hints that "modern times", the rule of the moneybag, is an un-Russian phenomenon, imposed on Russia by certain "dark-haired persons" who consider that, for 100 per cent, "one could even adopt the Orthodox religion".'[116] Here, as A. Anastas'ev indicated transparently enough in discussing books on Russian classical authors written by neo-Slavophils, anti-Europeanism comes very close to anti-Semitism:

> Here this 'dark-haired', 'swarthy' young man with a bald patch and gold-rimmed pince-nez was talking in a railway compartment with 'a sturdy old man with a broad, thick beard, wearing a close-fitting jacket made of blue silk'. This 'swarthy' fellow turned up again in the book. It was he who appeared to Ostrovsky in a bad dream, in the form of a producer who advocated biomechanics.[117]

As the reader will have perceived, Meyerhold is meant. But even that is not the heart of the matter. The blow is struck at the entire Europeanized intelligentsia. The 'Jew', the 'swarthy' person, appears here as a symbol – as an element not only culturally but also ethnically 'alien'. He is the incarnation of something we do not need, brought in from the West. We have already seen where this logic leads.

Karyakin once aptly remarked that for Dostoevsky the socialists, by virtue of their pro-Western cultural orientation, were an example of 'bourgeois-ness'. The neo-Slavophils see the cause of the development of the consumer society and the flourishing of 'bourgeois-ness' in –

Marxism. The ideal social structure for Russia they find somewhere in pre-Petrine times, in the Orthodox monarchy, linked with the traditions of Byzantine Eastern Christianity. This is the essence of what Batkin called their 'nostalgia for the East'.

The tradition in Russian thought that runs from Belinsky and Herzen posed the same questions as the Slavophils, but answered them differently. The idea that Russia has a special role to play in the world was by no means a fantastic Slavophil notion. The largest state in Europe and the whole world cannot but play a special role in the history of the continent and of mankind. Russian society was always developed enough to be able to catch up with the West. Moreover, the one who has to catch up undoubtedly enjoys some advantages. He can see the road traversed by his predecessors, learn from their experience, and traverse that same road more quickly. But these positive potentialities of Russian society were never fully realized. The country's despotic government was the obstacle. Consequently, as Belinsky and Herzen saw it, Europeanization of Russian life, leading to the emancipation of the people, would make possible a historical leap forward. To overcome 'bourgeois-ness' it was necessary to advance still further along the road of the democratization of society, the road of freedom.

On the other hand, in the course of many centuries of European history, now one country and now another 'came to the forefront'. That meant that the people of the country holding that position, in deciding their own fate, to some extent also decided the fate of other peoples. This idea was frequently repeated by Marx, as when he said that Poland had to be liberated in Britain, and Italy in France. Italy in the age of the Renaissance, France in 1789, Britain during the Industrial Revolution determined, in some considerable degree, the whole course of European history. It is not out of the question that events in the next few decades in the USSR will have similar significance. Every time a period of expectation began in our country – when the need for changes was obvious to all, but their precise outlines were not clearly visible – nationalist feelings were strengthened among us. There was an objective basis for this – a presentiment of the all-European importance of what would happen in Russia, its *supranational* dimension.

This does not, of course, signify that the nationalists are right or that nationalism is historically justified. On the contrary, by thrusting the country back and by imposing some 'higher', divine mission upon its people, the nationalists hinder the realization of real potentialities. The growth of Russian nationalism stimulates the development of anti-Russian feeling among the smaller peoples of our country, who are alarmed by this turn of affairs. The general effect of all this is to divide the working people, to disorganize the masses, instead of uniting them against the common foe. Increasingly we see exposed the 'respectable reactionary' essence of neo-Slavophilism of which Batkin spoke.

As the neo-Slavophil movement gathered strength, the idyllic aspect faded into the background and its Black-Hundred features showed through ever more openly.[118] The most reactionary tendency in the 'back-to-the-soil movement' was formed as early as 1968, around the journal *Molodaya Gvardiya*. The chief specific feature of this tendency was its open attempt to unite neo-Slavophilism with Fascism and Stalinism – or, more precisely, to proclaim openly the link between them and to reorientate the Stalinist ideology, strengthening the nationalist and traditionalist motifs in it. What the Stalinist of the 'classical' type keeps quiet about and hides between the lines, the *Molodaya Gvardiya* trend proclaimed openly.

It all began with M. Lobanov's 'Educated Philistinism', in which he spoke in a contemptuous way about today's left-wing intellectuals, giving as an example of an 'educated philistine' the distinguished Russian poet Bulat Okudzhava. Complaining of 'the overflow of so-called education', he fulminated against the non-Russian producers Meyerhold and Efros, as destroyers of traditional values.[119] The dangerous and utterly useless diffusion of knowledge, Lobanov considered, detaches culture from its soil among the people and leads to the destruction of tradition. 'Will there be an end to this havoc?' he asked dramatically, forgetting that he himself was acting as an extreme nihilist and vandal, attacking the best representatives of twentieth-century Russian culture. Just as Kozhanov usually does, Lobanov recalled that Herzen was disappointed with the West – 'forgetting' to mention that, still earlier, Herzen had become disappointed with Russia and never returned to his homeland. Lobanov's article was a first trial flight. Five months later V. Chalmaev published in the same journal his manifesto entitled 'Inevitability'.

This began with a crude mistake by the writer, when he called Faust 'a youth' who 'was ready to make a pact with the Devil'.[120] All that followed was in the same spirit. I do not know whether the millions of Russians who have fallen during the twentieth century in wars, revolutions and modern Thermidors would agree with Chalmaev, but with truly cannibalistic optimism he wrote: 'Fortunately, the history of our homeland is indeed filled with great volcanic eruptions.'[121] Later on we learned (as you see, the nationalists' books are full of discoveries) that everything harmful to us was brought in from the West, that 'realm of everything alien'.[122] Subsequently he summoned to his banner Lenin, Saint Sergius of Radonezh, Dmitri Donskoy, Nekrasov, Yermak, the Patriarch Hermogen, Stenka Razin, Prince

Yaroslav the Wise, Peter I, Ivan the Terrible and, of course, that singer of reaction Konstantin Leont'ev. Even such mutual enemies as 'the clever Patriarch Nikon' and 'Archpriest Avvakum who suffered death by fire' are together here, all expressing the greatness of the Russian soul, before which the European appears petty and 'bourgeois'. Over there they have parliaments, democratic movements and other 'amusing happenings', but in our country, 'once in a hundred years the Russian peasant, coarsely clad and flogged with the knout, stepped forward', and in one day so acted that the whole world was turned upside down.[123] In this, it must be said, there is some truth, but is it only a matter for rejoicing?

Chalmaev also calls Marx to his aid. It turns out that he did not write *Secret Diplomatic History of the Eighteenth Century* against Russia's Tsarist despotism (which is why this book has, to this day, not been published in the USSR) but, on the contrary, spoke 'with profound respect' of 'the soaring genius of the Russian state'.[124]

The main danger, according to Chalmaev, comes from the Left, from the *Novy Mir* crowd. 'Demagogic "progressive" slogans' seduce healthy youngsters, turning them into 'voluntary, selfless cannon-fodder for cynical corrupters'.[125] The struggle between the two systems is presented as a struggle between the Russian principle (which is also Communist) and the Western. Under Stalin and his successors we followed 'that historical track' along which, down to the revolution of 1917, our people 'marched for centuries' and 'are now on their way to Communism'.[126] So that if we are to believe Chalmaev, we have been moving towards Communism since the time of Ivan the Terrible, and Stalin was a great man precisely because he embodied this 'Russian idea'. There is an element of truth in Chalmaev's notions. Stalin was indeed much closer to Ivan the Terrible than to Marx, from whom he took only phraseology. It is to Chalmaev's credit that he was the first of the Stalinists to boast of this openly, but it was on this very point that the Lefts tried to take him at his word. A. Dement'ev, in *Novy Mir*, called Chalmaev & Co. anti-Marxists, and in reply came a collective letter signed by eleven reactionaries of various sorts, published in *Ogonyok*.[127] Yanov wrote that the statement in *Ogonyok* might have created an 'alliance of right-wing factions', but this did not come about, owing to the 'furious polemics' by the classical Stalinists of *Oktyabr'* against the national-Bolshevism of *Molodaya Gvardiya*.[128]

That may be true, but this explanation is insufficient. The essence of the problem was not that nationalist and even Fascist ideology was growing stronger in Russia. That is not a new danger for us: the Black Hundreds appeared in Russia long before Italian Fascism and Hitler's Nazism. The distinctive character of the new danger lies in the fact that out of disappointment with socialism, nationalist and even anti-democratic ideologies have, *for the first time in history*, found support among some groups of our intelligentsia.[129] And it is a question of a struggle for the intelligentsia, because in their struggle to win the masses, the Black Hundreds choose different means from the writing of literary criticism. Today they have turned their attention not to the declassed elements or even to the extreme reactionaries among the statocracy,[130] but to the intellectuals. In order to succeed among the intelligentsia they have, from time to time, to demonstrate opposition and independence. If, in 1969, the neo-Slavophils had united openly with the Stalinists, that would have been suicidal for them. On the contrary, the spiritual kinship between the two groups was carefully concealed.

In this sense, *Molodaya Gvardiya* acted very unwisely. By depicting Stalinism as 'the embodiment of the Russo-Byzantine tradition'[131] it revealed what others had hidden. The nationalists were strong in so far as they presented themselves as bearers of a spiritual alternative and tried to show the liberal Westernizers and Marxists as incapable of breaking with the system. That was why the Orthodox and oppositionist 'back-to-the-soil movement' of *Nash Sovremennik* had such success. True, *Molodaya Gvardiya* also won supporters among the intelligentsia. Solzhenitsyn liked their statements, although he had a number of reservations: the national idea had been 'wrenched into an officially acceptable form', and it was bad to see 'the author now and again rehearsing the Communist oath of loyalty'.[132] Nevertheless, Solzhenitsyn counted eleven (!) points of agreement with *Molodaya Gvardiya* (that is, let me emphasize, with open Stalinists who had even suffered for praising Stalin in their publication – not under Khrushchev but under Brezhnev![132]). The first of these was common hostility to the revolutionary democrats, 'the whole carnival procession from Chernyshevsky to Kerensky', and also contempt for 'this educated rabble which has usurped the title of the intelligentsia'.[134] Later he expressed his attitude to members of the intelligentsia still more sharply, saying that they 'labour day after day, conscientiously and sometimes even with talent, to strengthen our common prison.'[135] This view of the intelligentsia was due mainly to Solzhenitsyn's conviction that all ideas of progress and freedom, democracy and liberalism merely pave the way that leads to totalitarianism and terror. Solzhenitsyn is also indignant at the intellectuals' indifference to 'the national idea', their 'cosmopolitanism', and so on.[136] Curiously enough, many intellectuals applauded this charge, confirming once more the old truth that anti-intellectual sentiments can be fully developed in the minds of intellectuals as well.[137]

On the whole, according to Solzhenitsyn, *Molodaya Gvardiya* had failed to grasp only one thing: 'it is impossible to be both a Communist *and* a Russian.'[138] Consequently the accents should be changed once more, and this nationalism 'purged', for 'their hybrid of "Russianness" and "redness"' was a 'cross between a mongrel and a pig'.[139] Solzehnitsyn seems actually not to have noticed that this ideological miscegenation was not originated by *Molodaya Gvardiya* – that the combination to which he refers is the very essence of Stalinist propaganda. The *Molodaya Gvardiya* tendency merely changed the proportions a little, trying to increase the element of Russian-nationalist swinishness.

In 1969, however, Solzhenitsyn was still an exception. In that period the programme of *Molodaya Gvardiya* was too reactionary and – most important – too frank to win any sympathy from the intelligentsia. During the seventies the ideas of the New Right assumed a different form, more attractive to the intelligentsia. This anti-democratic ideology developed quite fast, in both legal and illegal publications.

As early as the sixties an underground organization was formed in Leningrad with the name All-Russia Social-Christian League for the Liberation of the People (VSKhSON). It preached nationalism and Orthodoxy and sought to base itself on the ideas expressed by Berdyaev in the twenties.[140] In the sixties an organization of this kind was, by general agreement, an exception, much more typical of the period being another Leningrad group – the 'League of Communards' of V. Ronkin and S. Khakaev (the neo-Communists). In the seventies, however, the nationalists already held stronger positions. It is highly instructive that their *samizdat* journal *Veche* was founded by a former socialist, V. Osipov. He still tried to give it at least an outward appearance of liberalism, but suffered defeat, and the journal was taken over by an openly Fascist group – which Yanov considers should be a lesson to moderate neo-Slavophils, if they still cherish 'the illusion that it is possible to combine their nationalism with liberalism.'[141]

The increase in the popularity of the Rights can be followed with particular ease through the example of Ilya Glazunov. In 1967 nobody took him seriously. Volynsky wrote of his lack of talent as an artist as something well known and taken for granted. Yet in July 1978 'Ilyushka' Glazunov was enabled to hold an exhibition of his work at the Manège. *Izvestiya* wrote in 1982 that 'it would be hard to find another artist whose work has attracted so much attention and aroused such lasting interest',[142] and misquoting – as was to be expected – the title of his book (in the newspaper it was given as *Doroga k tebe* [The Road to You]) said of him that Glazunov was a real 'master of painting with words'.[143] Although the book, when it appeared, had aroused only bewilderment, in 1982 this panegyric surprised no one. Glazunov was forgiven even for such flagrant cringing as his portraits of the builders of the Baikal–Amur Railway and the like. In *Sovetskaya Kultura* N. Malakhov praised Glazunov because his works were 'always socially active and sometimes even sharply agitational'.[144] His nationalist propaganda put Glazunov on a good footing: about 600,000 people visited his exhibition (although we do not know how many of them he succeeded in 'agitating').

A few months before the exhibition at the Manège, on 6 December 1977, the nationalists organized heckling of Anatoly Efros when he spoke at the Writers' Club. His only crime, it turned out, was that he, a Jew, had dared to produce classical Russian plays. From the publishing house of *Molodaya Gvardiya* the neo-Slavophils issued, in huge editions, books that gave a new interpretation of Russian literature. The petty tyrant Kabanikha in Ostrovsky's *The Storm* was presented here as 'a custodian of worldly wisdom and of the foundations of family life' (women's liberation being seen as undermining these 'foundations'). Belinsky, it appears, 'expressed lack of confidence in the Russian way of life, depriving it of positive content and significance', while Gogol's aim was to protect Russia from the costly experience of European civilization. And so on.[145] But the object of their special interest was Dostoevsky.

Objectivity demands that it be admitted that they were right to refer to Gogol and Dostoevsky. I have already written about that. However, something else must be borne in mind. The work of both these writers constitutes an extremely complex artistic system. It was not accidental that it was on the basis of Dostoevsky's writings that Bakhtin developed his theory of dialogue. Dostoevsky's books are polyphonic, and the voice of the writer himself is only one of the voices that make themselves heard in these works. The work is higher than the author: the dialogue form of creative thinking, demonstrated later by culturologists, makes this an inexorable law of all creative work (and not only of creative work). The neo-Slavophils fail to hear this polyphony in literature. For them there is only a monologue, a sermon, where actually there is dispute. 'Any multisemantic artistic structure', wrote I. Volgin, in opposition to their view,

> can be subjected to a more or less monosemantic interpretation. *War and Peace, Anna Karenina, Fathers and Sons, Crime and Punishment*, all can, if one so desires, be interpreted (and they often have been) as reactionary works.[146]

The thing is, though, that with such an interpretation, the very essence of art is lost. Sartre once said that it is impossible to write a good anti-Semitic novel. Culturology provides the essential explanation for this. Creative thinking takes the form of a dialogue, whereas reactionary consciousness is always a monologue, the consciousness of a preacher. Sooner or later, this inevitably kills creativity. For this reason, while swearing by the name of Dostoevsky, the neo-Slavophils proved incapable of understanding the artistic meaning of his work.

Which, however, does not prevent them from claiming him as their forerunner. This applies particularly to the group around Solzhenitsyn and Shafarevich, who came together in the symposium *From Under the Rubble* and subsequently expressed their views in a very consistent way in Russian books published abroad. The symposium begins with the excellent words: 'The universal suppression of thought leads not to its extinction, but to distortion, ignorance and the mutual incomprehension of compatriots and contemporaries.'[147] Solzhenitsyn complains that

> the stereotypes of required thought, or rather of dictated opinion, dinned into us daily from the electrified gullets of radio, endlessly reproduced in thousands of newspapers as like as peas, condensed into weekly surveys for political study groups, have made mental cripples of us and left very few minds undamaged.[148]

Alas, all the rest of the symposium, which opened with such a ringing declaration, is written as though to demonstrate, by its own example, how sadly true this is.[149] On all serious theoretical questions Solzhenitsyn and his friends speak from the position of the official ideology:

> *There never was such a thing as Stalinism* (either as a doctrine, or as a path of national life, or as a state system), and official circles in our country [!] as well as the Chinese leaders, have every right to insist on this.[150]

In general, in all controversies, Solzhenitsyn invariably refers to Soviet political textbooks of Stalin's time as books that contain indisputable truth. How could it be otherwise, if such and such a statement appears in the *History of the CPSU: Short Course*? Fully in the spirit of orthodox dogmatics he subverts bourgeois democracy, for the Twentieth Party Congress showed its 'defects' and today the West is 'in a state of political crisis and spiritual confusion'.[151]

Solzhenitsyn directs his hatred against the idea of democratic socialism and Communist reformism, insisting 'that socialism is inherently flawed, that it is altogether unrealizable in a pure form.'[152] Whenever something is said in *samizdat* that is favourable to Marx or Lenin, he sees in this the 'thought processes' of people 'who write for the censor' – even though he had acknowledged that for the opposition of the sixties, 'Marxism was not compulsory ballast required by the censors.'[153] Hatred of socialist ideas easily develops into hatred of democracy – which shows very well, *a negativo*, the profound kinship between the two ideas.

Solzhenitsyn, Shafarevich and the national-Christians see themselves as the heirs of Russian religious philosophy at the beginning of this century, but they are mistaken. The Russian religious philosophers were neither nationalists nor anti-socialists. Vladimir Solovev fought resolutely against nationalism. Berdyaev saw in nationalism 'the alluring temptation of imperialism' generated by Russian messianic thinking, a temptation which had to be overcome. In general he recognized 'the Russian idea' as a fact of national tradition, and tried to include it in a context that was 'universalist' (or, as we should say, internationalist). He was not anti-Marxist, for he frequently emphasized that he owed much to Marx.

The outstanding Russian idealists were opposed to anti-Semitism. Berdyaev considered the Jews the people nearest to the Russians in the spiritual sense: 'it is not merely a matter of chance that precisely in these two peoples there exists a vigorous messianic consciousness.'[154] By an irony of fate, the anti-Semitic VSKhSON proclaimed Berdyaev as its prophet. Such contradictions betray imposture, whether conscious or unconscious. Just as the Stalinists try to cover themselves with the authority of Marxism and socialism, the Rights exploit for their own ends the prestige of Christianity and the names of Berdyaev, Bulgakov, Solovev or Dostoevsky. Whether they actually are Christians is not for me to judge, but I am profoundly convinced that Christianity, like Marxism, is incompatible with nationalism, because they both start from the idea of the human personality, not from that of a chosen people. It is just this universalism of Christianity that has ensured its success as a world religion. The lie of the New Right about the 'Christian' character of their ideas is akin to the official lie about the 'Marxist' character of the neo-Stalinist despotism.

To Solzhenitsyn the ideology of the system is even more hateful than the system itself. In this respect he is a typical exponent of the world-view of the new 'back-to-the-soil movement'. Agursky, analysing their literature published legally in the Soviet Union, has noted the basic identity of their ideas with those of Solzhenitsyn. This literature 'is not aimed at those who are trying to change the political system. The political system is a matter of indifference to them.'[155] These ideas are not due to the barbed wire of the censorship:

It is not difficult to observe that the movement's positive programme coincides on many points with the ideas of Solzhenitsyn, especially as expressed in his *Letter to Soviet Leaders*. We find here the same indifference to the political system. They both hate the ideology alone. ...[156]

In fact Solzhenitsyn writes, summing up the significance of his *Letter to Soviet Leaders* – the first manifesto of the New Right to become known world-wide: 'I put it to them: get rid of the Communist ideology, if only of that for the time being.'[157] The quotation is interesting, not because it shows how Solzhenitsyn's style has degenerated since he has been living as an *émigré* publicist but because it is indicative politically. If it is only a matter of 'getting rid of the Communist ideology', the Soviet system may be fully transformable into an 'authoritarian order based on love of mankind'.[158] Thus Solzhenitsyn actually admits that the Communist ideology does not in the least express the essential nature of the system, but is some sort of extraneous 'weapon' it uses in fighting for the sympathy of Western public opinion, and so on. But the most important thing is that Solzhenitsyn's idea of resorting to the proposal of a dialogue with the statocracy is inherently logical: they have much in common,[159] above all – however paradoxical this may be – ideology. Ernest Mandel is quite right when he says that Solzhenitsyn is 'to a large extent himself a prisoner of the Stalinist ideology'.[160] The publication of the *Letter to Soviet Leaders* and the statements by anti-Marxist dissidents (especially the *émigrés*) evoked dismay and bewilderment not only among the Lefts but also in Western liberal circles and among Soviet intellectuals faithful to the ideals of 1956. 'Indeed, Solzhenitsyn appears to distrust the very freedom for which he has so long fought,' and his views 'in a curious way reflect the Soviet dogma on which he was raised,' we read in the American conservative periodical *Commentary*.[161] 'This is a kind of utopia in which the complex and dynamic problems of society are settled once and for all ...'[162] Thinking of this sort is typical of dogmatists. He seeks to oppose the Soviet ideology, yet 'he arms himself with the same weapons, uses similar techniques and adopts a comparable manner,' writes A. Besançon.[163]

Anna Akhmatova, too, 'when asked one day about Solzhenitsyn, uttered the words *sovetskii chelovek*, a Soviet man.'[164] In Besançon's view, Solzhenitsyn, having been formed in the Stalin school and by the official ideology, turns to nineteenth-century Russia in the hope of overcoming thereby his own 'Sovietness' but is capable only of seeing in past history, through an irony of fate, those ideas that are close to Stalin's.

'Certain accusations by Solzhenitsyn and Shafarevich oddly resemble in tone the ideological campaigns of the period between the thirties and the fifties,' wrote the Hungarian Marxists Bence and Kis.[165] 'The source, paradoxically, of Solzhenitsyn's notion is the vulgar Soviet view of 1917 as a milestone of good,' wrote the Soviet *émigrés* Solovyov and Klepikova in the American left-wing periodical *Dissent*.[166] 'Solzhenitsyn wishes to be an inverted Lenin,' concludes Besançon.[167] But the Lenin he imitates is not the real Lenin of history, it is the Lenin of the Stalinist textbooks.

Such quotations could be multiplied, for on this matter people of very different views find themselves in agreement. The real theoretical interest, however, lies not in polemicizing against the New Right and convicting them of repeating official dogmas, but in trying to understand how they 'came to this way of life'. People change, and their views with them. It is not enough for us merely to record the turn to the Right by many oppositionist intellectuals; it is more interesting to analyse the psychological and ideological mechanisms that have brought this turn about. Furthermore, when we look more closely we perceive that the 'Solzhenitsyn syndrome' is a very much more widespread malady among oppositionists than appears at first sight. Many even of those who do not agree with his views are very close to his method of thinking.

Official and Oppositional Dogmatism

I have already said that the spiritual crisis of the Russian intelligentsia after 1968 can be compared only with the crisis set off by *Vekhi*. The present crisis, however, is deeper and graver. It has been produced by the combination of two interacting processes of disintegration – the crisis of the pseudo-Communist official ideology and the crisis of Communist reformism, a sort of spiritual bankruptcy of both government and opposition. Isaac Deutscher wrote that almost all those who broke with Stalinism did so, in the first place, in the name of 'true Communism':

> Sooner or later these intentions are forgotten or abandoned. Having broken with a party bureaucracy in the name of Communism, the heretic goes on to break with Communism itself. He claims to have made the discovery that the root of the evil goes far deeper than he at first imagined, even though his digging for that 'root' may have been very lazy and very shallow. He no longer defends socialism from unscrupulous abuse; he now defends mankind from the fallacy of socialism. ... He remains a sectarian. He is an inverted Stalinist. He continues to see the world in white and black, but now the colours are differently distributed. As a Communist he saw no difference between Fascists and Social Democrats. As an anti-Communist he sees no

difference between Nazism and Communism. Once, he accepted the Party's claim to infallibility; now he believes himself to be infallible. Having once been caught by the 'greatest illusion', he is now obsessed by the greatest disillusionment of our time.[168]

Those prophetic words were uttered in 1955, before the Twentieth Party Congress, the Hungarian Revolution, the 'Prague spring' or the publication of *The Gulag Archipelago*. People shaped by Stalin's totalitarianism are often unable, despite all their efforts, to get rid of the birthmark of Stalinism. 'Character and psychological make-up remain the same as a rule, whatever the changes in ideology', wrote L. Kopelev.[169]

Stalin in his underground activity, in the civil war, and at the peak of his autocratic power, never lost the rhetorical style, the oily cunning and the boorish rudeness of the seminarist. Something similar is observable in our own day in the case of many deserters from Stalinism and Leninism. The more radical and fanatical their new views, the more firmly they retain many of the distinctive features of the world-view and moral consciousness – or, rather, subconsciousness – they acquired in Soviet schools and institutes.[170]

This was said about Maksimov, after *Saga About Rhinoceroses*. When Zhores Medvedev asked a mutual acquaintance to describe Maksimov to him in a few words, he got more or less the same reply: 'Even after rejecting the ideology, symbols and sacred objects of the Stalin system', Maksimov 'fully retained the same method of thinking.'[171]

Plekhanov frequently reminded his readers that ideology cannot be understood in isolation from psychology. Stalinism suppressed reason, replacing it with irrational emotions and faith in absolute ideals. 'This irrational emotionalism dominates the evolution of many an ex-Communist', wrote Deutscher.[172] To Maksimov and to many opponents of the system we may apply the words of this British historian, written in 1955:

His emotional reaction against his former environment keeps him in its deadly grip and prevents him from understanding the drama in which he was involved or half-involved. The picture of Communism and Stalinism he draws is that of a gigantic chamber of intellectual and moral horrors. Viewing it, the uninitiated are transferred from politics to pure demonology. Sometimes the artistic effect may be strong – horrors and demons do enter into many a poetic masterpiece; but it is politically unreliable and even dangerous. Of course, the story of Stalinism abounds in horror. But this is only one of its elements; and even this, the demonic, has to be translated into terms of human motives and interests. The ex-Communist does not even attempt the translation.[173]

Evidently Trotsky was not exaggerating when he warned that if such men as Stalin come to power, socialism will be compromised for ever. The spectacle of a revolution degenerated and of Thermidorian terror undermines faith in revolutionary ideals more than any hostile propaganda and more, even, than military or political defeat of socialism. Karl Radek was prophetic when he said in 1918:

> If, contrary to expectation, the Russian Revolution loses its socialist character and betrays the interests of the working class, this blow will have the most frightful consequences for the future of the revolution in Russia and throughout the world.[174]

But of course, it is not only a matter of the compromising of an idea. The bureaucratic system deprived many, including our intellectuals, of the habit of thinking objectively, calmly and without prejudice. From tendentious exaltation of 'true Bolsheviks' in the sixties they hurtled in the seventies into no less tendentious anti-Bolshevism. After the publication of *The Gulag Archipelago* they started to talk about the Red Terror. That was indeed a terrible page in the history of the revolution. Lenin's terror did really prepare the way for Stalin's and it was no accident that such Marxists as Rosa Luxemburg, Karl Kautsky and L. Martov, regardless of the difference in their political views, all condemned the terror. Not to mention the terror, or to play down its importance, is dishonest, but those who wish to see in it the essence of the revolution show bias. After all, there was also a White terror, about which now the same people who were previously silent about the Red Terror prefer to say nothing. Their bias obliged the New Right to discard 'unacceptable' facts.[175] They do not even try to answer the question: Why was Bolshevism victorious? (Was it not because the Whites showed themselves to be even worse than the Reds?) They are incapable of looking at events *historically* – that is, from a position above the contending sides of the past. Trotsky's cruelties enable them, so to speak, to forget about the savageries of General Slashchev. The Red Terror is condemned not because it was terror but because it was Red. The humanist point of view is quite alien to the New Right, as Roy Medvedev points out: 'They find Kornilov or Denikin preferable to Lenin and Sverdlov, White terror preferable to Red.'[176] Hence the amazing statements by Solzhenitsyn, Bukovsky, Maksimov and even Brodsky[177] concerning terror in Latin America. The atrocities of the military junta in El Salvador, which has turned the entire country into a real Gulag, can in their view be justified in the name of the 'sacred' cause of a struggle against Communism. The end justifies the means; of that they have no doubt, despite what history teaches us. The ends change; the means remain.

Sometimes, to cover themselves, they claim that things are 'better' in El Salvador or in Chile than in the Soviet Union. That is, frankly, a lie: socialist oppositionists, Christian democrats and liberals are murdered in their dozens every day in Latin America.[178] To justify these murders by reference to the Stalin terror is sacrilege, but it is a fully logical procedure. The Stalinists always considered that repressions in their own country could be justified by repressions elsewhere. Here again the New Right is imitating the Stalinist type of thinking, without considering that *no* political murders can be justified.

Anti-Stalinism will not, in itself, make someone either a humanist or a democrat. 'The anti-hangman', wrote Pomerants, 'bears within himself a charge of fury that will tomorrow produce a new hangman. ... In the realm of the soul, *anti* will not do at all.'[179] Rebels themselves feel the need for some positive idea. It is natural for human beings to strive towards ideals, and when an ideal collapses the world begins to seem insipid and meaningless. 'It is difficult', writes the British philosopher-economist Schumacher,

> to bear the resultant feeling of emptiness, and the vacuum of our minds may only too easily be filled by some big, fantastic notion – political or otherwise – which suddenly seems to illumine everything and to give meaning and purpose to our existence. It needs no emphasis that herein lies one of the great dangers of our time.[180]

There have been people like Bukovsky who have tried to get by without any ideology at all, but the experience of Bukovsky himself, who eventually turned into an *ideologist*, showed that this does not work. Spasmodic attempts are begun to find or construct such an idea, but naturally, it is constructed from the ideological and philosophical material that is to hand. 'Primitive people, without intellectual needs,' writes Bukovsky,

> are inclined to interpret the Soviet newspapers simply *à rebours*, as though seen in a mirror, so to speak. If somebody is denounced, that means he must be a good man, and if he is praised, he must be bad. ... All of which is partly true, but such over-simplification deprives the reader of much of the news, leaving only the bald fact. What remains important are *nuances*, scales, degrees – in short, information.[181]

Although Bukovsky is trying to better his world-view, he takes the official propaganda as his starting point. If you reverse this, you see 'the bald fact', and later you can improve on this with 'nuances, scales, degrees'. He 'knows' how to read the newspapers, and is sure that he can extract correct information from them. Here he shows himself to be a slave to propaganda, for he agrees to form his view of the world on the basis of the picture presented to him. *He does not think about the world but, instead, rethinks propaganda.* In this respect the ordinary Soviet person, who believes some things he reads in the paper but not others, is much more of a critic than is a dissident of the Bukovsky type, who believes everything, but in his own way. In starting to form his 'new' ideology in this way, the dissident resembles those thinkers of whom Marx wrote that in their revolt against the dominant theory, they 'contest it from its own standpoint'.[182]

The logic of the history of ideology – and, more precisely, the inertia of thought – means that although dogmas fall, dogmatism remains. The dogmatic type of thinking proves highly tenacious of life, and new dogmas arise to replace the discredited ones. Thus criticism of ideology is accompanied by the creation of dogmas, the creation not of new ideas but of an anti-ideology which lives by that same logic of *unilinearity* as the official doctrine. In place of the 'absolute' values consecrated by the state we get anti-values, and as an ideal of human conduct, instead of the Semitic commissar of 1918, the anti-Semitic Black-Hundred-ist of 1908.

What is this dogmatic style of thinking? Its main feature, in my view, is an endeavour to understand the world by starting from some ready-made general formula which 'explains everything' and cannot be doubted. It is impossible to refute such a formula by rational arguments, because any rational information that contradicts the dogma is re-thought from the standpoint of that dogma and thereby rendered harmless to it. Debates with a dogmatist are fruitless: in his own eyes, at least, he always emerges from them victorious. The formula must be simple and extremely general. For example: 'all Jews are dishonest', or 'all Bolsheviks are scoundrels'. You may adduce as many counterarguments as you like – talk about Jews who were renowned for their honesty, or about Bolsheviks who never committed any scoundrelism. In reply you hear that of course, the Jews mentioned were just hypocrites who carefully concealed their dishonesty and the Bolsheviks of whom you spoke simply committed their scoundrelly acts in such a way that nobody noticed. No rational arguments can take effect in such a debate.[183]

Here, for example, we have Bukovsky, who is convinced that 'Stalin, with all his brutality, was an organic consequence of Leninist ideas and of the very idea of socialism itself.'[184] If that formula is beyond question, then all the ideas of 'Eurocommunism', the 'Prague spring' and so on, are so much idle chatter and dangerous demagogy.[185] Hence the 'self-evident' conclusion, which is specially formulated in Bukovsky's book *Pis' ma russkogo puteshestvennika*,[186] that the Western socialists, and even Social Democrats, are no better than the Communists: they are all tarred with the same brush! Here we have a generalization of the 'You're-all-swine' type, and here lies the root of the evil. This is, if you like, the methodological foundation of foundations of dogmatism, its 'cage': all ideological phenomena that are alien to you are thrown into one heap and without further analysis, without proof, are wiped out. It is the same logic that enabled Stalin and his assistants to set up the 'amalgam' trials. If you do not agree with the Party line, you are not a Communist. If you are not a Communist, that means that you are a supporter of capitalism. A supporter of capitalism – that means an enemy of the people, and ... to the execution wall with him! We see the same logic in the case of the Russian New Right, only now 'all the other way round'. Every Communist without exception bears, for them, responsibility for the crimes of Stalin: between Lenin, Trotsky, Gramsci and Togliatti, on the one hand, and Stalin, Beria and Yezhov on the other, there is no difference. 'Socialism with a human face' is based, as they see it, on the same principles as the Gulag, and Western socialists are preparing 'an easy transition to Communist rule'.[187] All Lefts are Communists, all Communists are hangmen, and ... to the wall with them! He has yet to reach that final generalization which was made in the immortal novel by Ilf and Petrov, *Diamonds To Sit On*: 'All Jews are lefties', although some people are even now ready to draw that conclusion, too. To be sure, nobody has gone to that wall yet; nor, God grant, will they. But Maksimov is already threatening to put the Social Democrats on trial. One is made a little uneasy when one reads in Bukovsky's book how he and his friends, when young, dreamed of being issued with 'brand-new machine-guns'.[188] To tell the truth, I should not want to see a machine-gun in Bukovsky's hands.

However, it is not Solzhenitsyn, Bukovsky and Shafarevich who ought to be blamed here, but the system that disfigured their minds. Given the personal qualities of each of them – bravery, frankness, resolution – we should have preferred to have these men on our side. Reactionary ideas are often upheld by honest and talented people. As Yanov has written, 'for people in Russia, Solzhenitsyn was – and for many remains – the conscience of the nation.'[189] 'Isaich' can be happy: he has managed to do what *Vekhi* could not do – turn rightward at least a section of the Russian intelligentsia. But that was possible only when a despotic state was striving with all its might to present itself as 'Left', 'progressive', and so on. I have already said a great deal here about the limitedness of the ideology of 'true Communism' and the fact that it was just that limitedness of the opposition's ideas in the sixties that prepared for the growth of the New Right ideology in the seventies. It needs only to be added that *in a certain way* the ruling ideas of the opposition in the seventies were already a step backward in comparison with the previous period. 'True Communism' was connected with East European 'revisionism' and questioned, first, the legality of official practice and, later, some elements of official theory. There was a critical principle at work in it, even if this was insufficiently developed. The new anti-Communism lacks that critical 'sense of questioning'. It may therefore be the case that, in fact, the liberation of consciousness played a greater role in the sixties than in the seventies. Among the illusions of the sixties there was evidently the illusion of victory over dogmatism. The Brezhnev era showed that dogmatism was still powerful in the minds of the opposition intelligentsia.

What is worst is that the dogmatist has been convinced only of the practical and outward collapse of his dogma. This does not always lead to his recovery, for the dogma may easily assume a new form. The difference between official and oppositional dogmatism[190] is that the former is more fully worked out and, if you like, richer in ideas. Down below, several different antagonistic forms of dogmatism are found. Thus, a single official ideology engenders several shadow ideologies at the same time. Such pluralism is said to be a positive phenomenon, but dialogue is impossible between the opposition dogmatists and theoretical discussion always degenerates into ill-tempered squabbling (only Western observers, it seems, cannot understand 'why Russians quarrel so much'). The diversity of the opposition's dogmatisms can, in its turn, be explained by the specific character of the official dogmatism.

The revival of Russian nationalism, for example, is not – as Yanov supposes – connected with a survival into our time of the tradition of Leont'ev and Pobedonostsev, but with the crisis and *break-up* of the official ideology. A. Lim wrote that Stalinist 'Marxism-Leninism' was in fact a 'complex conglomerate' of various ideological elements – nationalism, autocracy, socialism, Russian religiosity and so on,

> cemented into a whole by hatred of the representatives of all the listed tendencies to liberalism in the nineteenth and twentieth centuries. When Stalin and his doctrine were dethroned, this caused a deep crack to appear in the conglomerate, and the Stalinist ideology quickly began to break up.[191]

During the 'purges' of the thirties and the 'struggle against cosmopolitanism' the official doctrine absorbed elements of Pobedonostsev's national demagogy, the idea of 'the Russian soul' and 'popular' despotism (glorification of Ivan the Terrible, and so on). In the period when the official ideology was breaking up, losing its integral character, those elements recovered independent existence, detaching themselves and acquiring new life. A 'Thermidorian' ideology cannot, by virtue of its historical nature, be anything but an attempt to synthesize revolutionary and reactionary ideas. 'True Communism' tried to separate out the revolutionary ideas, while the New Right tries to develop the reactionary part of the official 'heritage'. But both try to find an alternative to the ruling ideology within the framework of that ideology. Both groups look back and see a golden age in the past, 'some before Stalin, some before Lenin, yet others before Nikolai, and still others before Peter, or before the Tatars, or even before Prince Vladimir in the tenth century'.[192] Solzhenitsyn, for example, blames a lot on Patriarch Nikon and the church reform of the seventeenth century, which undermined old-time piety.

For all the diversity of oppositional dogmatics, it is possible to discern in them some obligatory basic ideas borrowed from the official dogmatism.

1. The way the world is developing is seen as a conflict between two systems. The world's future depends on the outcome of this conflict and it is perceived in absolute moral categories, as a conflict between good and evil. This idea has been formulated most categorically by A. Zinoviev, who says that it is a conflict 'between two powers – the power of civilization (anti-Communism) and the power of anti-civilization (Communism).'[193]

2. The USSR is a model of victorious socialism and is its *classical* model. We can again quote from Zinoviev: 'Just as England was, in its time, the classical model of capitalist society, so the Soviet Union now presents the classical model of Communist society.'[194] Zinoviev stresses that he sees no difference between socialism and Communism. Every assertion that the Soviet system is not fully socialist, or that it is not socialist at all, is, for Zinoviev, 'either the result of clinical imbecility or else simply a dishonest allegation made in order to secure a more comfortable and prominent position in society'.[195] Such 'delusions' are punished by the statocracy with compulsory confinement in psychiatric clinics (clinical imbecility) and with imprisonment (dishonest allegation). Fortunately the New Rights have, as yet, no such possibilities available to them.

3. Parliamentary democracy is possible only as part of the capitalist system. V. Sokirko (Burzhuademov) devoted a whole book to supporting this idea – the cornerstone of Stalinist ideology – and showed that socialist democracy 'cannot exist'.[196] There is no democratic road to socialism, and in any country where the Lefts come to power 'the results will be similar to what happened in our country' (A. Zinoviev). In short, democratic socialism is inconceivable.

4. The present regime in the USSR is the legitimate heir of the 1917 Revolution and its leaders are 'true Leninists'.

Under pressure from socialist criticism, the New Rights appear more and more often in the unenviable role of last defenders of the ideological dogmas of Stalinism. All these ideas can be found, in a different formulation, in the official textbook on the Party's history, and the present state ideology is unthinkable without them. They are all in flagrant contradiction with reality. It is hard nowadays to find serious political scientists who would say that political conflict in the world can be reduced to the conflict between two systems (because new centres of gravity have appeared) or who would doubt that the social processes going on *within* the societies of East and West are of more decisive importance for the future of mankind than is the opposition between these two societies. But that is not the point. Of Solzhenitsyn it has long been known that his ideology is Stalinism inside out. However, he is not alone in this. The ideas of Burzhuademov or Zinoviev can provide a much more significant example of hopeless dogmatism.

Among the opposition's ideologues Zinoviev appears rather in the role of sceptic, but his statements excellently illustrate E. Il'enkov's idea that 'scepticism is the reverse side of dogmatism.'[197] The same thing has happened with Zinoviev as happened once with Proudhon. Marx observed that for the French Proudhon represented 'German' philosophy, while for the Germans he stood for French political economy.[198] It is like that with Zinoviev. Literary critics say that his books are worthless from the literary point of view, but not a great deal ought to be expected of them because they are not so much literature as sociology; whereas sociologists and historians say that in his works there are, of course, no original or valuable sociological ideas, but, after all, they are not sociology but satire, and one ought not to expect to find ideas in them.[199] Here it must be noted that banality does not mean at all an absence of social ideas: banal ideas are the easiest to master, especially if they are presented in an unusual form. Banality is something which is self-evident and has no need to convince the reader of its truth. For Zinoviev it is enough merely to set forth in a more amusing way *those very ideas* which the state propaganda apparatus already makes it its business to drum into our poor heads.

When we read Zinoviev's books, what is most immediately striking is the psychological kinship between the author and some of his heroes. Zinoviev's own world-view is analogous to that of official statocratic circles – or, more precisely, of a certain section of the statocracy. The key figure at the end of the seventies and in the eighties is not the old Stalinist but the young (not over sixty) careerist of the Brezhnev era, the 'young guard' of the statocracy. This man knows all about the system but coexists cynically with it, exploiting its benefits while at the same time sneering at the 'cattle' – that is, the masses at whose expense he lives (these masses, in his opinion, deserve nothing better). The readership among whom Zinoviev's books had a phenomenal success consisted of young people from privileged families who were taking their first steps on the glorious road of a bureaucratic career. They are ironical, but their irony is that 'drug for the privileged' of which I wrote earlier. In Zinoviev's books these young people found their New Testament and guide to action. This it was that created the fashion for 'Zinovievism' among Moscow's elite. Most probably Zinoviev did not plan this turn of events, but it could not have gone any other way. Let us look at him more closely.

There is one small defect in this writer's satirical works: they are not funny. This quality cannot, of course, be asked of a writer of 'strictly scientific' works on Soviet society, and it is not asked. True, Zinoviev's cynicism is sometimes taken for irony, but that is a mistake. Irony is constructive to the extent that it is *self-critical.* The history of German Romanticism showed that irony is capable of producing long-lived philosophical ideas and stimulating the development of social consciousness in so far as it brings everything into doubt, itself included, constantly refuting its own conclusion, schemas and dogmas. It is fluid. But Zinoviev's works, despite the high-flown anti-dogmatist rhetoric, constitute a unique example of *pure* dogmatism. This dogmatic consciousness, like the Stalinist variety, is *self-canonizing.* Unlike the 'run-of-the-mill' dogmatist, who relies on some past authority (Jesus, Mohammed, Marx, Lenin, Bakhtin, and so on), Zinoviev and Stalin have no need of that, for both utter finished formulas which are held to be great 'discoveries' and the highest truth. Each builds an elementary schema which seems to him self-sufficient, and all his further constructions stay within its framework. For any 'new' idea to be proved it is enough that it be brought within the already-formulated schema. Arguments, analysis of social processes, generalizing of facts, study of other people's views and examination of the constructive information contained in them (without which science is inconceivable) – all of that is unnecessary. A different point of view is declared to be false as soon as it fails to correspond to the schema. Such a theoretical 'model' is indeed logical in its own way, but Stalin's works and the official textbooks are very logical! Zinoviev's 'logic' is of the same sort as Stalin's. It is often said that our official publications are full of absurdity. That is not true. They are extremely logical. They have only one thing wrong with them: they contradict reality, but they contain no other contradictions. Reread *Problems of Leninism* or any of Stalin's speeches and compare it with any statement by Zinoviev, and you will see that the one 'great theoretician' is like the other. The 'friend and teacher' has found a worthy pupil.[200]

Stalin's dogmatism is, of course, somewhat more creative – after all, it is the original from which the copy was taken. But Zinoviev's cynicism turns this dogmatism inside out – or, rather, turns it over and *stands it on its feet*. Just that, for every other Soviet statocrat who began his career after 1953 thinks in this way. In that sense, at least half of our bureaucratic apparatus consists of convinced 'Zinovievists'.

'I consider that our society and our government are healthy phenomena. This does not mean that I like them. Nor that I dislike them,' says Zinoviev. 'My attitude to them is that of an observer. ....'[201] The existing system is an objective reality. It has to be accepted as it is, and attempts to change it are senseless. Nobody needs such change, either, apart from a handful of intellectuals who have adopted Western ideas: 'The majority of our country's inhabitants have no need of that.'[202] In the last analysis, what we have is 'genuine sovereignty of the people'.[203] There are 'no grounds for hoping' for any changes, and with this system and this society they are essentially impossible.[204] Talk to any successful bureaucrat of the post-Stalin generation and you will hear the same, only better put, because Zinoviev's frightful style makes it rather hard to read him.[205] Today's statocrats are by no means hostile to freedom, in principle. They merely 'know very well' that in our country democracy 'is out of the question'. They are not hostile to the West – indeed, they idealize it. Wolfgang Leonhard has observed that where Soviet bureaucrats of the post-Stalin generation are concerned, 'nobody thinks about pollution of the environment, alienation and relative impoverishment' in connection with the West.[206] Sometimes they frankly admit that they might prefer to be managing directors of concerns or deputies of some right-wing party in the West rather than members of the CPSU, but since they live here, they have to conform to the rules of the game (it's all the same, anyway, since no change is possible) – 'if you live with the wolves you have to howl as they do,' and so on. Just as in Brecht's *Threepenny Opera*: we, too, would be good if circumstances were not as they are.

The official ideological schema aspires to 'a Marxist aspect', but Zinoviev simply tears off the illusory 'Marxist' wrapper and shows us this conception of Soviet society without any celebration-day rhetoric. He deals with Stalin as the young Marx dealt with Hegel. He does this, to be sure, unconsciously and therefore foolishly. It is unfortunate, too, that the material is of different qualities in the two cases, and the level of philosophical knowledge involved is, to put it mildly, not the same.

At first sight Zinoviev is like the boy in the fable who shouted out that the King was naked. But what is specific to the situation is that the King in the fable thought that he was clothed, whereas the Soviet 'Kings' ostentatiously stroll about stark naked, although they cannot themselves announce the fact. In the Soviet case the 'boy' and the 'naked King' think in the same way. What the crowd thinks in this case is another question.

Zinoviev's initiative is, of course, also useful and proper. But it does not provide us with a spiritual 'way out, and he does not try to provide this. He argues that the system will last for centuries, nay longer: 'the thing may go on for thousands of years',[207] because he shares all the illusions of the ruling statocracy concerning the unshakeability of the regime. But even if he is right, even if it lasts for ever – where is the *spiritual* alternative,[208] where is the critical analysis of *real* social processes, of technology, economics, social structure? Zinoviev, like the Soviet ideologues, is incapable, with the best will in the world, of undertaking that task, because he sees his task as fitting the facts into a preconceived scheme, and not as analysing them. This results in terrible short-sightedness. Discussing the impossibility or the needlessness of 'a positive programme of change',[209] he omits even to mention how the very acute economic crisis of the 1980s put the question of a reform programme on the agenda not only for the opposition but also for the statocracy. It must again be stressed that this is not due to any feeble-mindedness on Zinoviev's part – that is how he prefers to explain opinions different from his own, by stupidity and mercenary considerations – but to the faultiness of the entire system of thinking he has adopted.

He says much and at length about the difference between the 'ideology' and the 'scientific' approach (the sole representative of the latter in relation to the USSR is one A. Zinoviev). But he does not even mention the chief difference – namely, that the former relies on intellectual schemas and the second on scientific facts.[210] In Zinoviev's books we simply cannot find any sociological information other than what any of us obtains from everyday life. But such examples taken from the life of a highly paid Moscow intellectual worker are useful as illustrations – no more than that. Such examples and illustrations can always be fitted into practically any schema (life is so variegated). Soviet official ideologues always proceed in this way: as a rule, they do not lie but cite a certain number of *selected* real facts.

Thus Zinoviev alleges, categorically, that most of the people of the USSR prefer the one-party system. It may be that this is indeed the case, although in reality the one-party system causes a good deal of irritation among the working class – which consists (contrary to Zinoviev's view) not only of idiots – since it crushes more and more painfully their *political* rights.[211] But what is most important is not this but the fact that Zinoviev overlooks something which has been generally known for the last two or three thousand years: that *people's views change*. On the eve of the 1905 Revolution 'the majority' of Russians were supporters of the autocracy, but eighteen months of political crisis radically altered their ideology and even their psychology. In one day, the shooting on 9 January 1905 turned hundreds of thousands of previously loyal subjects into enemies of the throne. We should not wish our people to learn through such bloody lessons, but in any case the political and economic crisis is leading to an immense and *rapid* social enlightenment of the masses.

But here we have Zinoviev saying:

> The overwhelming majority of the Soviet people would reject a system of self-management in the enterprises, even if it were to be imposed on them by force, and such a system would degenerate into an empty formality, or else into a system of gangsterism.[212]

In reality, experiments in self-management have frequently been carried out in the USSR and have produced excellent results. Even in official circles they recognize that, given the increased cultural level of the workers, it is necessary to tackle afresh 'the question of their participation in the management of social production',[213] and that without this it will be difficult to count on serious progress in either the economic or the social sphere. The journal *EKO* wrote about 'the great social repercussions and growing number of supporters' of these experiments,[214] but admitted that they were usually cut short by the apparatus. At a certain stage of the experiment self-management inevitably comes into contradiction with the existing system of economic and political organization, and is therefore dangerous to the statocracy. Zinoviev is not interested in such facts; for him schemas are enough. Incidentally, note this about the way he writes: he never says 'from my personal observation', 'possibly', 'it seems to me', 'I am afraid that', and so on. No, he at once gives a conclusive decision in the name of 'the overwhelming majority of the Soviet people'. Such clichés seem convincing to us because they are familiar: this is how *Pravda* speaks.

Every society, of course, generates certain social types in massive numbers. Zinoviev constantly repeats this idea as though he himself had discovered it, although the problem of *social character* was studied in Marxist social science a very long time ago.[215] In complex systems like the Soviet one, however, one is obliged to deal with many different types: all the more because even in simpler systems, a particular type of *dissident* is always formed. Finally, among the many types shaped by the system, there is also the type of civilized conformist. He cannot fail to be aware of the crying defects in the regime, but conviction that it is impossible to change the system gives him the opportunity for moral self-justification. The ineradicability of social baseness is made the explanation of individual baseness. Consequently, as L. Kolakowski has noted, propagating the idea that the statocratic system is firm and unreformable is not only contrary to the facts but also immoral[216] – besides, Zinoviev's ideology ultimately assumes conservative features[217] which ensure its success among the Soviet middle strata and the 'enlightened' bureaucracy. Essentially, this is no special ideology but a mere collection of commonplaces.

And so the circle is closed. From denial of the system we arrive at acceptance of it as an accomplished fact. Zinoviev's views constitute one attempt – God grant that it be the last – to explain what has happened in the USSR by turning the state ideology inside out (in this case, openly and consciously). These intellectual games played with dogmatism are futile. Zinoviev and Solzhenitsyn cannot stand each other, but they have something in common: the official ideology hypnotizes them, as a snake does a rabbit. They approach it from different sides, but cannot tear themselves away from it.

On the whole, the politico-ideological principles of Stalinism have proved less tenacious of life than its philosophical *conception of the world* (if one can speak of philosophy in this connection) – its presentation of 'socialism' and 'Marxism'. A factual lie is always easier to refute than a 'theoretical' one. As Schopenhauer said:

> If in the representation of perception *illusion* does at moments distort reality, then in the representation of the abstract *error* can reign for thousands of years, impose its iron yoke on whole nations, stifle the noblest impulses of mankind; through its slaves and dupes it can enchain even the man it cannot deceive.[218]

A paradoxical question arises. Democratic man and democratic ideology can develop only under democratic conditions. But if this were so, not a single democracy would ever have appeared. It is not a simple matter at all.

The history of Soviet dissidence in the 1970s confirms once more, albeit in a very special way, the classical Marxist idea that the ruling ideas of every society are the ideas of the ruling class. In trying to create an opposition ideology or to work out a new way of thinking, Soviet man is obliged to use the cultural material of the official ideology. This is the logic of history. Philosophy and culture have to use the material left to them by their predecessors. Literature brought in illegally from abroad, together with *samizdat,* were – in any case in the seventies – unable to *shape* the spiritual climate in the country; they merely *reflected* it. Is there no way out?

There is a way out. The official ideology is not the only possible source of cultural material in our society. The alternative sources are limited, but they do exist. The opposition can derive this material from the traditions of European (including Russian) humanist culture, from its own history, and also from the accessible works of classical and contemporary Marxist thinking on history and philosophy. Finally, the very fact that in place of one universally obligatory dogmatism there have come into being several contending dogmas is itself significant: it points to the approaching decline of the Stalinist pseudoculture and the beginning of a real spiritual emancipation.

Notes

1. Zhores Medvedev, 'U istokov geneticheskoy diskussii', *Novy Mir,* no. 4, 1967.
2. Shatz, *Soviet Dissent in Historical Perspective,* Cambridge 1981, pp. 119–120.
3. Rubenstein, *Soviet Dissidents: Their Struggle for Human Rights,* Boston 1980, p. 40.
4. E. Gnedin, *Novy Mir,* no. 3, 1966, p. 51.
5. Ibid., p. 54.
6. Rubenstein, p. 42.
7. R.A. Medvedev, *On Stalin and Stalinism,* pp. 177–8.
8. Ibid., p. 178.
9. *Novy Mir,* no. 8, 1970, p. 167.
10. Of most importance were two works which became widely known in the USSR: J. Kornai, *Overcentralization in Economic Administration (1959),* and O. Šik, *Plan a trh za socialismu,* Prague 1968.
11. *Novy Mir,* no. 1, 1967, p. 184.
12. Ibid., p. 187.
13. *Novy Mir,* no. 2, 1966, p. 206.
14. *Novy Mir,* no. 9, 1965, p. 226.
15. Ibid., p. 212.
16. *Novy Mir,* no. 4, 1967, p. 168.
17. R.W. Campbell, *Soviet-Type Economies: Performance and Evolution,* Boston 1974, p. 199.
18. G. Lisichkin, *Chto cheloveku nado?,* p. 45.
19. Manuel Azcarate, 'The New Role of Science', *Marxism Today,* vol. 17, no. 3, March 1973, p. 79.
20. G. Lisichkin, *Plan i rynok,* Moscow 1966, pp. 11–12.
21. Ibid., p. 21.
22. Ibid., p. 50.
23. Ibid., p. 60.
24. Ibid., p. 60–61.
25. This idea was first formulated by an Italian economist, Barone, at the beginning of this century.
26. Lisichkin, *Chto cheloveku nado?,* p. 173.
27. Lisichkin, *Plan i rynok,* p. 83.
28. V. Bukovsky, *To Build A Castle,* 1978, p. 151.

29. Loren R. Graham, *Science and Philosophy in the Soviet Union*, 1973, p. 329.

30. Šik, p. 78.

31. The journals *Socialist Czechoslovakia* and *Czechoslovak Trade Unions* were published in Russian, and materials on the 'Prague spring' were printed in *Problemy mira i sotsializma*. Besides this, Czechoslovak publications – periodicals, newspapers and books in Czech, Slovak, German and English – were freely available in our libraries.

32. *Politichesky Dnevnik*, vol. 1, p. 336.

33. J. Kalvoda, *Czechoslovakia's Role in Soviet Strategy*, Washington 1978, p. 264.

34. Rakovski, *Towards an East European Marxism*, 1979, p. 19.

35. An unambiguously pro-reform position was assumed, for instance, by the Novosibirsk journal *EKO*, which published articles that were honest and bold.

36. Rakovski, p. 19.

37. V. Mayakovsky, 'To Comrade Nette' (1926), in Herbert Marshall, ed., *Mayakovsky and his Poetry*, 1942 (?), p. 112.

38. *Problemy Vostochnoy Evropy*, no. 1, 1981, p. 10.

39. Ibid., p. 8.

40. Solzhenitsyn, *The Oak and the Calf*, 1980, p. 220.

41. *An End to Silence*, pp. 213–14.

42. See the symposium *From Under the Rubble*, 1975.

43. *Sovetskaya Kultura*, 1 December 1981.

44. *Politichesky dnevnik*, vol. 1, p. 270.

45. Ibid., p. 186.

46. *Le Monde*, 22 March 1974, p. 17.

47. *Novy Mir*, no. 11, 1971, p. 191.

48. Ibid., p. 198.

49. Ibid., p. 202.

50. Later an article on Suvorin, by I. Solovekova and V. Shitova, was published, with severe cuts by the censor, in *Voprosy Literatury*. Its conclusions were much the same as Granin's.

51. *Novy Mir*, no. 11, 1971, p. 203.

52. *Novy Mir*, no. 1, 1968, p. 192 (the book was published in 1969).

53. Klaus Mehnert, *Moskau und die neue Linke*, Suttgart 1973, p 41.

54. *Novy Mir*, no. 1, 1968, p. 179.

55. Brzezinski and Huntington, p. 54.

56. Ibid., p. 109.

57. The experience of Poland in 1981 showed that the development of new, informal bonds threatens the system with complete collapse.

58. *Novy Mir*, no. 1, 1968, p. 188.

59. Ibid., pp. 188–9.

60. *Novy Mir*, no. 10, 1970.

61. *Novy Mir*, no. 1, 1968, p. 190.

62. Ibid., p. 196.

63. A. Lim, 'Intellektualy i novyi obshchestvennyi dogovor', in *Problemy Vostochnoy Evropy*, no. 2, 1981. See also V. Zaslavsky, *Il consenso organizzato: la società sovietica negli anni di Brezhnev*, Bologna 1981.

64. The conception of the 'preventive counter-revolution' was very aptly applied by Marcuse to the development of the world political situation between 1968 and 1973. See H. Marcuse, *Counter-Revolution and Revolt*, Boston 1972, p. 2.

65. Rakovski, pp. 51–2.

66. *Problemy Vostochnoy Evropy*, no. 2, 1981, p. 53.

67. *Socialist Register, 1980*, p. 281 (G. Bence and J. Kis, 'On Being a Marxist: a Hungarian View').

68. Rakovski, p. 67.

69. *Poiski*, no. 1, 1978, Moscow (*samizdat*), p. 43.

70. Zh. Medvedev, p. 130.

71. Privileges influence the conduct of scientists in two ways. On the one hand, people who have attained a certain position must make some concessions to the statocracy; but

on the other, scientists with a world reputation, such as A.D. Sakharov, quickly reach a level at which nothing can be done to them (the exiling of Sakharov to Gorky was more of a gesture of despair by the rulers). And intellectuals of the young generation, who have not yet achieved high position and have made no moral concessions to the rulers, are potentially dangerous. (The most loyal are often those of middle age and middle rank in science.)

72. *Neues Forum*, May–June, 1979, p. 35.

73. I refer here to the dissidents in the strict sense – that is, *the defenders of civil rights*. Among the *émigrés* there are serious specialists – V. Zaslavsky, M. Voslensky, L. Tykotsky, A. Yanov and others – but they were not dissidents. On political dissidence, as against the movement for the defence of civil rights, see below.

74. Elleinstein's preface to the French edition of Voslensky's *Nomenklatura*.

75. Rakovski, p. 68.

76. A. Yanov, *The Russian New Right*, Berkeley 1978, p. 12.

77. Ibid., p. 6.

78. A very important condition for totalitarianism is economic autarky – that is, a country's maximum independence of the external market. Stalin succeeded in achieving this in the course of seven or eight years:

> Thus, for example, in 1928 the country's requirements in the sphere of mechanical engineering were met to the extent of 69.6 per cent by our own production, in 1932 this share rose to 87.3 per cent, in 1933 to 95.6 per cent, and in 1937 to 99.1 per cent. The share of net imports in our consumption of rubber was 99.6 per cent in 1932 and in 1937 23.9 per cent. In the case of aluminium the corresponding shrinkage was from 92.2 to 4.9 per cent: and so on. (E.D. Kaganov, *Sotsialisticheskoe vosproizvodstvo i rynok*, Moscow 1966, p. 40)

The present-day Soviet economy is linked closely with the West, and it would be more difficult than in 1928 to break this link because the new level of technology rules out Stalinist 'simple solutions'.

79. L. Batkin, 'Third Lecture on Leonardo', Pushkin Museum, Moscow, 24 December 1980.

80. Wolfgang Kasack, *Lexicon der Literatur ab 1917*, Stuttgart 1976, p. 254.

81. 'Soviet Authors Question Expansionism', *Soviet Analyst*, vol. 10, no. 9, 1981, p. 5.

82. For comparison, see the Green Party in West Germany, in which conservatives rub shoulders with Left radicals and neo-Communists like R. Bahro.

83. See *Oktyabr'*, no. 4, 1963; no. 4, 1965.

84. V. Komarov, *Unichtozhenie prirody*, Frankfurt-am-Main 1978, p. 208.

85. Ibid., p. 109.

86. Ibid., p. 113.

87. *Izvestiya*, 8 October 1981.

88. *Sovetskaya Kultura*, 9 October 1981.

89. Ibid.

90. *Izvestiya*, 8 October 1981.

91. See V.A. Kuvakin, *Religioznaya filosofiya v Rossii*, p. 296.

92. Hollander, *Soviet and American Societies: A Comparison*, New York 1973.

93. Ibid., p. 191.

94. Ibid.

95. *New York Times*, 12 November 1978, p. 14.

96. *Voprosy Literatury*, no. 5, 1969, p. 90.

97. *Studies on Soviet Thought*, vol. 20, no. 1, July 1979, p. 33.

98. *Voprosy Literatury*, no. 5, 1969, p. 98.

99. Ibid., pp. 115–16.

100. *Voprosy Literatury*, no. 10, 1969, p. 115.

101. Ibid., p. 116.

102. Ibid., p. 118.

103. *Studies on Soviet Thought*, p. 32.
104. *Voprosy Literatury*, no. 10, 1969, p. 128.
105. *Nash Sovremennik*, no. 11, 1981, p. 155.
106. Ibid., p. 159.
107. Ibid., pp. 159, 160.
108. Berdyaev, *The Russian Idea*, 1947, p. 43.
109. J.L.I. Fennell, ed., *The Correspondence between Prince A.M. Kurbsky and Tsar Ivan IV of Russia, 1564–1579*, Cambridge 1955, p. 189.
110. Ibid., p. 19.
111. *Nash Sovremennik*, no. 11, 1981, p. 173.
112. Ibid.
113. Ibid., p. 164.
114. Ibid., p. 169.
115. Berdyaev, *The Russian Idea*, pp. 4–5.
116. *Voprosy Literatury*, no. 9, 1980, pp. 223–4.
117. Ibid., p. 224.
118. See, on Black-Hundred anti-Semitic publications in the USSR, Mikhail Agursky's paper *Contemporary Russian Nationalism*. There are, however, some inaccuracies in this valuable work. For instance, V. Turkov and V. Soloukhin are well known for statements opposed to anti-Semitism and among the Neo-Slavophils they are regarded as 'pro-Jewish' deviationists, but Agursky does not take this into account. On the whole, I think, he dramatizes the situation somewhat. See M. Agursky, *Contemporary Russian Nationalism – History Revised*, Research Paper no. 45, Soviet and East European Research Centre, Hebrew University of Jerusalem, January 1982, p. 48.
119. *Molodaya Gvardiya*, no. 4, 1968, p. 299.
120. *Molodaya Gvardiya*, no. 9, 1968, p. 259.
121. Ibid., p. 262.
122. Ibid., pp. 264–5.
123. Ibid., p. 264.
124. Ibid., p. 267.
125. Ibid., p. 274.
126. Ibid., p. 288.
127. *Ogonyok*, no. 30, 1969. For more details see Yanov, pp. 50–52.
128. Yanov, p. 51.
129. This needs to be emphasized: what matters is the process going on in the intelligentsia and semi-intelligentsia, and not the struggle for the lower orders, as Yanov thinks. We can comfort him – it will not be easy to raise a revolt of the masses with anti-Semitic appeals alone. The poet Joseph Brodsky says that 'in factories, villages, even in prison, I found surprisingly little anti-Semitism. Where I did find anti-Semitism strongest was among the literati, the intellectuals' (*Observer Magazine*, 25 October 1981, p.37). Sociologists sometimes confirm this. Among the workers the degree of nationalistic prejudice declines in proportion to the increase in their degree of education, but among intellectuals it is 'higher than among workers though still not by any means overwhelming' (Horace B. Davis, *Toward a Marxist Theory of Nationalism*, 1978, p. 111). This can be explained by the serious competition among intellectuals and by the general processes of the crisis of consciousness in their milieu, which favour the growth of nationalism, along with other factors. On the whole, according to Davis, sociologists 'find extreme national chauvinism among 5 to 10 per cent of the Soviet population' (ibid., p. 112). It is difficult to judge what the American scholar understands by 'extreme' national chauvinism, especially as he says nothing about any 'moderate' variety. In any case, the percentage mentioned is high enough; all the same, it cannot be regarded as catastrophically high.
130. A bloc between a section of the ruling group and the 'lower depths' of the people seems to me to afford the only possible social basis for Fascism in Russia, but neither group reads articles of literary criticism.
131. Yanov, p. 61.
132. Solzhenitsyn, *The Oak and the Calf*, p. 245.
133. *Molodaya Gvardiya* had published an article by S. Semanov, 'On Values

Relative and Eternal', which eulogized Stalin. R. Lert called it a treatise on 'the charms of the whip' (*An End to Silence*, p. 189). This caused a scandal. The journal *Kommunist* launched a direct attack on *Molodaya Gvardiya* and some organizational changes were made, although these did not go very far.

134. Solzhenitsyn, *The Oak and the Calf*, pp. 246, 247.

135. Solzhenitsyn, in the symposium *From Under the Rubble*, p. 249.

136. Ibid., pp. 261–2.

137. An idea often voiced by Maxim Gorky.

138. Solzhenitsyn, *The Oak and the Calf*, p. 245.

139. Ibid., p. 248.

140. Yanov mentions that in the 1920s Berdyaev was strongly influenced by Mussolini, but at that time an attraction to Italian-style Fascism was common to many radical intellectuals, who saw in it a variant of the Left-wing movement. Bernard Shaw was an example of this trend. Fascism had not yet given itself away – Hitler had not yet come to power in Germany. And Berdyaev was never a Fascist. He underwent serious waverings and made serious political mistakes, but he recognized these himself and tried to correct them in his lifetime. If the VSKhSON interpreted Berdyaev's ideas in a Fascist and anti-Semitic sense, the Russian thinker himself cannot be made responsible for that, any more than Marx can be blamed for the crimes of Stalin.

141. Yanov, p. 63.

142. *Izvestiya*, 6 February 1982.

143. Ibid.

144. *Sovetskaya Kultura*, 10 March 1982.

145. See *Voprosy Literatury*, no. 9, 1980, pp. 195, 211–13, etc.

146. *Voprosy Literatury*, no. 6, 1980, p. 191.

147. *From Under the Rubble*, p. ix.

148. Ibid., p. 4.

149. The contributors to the symposium are not all of one mind. On its own stands the technocratic utopia of Mikhail Agursky, which, broadly, reiterates the ideas of reformist Communism (although the reformist Communists go further in the matter of democracy).

150. *From Under the Rubble*, p. 12.

151. Ibid., p. 22.

152. Solzhenitsyn, *The Oak and the Calf*, p. 284.

153. Ibid., pp. 248, 283.

154. Berdyaev, *The Russian Idea*, p. 2. See also pp. 8, 9.

155. M. Agursky. *The New Russian Literature*, p. 61.

156. Ibid., pp. 62–3.

157. *Vestnik Rossiiskogo Khristianskogo Dvizheniya*, no. 131, 1980, p. 208.

158. Ibid., p. 210. Yanov (p. 36) considers that liberalism can be combined with an authoritarian regime 'only in the framework of a *utopia* which is to say an ideological construct, unrealizable in practice'. That is not true. Liberal-authoritarian regimes have existed and succeeded quite well in the twentieth-century. One can enumerate a number of such regimes, from the most authoritarian – Franco's Spain in the 1960s – to the most liberal – Yugoslavia under Tito, Mexico in the 1960s, Kádár's Hungary, and so on. The specific feature of these regimes is that they leave open the possibility of an evolutionary transition to democracy. The problem is not whether such a form of government is possible in general, but whether it is possible in the concrete conditions of Russia. I think it is impossible, for two reasons. The first is that liberal authoritarianism arises in countries with a more developed democratic (and legal) tradition than ours, which influences the ideology of the ruling social strata. The second is that the ideology and psychology of the Russian nationalists is, in itself, too aggressive, too closely linked with Stalinism and the reactionary ideas of the extreme Right. It is not suitable as accompaniment to a liberal policy, it is totalitarian. Solzhenitsyn is not the first to have tried to transform Russia on the basis of humaneness while retaining an authoritarian order. Gogol dreamed of doing that in the period of his *Select Passages From Correspondence With My Friends*. Berdyaev said of 'Gogol's utopia' that it was 'abject and slavish' and was rejected by all thinking

people in Russia (*The Russian Idea*, p. 82).

159. In 1979 a left-wing *samizdat* journal wrote of the possibility of a 'historic compromise' between nationalists of the Solzhenitsyn type and the Stalinists. A cry of protest against this suggestion went up in Moscow's Christian circles, yet both Solzhenitsyn and *Veche* quite frankly proclaimed such a compromise as their aim. Solzhenitsyn himself acknowledges that the *Letter to Soviet Leaders* was not a propaganda document but a genuine proposal for dialogue.

160. Ernest Mandel, *Die Sowjetunion, Solschenizyn und die westliche Linke*, Reinbek bei Hamburg 1975, p. 224.

161. *Commentary*, vol. 57, no. 5, May 1974, p. 35.

162. Ibid., vol. 58, no. 3, September 1974, p. 12.

163. *Survey*, no. 1, 1979, p. 134.

164. Ibid.

165. *Socialist Register 1980*, p. 281.

166. *Dissent*, Winter 1981, p. 66 ('Solzhenitsyn: Prisoner of Chillon').

167. *Survey*, no. 1, 1979, p. 134.

168. I. Deutscher, *Heretics and Renegades*, 1955, pp. 14–15.

169. *Sintaksis*, no. 5, 1979, p. 157.

170. Ibid., p. 158.

171. R.A. and Zh. A. Medvedev, *V poiskakh zdravogo smysla*, Moscow (*samizdat*), p. 13.

172. Deutscher, p. 14.

173. Ibid., p. 13.

174. Quoted in Scharndorf, *Istoriya KPSS*, Moscow 1962, p. 36.

175. This problem is discussed in a sensible article by G. Pomerants, 'A Dream of Just Revenge', in *Sintaksis*, no. 6, 1980. It is difficult to estimate the true scale of the White terror, for oppositionist historians do not concern themselves with the subject, having no wish to give pleasure to the authorities, and one cannot rely on the honesty of the Stalinists – who also stay away from the subject. I lack the necessary information, but according to my calculations the number of victims of the White terror was *at least* three million, while the *maximum* number of victims of the Red terror has been estimated by Western historians at two million. In any case, one cannot understand the Red terror without studying the White.

176. R.A. Medvedev, *On Stalin and Stalinism*, p. 186.

177. Solzhenitsyn, *The Oak and the Calf*, pp. 526–7. Brodsky, whom nobody will accuse of sympathy with Fascism, declared that, since the USSR is 'so huge that to accept that its regime is bad is to accept a bigger notion of evil than these people can stomach', Western public opinion, when desiring to condemn Fascism, turns to 'more manageable cases – in Latin America or Asia or wherever – where expressing your outrage can bring results' (*Observer Magazine*, 25 October 1981, p. 41). One recalls Roger Garaudy's observation that the dogmatist always sees the world in criteria of absolute good and evil: he fights against nothing less than absolute evil.

178. *Za rubezhom*, no. 10, 1982, quoting *Le Monde*, states that in Guatemala 'in recent weeks there have been an average of fifty to sixty killings every day' (p. 9).

179. *Sintaksis*, no. 6, 1980, p. 19.

180. E.F. Schumacher, *Small Is Beautiful*, 1973, p. 75.

181. V. Bukovsky, *Pis' ma russkogo puteshestvennika*, New York 1981, p. 40.

182. Marx, *Theories of Surplus Value*, 1969, Part I, p. 345.

183. The examples given were not invented but taken from life.

184. Bukovsky, *To Build A Castle*, p. 108.

185. Bukovsky writes that 'we Russians ... listen sadly to all the chatter about Eurocommunism and socialism with a human face. Why is it that nobody speaks of Fascism with a human face?' (ibid., p. 89). Bukovsky imagines that by this argument he has annihilated the left-wing 'chatterers', never suspecting that he has thereby demolished his own arguments. If he had not asked that question himself, we should have asked it of him. Why, indeed? For a very simple reason: the one is possible, the other not. Fascist ideology and psychology leave not the slightest possibility for the existence of democratic

ideals, but their Communist counterparts, even in official Soviet form, not only allow but constantly engender a variety of democratic 'deviations', because in them the democratic ideal – albeit disfigured and maimed by Stalin, shot down a thousand times or left to rot in the camps – nevertheless lives on. It lives in the illusions of young Ulyanov, in the disappointments of the later Lenin, in the tragic fate of Imre Nagy ... precisely because democratic reformism is continually being generated within the framework of official pseudo-Communism. As for those movements which were not much influenced by Stalinism – such as the Italian Communist Party, or the socialist parties which have always combated barracks-Communism – in them the democratic ideal never died. There is one detail on which I in my turn would ask Mr Bukovsky to ponder. What real Fascism do we know, and what 'real' socialism? He can hardly give a satisfactory answer, for the simple reason that up to now there has been no real socialism anywhere. Will there be? We shall see.

186. See V. Krasnov, *Otvet V. Bukovskomu* (*samizdat*).

187. Bukovsky, *Pis'ma ...*, p. 204.

188. Bukovsky, *To Build A Castle*, pp. 90, 92ff.

189. Yanov, p. 85.

190. Oppositional and even liberal dogmatism is no new thing in Russia. A.F. Koni wrote, of the nineteenth-century liberals: 'It is hard to imagine greater discord, intolerance, and blind liberal orthodoxy than prevailed amongst them' *(Sochineniya,* vol. 2, p. 183).

191. *Problemy Vostochnoy Evropy*, no. 2, 1981, p. 46.

192. Yanov, p. 98.

193. A. Zinoviev, *My i zapad,* Lausanne 1981, p. 89.

194. *Corriere della Sera*, supplement, 5 November 1977, interview with A. Zinoviev.

195. A. Zinoviev, *My i zapad,* p. 118.

196. K. Burdzhuademov, *Ocherki rastushchey ideologii*, Munich 1974, p. 6.

197. E. Il'enkov, *Ob idolakh i idealakh*, Moscow 1968, p. 183.

198. Marx and Engels, *Collected Works*, vol. 6, p. 109 (*The Poverty of Philosophy*)

199. See, for example, the very strange concluding words of Roy Medvedev in his talk with A. Zinoviev and P. Ostellino.

200. The Stalinist mentality is the guarantee of Zinoviev's success. In the West they have not read Stalin and Soviet textbooks, but they read Zinoviev. His seems an original, distinctive way of thinking. But in the USSR it all appears familiar and understandable – 'our own'!

201. Zinoviev in *Corriere della Sera.*

202 Ibid.

203 Zinoviev, *My i zapad,* p. 8.

204. Ibid., p. 57 ff.

205. Such phrases as these, for instance: 'It is not enough to say that this conception is stupid. It is stupid in the highest degree, i.e., idiotic' (ibid., p. 87). Like a bad translation from German. I deliberately refrain from quoting here from Zinoviev's 'artistic' works, lest I resemble those critics who, as Oscar Wilde put it, 'are apparently reduced to be the reporters of the police-court of literature, the chroniclers of the doings of the habitual criminals of art' (*The Critic As Artist*, Utrecht 1957, p. 28).

206. *Die Zukunft*, no. 11, 1980, p. 30.

207. Zinoviev, *My i zapad,* p. 58.

208. It is amusing that Zinoviev constantly rebukes the dissidents for their lack of theory, mentioning that they have no sociological training (but has he?). That is not the point. Many discoveries in the social sciences have been made by dilettanti (Marx was a philosopher who wrote a work of genius on political economy; Freud was a doctor who opened a new epoch in philosophy; Marcuse, though not a Sovietologist, wrote the best work of Sovietology; and so on). Contrariwise, A. Amalrik, a professional historian, failed to create a scientific theory. The ideological weakness of the dissidents lies in their inability to transcend the narrow horizon of neo-Stalinist dogmas, but lack of special training explains only a few concrete cases. Furthermore, Zinoviev himself is an example of this weak side of the dissident movement. With many dissidents, personal heroism

compensates for lack of theoretical knowledge. Zinoviev has performed no acts of heroism. For this there is, of course, no reason to 'blame' him; it was our rulers who decided not to make a martyr of him. Alas, it has to be admitted that our system produces martyrs not only for internal consumption, but for export – in excess of demand.
209. Zinoviev, *My i zapad,* p. 57.
210. Zinoviev frankly admits that the results of his 'scientific investigations'

do not coincide immediately with the observed facts. They are not simple generalizations from facts. They merely provide the means with which to explain facts and predict them. (ibid., p. 9)

As to how Zinoviev predicts facts we may judge by his assurance in May 1980, when the Polish revolution was already on the way, that this year could see only something 'deserving of sneers and contempt', 'evoked by apathy and disillusionment, but most improbably by hope. An ordinary, dull year' (p. 153). As regards ability to explain, in the last analysis all ideologues do is to explain facts in accordance with their preconceived schemas and try to predict them. But facts require not to be 'explained' but to be assembled, generalized, studied and analysed; and only then can they be understood.
211. It was no accident that the idea of free trade unions began to spread among us even before the Polish events of August 1980. It may be supposed that my personal experience differs markedly from that of Mr Zinoviev (even though I do not build my 'original' theories on this ground). But here before me lies a very interesting *samizdat* document, a long manuscript entitled *Repairs*, written by some provincial engineer. The author of this paper is not a dissident: indeed, he dislikes dissidents. He reads no opposition literature and gets his information from the official newspapers. He approves of the invasion of Czechoslovakia in 1968 and thinks the censorship very useful: 'Permit wide and open criticism of the negative factors in our life, and within a week anarchy would reign in the country' (*Repairs*, copy no. 3–1, p. 4). He explains the suppression of criticism by 'a sound protective instinct' (ibid.). He fully supports the official ideology in its school-book version. In the level of his political knowledge he, though an engineer, is much lower than many workers (for during the last three years the workers have put into *samizdat* a number of rather interesting documents, including some composed in the provinces – see *Socialism and the Future*, no. 10–11, Summer 1981). He might seem to be the ideal 'Soviet man' according to Zinoviev. What made him write for *samizdat*? The fact that in the entire system there is only one thing he rejects: the one-party principle, in which he sees the cause of all our woes. A second 'Communist Party' must be formed, a twin to the first with exactly the same ideology, and then all will come right. The author has not perceived that he has encroached upon the very basis of the statocratic regime. But how did such an idea enter his head? Here it has to be made clear that not only in the works of Lenin but even in the official manuals of 'Marxism-Leninism' we fail to find a developed justification for the one-party system. Even fervent Stalinists cannot bring themselves to assert that the one-party system is a 'law' or principle of socialism. This is only implied, hinted at, when they talk of the leading role of the Party (but the leading role of one party does not rule out the existence of others). For the official ideology the one-party system is a sort of 'skeleton in the cupboard' about which everyone knows but no one ever speaks. True, in Brezhnev's constitution the one-party system was given a 'juridical' basis (for the first time in sixty years!) but it still lacks any theoretical justification. It is not surprising, therefore, that even those loyal to the official ideology more and more often arrive, through their own thinking, at the idea of a multiparty system (which is not yet the same as political pluralism, since that presumes competition between different political and ideological tendencies), without seeing in this a break with Communism. Propaganda for 'the ideals of October' is also dangerous to the statocracy, because society has diverged from these ideals. The statocracy would like to put an end to them, but this gets more and more difficult. As for the author of *Repairs*, he complains that the dream of Soviet people is now 'the dissolution of the CPSU, a tempting prospect for "unburdening the heart" of the non-Party people whom the Party exasperates, but *also for the rank-and-file members of the party itself*' (p. 84; emphasis added). In the

same way, while remaining an adherent of the official ideology, the author advocates 'election to all posts in the economic and technical leadership' (p. 82) and 'workers' control over production' (p. 86). Neo-Stalinism cannot resolve openly to repudiate these principles, either, but simply refuses to put them into practice.

212. Zinoviev, *My i zapad*, p. 60.

213. *Voprosy Filosofii*, no. 5, 1980, p. 95.

214. *EKO*, no. 7, 1980, p. 80.

215. See Erich Fromm, *Agression und Charakter: ein Gespräch*, Zurich 1975; and his *Marx's Concept of Man*, New York 1963.

216. L. Kolakowski, 'Tesi sulla speranza e sulla disperazione', in *Elogio dell'incoerenza*.

217. Zinoviev himself said that his social ideal is 'the world as it exists today' (*My i zapad*, p. 97).

218. A. Schopenhauer, *The World as Will and Representation*, trans. E.F.J. Payne, Indian Hills (Colorado) 1958, vol. 1, p. 35.

6

Looking for a Way Out

The 1970s: New Cultural Currents

Dogma-creation was by no means always capable of satisfying the 'hunger for ideology'. In any case it would be wrong to suppose that the overwhelming majority of the intelligentsia took that road. On the contrary, in the seventies the quest for new ideas was quite fruitful, but now the critically thinking intellectuals no longer hastened to publicize these ideas. In the art of the seventies, in all its genres, there was less pathos and emotion but more objectivity and analysis. Distrust in emotionalism became so widespread that it even affected the statocratic pseudoculture.

At first, official art reacted to the ideological crisis merely by increasing the number of propagandist films and 'artistic' canvases in the spirit of the old 'socialist realism', but this propagandist pressure proved only counterproductive, displeasing not merely intellectual circles but also the broad masses. Then another tendency, especially noticeable in the cinema and on television, began to gain ascendancy. They began to make deliberately problem-free films in the style of the worst clichés of Hollywood – 'hits' like *Pirates of the Twentieth Century* or *The Crew*, or melodramas (*Moscow Doesn't Trust Tears*, and so on) – all with an obligatory happy ending. Such commercial products met with a favourable response among some viewers, who wanted 'just to be entertained', 'to be relaxed, relieved of their worries'. The technical level of these films was higher than in the old propaganda jobs, and the approach different, Americanized. Nevertheless, the purpose was the same. It was obvious, frank propaganda for lack of spirituality – ideological opium.

In 1979–81 such commercial films flooded on to our screens, to an extent that aroused serious concern in intellectual circles. Figures from the world of art and criticism protested in the pages of *Literaturnaya Gazeta* and *Sovetskaya Kultura* against this encroaching 'Hollywoodization'. It was mentioned, in particular, that the propagation of violence in Soviet commercial films was having the same consequences as in the West. Militiamen acknowledged that 'the number of acts of hooliganism committed by young people increases sharply when a film like *Pirates of the Twentieth Century* is shown, especially in a small town.'[1] Well-known producers complained that the screen was being filled with Soviet-produced films that had been made 'according to the outdated patterns of the American conveyor-belt of the forties and fifties'.[2] V. Motyl' wrote, bitterly: 'It appears that some novelty or other can simply be organized, its success planned and also organized, and then it is "issued in many copies".'[3]

In the seventies Soviet society increasingly assumed the characteristics of a consumer society, with all the ensuing consequences. Cultural values were also transformed into objects of mass consumption. *Izvestiya* wrote that 'into the category of "prestige articles" have moved not only cars, flats, clothes, furniture and rings but also books, shows and concerts.'[4] The transformation of cultural objects into commodities, objects of speculation, is certainly not a very positive phenomenon, even though it is quite logical under the new conditions. It is felt especially painfully in a society where traditional values are not moribund but still alive. Some social strata are becoming *embourgeoisé* (which is sometimes mistaken for 'Europeanization'). But these processes must not be viewed in a one-sided and moralizing way. The development of a consumer society in a country chronically suffering from shortages of consumer goods will have far-reaching – perhaps revolutionary – consequences. It is in consumer society that culture acquires 'prestige' and whole social groups come into contact with art for the very first time. Many people speak of a 'book boom' in our country (actually we had two such booms, the first at the end of the fifties, the second after 1967). It was noted that the increased interest in books was connected with an improved standard of living, and especially with improved housing conditions. The complaint is heard that many people buy books but do not read them. All the same, there are now more books in people's possession, and that cannot fail to have consequences. Moreover, note this – the 'book boom' did not apply to the works of the official ideologues. People not only do not read them, they do not even buy them. They do not regard them as 'books'!

In the same way, the commercial cinema played a role more complex than the one assigned to it by the heads of the propaganda department. It finished off 'socialist realism'. More precisely, 'socialist realism' was dead and buried by the seventies as a result of the objective development of events. But the commercial art of the late seventies drove the traditional aspen stake into its grave. That old thing would not rise again.

The spiritual emptiness of the commercial cinema reflected the ideological crisis in society. On the other hand there appeared the theatre of A. Efros, in which the problems of spiritual emptiness, stagnation and bankruptcy were brought to the fore. The spiritual vacuum became, so to speak, the content and theme of art, and a matter for study. Efros created a sort of poetry of stagnation. From one performance to the next there floated an atmosphere of enigmatic expectation, but it was still not known what was being expected or whether, anyway, there was any sense in this expectation. A similar motif was present in all the productions. Perhaps one might name Samuel Beckett the most 'Efrosish' playwright. His plays could not be seen in the official theatres – except in the Baltic republics, where the local bureaucracy is a little more liberal, or just wiser. Efros's theatre shows people at a turning point in their lives, but that moment, it seems, goes on for ever. The heroes continually balance between belief and unbelief, awareness and unawareness, and are incapable of making the only right choice. This was remarkably poetic art, but it faced towards the past.

At the same time a different tendency made its appearance – one objectively turned towards the future, even though the material used in its art was often not the present day only, but history as well. This was what could be called, for convenience, 'the analytical tendency'. In prose its strongest representative was, perhaps, Yuri Trifonov, while in drama this role was played, each in his own way, by M. Shatrov and A. Gel'man. For lack of space I can deal only with these three, although many others deserve to be discussed – the Azerbaijan film *Interrogation* (scenario by Ibragimov), about corruption in leading circles; V. Fokin's play *And in the Spring I'll Come Back to You,* which showed, so to speak, the anatomy of the Soviet Thermidor of the 1920s; and so on.

Trifonov's task was akin to that of a researcher: to understand, to analyse history, to re-establish the truth – not only to reconstitute true situations, but also to discover historical tendencies, to perceive the genesis of a society. In *The House on the Embankment,* the establishment of a new ruling class, the *nomenklatura*; in *The Old Man,* the development of anti-democratic tendencies and forces within Bolshevism. Trifonov's novellas are written in an offhand sort of way; their form is not carefully realized, and sometimes – as for instance in *The Old Man* – matters appear that are incongruous with the subject: whole sentences taken from his book *The Campfire's Gleam.* The author is in a hurry; it is as though he knows that he is doomed not to live to sixty. In this situation the refining of artistic forms has no place. What matters above all is to provide a snapshot of social history. This photograph is imprinted in the destinies and personalities of the characters – hence the image 'the campfire's gleam'. History advances through Trifonov's heroes. The main thing is to understand, and to explain to others. These are, in their way, the notes of an eye-witness, reconstituted with hindsight.

Analytical reconstruction of history is the essence of the work of M. Shatrov, the author of a series of plays about Lenin. Shatrov's works flatly contradict official historical accounts. Here also we have a quest, the quest for 'the real Lenin'. Shatrov turns his attention to crucial moments in the history of Bolshevism: 6 July 1918, the revolt of the Left Socialist-Revolutionaries, which led to the initiation of the one-party system and the restriction of Soviet democracy; 5 September 1918, the Council of People's Commissars discusses the question of Red terror. In his later plays, in the seventies – *Revolutionary Etude* and *This is How We'll Win!* – the subject is Lenin's clash with the new bureaucracy. Shatrov undoubtedly idealizes Lenin; nevertheless, his hero differs markedly from the official 'honeycake Ilyich'. Lenin's revolutionary spirit is contrasted with the bureaucratized Communists whom Lenin sees as the worst enemies of the proletariat.

This theme of moral and political disparity between Lenin and his 'heirs' gave Shatrov no rest. His plays had great difficulty in getting past the censor: the latest of them, *This is How We'll Win!*, was for some time thought to be doomed. The question of letting it be performed was decided at the highest level and was the occasion of a clash between 'hard' and 'soft' members of the state leadership. The 'softs' won the day: the statocratic upper circle preferred to put a brave face on what for them was a sorry business. On 3 March 1982 the Political Bureau, with Brezhnev at its head, went to the Moscow Art Theatre to see Shatrov's play as produced by O. Yefremov. In its report, *Sovetskaya Kultura* added that the performance enjoyed 'great success'.[5] To be sure, the paper did not indicate precisely with whom.

The struggle for power at the top had caused yet another ideological crack to appear, into which Shatrov and Yefremov inserted themselves. The long review by M. Stroeva in *Literaturnaya Gazeta*, which millions of people had been able to read even before the 'historic' visit to the Moscow Art Theatre by Brezhnev & Co., was in its way no less an event than the performance itself. The theatre, wrote Stroeva, had resolved to show a Lenin who was 'suffering and unable to understand'. There stood before the audience 'a Lenin who was the victim of a tragedy'.[6]

Writing honestly about Lenin meant speaking up about the tragedy of Bolshevism; meant judging, on Lenin's behalf, those who declared themselves his loyal successors. The performance ended with the words: 'No one in the world can compromise the Communists unless the Communists compromise themselves. No one in the world can prevent the victory of Communism unless the Communists themselves prevent it.'[7] Shatrov's tragedy, however, was quite different from Lenin's and the point here is not that the author, in trying to re-establish the truth, has constantly to add in his work at least a little of the official falsehood, for unless he did that he would not have been allowed to say *anything*. What is more important is that the author, when he wrote those lines just quoted, and the critic Stroeva, when she reproduced them for readers of *Literaturnaya Gazeta*, could not be unaware that Communism has indeed already been compromised, that the realization of Lenin's hopes has already been prevented. It remained only to dream that new generations will be able to distinguish between the historical truth and the official lie – although the shadow of that lie falls upon those who try to re-establish the truth.

The history of Bolshevism is a question that is currently relevant in the highest degree for the fate of our society. Understanding it means finding the key to present-day reality, finding the method for interpreting it. In his plays Shatrov tried to understand the past through the present and the present through the past. He is not the only one working in thst direction. Of even greater importance are the plays of A. Gel'man, which are set in the present day.

Gel'man made his debut in the theatrical world as the author of 'plays about production'. That sort of work was strongly fostered by the authorities, who saw in it a 'healthy alternative' to the problem plays of Rozov and other playwrights of the sixties. What was wanted was to take up problems of production rather than spiritual problems. But as things got worse in the economy, the sphere of production exhibited more and more those general social and psychological conflicts that were typical of the country as a whole. It became harder and harder to cover them up. The myth of the 'socialist' character of labour in the USSR collapsed in ruins. Gel'man, himself a 'production writer', showed that the economy is a field of fierce conflict of interests – between departments, between branches of industry and between classes.

A number of writers before Gel'man had already tried to deal with the 'production theme' from this standpoint. Very interesting in this connection was Shatrov's play *The Weather for Tomorrow*, staged at the Contemporary Theatre. The economic discussion in the sixties revealed to the Soviet intelligentsia as a whole new problems and new ideas which had previously been the property of a narrow circle of people only. This discussion not only influenced the development of political thought among Soviet Marxists, it also had a certain cultural importance. This made itself felt in the 'production' writings of the seventies. Shatrov's *The Weather for Tomorrow* was a sort of technocratic utopia, and interesting from that standpoint.

The play's ideas are close to those of wide circles of the Soviet intelligentsia and middle strata who, although no longer satisfied with the system, at the same time lack the strength to break with it. Along with the idea of 'true Leninism', technocratic utopianism constitutes a definite ideological complex – albeit a very contradictory one, for Lenin's thought constantly revolts against attempts to interpret it from the position of technocratic pragmatism or even Shatrov's 'technocratic humanism'.

The Limits of Technocracy

The expression 'technocratic humanism' sounds so unusual that it calls for examination. In *The Weather for Tomorrow* we see depicted one day in the life of a Volga motorcar factory. Before us are up-to-date production methods, Western technology. The heroes of the play are ideally Europeanized technocrats. They are shown with great sympathy, but for some reason they all seem the same. If what interests you is individual characterization, you will not find it in this play.

We discover that the factory is in constant conflict with the whole economic system, to which it cannot adjust. We see with our own eyes the conflict between the productive forces and the relations of production. This is no longer an abstract notion, but a concrete reality. Owing to defects in supply and organization the conveyor belt keeps having to stop, but competent technocrats always find a solution: they wage a ceaseless battle and invariably triumph. The factory on the Volga is the weather for tomorrow – it and similar enterprises will force a change in the system of management. The technocratic revolution will itself inevitably lead to democratization: techniques, as such, can free us.

There is, of course, no social struggle here, and Shatrov's technocrats are in no way social fighters. They have to change society not through their protest but through their own activity. Workers and engineers appear only as extras. On the whole, this has a depressing effect on audiences of the 1980s.

We must look more closely at the question of Soviet 'technocracy'. In practice it is closely connected with the problem of experts, which has become very acute in the USSR (although not all experts are technocrats). In a work by a group of Western Sovietologists we read:

> Social scientists and other experts could easily adjust to a rationalized authoritarian environment where decisions were reached solely on a national-technical basis divorced from the influence of bureaucratic interests and other political considerations.[8]

This argument is astonishingly feeble. In the first place, the very idea that an authoritarian society can exist in which decisions are taken without regard to political considerations is absurd. In general, the very idea of pure 'rationality', when applied to the contemporary world, sounds like a joke. All decisions in society are taken in somebody's interests. It is impossible to rule without a purpose, different people have different purposes, and for almost any of them one could find rational means.[9] In any case, a ruling class *nowhere and never* allows 'rational-technical management' in any interests but its own. If we assume that society has already overcome the narrowness of class interests, and that bureaucratic limitations no longer affect decision-making, then such a society will inevitably be not authoritarian but democratic and socialist.

In short, technocracy and bureaucracy are incompatible for a number of reasons. *The tragedy of the Soviet technocrats is that they are compelled to place their rationalism at the service of bureaucratic irrationality.* But the bureaucracy itself is guided by its own laws, which do not coincide with those of technical rationality and have little need of technocrats for attaining their ends. The bureaucracy strives to keep as much power as possible in its own hands, and an increased role for experts would restrict its power. Consequently, although many experts belong to the statocratic corporation of the class type, they feel that they are pariahs. 'Increased professional autonomy', writes Rakovski, 'encourages this or that expert to try and influence social decisions which concern his own speciality.' However, this attempt always fails:

> The post-Stalinist system produces but does not tolerate the type of expert who is well known in Western society, who – conscious of his own scientific competence – intervenes in social questions with a great deal of naïvety but also with a great deal of courage.[10]

An example of an unsuccessful expert-technocrat is the sociologist F. Burlatsky, who made a rapid advance in his career under Khrushchev but later lost his position.

To begin with, the experts had to fight for the mere right to exist of such sciences as sociology, social psychology and political science.[11]

Soviet sociologists appealed to the writings of Lenin, and it was with the study of Lenin's works that these sciences began their development here. One may laugh as much as one likes at this 'quotation-digging', but without it no sociological research would have been possible in the USSR. Lenin included in his articles a great number of valuable ideas which made even the first Soviet sociological writings extremely interesting. Burlatsky tried to counterpose modern sociological science to the schemas of the official textbooks, but without engaging in a direct polemic with the official dogmas. He drew attention to the absence in the Soviet Union of any serious works on the political life of our own country:

> It must be said that there exists an immense amount of information describing the political process, accumulated in state, Party and other organizations, which has hardly yet been generalized and studied. Groups of sociologists working in some committees, ministries and departments are only beginning to get to work. But they, too, hardly concern themselves with the political aspect of the work of these organizations.[12]

He tried in his own writings to formulate in a more or less clear-cut way the ideas of rationalizing the system and introducing liberal reforms. In particular he spoke up for democracy at the point of production, urging study of various forms of worker participation in the management of enterprises, and 'publicity for the most effective of these'.[13] He also recalled Lenin's saying that the Soviet trade unions must wage 'economic struggle' against the bureaucratic apparatus, 'safeguarding the working people's material and spiritual interests in ways and means inaccessible to this apparatus'.[14] In his books we find sharp criticism of the bureaucracy, based on the ideas of the young Marx and having much in common with the ideas of E. Gnedin:

> As Marx observed long ago, it is always a characteristic of bureaucracy that it identifies the processes of society and even those of the class whose interests it represents with its own specific interests and that it tries to ignore society's requirements. As the functions and scope of action of the bureaucratic apparatus expand, so these tendencies become all-embracing. The danger of bureaucratic dictatorship arises: there appears and becomes dominant a striving to break free from all control. The bureaucratic apparatus retires into itself, so to speak, and begins to develop according to its own laws. And, correspondingly, the bureaucratic caste becomes exclusive.

From this Burlatsky concludes:

> The basic evil in the inflation of the bureaucratic apparatus is not that it is

very expensive to maintain, even though that is also hard to put up with. The worst aspect lies elsewhere. Being constructed on purely official-hierarchical principles, the bureaucratic mechanism soon ceases to perform the social functions for which it was actually created.[15]

Burlatsky's ideas are thus radical enough, but he does not contemplate their fulfilment otherwise than through a rationalization of the existing statocratic system; and, consequently, he accepts all the rules of the game. In his books every original and fresh idea appears like a gold coin in a heap of rubbish; every scientific conclusion is situated amid a mess of lying ideological verbiage, whose emptiness the author appreciates even better than the reader.[16] He is obliged not only to put up with the usual restrictions imposed by the censorship but also to talk in bureaucratic language; this means that his ideas cannot be expressed plainly. Burlatsky's practical work in the state apparatus was no more successful than his theoretical work; he remained a reformist without reforms. This tragedy of technocratic reformism he tried to describe in a book with the expressive title *The Riddle and Lesson of Niccolò Machiavelli.* In writing about the great Florentine, the author essentially drew a psychological portrait of himself.

The picture presented to us is roughly this. The state requires loyalty, above all, but the expert, the adviser, endeavours to serve the state while preserving his independence and not becoming the state's slave. The expert is essentially apolitical, alien to any ideological sympathies: 'Be clear about this – I am not for anyone in particular, I am for everyone. I am an adviser: an adviser, nothing more.'[17] But the state does not want independent advisers, it wants people who will promote its policy and ideology. The rulers fear that the adviser wants to share their power, to lay claim to their rights. The opposition also requires him to perform ideological acts. The position of the 'pure expert' becomes hopeless.

The rulers do not tolerate his independence, while the people have not yet matured to the stage where they can use his services; have not yet become a political force with which Machiavelli-Burlatsky can collaborate and which needs his collaboration. The state is still the only political force in society. As professional politicians, neither Burlatsky nor his hero can simply 'retire'. They have to play to the end their tragic game with the authoritarian state. This is why the republican Machiavelli turns to the 'princes' and the democrat Burlatsky to aged bureaucrats (it is well known that it was he who dubbed the Soviet leaders a 'gerontocracy', describing the system of rule within the CPSU as rule by old men). For Machiavelli-Burlatsky the tragic conflict is bound up with their understanding of the need for changes together with inability to find an agent capable of effecting these changes, a force that can change something: 'In the course of these quests he passes from hope to delusion and disappointment, from confidence in the real possibility of success to understanding of its complete hopelessness.'[18]

At the end of the book the author himself enters, and Machiavelli gives him a lesson in politics. The conversation between the two is conducted in absolutely 'Soviet-Russian' language, which makes the whole dialogue resemble a scene from the theatre of the absurd:

> AUTHOR: Your occupation?
> NICCOLÒ: Official. Diplomat. Publicist. Historian. Writer. ...
> AUTHOR: Sorry, I'll be more precise: your vocation?
> NICCOLÒ: Reformer.
> AUTHOR: Reformer of what?[19]

The trouble is that both Niccolò and the author have spent their whole lives trying to effect reform *from within* the system, which has proved to be unreformable (by *their* methods, at any rate). Nevertheless, the political failure of reformism is, for Burlatsky, not equivalent to complete shipwreck:

> AUTHOR: So, then, did you succeed in your reforming activity?
> NICCOLÒ: We awakened ourselves and gave new life to Time.[20]

If the reformers were listened to, it was certainly not by those whom they were addressing. They tried to influence members of the ruling statocracy by showing them that timely reforms were the best way to safeguard their power, whereas a conservative policy would eventually undermine it. They warned that 'standing firm on the maintenance of a status quo which has been overtaken by the course of development will lead directly to the shattering of the system.'[21] But the warnings were in vain, for *the conservative statocracy is its own gravedigger.*

We see now how naïve were Shatrov's technocratic-reformist illusions. Gel'man was different. His first play, *A Meeting of the Party Committee*, which was put on by Tovstonogov in Leningrad and by Yefremov in Moscow, was much discussed both here and in the West. Gel'man is free from naïve technocratic illusions; he knows economic reality otherwise than by hearsay. But the conflict in his play is not economic in the narrow sense; this was the first fictional work to deal with the class struggle in the USSR. Not without reason did many people say, later, that *A Meeting of the Party Committee* was prophetic, presaging the strikes of summer 1980 and the workers' movement in Poland.

The situation in the play, when the workers refuse to accept a bonus as a way of protesting against an action by the management – and, as is made clear in the course of the affair, against the whole system of economic leadership – is improbable in real life. The actual forms of the class struggle in the USSR are different. But the exceptional situation throws especially clear light upon typical conflicts. Herein lies the essence of Gel'man's aesthetic. *A Meeting of the Party Committee* stands out from the general background not only through the 'novelty' of its conflict. Real people appear on the stage. Instead of Shatrov's faceless technocrats we see live production-workers who turn out to be very different, unlike each other, complex, unexpected. Gel'man gives a precise answer to history's question. He sees the only hope for society in the movement of the proletariat. Russian culture has actually performed a spiral circuit, and the conclusions at which social thought arrived at the beginning of our century have become significant for us once again.

Gel'man's most recent plays – not including his less successful *Feedback* – localize the conflict, so to speak – confine it to a small group of people. More and more attention is paid to the conduct of particular individuals. The time and place of the action are confined within the unities of the classical theatre, and thus concentrated. Different types of people are put to the test in tense situations. The lovers of truth, the fighters for justice usually suffer defeat. Those who try to retain some vestiges of spirituality, or who try to restore that quality in themselves, rarely meet with success. There are no workers here. This is the world of lower and middle-ranking 'chiefs'. Bureaucracy. A milieu in which honesty is impossible, unattainable, having been eradicated. Love for one's job and confidence in one's rightness are also unattainable. What prevail here are the rules formulated in the play *We, the Undersigned*:

> If a man is sensible, they get rid of him all the same. And, incidentally, that is the right thing to do. Because being good and honest is, pardon me, a pleasure for the soul! Isn't that so? It is. And if you are honest, and a chief as well, that's too much pleasure! Life is just. To one it gives a conscience – and he's happy. To another it gives a position – and he's happy too. It's necessary that things should be right for everybody![22]

We behold the anatomy of the bureaucratic world, its mechanisms, the Mafia-like bonds among the bureaucratic cliques, the formation of a 'clientage', and all the relationships that result. In art like this there is no room either for hope or for illusions. Art – and this does not apply only to Gel'man – becomes ever harsher; in it we hear the voices of rage and despair sounding louder and louder. But this is itself a sign of hope. Liberation from illusions is painful, but a fine thing. What is happening now could be called an ideological catharsis. The downfall of the old ideology and the old morality certainly entails a crisis of all ideology and all morality, but at the same time it liberates. Art no longer shows the way out; it does not summon us in any particular direction. It does not confer hope, does not soothe. It analyses, judges, diagnoses. The way out has to be sought not in art but in life. Problems must be solved not in the pages of novels, not on the stage or the screen, but in reality. And the less artists comfort us, the greater is our wrath and our resolution. This art is uncompromising and for that very reason it looks towards the future.

Of course, a certain section of the public – the one which is delighted with commercial art – is angry with the new analytical works, especially when some productions connected in this spirit find their way on to the cinema or television screen. 'What does it matter that now I know all this?' we read in one viewer's letter. 'I personally can't do anything about it, but, with such films, life gets very depressing. We have enough of these "serious problems" in real life, and yet here they are again, on TV.'[23] But what matters is that more and more people are becoming aware that changes are not only necessary but possible – that we can no longer put up with what is going on around us. And the new art is playing no small part in forming the new mood in society.

Art, wrote the well-known commentator A. Vaksberg, replying to viewers' letters,

> fulfils its great mission only when it addresses itself to the complex problems of its time in all their depth and variety. Not because it can *solve* these problems, if we understand that in too utilitarian, administrative-departmental a sense.[24]

Nevertheless, in its own way it does solve them, 'by forming public opinion, drawing attention not only to the event but to the phenomenon, examining it in the way that only art can'.[25] Let us not entertain any illusions. Public opinion by itself cannot alter the nature of society, but the fact that it exists is significant. It bears witness that there are in our country healthy forces which are capable of fighting for a new life.

Art cannot provide answers to the questions of theory, cannot even formulate them as such. It transforms them into moral questions, creates a new psychological atmosphere, and in a certain sense also a new type of intellectual who is able to solve these problems, to contribute to an intellectual rebirth after a quarter-century of Stalinism.

Philosophical Trends

However, one important consequence of the break-up of the united cultural front was theory's emergence into the foreground. We saw that at the beginning of the sixties fresh ideas were first proclaimed by writers and later taken up by theoreticians. The articles by Lakshin and Karyakin came after, not before, Solzhenitsyn's book. After the united front ceased to exist several ideological tendencies started to take shape, and each of these sought to create its own theory. In this situation it was general philosophical ideas that began to determine the way art developed, not the other way round.

Doubts were sometimes voiced in *samizdat* writings as to whether there was any philosophy at all in the USSR. In *Poiski* the democratic socialist P. Tamarin complained:

> Dystrophy of the soul became a universal phenomenon among us. The entire social organism was affected by it, every sphere of public activity. The sphere most sensitive, most predisposed to dystrophy was that of the humanities.[26]

And especially, according to Tamarin, philosophy. A certain kind of '*samizdat* patriotism' is apparent here, for it turns out that for him only in the underground is creative thought alive among us. I beg to differ with Comrade Tamarin: all the most important phenomena in *samizdat*, including the journal *Poiski*, were engendered by processes that began in the *legal* culture. This does not mean, of course, that everything there is plain sailing. Philosophy does indeed encounter serious difficulties in the USSR.

In our country one can only be a *Marxist* philosopher, but it is hard even to be that, since every new idea is liable to be denounced as 'revisionism'. 'Scientific discussion,' wrote P. Egides,

> in my view, can be sharp, one can 'incriminate' an opponent for breaches of logic, for contradicting himself, one can even wax ironical at his expense, and so on, but such discussion must not transgress the ethical standards of a scientific dispute: opponents must not be accused of writing what they have not written. Such methods as that merely hinder the development of Marxist philosophy. The time has come, at last, for everyone to understand this, but some are set in their ways. ... In words they are for development, but any new idea causes them to tremble. In short, they are 'for' development, but ... without development.[27]

The official ideological interpretation of dialectics stripped it of every element of critical method. What suffered especially, it was said, was the principle of dialectical negation, which was reduced to a set of examples in books on 'diamat'. Altogether, dialectical thought was formalized and subjugated, adapted to the requirements of the conservative, statocratic state: in the words of J.N. Findlay, the 'Hegelian machinery' was forced 'to operate ... with a quite alien and unsuitable fuel'.[28] Nevertheless, in the sixties, and even more in the seventies, some quickening of dialectical philosophical thought was observable in our country.

A certain role in this was played by Lenin's *Philosophical Notebooks*, which, under Khrushchev, were included in the 'canonical' texts of official 'Marxism-Leninism'. On the one hand they helped to revive interest in Hegelian dialectics; but on the other they imposed upon Soviet philosophers a kind of universally obligatory way of interpreting Hegel, even though it is clear that Lenin's treatment of him is not the only one possible.

Lenin, of course, did not know, when making his transcripts from notes on Hegel, that these would be transformed into a universally obligatory philosophical gospel for future generations. He did not regard himself as a philosopher. But in the perspective of Soviet philosophy Lenin pushes Marx into the background and casts his shadow over Hegel. Consequently, as we shall see, serious works on dialectics usually include a hidden polemic with Lenin – with the *Philosophical Notebooks* or with *Materialism and Empiriocriticism*.

Of substantial importance, too, was the criticism of Stalin in philosophy which began after the Twenty-Second Party Congress. However, on the whole this criticism was unproductive and abstract. Soviet philosophers were not allowed to go as far as Lukács or the Yugoslav journal *Praxis*, let alone the 'Frankfurt School'.[29]

A serious stimulus to the development of dialectical thought was given by F. Il'enkov's works, especially his book *The Dialectics of Abstract and Concrete in Marx's 'Capital'*, published in 1960. Later, in the view of many philosophers, E. Il'enkov failed to follow up his own conclusions but tried instead to reconcile his dialectics with the official schemas, mitigating its critical sense of the negation of reality. From this standpoint his book *Dialectical Logic* (1974) was already a step back. All the same, Il'enkov's works served as a school of critical thinking for a whole generation of Soviet Marxists.[30] It is highly significant, too, that in his book *On Idols and Ideals*, this Soviet philosopher arrived, on many points, at the same conclusions as the 'Frankfurt School' when they dealt with the problem of the alienation of the personality and the humanistic tasks of socialism. It is hard not to compare his works to those of Erich Fromm: a similarity can be observed not only in the general ideas but even in the style.

After dialectics had been restored to its rights, even if only formally,

Marxist philosophers tried to free themselves from Lenin's 'theory of reflection'. Lenin himself considered the very expression a most unhappy one, because it implies that consciousness merely reflects reality in a passive way: he realized this, and tried to make the necessary correction himself, speaking of 'active' reflection: 'Man's consciousness not only reflects the objective world but creates it. ...'[31] But 'active reflection' sounds rather like 'salty sugar'. In his *Marxism in the Twentieth Century* Roger Garaudy tried to resolve this contradiction but was unsuccessful, for it turned out that the more active the reflection, the less accurate it is (distorting mirrors reflect 'more actively' than ordinary ones). Actually, consciousness does not 'reflect' the world but cognizes it, trying actively to penetrate into the depths of things, without confining itself to mere reflection of what is visible. Of course, cognition is a historical process, with all the ensuing consequences. Marx understood the problem in this way when he wrote his *Theses on Feuerbach*.

An open onslaught on the theory of reflection was launched in 1968 by P. Egides, who later became editor of the *samizdat* journal *Poiski*. He wrote:

> In order that thinking may be dialectically identical with being, dialectically coincident with it – that is, in order that thinking may follow all the slightest twists and turns of being, its versatile and complex dialectic, it must indeed be highly active. It must create, transform the world, it must be free, rejecting in a revolutionary way everything that prevents it from grasping the truth in all its fullness.[32]

He showed that the question of 'reflection' is closely connected with the philosophical question of freedom and necessity and that, in its turn, with the question of political freedom:

> Without cognition of necessity there is no freedom, but freedom itself, the essence of freedom, is not the knowledge of necessity but mastery thereof, the controlling and overcoming of necessity. All freedom is cognized necessity, but not all cognized necessity is freedom.[33]

Official philosophy, in calling for submission to necessity and seeing that as freedom, 'may turn into an apologia for slavery.'[34] For Egides, 'freedom means the creation of something new – otherwise, it is not freedom', and alienation reigns: 'Alienation is the antipodes of freedom. Alienation is also connected with that frame of mind in which one does not even dare to think of overcoming necessity.'[35] Genuine freedom of thought means ideological breakthrough, the overcoming of dogmatic schemas which fetter the intellect.

Egides, G. Batishchev and P. Naumenko endeavoured to revive dialectical thinking by turning to Hegel and early Marx, counterposing their ideas on freedom and alienation to the official schematism of the state philosophy. An American philosophical journal described their works published in 1967–68 as blows struck 'against dogmatism, conservatism and the apologetics of official Soviet philosophy'.[36] Their positions, it said, are reminiscent of 'the criticism of industrial society and official Marxism by the philosophers of the "Frankfurt School" (M. Horkheimer, T. Adorno, E. Fromm, H. Marcuse, J. Habermas) and the Yugoslav philosophers grouped around the journal *Praxis* (C. Petrović, R. Supek, M. Marcović, P. Vranitskiy).'[37]

Of greatest interest was the article by G. Batishchev, 'The Active Essence of Man as a Philosophical Principle', in which he declared that Marxist philosophy 'is the philosophy of man in his entirety, with his whole content intact, as a system'.[38] Both nature and society are fields for Marxism, in so far as man himself is both a natural and a social being. In contrast to the determinist-teleological fatalism of the official ideology, which sees the history of mankind as proceeding in accordance with a sort of strict schedule (the stops on the line nearest to us being capitalism, socialism and Communism), and people as merely slaves of objective forces, Batishchev sees humanity as free, and grasping the world through active behaviour and choice. The human personality is in principle creative, and whenever this creative principle is artificially restricted we encounter alienation and depersonalization. The creative process of mankind as a whole is 'a cultural-historical process':[39] not only growth of the productive forces but also development of mankind as a whole, of 'human nature'. In so far as freedom constitutes the essence of man 'as a self-acting subject', it cannot be merely 'freedom *from*' or 'freedom *for*'. This twofold definition given by Fromm is, for Batishchev, not radical enough, for freedom 'can have a purpose in itself alone'.[40]

He attacks simultaneously both capitalism and 'barracks-Communism', the bourgeoisie and the bureaucracy, to whom he counterposes Marxist 'humanist revolutionariness'.[41] Incidentally, he stresses that 'barracks-Communism' is even worse than capitalism, since it expresses the attitude of those individuals and classes who, in Marx's words, have 'not only failed to go beyond private property but [have] not yet even reached it.'[42] In general, Batishchev develops Karyakin's ideas and at the same time makes them concrete emphasizing that 'barracks-Communism' is 'reactionary, being orientated on patently pre-bourgeois forms and re-establishing the "Asiatic mode of production".'[43] He insists that both capitalist and bureaucrat are 'secondary personages' because they rule over production without participating in it, are external factors counterposed to free creative activity. Their own roles are irrational, especially if they are also estranged from the direct process of management: 'Their activity is *formal*, it is pursued only on the basis and within the limits of alienated roles which radically separate them from the cultural-creative process.'[44] Worst of all, though, are not these people but 'secondary personages' of the second order, who are alienated from direct participation in alienated activity – 'all sorts of utilitarian-institutional pen-pushers and security-and-punitive functionaries (including also the honoured group of reliably venal specialists in "brain-work", the ideologues). ...[45]

Thus contemporary society, both Soviet and Western, seems to Batishchev a world of universal alienation, an anti-human and 'false' society which needs to be fundamentally transformed on the principles of freedom and socialism. All these ideas are splendidly inserted into a framework of critical theory as conceived by Marcuse or Adorno, although in this case Batishchev takes up a position on the theory's extreme left wing. Taken as a whole, the philosophical works of our Marxist theoreticians at the end of the sixties, which complement each other, form a fully integrated picture. Nevertheless, the question arises of how original these ideas of theirs are: after all, the 'Frankfurt School' had already formulated them earlier and more completely (of course, neither Marcuse nor Fromm had to worry about a censor).

In the field of the philosophy of nature Soviet thinkers have evidently been somewhat more original, as Western scholars acknowledged. Graham notes that:

> despite the bureaucratic support of the Soviet state for dialectical materialism, a number of able Soviet scientists have created intellectual schema [*sic*] within the framework of dialectical materialism that are sincerely held by their authors and that, furthermore, are intrinsically interesting as the most advanced developments of philosophical materialism. These natural scientists are best seen, just as in the case of the fourteenth-century scholastic thinkers, not as rebels against the prevailing philosophy, but as intellectuals who wish to refine the system, to make it more adequate as a system of explanation.[46]

At first glance this testimonial may not seem, to the Soviet reader, a very flattering one, but Graham is trying to underline the merits of the Soviet philosophy of nature. An important factor needs to be mentioned here. Engels's theory of the dialectics of nature, being most remote from the interests of the social struggle, was the least distorted aspect of Marxist theory in Soviet textbooks. *These* ideas were not subjected to any special 'reworking' – unlike, for example, the Marxist theory of the state. It was thus possible to do serious philosophical work, up to a certain stage, on problems of the natural sciences within the framework of the official ideology. Doubts exist, to be sure, as to the correctness of Engels's approach to the study of nature. These doubts were voiced by Lukács and by the *Praxis* philosophers in Yugoslavia (who saw in Engels's ideas a revival of Hegel's philosophy of nature), but in my view their attacks on Engels were groundless, dogmatic and extremely abstract. In any case, the fruitful development of Engels's ideas by Soviet scholars can serve as a very strong argument against the views of the *Praxis* group.

Dialectical materialism, based on the ideas of Hegel and Engels on the philosophy of nature, was a powerful weapon in the hands of scientists battling against Lysenkoism. It is interesting that in the discussion about genetics both Stalin and Khrushchev showed themselves equally hostile to materialist dialectics (just as the Soviet system as a whole, with its *single* party, which rules out any possibility of the dynamic resolution of contradictions, is ignorant of the dialectical principles of history and is consequently doomed to eventual collapse). The lack of dialectical thinking on the part of the rulers obviously set them against scientific cognition, which requires that the world be seen in all its contradictoriness. It is therefore not surprising that in scientific debates the rulers often supported plainly un-Marxist views, and the fact that these views turned out to be 'also' incorrect produced a particularly grotesque situation. 'Nothing in the philosophical system of dialectical materialism lends obvious support to any of Lysenko's views', observes Graham.[47] It was no accident that such a prominent role in the fight against Lysenko was played by the Marxist dissident Zhores Medvedev. In situations like these the ideas of Engels, even if debatable, proved their scientific worth and ideological usefulness. Thus the dialectics of nature is used by scientists for theoretical self-defence against the voluntarism of the statocracy and is a genuinely living doctrine in the USSR. 'Marxism as methodology and socialism as the structure of social life are not the political ideas which Soviet scientists believe because of official education only', Zhores Medvedev rightly observes. 'These ideas have a logic and scientific appeal which could attract scientists – and not in the USSR alone.'[48] Graham came to similar conclusions:

Marxism is taken quite seriously by some Soviet scientists, less seriously by others, disregarded by still others. There is even a category of Soviet philosophers and scientists who take their dialectical materialism so seriously that they refuse to accept the official statements of the Communist Party on the subject: they strive to develop their own dialectical materialist interpretations of nature, using highly technical articles as screens against the censors. Yet these authors consider themselves dialectical materialists in every sense of the term. ... I am convinced that dialectical materialism has affected the work of some Soviet scientists, and that in certain cases these influences helped them to arrive at views that won them international recognition among their foreign colleagues.[49]

On the whole, Graham evaluates very positively the results of the development of dialectical materialism, and hopes 'the day will come when ... further development of dialectical materialism can take place under conditions of free debate.'[50] When that day arrives, Graham considers, the Western scientific world will be able properly to estimate the achievements of the Soviet philosophy of nature.

Bakhtin and the Culturological School

New ideas in the sphere of the dialectics of nature influence only indirectly the development of social thought in our country. The most original ideas, in my view, relate nevertheless to the philosophy of culture. I have already spoken about the role of cultural traditions in the fight for spiritual emancipation. The rapid growth of the science of culture in the USSR seems therefore not to be accidental.

The point of departure for the beginning of intensive culturological research was the appearance of M. Bakhtin's theory of dialogue. Bakhtin's ideas were actually formed as far back as the 1930s, but they became known to wide circles of the intelligentsia only much later. 'In the sixties and seventies,' wrote the prominent dialectician V.S. Bibler in his *Myshlenie kak tvorchestvo* [Thinking as Creativity],

> the attention given in philosophical literature to the problems of dialogue as the basis of creative thinking sharply increased. The role of a sort of culturological introduction was played here by the works of M.M. Bakhtin, especially *Problemy poetiki Dostoevskogo* (republished in 1972). What counted here was that Bakhtin's books themselves became a most serious cultural event, which in many ways determined the direction of the thinking of a wide variety of theoreticians in the most diverse spheres of research – in philosophy, linguistics, art history, logic. ... But, besides this, Bakhtin's books 'entered into our language, our thought': written much earlier, they unexpectedly became a typical phenomenon of the present cultural epoch. Alongside Bakhtin's books, both before their republication and after, there appeared and are appearing books, articles and symposia devoted to the same problem – dialogue as a cultural phenomenon.[51]

Bakhtin's basic principles are simple enough: 'Other people's consciousnesses cannot be contemplated, analysed, defined as objects, as things – one can commune with them only through dialogue.'[52] One can understand a person only through conversation with him, putting one's own questions to him and answering his. But this applies also to works of art, to philosophical treatises past and present – to *culture* in general, as a sphere of subjective activity. In 'studying' our interlocutor through dialogue, however, we at the same time get to know ourselves. Furthermore, the measure of our self-knowledge corresponds to the depth of our penetration into the soul of 'the other'. This, strictly speaking, is the departure point of the entire culturological school.

It must be appreciated that the concept 'culture' is used here in a rather broad sense. In his lecture on Bakhtin, Bibler defined it as a sort of historical 'sediment'. Culture is everything we have inherited from past epochs, from social formations that no longer exist. To it belong philosophical works, art, traditions, the people's historical experience, science and the level of technology that has been attained. In so far as all this can be looked at and studied as a whole, we can speak of 'culture'. This approach makes the theory of culture a very important element in sociohistorical theory. It is quite natural that the culturological school should be in resolute opposition to the official 'received wisdom', the whole essence of which comes down to the 'fitting' of all historical facts into a previously given schema.

The culturological school could, broadly speaking, be called Marxist-Bakhtinist. However, for some of its representatives, such as V. Bibler and A.Ya. Gurevich, Marx is perhaps given first place, whereas for L. Batkin the influence of Bakhtin is of central methodological importance. Very important in Gurevich's development of new historical and culturological ideas was the thought of the French historian Marc Bloch, and for Bibler this role was played by Hegel's philosophy. All these different sources can be brought into unity through an overall critical-dialectical and, above all, historical approach to culture. The special role of Marx is defined for the Moscow culturologists[53] as, first and foremost, that he began 'the transition to a historical science of a new type'.[54] At the same time, despite the differences between individual writers, the whole school is clearly working for the enrichment of method.

It is one of the ironies of history that it should be the Christian Bakhtin, a deeply religious man quite alien to Marxism, who has had an immensely stimulating effect on the development and revival of Marxist dialectics in the USSR. In 1936 Trotsky wrote that although everyone in our country considers himself a Marxist, not a single Marxist book gets published. That was true also of the 1960s, at least as far as the first half of that decade was concerned. The presence of quotations and references in general schemas was in no way proof of the flourishing of

Marxist thought, because the most important thing – namely, method – remained in oblivion.

In order to understand the methodological revolution brought about in the sphere of culturology one must compare Bakhtin with E.V. Il'enkov. Both men worked for the revival of dialectics, which had been reduced in the textbooks to a collection of examples (something to which Engels himself objected), and for its transformation into a way of thinking. Whereas Bakhtin's dialectics were rooted in the New Testament, Il'enkov's goes back to Marx's *Capital.* The culturologists of the seventies – being of a different generation, a different education, a different training – did not share Bakhtin's religious ideas, although they seized upon his scientific conclusions. A demand arose for a methodological 'correction' of Bakhtin's philosophy 'in accordance with Marx'. (Here a role was played by Il'enkov's works, which were examples of serious scientific thinking.)

The new school, following Bakhtin, formulated the fundamental conclusions of the theory of dialogue. First and foremost they formed the view that ordinary dialectics – the universal theory of development of nature and society – is inadequate for the explanation of thought. Thinking is more than dialectical, it is dialogical. It is not enough to establish the presence of 'two sides' to every concept, its inner contradictoriness. The contradictions of thought are much more fundamental. Creative thinking is based not on conflict between a thesis and the antithesis that this engenders, but on conflict between two initial theses, resulting in a synthesis. Consequently, *all* cognition is dialogical, and the cognition of culture especially so. But for dialogue, as we know, two sides are needed. It is necessary to recognize the cultural sovereignty of the past. 'Unless we realize that,' said Batkin in his famous lectures on Leonardo de Vinci, 'we cannot comprehend the originality and distinctiveness of our own epoch and our own method. The present is not the absolute criterion for history. ...'[55]

New tasks arise from this. We have to understand the culture of the past as a whole, as an independent system, and development not as a process of steady advance but as a more complex accumulation of historical experience through a dialogue of cultures. In his lecture on Leonardo, Batkin declared against the traditional academic idealizing of the past, against reverential 'rounding off' and excision of contradictions. For him it was important to know not only *what* people thought but also *how* they thought, and not only to establish this but also to understand it.

Here one finds oneself recalling Bertolt Brecht, the playwright – or rather the theoretician – with his 'alienation effect', looking from the side, objectivizing. The method of the Moscow culturologists is based on a threefold dialectical alienation. First, alienation of one's view of the past, purging it of stereotyped ideas, those prejudices about it which come naturally to us. The second alienation happens when, after jettisoning the most banal of our schemas, we still remain people of our own epoch and alienate the past itself, and then we sometimes see things that contemporaries did not see – when, to use Bakhtin's own phrase, 'we put to an alien culture questions which it did not put to itself.'[56] In this way we manage, now and then, to perceive new features in the culture of a past epoch. Thus, for example, the tragic nature of Leonardo's personality was clear to Batkin although he himself did not realize this. Lastly we have alienation of our own time: in studying the past we begin to look in a new way at the present. The 'alien' culture puts its own questions to us.

Here we perceive a manifest break with the official theory of culture and society. The writers of textbooks – and, of course, we have in mind here not only manuals for students but also some 'serious' works in the category of official 'education in historical materialism' – consider that investigation is complete when events have been reduced to a sociological-dialectical schema. Here we have everything – the productive forces, the relations of production, the social factors and even, sometimes, mention of cultural and religious traditions. One thing alone is missing: living interaction, movement, process: in other words, dialectics itself. M.Ya. Gefter noted that this whole schema is

> a distorted representation of the structure and logic of Marxism, in which the materialist conception of history becomes something secondary, derived from the philosophy of nature according to 'diamat'. The true picture of the genesis of materialist dialectics is distorted; but what is even more important is that this merely instructional schema, when implanted in people's minds, maintains the isolation of contemporary historical materialism both from dialectics and from concrete study of society in past and present alike.[57]

The culturologists, on the contrary, address themselves both to dialectics and to concrete study. For them scientific work begins precisely where, for the dogmatists, it stops.

It is of major importance that from now on theoretical thinking is not only revealing afresh truths which had been 'closed' under Stalin but also creating something of its own, something new and original, carrying on scientific research in the full sense of the word. The preparatory period is past; philosophical science has reached maturity.

Batkin's article 'The Uncomfortableness of Culture', published in the uncensored symposium *Metropol'*, was a sort of manifesto of the philosophical ideas of the culturologists. It was written originally for the official journal *Voprosy Filosofii* and failed to be published there for quite accidental reasons. Nevertheless it was symbolic that this programmatic declaration of the culturological school should have appeared in an uncensored publication. Batkin insisted on regarding culture as a tragic process of self-negation and self-renewal, in constant conflict with the conservatism of official society and with itself: 'Enclosure in itself as complete as possible, dialogue without limits, that is what is needed for culture: any mechanical reduction or exclusion from internal debate, that is what really emasculates culture. But how frightened we are to linger for a breath of air!'[58] Culture constantly fights also against the 'guardians' of culture, who prove to be, in reality, prison warders protecting the official ideology, for culture is a challenge to dogmas, a revolt against tradition, against everything stagnant and immobile. 'There is no way out except oblivion. Seriously to "rest" the whole weight of the present upon tradition means to refute it.'[59]

The culturologists struck a powerful blow at the dogmatic consciousness – not only at particular dogmas but at this type of thinking generally, at positivist or national-'Christian' dogmatism no less than at the 'Marxist' variety. From now on it was impossible to work in the old way. On the other hand the culturologists, especially A. Gurevich, did a great deal to reconstruct historical materialism, eradicating various outworn schemas and pseudo-determinist notions.

The role played by members of the culturological school in public life is quite important. They *teach how to think*, and on that plane their significance is not reducible to their contribution to science. It is hard to define the ideological position of the culturologists. This school is resolutely opposed to every sort of reactionary nationalist tendency and at the same time its ideas are closely linked to Marxism, even though this link is not, as a rule, given much emphasis. Without the contribution to science made by Marx and Gramsci the new culturology would have been as impossible as if Bakhtin had never existed. However, it is risky to talk openly about that in some circles.

Critical Marxism

The crisis of the oppositional ideology in the Khrushchev period left the word 'Marxism' extremely unpopular among a certain section of the intellectuals. Rakovski regrets that since 1968 not only are serious works on the development of Marxist thought difficult to find – 'it is Marxists themselves who are now difficult to find in Eastern Europe'. Nevertheless, in the sixties and seventies oppositional Marxist thought not only went on developing in the USSR, it achieved some great successes. Apart from anything else, it became more Marxist and acquired the opportunity to constitute a real alternative to the dead official ideology and the neo-dogmatism of the Right opposition.

It is possible to distinguish between legal and illegal Marxist thought in the USSR. Legal does not mean official: on the contrary, the legal Marxists carry on a systematic struggle against official dogmatism, but prefer to do this in censored publications which are available to the general public, although many of them also express themselves in *samizdat.* Thus P. Egides and M. Gefter moved in the seventies from censored publications into the uncensored Moscow journal *Poiski.*

I have already spoken here about the unity of the cultural-political process and the close link between censored literature and *samizdat.* It is easy to observe how legal and illegal literature supplement each other. In any case, Marxist *samizdat* owes a great deal to legal Marxism.

In the West, Roy Medvedev is seen as practically the sole supporter of Marxism in our country. Some *émigrés* also try to depict the situation like that,[61] but this does not fit the facts at all. Of course, Roy Medvedev deserves the international recognition given to his works of research, which differ so markedly from the dogmatic philosophizing of the Soviet New Right, but he is far from being a lonely Don Quixote or a fighter defending the last barricade. On the other hand, although Medvedev's writings are published abroad, he can be regarded rather as a representative of legal Marxism in the USSR. He expounds the same system of ideas that we can find in the works of Karyakin, Batishchev, Butenko or Vodolazov, except that because his books are not subject to censorship, he is able to formulate his conclusions openly.

Moreover, Medvedev is one of the theoreticians of a moderate tendency. There are among Soviet Marxists, including those who publish legally, theoreticians who draw more radical conclusions and go much further in their critique of statocracy and neo-Stalinism.[62] *Samizdat* helps to formulate the ultimate conclusions drawn by these critics. At the end of the seventies a number of periodicals of a socialist tendency appeared together. The best-known of these was the journal *Poiski,* which carried articles not only by Marxists but also by representatives of other trends (for example, V. Sokirko-Burzhuademov collaborated with *Poiski*). In Leningrad the New Left published the journal *Perspektivy.* Both journals later ceased to appear, as a result of repressive measures. Leningrad socialists belonging to the *Kolokol* group (Ronkin and Khakhaev) issued in *samizdat* the symposium *Cherez Top'* [Through the Swamp], in which they tried to revive the 'orthodox Marxism' of G.V. Plekhanov. In Moscow in 1977 an almanac of socialist thought appeared, under the title *Varianty.* Between 1977 and 1980 four issues came out, but in 1981 publication ceased. Although much of its material could have been better, *Varianty* was a very interesting and successful attempt to enliven the theoretical discussion in *samizdat*.[63] Typical of *Varianty* was its endeavour to utilize the ideas of Gramsci, of Western neo-Marxism, Kardelj and other Yugoslav theoreticians, and also, in some articles, contemporary Social Democratic ideas. The new achievements of socialist thought in the West were bound to be of help in studying Soviet problems, but most of the articles in *Varianty* were not mere students' expositions of foreign works. Besides *Varianty*, several other *samizdat* publications of a Left tendency appeared at the end of the seventies.

However, legal Marxist literature differs in many ways from *samizdat*, and for the better. Some of the wiser dissidents have admitted the superiority of a number of censored publications. V. Chalidze writes that in legal literature, authors and scholars wage a constant struggle for culture against the statocracy:

> This is that section of the intelligentsia which, in full continuity with previous generations, is creating and upholding Russian culture and the culture of other peoples. Although the *émigrés* boast of famous names and of the uncensored character of their work, our country's culture is being created by the group mentioned, and not by the *émigrés*, despite the need sometimes to use phraseology acceptable to the authorities.[64]

There is no abuse of the authorities in legal literature, but from time to time its contributors show great intellectual boldness, bringing forward new ideas, which *samizdat* often fails to do.

What I have here called 'legal Marxism' is diverse. In the first place we find in this category a right wing, consisting of those whose views could be described as Social Democratic or technocratic. When publishing their works legally they doubtless have to give them a 'Marxist look'. As an example of a technocrat one may take V. Lukin. Generally speaking, the Institute for Study of the USA and Canada is a place where openly pro-American and technocratic attitudes predominate. However, the representatives of this trend are the most loyal to the statocracy and restrained in their criticism. Also among the legal Marxists there is a neo-Communist centre – G. Vodolazov or M. Cheshkov – and an extreme left wing, close to K. Maydannik. This schema does not exhaust the differences among them; nevertheless, the existence of a common problematic and the similarity between many of their chief conclusions enables us to speak of legal Marxism as a single entity.

Legal Marxism proved able to raise and answer a number of historico-social questions. Above all it was necessary to look into the essence and history of socialist doctrine. An important consideration was that the big question always remained 'outside the frame': How did it happen that, under the slogan of emancipation of labour and amid talk about 'socialist construction', we arrived at totalitarianism? This is the question of questions and although it is never even mentioned in so many words, it determines all the other questions. Whether writers realize this or not does not matter. A general scientific context arises which no serious scholar can avoid. The content of this scientific context consists precisely of the 'accursed' questions of our time, the most acute and painful social problems, and there is no getting away from them. We have to keep on coming back to them so long as life has not set new tasks before us. For this reason one can well understand A. Tsipko's confidence when he wrote, at the end of his book, that the necessary conclusions 'will be drawn by the reader for himself'.[65]

The question of socialism thus became very acute. It was necessary to analyse the history of the struggle for socialism in order to discover the roots of the 'totalitarian degeneration'. In the seventies and eighties it was already not enough merely to say that Stalinism was inimical to Marxism: one had to track down the ideological and historical roots of Stalinism and at the same time discover the spiritual foundations, the general principles for overcoming it. For both purposes it was necessary to study the history of socialism.

What has especially attracted researchers' interest is the concept of utopia. One can read about this in Tsipko's *Optimizm istorii*, G. Vodolazov's *Ot Chernyshevskogo k Plekhanovu*, Yu. Kagarlitsky's *Chto takoe fantastika?* and many other books. As an example, I will take Tsipko's writings. It has to be said that in them, as also in Vodolazov's, we encounter some highly tendentious appraisals of certain Western thinkers. It is difficult to make out whether this is a gesture of submission to the censors or whether the two authors sincerely do not accept ideas which lie outside the framework of the 'classical' Marxism of the beginning of this century. However Tsipko, and M. Barg before him, raised a very pointed question: What criterion must be used to decide whether certain ideas are or are not 'socialist'?[66] According to Tsipko, 'the criterion for the socialist character of an idea has to be sought, above all, in the degree of humanism',[67] and there can be no question of socialism where there is no *humanist ideal of society*. This ideal is not an 'ultimate aim' but accompanies the movement, becoming perfected and changing at each stage. Engels wrote that socialists 'have no ultimate aim. We are for constant, uninterrupted development and have no intention of dictating to mankind any definite laws.'[68] Tsipko notes that Marx ascribed enormous importance to trying to 'safeguard the humanist essence' of his philosophy.[69] For this reason the democratic ideal was necessary to him, because it enables one to choose the means and tasks of the current moment and establish a criterion for self-appraisal. Forgetting the humanist ideal of Marxism or transforming it into a formal 'ultimate aim' (which, as we know, was what happened in the Communist movement in the 1920s) can mean that 'the means of socialism are brought into contradiction with its aim, and thereby lose their "socialist" character.'[70] Such a breach between the ideal and the means is a constant danger for any revolutionary movement and an effort to overcome it was made by Marxism, which 'from the outset linked, in its teaching, revolutionary methods with the humanist ideal of the genuine emancipation of mankind'.[71]

When he turns his attention to utopias, Tsipko does not merely criticize them. Whereas Karyakin concentrated primarily on the ideas of barracks-Communism as put into practice by Stalin, Tsipko, on the contrary, stresses that democratic ideas were also present in utopian socialism. It was these that Marx utilized, while rejecting the means proposed by the utopians. *Thus the defect of the utopias is not that they are unrealizable but that their realization leads to consequences quite different from what had been hoped.* In so far as the corresponding means are not available, 'the demand for freedom of association is a declaration rather than a practical principle'.[72] At the same time, Marxists must strive towards a society wherein 'the genuine and free development of individuals ceases to be a mere phrase'.[73]

Tsipko's book replied to the very questions that had been raised by Shafarevich. The censorship situation renders unthinkable either an open polemic (opposing a dissident in a legal publication means siding with the rulers) or a clear-cut formulation of one's replies. But replies were certainly given, albeit only in descriptive form. Tsipko's work shows that Shafarevich not only confused the Asiatic mode of production with socialism but also *social* utopias with *socialist* ones.[74] Tsipko's historical approach reveals that many utopian projects, which to us seem despotic, left the individual more freedom than did the actual society of their time. In general, he seeks to 'rehabilitate' the humanist utopia, defending it against Soviet dogmatists – from whom, incidentally, Shafarevich borrowed his general treatment of the problem. However, the merit of Tsipko's book is that he neither praises nor curses utopia, but looks at the idea objectively. He shows that the ideology of barracks-Communism is formed by proclaiming extreme means as its ultimate aim, and normal socialist practice as a retreat from the ideal, and raises the question of how to avoid such 'degeneration'. Tsipko sees the development of culture and democracy in production as guarantees against totalitarianism. The one is closely bound up with the other, and without them there can be no socialism:

An indispensable condition for the socialization of the means of production is socialization of the management of production and assimilation of all the achievements of civilization and culture by the working people themselves. Only when the direct producer takes a very active part in the organization and management of production can we count on the awakening in him of the sentiments of a master of production, and thereby the establishment of a new, direct bond between him and the nationalized means of production.[75]

The abolition of private property leads to socialism only if it be complemented by a 'restructuring of society as a whole in the interests of the development of the human personality'.[76] But the new socialist 'mechanism' will not function without a great number of civilized people, bearers of up-to-date culture. Clearly present-day Soviet society, in which there is neither self-management in production nor political freedom, fails to correspond to the principles of socialism enunciated here. In Tsipko's opinion, however, the development of culture sharply increases the chances of a socialist transformation. Culture makes possible the overcoming of utopian illusions, which are fraught with much danger.

The heart of the problem amounts to this: born as a mythological embodiment of the working people's hopes for deliverance from their day-to-day burdens, utopian collectivism becomes in practice, when it is put into effect, worse in many ways than slavery. Inherent in utopia are both the basis for the future movement of liberation and an internal danger thereto. And inasmuch as the future is always imagined in the consciousness of the masses in a way that is to some extent utopian, any party that is orientated on the future constantly comes up against the phenomenon of utopianism. No scientific knowledge can guarantee against this. Bernard Shaw, discussing Darwinism, remarked that any science can become an ideology in itself – even a religion (and can consequently engender utopian illusions). In the twentieth century, he observed, we see 'the revival of religion on a scientific basis'.[77] Even where scientific ideas have triumphed, in the shape of Marxism, nothing yet ensures that utopian thinking will not make a comeback, assuming different forms. A relapse from science to utopia is sometimes expressed in a false interpretation of scientific conclusions. 'The correctness of a principle does not guarantee the correctness of its application,' wrote G. Vodolazov.[78] An objectively reactionary utopia can adopt scientific terminology and acquire an appearance of soundness. The utopianism of the mass consciousness helps totalitarianism to subject the people, if only at first, but that is not the whole story. Totalitarianism sometimes performs really necessary work. The only question is *how* it does this.

According to Cheshkov and Vodolazov, for example, there are

objective historical tasks that confront every society – tasks which are, so to speak, supra-class. But the means and methods for accomplishing these tasks possess a class character. Such a task is the modernizing of a backward country. In its own way, totalitarianism copes very well with that task. The point is, though, that it does this at man's expense. 'If this condition is not "stipulated",' wrote Vodolazov,

> the problem is rendered extremely simple. All 'subtleties' are then eliminated from the problem with all the complications of transitional stages and measures, the solution to the problem is set out in straight lines, and a system made up of these lines is realized in the form of a system of barbed-wire fences, places of detention, prisons, concentration camps, and so on.[79]

On History and Historiography

All these general-theoretical conclusions became concrete in discussions among historians. One can even speak of a renaissance of historiography in the USSR at the end of the sixties and the beginning of the seventies. The acuteness of the problems, their 'non-theoretical' significance, compelled the historians to think very intensely and productively.

In the 1940s George Orwell wrote that 'what is peculiar to our own age is the abandonment of the idea that history *could* be truthfully written.'[80] After Stalin's death it fell to the historians to rectify a situation that seemed irremediable: they had to rehabilitate not just this or that person, but historiography as a whole in the USSR. Later, in 1965, a group of historians, replying to *Izvestiya*'s attacks on *Novy Mir*, wrote that they regarded it as their duty 'in the name of the past and of the future, to comprehend historical truth in all its fullness.'[81] But it was impossible to tell the truth about the past without affecting certain interests that exist in the present. At first, however, the government itself encouraged the search for new ideas in history. Soon after the Twenty-Second Party Congress an All-Union Conference of Historians was held and was addressed by B.N. Ponomarev, who at that time was already a prominent ideologue of the CPSU. He blamed Stalin for having 'placed the study of historical problems under his own supervision, subordinating it to the task of glorifying his personality', and even spoke of 'the Procrustean bed of Stalinist schemas and formulas'.[82] This sharply anti-Stalinist speech set the tone for the whole conference. A.K. Kasimenko said that

> it would be difficult to name any stage in the history of the Ukrainian people in the Soviet period when serious deviations from historical truth were not

committed in the service of the cult of Stalin's personality or to please his henchmen, like Kaganovich,

and called for historical science to be 'purged' of the 'deposits' left by Stalinism.[83] V.G. Trukhanovsky distinguished among (Western) Sovietologists 'honest scholars' with whom 'we need to talk in a different language from that which we use with falsifiers.'[84] It was clear that many Western scholars were honestly trying to get at the truth about the events of the revolution at a time when Soviet historians were distorting it. I.M. Maisky said that 'the period of the personality cult', as he called it, 'simply killed off the memoir genre.'[85]

A re-examination of the Stalinist schemas of history was begun. Thus, after 1961, theories which depicted the conquest by Tsarist Russia of the 'border peoples' of Central Asia, Caucasia and other parts of the present Soviet Union as historical good luck – almost a boon – for these peoples were condemned. It was officially recognized that such an interpretation of events was mistaken.[86] It was at last permitted to curse tyrants like Ivan the Terrible, Stalin's favourite hero. In the symposium *Evropa v novoe i noveyshee vremya* V.A. Dunaevsky criticized Stalin's famous letter to the editors of the journal *Proletarskaya Revolyutsiya*, in which he accused the journal of following an incorrect line on the history of Bolshevism. For many years this letter was regarded as a basic document of Party history. Now it was itself declared wrong. Dunaevsky mentioned that Stalin put an end to discussion about the history of the revolution at the very moment 'when Soviet historiography was beginning to arrive at a number of constructive solutions.'[87]

The start thus made looked very promising. However, while there were many anti-Stalin declarations, not much actual work was done. V. Danilov, Party organizer at the Institute of History at that time, spoke frankly about this at the historians' conference. He recalled that the 'filling-in of the gaps' had only begun, that 'the most important archives' were still closed, and so on.[88] Danilov's speech struck a discordant note, because he did not so much expose the accursed past as talk of 'serious difficulties' in the present.[89] He himself tried to overcome these difficulties – that is, the obstacles presented by the censorship and the official ideology – by intensified study of particular problems of socioeconomic history. He was mainly interested in the fate of the Russian peasantry. The starting point of Danilov's reflections was a critique of Stalin's ideas, according to which the relations of production among the Russian peasants before collectivization were capitalist. It was on the basis of this theory that the case for collectivization was argued, as a necessary stage on the road to socialism in the USSR. Danilov doubted the correctness of this idea, which was usually not supported by any facts. 'In works on the class struggle,' he wrote, 'we cannot find any serious scientific account of the social forces in the countryside and their distribution.'[90]

After closer study of the question, he came to the conclusion that the relations of production prevailing in Russia's countryside in the 1920s could not be called capitalist. Stalin spoke of 'capitalism' in the villages on the grounds that private property existed there. Danilov based himself on Marx's idea that 'according to whether these private individuals (who own property) are workers or non-workers, private property has a different character.'[91] The petty peasant production that existed in Soviet Russia in the 1920s was therefore not capitalist. But in any case, could one speak of 'private property' in relation to that period? 'The nationalization of the land meant that one of the basic means of production in agriculture had been brought under state-social ownership and this was therefore an important step on the road to socialism.'[92] Danilov also mentioned the growth of co-operation and the decline in the relative importance of private trade. Thus in the circumstances of the post-revolutionary society of the 1920s, in the countryside, 'socioeconomic relations of a new type which could not be regarded as bourgeois' were beginning to arise.[93]

The question consequently arose: Was collectivization really necessary? Soviet historians could not and cannot, of course, discuss that question openly. Under Khrushchev all that was allowed was criticism of particular mistakes, but this criticism went quite a long way and as a result it became possible to draw, if not a complete, then at least a fairly reliable picture of collectivization and to subvert the Stalinist myth of the 'great turning point'. Soviet historians showed that the process of collectivization proved extremely harmful both to the peasantry and to agriculture as a whole – to such a degree that, as it was agreed to put this, there had been violation of 'Lenin's principle of voluntariness in bringing peasants into collective farms and providing material incentives for the peasant masses'.[94] This formulation may seem too mild, but it was the most that the censorship allowed. It made possible the setting forth of historical material with comparative accuracy, quoting important facts which had previously been concealed.[95] The role played by Stalin, his personal responsibility, was established more or less precisely. This was of particular importance for understanding collectivization, because the question inevitably arose: Where does the boundary run between 'mistakes', 'distortion' of the Party line and the 'Party line' itself? What the historians could not say was said by writers. The years 1964 to 1968 saw the publication of A. Alekseev's *Bread, Noun Substantive*, Tendryakov's *Decease*, and many other works dealing with the collectivization period. Those books which failed to pass the censor went into *samizdat.* Works of fiction and works of research complemented each other. Roy Medvedev could quite correctly observe later that the outrages of Stalin's collectivization 'have frequently been subjected to critical analysis in our historical, political and fictional literature.'[96]

The truth was restored bit by bit, like a broken mirror. No question was 'seditious' in itself, but the mosaic picture thus assembled formed an integral representation of the past which utterly refuted the statocratic ideology. However, the demand that the knowledge which had been accumulated should be generalized remained largely unfulfilled. The facts had to be thought over in a theoretical way, but the methods employed at the beginning of the sixties for this purpose were not adequate to the task. History had to become theory. The ideological crisis which broke out after 1968 raised this question with particular sharpness, and it was as a result of this that legal Marxism began to develop new ideas.

The role of manifesto of legal Marxism was played by the book published in 1969, under the editorship of M.Ya. Gefter, with the title *The Science of History and Some Problems of the Present Day.* This symposium began with a preface which dealt with general problems of historiography in the USSR. The writers acknowledged that the initial reaction against Stalinist dogmatism in this sphere had been purely negative. Some of the most offensive conceptions had been cast out (such as that the Roman Empire fell as a result of a 'revolution of the slaves'), quotations from the works of 'the friend and teacher' had been removed, and at a certain moment there had arisen a movement to 'get back to Lenin'. This constituted a beginning of the transition to working out a positive Marxist theory but, as soon became clear, going 'back to Lenin' was not enough by itself. This slogan was replaced by another – forward to Marx. Marx, unlike Lenin, was studied as the founder of a method. From Lenin they tried to find answers to problems of the present day, which, in a certain sense, impelled them back to the past – although, after Stalinism, even this was a huge step forward. From Marx they learned, above all, the culture of historical thought. Paradoxical as it may seem, Soviet historiography discovered Marx not in the fifties but at the end of the sixties.

The ideological legacy of Gramsci was appreciated even later. A three-volume edition of his writings had appeared in Russian translation in 1959, but the importance of his *Prison Notebooks* actually began to be understood only in the seventies, in connection with a growth of interest in the Italian Communist Party and Eurocommunism. One of the first to popularize Gramsci's ideas was G.

Vodolazov. In 1968 he published in *Novy Mir* an article on Gramsci's legacy in the field of aesthetics. In this article he wrote mainly, however, on the historico-philosophical reflections of the author of the *Prison Notebooks*. Vodolazov was principally interested in Gramsci's ideas on the destiny of the revolution, which had much in common with the Russian experience. Gramsci observed that 'a revolution is not proletarian and Communist, even if a wave of popular revolt has placed in power men who call themselves Communists (sincerely too)'.[97] If the proletariat *as a class* is not ready to take power, then the victory of the Communists, despite all the enthusiasm of the worker masses, will not lead to socialism and will require 'further and even more frightful sacrifices' in order to ensure the establishment of a democracy of the working people.[98]

After the events of 1968 the left-wing intelligentsia gradually began to realize how true these views of Gramsci's were. But it was not possible to look for answers to our present-day problems in the work of a thinker of the past. One had urgently to make up for past neglect, and go forward. 'Consequently,' we read in Gefter's symposium,

> if our assimilation of the heritage is to be creative, it cannot be restricted to mobilizing 'quotations' directed against particular oversimplified schemas and propositions. It has to be – and the crucial character of our epoch necessitates this with special force – a fresh reading of the historical conceptions of Marx, Engels and Lenin.[99]

The old Stalinist historiography combined magnificently a bald empiricism with speculative 'general laws' – only at best, however, for most often there was mere falsification under both heads. The task of the legal Marxists was to renew theory and develop method through concrete historical research. In a certain sense they had to open afresh the road traversed by Marx in such works as *The Eighteenth Brumaire of Louis Bonaparte*. The principal problem, on the general plane, which faced historians (and brought them up against the 'accursed' questions concerning Russia's fate in the twentieth century) was that of *how the world of today came to be*. Here the field of activity was broad, to say the least. It included the origin of socialist ideas, the origin of the revolution in Russia, the formation of nations in modern Europe, the establishment of 'Faustian civilization', and so on. In this context even works devoted to medieval subjects (such as A. Gurevich's notable book on the origin of feudalism in Western Europe) appeared highly topical and far from boringly academic.

Official 'istmat' (historical materialism), as M. Markus and A. Hegedüs observed, constantly proclaimed its scientific character, but in reality it rejected science to the extent that it refused to confront theory with social reality, and did not recognize the necessity for social theory to develop any further.[100]

The most important problems of Marxism – alienation, for example – were simply omitted from the official textbooks. What was needed, however, was not merely to restore Marx's original theory of history but also to renew it. Accumulated experience does not permit one just to 'go back to Marx'. Marc Rakovski noted that in so far as most East European Marxists characterize societies of the Soviet type as '*sui generis* class societies existing alongside capitalism',[101] it is necessary to take a fresh look at all the traditional schemas of history:

> Within the traditional structure of historical materialism there is no place for a modern social system which has an evolutionary trajectory other than capitalism and which is not simply an earlier or later stage along the same route.[102]

Since Kautsky's time Marxists had perceived history as a kind of unilinear process in which social formations replace each other in strict order of succession. Marx must be given credit for never having said this, but Kautsky's interpretation of his ideas could be considered quite admissible from the standpoint of the inner logic of Marx's materialism (which does not mean that Kautsky's version was the only one possible). Experience in our century has compelled us to start thinking once more about the limitedness of such a conception of history, and Gurevich's book *Problemy genezisa feodalizma v Zapadnoy Evrope* (1970) was the most interesting and strikingly successful attempt to overcome the unilinearity of 'classical' Marxism. Gurevich showed that feudalism was by no means the inevitable outcome of the development of slave-owning society, but arose in concrete and highly specific historico-social circumstances. Thereby he raised the question of the possibility that more than one mode of production can exist on the basis of the same level of development of the productive forces.[103] Naturally, this book was furiously attacked by the dogmatists, who charged it with all the mortal sins. Some of them were particularly angry about those passages in it where they perceived hints at our own time, such as: 'The present-day conception of freedom presumes independence from anybody whatsoever.'[104] The accusation was brought against Gurevich that 'essentially, he is unwilling to take account of the Marxist-Leninist teaching on socioeconomic formations.'[105] Although the book had been written as a textbook for students, it was not accorded that honourable status. However, it was not withdrawn from the libraries, and despite all warnings it became classical material on which a new generation of Marxist historians was raised. Thus problems of medieval history can, with us, prove topical and even politically pointed.

'To the pragmatic, utilitarian and conjunctural approach to history,' declared the contributors to Gefter's symposium,

> we oppose not pretended neutrality and hypocritical indifference, but concern to obtain scientific truth and serve the cause of progress, the twofold task which constitutes the heart and meaning of the historical form of mankind's cognition of itself: the extraction of experience, and learning from the lessons of the near and distant past.[106]

In his writings Gefter has done much to show the specific character of Russian capitalism – namely, its barbarousness. He has examined in detail the question of the presence of several different economic structures in Russia. This was not merely a matter of technological backwardness and insufficient development of industry, but of the specifics of the structure of Russian capitalism itself – of *its* barbarousness. It was not a poorly developed capitalist structure but a structure which, in its own way, was even highly developed, but of a different type from elsewhere. As a result of his study of this phenomenon Gefter came to the conclusion: as the capitalism was, so was the revolution. Socialist revolution was impossible where what still needed to be done was the 'clearing' of society by putting an end to the multiplicity of economic structures within it. Further conclusions inevitably follow. Stalinism fulfilled this function very well indeed. Not only was the country industrialized but a comparatively more up-to-date social structure was created, with an advanced degree of proletarianization of the population and the predominance of wage-labour relations, and without patriarchal forms of exploitation. Stalinism was a modernizing despotism – and here we come back to Vodolazov's problem of the 'simple' totalitarian solution. True, variety of economic structures has been re-established at a new level in the form of the contradiction between the state-run economy and the black market, but that is another question. ...

Legal Marxism in the USSR has come to the same conclusion as the Western Marxism personified in Deutscher, which was banned in our country. History has become politics. Soviet historians are confronted with a serious problem to which they continually address themselves in one way or another. On the one hand, morality in historical science means objectivity, impartiality. On the other, the position of someone who is looking at history from the standpoint of the interests of the future, thinking about the emancipation of society, cannot but be moral. Does the adjective 'impartial' apply to him? His is a 'passionate' [*strastnaya*] position – even, if you like, a 'partial' [*pristrastnaya*] one. The matter is further complicated by the fact that man, by his very nature, cannot be absolutely objective: in so far as he is an individual, he is a subjective being.

However, reality, which has set us this problem, has also created the conditions for solving it. In combating the official ideology, left-wing historians see their task as restoring historical truth. In this their partiality finds expression, their *engagement* – their 'partisanship' [*partiynost*], if you care to put it that way.

The problems of methodological principle were presented in Ya.S. Drabkin's lecture on 'Unsolved Problems in the Study of Social Revolutions'.[107] The title speaks for itself. In a comparatively brief talk, Drabkin tried to formulate – or at least to enumerate – the fundamental problems which twentieth-century experience has set before Marxists (and, indeed, before all serious thinkers on social matters). On the plane of general theory this means: the problem of the dialectics of reform and revolution, which later confronted the Western Left – no less than the Soviet socialists – in a very acute form: the problem of 'peaceful evolution' from one mode of production to another – examples might be the transition to capitalism in Sweden, or the problem of the 'socialist' Thermidor.

All these are very serious problems – that is, of course, if they are to be solved not 'ideologically', disposed of with general phrases, but scientifically. As for Thermidor, this problem now arose for the first time for legal Soviet historiography. Drabkin recalled that Lenin did not deny the possibility of a Soviet Thermidor,[108] but naturally the lecturer left the question open. Of course, all these important problems could be examined in the lecture only in an extremely abstract way, on the plane of general methodology, deliberately 'without coming to any conclusions'. Besides, Drabkin could not have given any answers, even if he had them. The censorship allows (though not always) questions to be put, but disallows answers. Consequently, Drabkin considered that his task was merely to 'focus attention on the most acute unsolved problems of research'.[109]

Nevertheless, it cannot be said that these problems remained totally unsolved. Discussion of the lecture gave rise to fresh debates, in which the participants got to grips with the conclusions to be drawn in principle. G.G. Diligensky concentrated on the subject of 'Thermidor'. He declared that

neither the leading role of the working class in the revolutionary movement nor even the adoption by that movement of the programmatic principles of scientific socialism can guarantee, by themselves, that the aims of the movement will not become distorted.[110]

The only guarantee lies in *conscious* participation by the masses. And for that, 'incidentally', it is necessary that the masses themselves be capable of such conscious participation – that the country be ripe for revolution not only economically and politically but also socially and culturally. This consciousness (and of course, Diligensky meant by 'consciousness' not readiness for unquestioning submission but, on the contrary, capacity for independent action and decision-making) signifies that the working classes are mature and is the guarantee against utopianism, against descent by the revolution to totalitarian decisions, against a bureaucratic Thermidor:

> A complex combination of factors: scientific and technological progress, new social experience by the masses, their increased education and culture, the decrease in the former social and cultural isolation of the working classes – all this has reduced the susceptibility of the ordinary person to a number of social illusions. The masses are no longer satisfied with mere promises, with more or less vague depictions of a happy life in the future. They more and more insistently demand rational, logical, convincing means of solving concrete problems. And the masses will march behind those persons and parties who offer them such means.[111]

At a certain stage the growth of consciousness leads not directly to revolutionization but to rejection of politics, to scepticism and indifference, as we have seen in the case of Soviet society. But this is a crisis of growth, which is followed by a fresh revolutionary upsurge.

K.L. Maydannik, representing the 'extreme left' wing of the Soviet legal Marxists, expressed himself still more definitely. The guarantee against Thermidorian dictatorship in post-revolutionary society lies in democratic forms of government: 'The revolutionary struggle for democracy is a constituent part of the struggle for socialism, not *a stage precedent thereto.* ...'[112]

Drabkin, Diligensky and Maydannik all used examples taken from the history of the West and of the 'Third World'. But although considerations of censorship dictated avoidance of any direct reference to the connection between the problems under discussion and our own society, in Gefter's lecture the discussion of Thermidor and revolution returned to primary sources and inquiry into concrete Russian material on social history. The lectures complemented each other, the conclusions to be drawn remaining somewhere in the spiritual space between them.

The Soviet State and the Asiatic Mode of Production

There was nothing surprising in the fact that questions raised by Russian history should eventually have brought the historians back to Russian material. What was important was something else – that material concerning *other* societies should provide so much for reflection about our own history. Gefter wrote later that 'Russia at the beginning of the twentieth century was "a model of the world".'[113] In our country the tragic contradictions of the world as a whole reached their culmination. This was why, for example, discussion of the 'Third World' and 'the Asiatic mode of production'; had and has such importance for the understanding of historical processes in Russia.

As a matter of fact, the problems of the 'Third World' are constantly raised not only by specialists in that field such as Maydannik, Mirsky and others, but also by theoreticians working in related fields – Vodolazov, Lukin, Burlatsky. Above all, the history of the 'Third World' countries makes it easy to find material for criticizing the vulgar schemas of official teaching. In this way the attempt to divide the whole history of the world into five phases – primitive society, slavery, feudalism, capitalism, socialism – collapses like a house of cards. 'It is hardly necessary to speak of setting up such constructions on ground so shaky,' wrote the Sinologist L.S. Vasil'ev.

> After all, facts are stubborn things, and take harsh revenge on those who disdain them. Here one bold hypothesis is quickly replaced by another, the 'serfdom' of one writer is easily transformed into the 'slavery' of another; but nothing is gained from all this for a scientific solution of the problem. Evidently, the time has come to say, frankly, that the entire three-thousand-years' history of China – and, in the first place, the history of ancient China – testifies convincingly against any automatic application of a priori schemas.[114]

The authors of a work on the Asiatic mode of production made the following observation:

> In contrast to what happened in the Graeco-Roman world, in most of the countries of the East a different process took place, the gist of which was this, that, given the absence (or only very slight presence) of private property, the management of a growing social organism, together with a number of purely political factors (conquests, necessity of defence against invasion, etc.), stimulated the development of state power on the basis of the absence (or slightness) of economic and property-owning differentiation in society.[115]

During the discussion on the Asiatic mode of production the Orientalist historians confirmed that appropriation of surplus product was effected in these societies not on the basis of private property but on that of state monopoly. An estate of officials became transformed everywhere into a class of exploiters. One and the same picture is seen in Egypt, in Persia [Iran] and to some extent in the Byzantine Empire. The countries of Southeast Asia – Cambodia [Kampuchea], Java, Burma – also knew exploitation of the people by a 'temple-bureaucratic aristocracy' and, directly, by a bureaucratic apparatus, 'the apparatus of officialdom coinciding with the ruling class'.[116]

Thus, long before Shafarevich undertook his amateurish attempts, Orientalists had already begun to study the bureaucratic state of the past. They were not, of course, out to look for socialism in Byzantium: rather, their researches revealed the similarity between the Soviet state and the Byzantine system, a similarity which cannot be concealed under any 'socialist' phrases. M.A. Vitkin even sees a special category of 'primary formation' which includes all varieties of the Asiatic mode of production. This formation is connected not with the development of private property but with the growth of the state; in general, private property really develops only with transition to a higher 'secondary formation': 'After concentrating in its hands the accumulated surplus product extracted on the basis of its power over the persons of the producers, the state distributes this surplus product among the members of the corporation of rulers'.[117] The real question is not why the East hardly knew private property but why it developed in Greece. This was presumably connected with the collapse of the archaic bureaucratic monarchy of Mycenae and with the shortage of land needed for growing corn, which gave rise to an acute need for commodity exchange.

European feudalism had some features in common with the East, but these were overcome: 'in this case we should not speak of an Eastern variant of feudalism but of a rebirth of the Asiatic system in the West.'[118] I.F. Kosesnitsky wrote that in the West, too, in the early Middle Ages, the state emerged as exploiter of the direct producers, which corresponded to a 'still undeveloped form of economic relations'.[119] In Europe, however, the small size of the territory, along with a relatively rapid growth of population – especially after the tenth century – evoked a need for commodity exchange. And here those immense spaces in which a mighty bureaucratic apparatus found its justification were lacking. Here there was no objective necessity for it.

Everywhere, in circumstances of undeveloped commodity–money relations, the apparatus of government began to be transformed into a ruling class. But in the West this happened differently. Here the barons were quickly transformed from officials into feudal lords. The same tendency existed in the East but did not reach fruition, for the immense spaces made it inevitable that government of the social organism should be connected with the growth of a special apparatus, constantly undergoing organizational consolidation. The centripetal forces prevailed over the centrifugal ones.

Vasil'ev traced the formation of the official class [*shi*] in ancient China, the distant predecessors of our *nomenklatura* and the *hanbu* of present-day China. He showed how, in the Chinese Empire,

> the role of highest and most important estate, guiding the country and fulfilling the functions of a ruling class, fell to the lot of the stratum of administrative officials – widespread, numerous and organized on strictly hierarchical lines – who were headed by the Emperor and his ministers. Real power was in the hands of this estate of officials who served the bureaucratic Empire, and they used it in the name of the Emperor and of 'the well-being of the state and the people'.[120]

It is important that we come here upon a ruling class which is not formed on the hereditary principle. The right to appropriate surplus product was ensured in this case not by 'wealth' or by 'descent' but by office held, by 'rank'. There were only two real forces in society – 'the people' and 'the ruling bureaucracy'.

So, at the end of our inquiry, we come back to the same questions with which we began. These questions were not invented by the intelligentsia but were inherent in reality itself, arrived at through suffering: history and logic led to them through knowledge of our society and of ourselves. The discussion of the Asiatic mode of production is important from the standpoint of principle.[121] It is important that since Stalin's time the concept of socialism has been bound up with state ownership, which itself has become the basis for the activity of a huge, centralized apparatus of officials and an authoritarian – if not totalitarian – system. But it has now become clear that all this already existed in ancient China, long before the 1917 Revolution, and naturally has nothing whatsoever to do with socialism. Compare this with M. Cheshkov's conclusions, which I have already mentioned, about the statocracy. Reading reports of the discussion of the Asiatic mode of production one cannot help thinking: Isn't all this a case of 'modernizing'? Isn't it just an example of Aesopian language? No, this research is objective, and precisely because of its objectivity it can lead us to some fundamental conclusions of present-day importance. Understanding and knowledge of the past is here helping us to understand the present, and not vice versa.[122]

Vasil'ev finds in the history of China various 'models', historical archetypes: the patriarchal state (Yin), the transitional xenocratic state (Chou), totalitarianism (Tsing), conservative authoritarianism (Han).

The last-named system proved the most stable and well developed. Sinologists show how traditions of authoritarianism and obedience led 'to exaggeration of the personal authority of a deified personage and depreciation of the individual'.[123] Conclusions suggest themselves. Our notorious 'cult of personality' was not a disease of socialism, not a deviation 'from' socialism, but a phenomenon logically connected with a particular form of totalitarian and authoritarian state which had nothing in common with socialism.

Finally, the models of bureaucratic behaviour turn out to be similar. In statocratic society we find a high degree of social mobility. A person of peasant origin may become a minister. But there is one circumstance which

> sharply alters this whole idyllic picture. It is that every possibility is open to an individual only on this absolute condition, that he will humbly remain within the channel of conformism and never think of displaying his individuality.[124]

As a result society experienced on the one hand, many centuries of stagnation and, on the other, the suppression of all freedom of thought. The historical good fortune of the European peoples, a long-lasting condition of 'dual power' (in the period when the modern nations were being formed), the rivalry of church and state (poorly developed, alas, in Russia), was unknown in the East. This situation created in the West the possibility for the development of political and social alternatives, ideological conflict, innovation. Where that was not the case, hyperconservatism triumphed.

Fully comprehensible, therefore, are the conclusions of V. Lukin: that in the twentieth century the state has become an object of deification most often in countries which have

> very rich historical traditions of mutual relations between the state and its subjects, traditions connected with the retention of numerous survivals of what Marx called 'the Asiatic mode of production'.[125]

Again we move from ancient times to the problems of the present day. This actuality of historical investigations is especially evident in the books of Cheshkov, who, writing as both sociologist and historian, comes in the course of his research upon the coincidence between the basic features of the Asiatic mode of production and the contemporary statocracy. Studying medieval Vietnam, he arrived at the conclusion that its economic system could be called 'state feudalism':

> Its economic basis was the state's monopoly of land, a monopoly which made

the state a real, and not merely a juridical, landowner. This monopoly was realized in the existence of a substantial state revenue, in the organization of basic irrigation works by the state, in the predominance of a conditional form of feudal landownership, and the direct merging of the economically dominant class with the state as a whole – a 'state-class'. In consequence of this, the state appears not merely as a superstructural phenomenon but also as a participant, a subject in the relations of production.[126]

Such a 'state of feudalism' was, in essentials, closer not to Western feudalism (really it was *something quite different*) but to contemporary statocracy, whether in Algeria, China, Vietnam or the Soviet Union. One and the same phenomenon, the 'state class' or 'class-apparatus', appears in different forms in different epochs. In Cheshkov's works the discussions of present-day statocracy and of the Asiatic mode of production resemble each other closely. In fifteenth-century Vietnam Cheshkov reveals the existence of 'a stratum of *nomenklatura* officials' who possessed immense political and economic power.[127] In medieval Vietnam there was not only separation of the executive from the supervisory organs, something new for the Russian bureaucracy (it developed here only in the Soviet period) but there also appeared important political institutions that were absolutely similar to Soviet ones:

The central apparatus included also several (to use modern terminology) ideological institutions. Among them the most important was the Academy of Scholars (*Khan lyam v'en*), the Department for Compiling the State's History (*Kyok ty vien* or *Shui kwan*), the Imperial School (*Tkhay ty vien* or *Kuok ty zhyam*), the Department of Edicts (*Doung kak*) and a number of others.[128]

How reminiscent this is of the Soviet statocracy, with its Higher Party School and its departments for compiling the Party's history! 'Very important also', Cheshkov continues,

is the fact that in this particular social formation the class character of the state is concealed behind its governmental, administrative function, in that the feudalist is here 'aggregated' and acts as an official, as the state. Consequently, class antagonism manifests itself here as a contradiction between rulers and ruled, and not between exploiters and oppressed. This distorted (though formed on a quite real basis) idea of the state entered deeply into the psychology of the masses and of the feudal intelligentsia, and stood firm even when social antagonism showed itself pretty clearly.

In its turn, this 'distorted idea of the state was the ideological foundation for the reform tendency in the political thinking of the feudal intelligentsia of Vietnam.'[129] When we delve deep in our study of the past, we become convinced that history repeats itself. It repeats itself not only as historical experience but also as historical illusions. But understanding the past helps us, in each instance, to become aware of our mistaken ideas and so to overcome them.

We can easily follow the genesis of modern statocracy in the countries of the 'Third World' and watch the process of which Russia has already reaped the fruits. When F. Abramov went to Portugal immediately after the fall of the dictatorship there, he said that as a Russian writer he would have liked to understand better what happened in our country between February and October 1917: Portugal might serve as an illustration. Cheshkov and other specialists on the 'Third World' help us to understand what happened here after October.

The discussion on the Asiatic mode of production and on present-day bureaucracy has focused on serious Soviet Sinology. In this sphere we can encounter the same problems as when studying Russia, except that they spread more widely and became even more acute. The similarity of the statocratic regimes in the USSR and China means that research in this field is especially productive.

Soviet specialists on China have raised important questions concerning the special problems of 'building socialism in a "petty-bourgeois country"', without having inherited from the previous society the appropriate material and technological preconditions'.[130] There is also the problem of several different economic structures coexisting which is so important for Gefter. Then, we have

> the degree of correspondence between the proclaimed rights of the working masses and their actual influence on the formation of the state's domestic and foreign policies, their actual participation in the work of the state and Party apparatus.[131]

Furthermore, there is the problem 'of the character of the socialization of the means of production'.[132] Here the question of what constitutes the actual essence of socialism comes up once more.

Interestingly, it was F. Burlatsky who took up the most definite position with regard to the 'Chinese problem'. He begins his evaluation of the social processes with the correct observation: 'Socialism has become the banner of the twentieth century just as democracy was the banner of the nineteenth. Nobody is surprised nowadays to hear socialist slogans.'[133] For this very reason, groups which are actually very remote from socialism seek to use the slogan of socialism for their own ends: 'What is left of the socialist idea if people are made victims of the adventuristic experiments of the uncontrolled government of the leaders, who claim to be the creators of a new symbol of belief?'[134] The answer to that question can be found in the history of China and in the history of Russia. Under conditions of bureaucratic rule, Burlatsky emphasizes, state property 'is not automatically socialist.'[135] It 'is socialist not because it belongs to the state but because it is in the hands of a *socialist* state, which disposes of it in the interests of the working class and all the working people.'[136] But how is the nature of the state to be determined? The question arises:

> Who disposes of this property? Do the working people participate in the running of the state, in deciding the economic and social purposes of development? In other words, is there socialist democracy?[137]

The Party-state upper circles in China (and not there alone) 'actually dispose of state property.'[138] Hence the conclusion:

> The most important criterion for socialist society is: whether power is in the hands of the working class and all the working people. But in this respect China is particularly remote from the socialist ideal.[139]

This formulation makes one reflect that other countries of so-called 'actually existing socialism' are also pretty remote from that ideal, and China just happens to be worse than the rest – in that it is *particularly* remote. Statocracy, says Burlatsky, is

> socialist without any well-being, without any democracy, without any participation in government by the masses, without any freedom of the individual. This is 'socialism' based on exploitation of the working people in the interests of the ruling military-bureaucratic group ... which formulated its social aims (war production and national greatness).[140]

Analysis of the social structure provides a fresh stimulus to ideological criticism. Whereas previously liberal publicists demonstrated the falsity of this or that idea, this or that approach, legal Marxism goes further and examines the ideological phenomenon itself. Lukin writes:

> The ruling elite sometimes cannot but yield to the temptation to use the prestige of the scientific world-view, exploiting its external aspects and transforming it into a metaphysical optimistic schema, in order to legitimize the existing order and offer the masses 'radiant horizons', sometimes departing openly from 'inconvenient' objective reality.[141]

Vodolazov speaks frankly of attempts by the ruling class to cover themselves with Marxism as their banner:

> But are these people really Marxists? Is their idea Marxism? ... But what does it matter what flag pirates nail to their mast? We have to eradicate piracy, not the country whose flag they have stolen.[142]

The point is, though, that Marxism does not merely have to be separated in people's minds from the bureaucratic class and counterposed to the rulers. We find in Marxism the basic principles on which to rely in the fight against the statocracy. It is no accident that book after book repeats that proposition which Marx and Engels themselves repeated – that the new society must make the free development of each the guarantee for the free development of all.

Freedom remains the criterion of progress, the measure of development of human society. 'I mean', wrote Tsipko,

> the growth of real freedom, the practical manifestation of which, according to Marx, is labour. To achieve real freedom, Marx considers, it is not enough to perceive that one is free or to possess the right to act freely, to enjoy the possibility of freedom, though this is important in itself: it is further necessary to possess real possibilities to act freely, to be free in work, in political life, freely to develop one's abilities and inclinations. Without that, progress is inconceivable.[143]

This means that both democracy in production and political rights are needed. 'Paramount attention must be accorded' to increasing social and political liberties.[144] But this signifies not only the victory of workers' self-management over bureaucratic tyranny, but also the triumph of culture over barbarism. Without culture there can be no lasting democracy. Without democracy culture cannot triumph. Nowhere and never were Engels's words so true as in Russia: 'Each step forward in civilization was a step towards freedom.'[145]

Notes

1. *Literaturnaya Gazeta*, 21 October 1981.
2. Ibid.
3. Ibid.
4. *Izvestiya*, 10 December 1981.
5. *Sovetskaya Kultura*, 5 March 1982. The visit to the Moscow Art Theatre by the leaders of the CPSU had originally been planned to take place earlier, but was postponed owing to the illness and death of M. Suslov.
6. *Literaturnaya Gazeta*, 20 January 1982, p. 8.
7. Ibid.
8. R.B. Remnek, ed., *Social Scientists and Policy-Making in the USSR*, New York 1977, p. vii.
9. The experience of Hitlerism showed that rational and effective means can be found even for the realization of irrational ends. The fearful possibility exists, even, that

Fascism's ends would have been realized if the other side had not found effective means of self-defence.

10. Rakovski, *Towards an East European Marxism*, p. 55.
11. See B.F. Porshnev, *Sotsial' naya psikhologiya i istoriya*, Moscow 1966, pp. 3–10.
12. F. Burlatsky, *Lenin, gosudarstvo, politika*, p. 69.
13. Ibid., p. 65.
14. Lenin, *Collected Works*, 4th edn, English version, vol. 32, p. 100.
15. F. Burlatsky and A. Galkin, *Sotsiologiya. Politika. Mezhdunarodnye otnosheniya*, Moscow 1974, p. 193.
16. It is interesting that although Burlatsky transcribed, in the book he wrote jointly with Galkin, whole paragraphs from his book about Lenin and the state, he did not include it in arguments about the Soviet state 'of the whole people' and the 'revisionism' of 1956 and 1968 in Eastern Europe. It is easy to imagine what his real attitude must be to all that.
17. F. Burlatsky, *Zagadka i urok Nikkolo Makiavelli*, Moscow 1977, p. 57.
18. Ibid., p. 67.
19. Ibid., p. 248.
20. Ibid., p. 249.
21. Burlatsky and Galkin, p. 269.
22. A. Gel'man, *My, nizhepodpisavshiesya*, Moscow 1980, p. 40.
23. *Sovetskaya Kultura*, 3 April 1981.
24. Ibid.
25. Ibid.
26. *Poiski*, no. 1, 1978, p. 30.
27. *Filosofskie nauki*, no. 4, 1968, p. 1–109.
28. J.N. Findlay, *Hegel: A Re-Examination*, New York 1958, p. 59.
29. See *Voprosy filosofii*, no. 4, 1962, pp. 27–65. It is nevertheless noteworthy that in many cases Soviet philosophers, and especially historians, arrived at the same conclusions as Lukács. He considered that the main feature of Stalinism as method was the attempt to leap from a listing of facts to a formulation of abstract laws which 'explain everything', avoiding concrete analysis. A similar idea was expressed by M. Gefter. However, under 'real Stalinism' it was easy to bring the facts under a general law, because 'unnecessary' facts were simply removed from the scene, along with the people who knew them. See G. Lukács, 'On Stalinism', *Soviet Survey*, no. 10, 1956, and 'Reflections on the Cult of Stalin', in ibid., no. 47, 1964.
30. Il'enkov's principal works are *Dialektika abstraktnogo i konkretnogo v 'Kapitale' Marksa*, Moscow 1960; *Ob idolakh i idealakh*, Moscow 1968; *K voprosy o prirode myphleniya*, Moscow 1968; *Dialekticheskaya Logika*, Moscow 1974.
31. Lenin, *Collected Works*, vol. 38, p. 212.
32. *Filosofskie nauki*, no. 4, 1968, p. 106.
33. Ibid., p. 111.
34. Ibid., p. 112.
35. Ibid.
36 *Studies in Soviet Thought*, vol. 18, no. 2, May 1978, p. 105.
37. Ibid.
38. *Problema cheloveka u sovremennoy filosofii*, Moscow 1969, p. 76.
39. Ibid., p. 90.
40. Ibid., p. 109
41. Ibid., p. 136.
42. Marx and Engels, *Collected Works*, vol. 3, 1975, p. 295.
43. *Problema cheloveka v sovremennoy filosofii*, p.138.
44. Ibid., p. 119.
45. Ibid., p. 124.
46. Loren R. Graham, *Science and Philosophy in the Soviet Union*, 1973, pp. 3–4.
47. Ibid., p. 6.
48. Zhores Medvedev, pp. 168–9.
49. Graham, pp. 5–6.

50. Ibid., p. 9.

51. V.S. Bibler, *Myshlenie kak tvorchestvo*, Moscow 1975, p. 7.

52. M.M. Bakhtin, *Problemy poetiki Dostoevskogo*, Moscow 1963, p. 92.

53. Because of their frequent appearances together in public, A. Gurevich, V. Bibler and L. Batkin are regarded by many as a sort of trio – 'the Moscow virtuosi'. S.S. Averintsev and Yu. Lotman stand somewhat aloof.

54. A. Gurevich, in M. Blok (Bloch), *Apologiya istorii*, p. 179.

55. L. Batkin, *I lektsiya o Leonardo*, A.S. Pushkin Museum, Moscow, 10 December 1980.

56. *Novy Mir*, no. 11, 1970, p. 240.

57. *Istoricheskaya nauka i nekotorye problemy sovremennosti*, Moscow 1969, p. 354.

58. *Metropol'*, Paris 1979, p. 751.

59. Ibid., p. 747.

60. Rakovski, p. 8.

61. See R.A. Medvedev, *Predislovie k nenapisannoy avtobiografii*, Moscow (*samizdat*); Also R.A. and Zh.A. Medvedev, *V poiskakh zdravogo smysla*.

62. Radical Marxists have criticized Roy Medvedev very strongly, and in some socialist circles it is almost considered *bon ton* to abuse him. I must admit that I went along with this fashion in my book *The Dialectics of Hope* (see the chapter 'Orchestra Rehearsal'). That was, of course, a manifestation of our purely Russian intolerance: I reacted too categorically to some of the expressions he used. I should add that I still disagree with him essentially on a number of matters, but the polemic ought to be carried on in a more good-humoured way than it has usually been in Russia. It is interesting, by the way, that the first issue of *Varianty* opened with a leading article aimed at Roy Medvedev.

63. Of the three journals mentioned, *Varianty* was the least known in the West and, consequently, in our country too. That is why I decided to deal with it in greater detail.

64. *Problemy Voitochnoy Evropy*, no. 2, 1981, p. 137.

65. A. Tsipko, *Optimizm istorii*, Moscow 1974, p. 179.

66. A. Tsipko, *Ideya sotsializma. Vekha biografii*, Moscow 1976, p. 25. See M. Barg, 'K voprosu o predmete i metode istorii sotsialisticheskikh idey', in the symposium *Istoriya obshchestvennoy mysli*, Moscow 1972, p. 432.

67. Tsipko, *Ideya sotsializma*, p. 42.

68. Engels, interview with *Le Figaro*, May 1893. [In the Dietz edition of collected works of Marx and Engels, vol. 22, pp. 538–43. The interview was given on 8 May and published on 13 May – *Trans.*]

69. Tsipko, *Ideya sotsializma*, p. 38.

70. Ibid.

71. Ibid., p. 41.

72. Ibid., p. 130.

73. Marx and Engels, *Collected Works*, vol. 5, 1976, p. 439.

74. Plato's *Laws* and *Republic* are an example of a social utopia.

75. Tsipko, *Ideya sotsializma*, p. 260.

76. Ibid.

77. G.B. Shaw, *Back to Methuselah* (preface), 1921, p. lxxix.

78. G. Vodolazov, *Dialektika i revolyutsiya*, Moscow 1975, p. 80.

79. Ibid., p. 71.

80. Orwell, 'Looking Back on the Spanish War' (1942), in *Collected Essays, Journalism and Letters of George Orwell*, Penguin, 1970, vol. 2, p. 296.

81. *Politicheskii Dnevnik*, vol. 1, p. 86.

82. *Vsesoyuznoe soveshchanie istorikov*, p. 19.

83. Ibid., pp. 69–70.

84. Ibid., p. 124.

85. Ibid., p. 148. Actually, of course, it was not the memoir genre that was killed off, but those who might have written memoirs. ...

86. See *Vestnik Akademii Nauk SSSR*, no. 1, 1962. This does not mean, in the least, that Great-Russian chauvinism ceased to be utilized officially. Thus in 1982 a book was

published in Kazakhstan (!) entitled *Thanks Be To You, Russian People.* This included 'passages from the classics of Marxism-Leninism and statements by representatives of many nations and nationalities of our country concerning the great Russian people, the exceptional importance of its historical role and its beneficent influence on the way other peoples developed' (*Knizhnoe obozrenie*, no. 6, 5 February 1982, p. 3). The Russian people was again spoken of as 'the elder brother'. Naturally, none of the critical statements made by Marx and Lenin about the Russians was included in the collection.

87. *Evropa v novoe i noveyshee vremya*, Moscow 1966, p. 513.

88. *Vsesoyuznoe soveshchanie istorikov*, pp. 358–9.

89. Ibid., p. 359.

90. V.P. Danilov, *O kharaktere sotsial'no-ekonomicheskikh otnoshenii sovetskogo krest'yanstva do kollektivizatsii sel'skogo khozyaistva*, Moscow 1961, p. 7.

91. Marx, *Capital*, vol. 1, Penguin/NLR, 1976, p. 927.

92. Danilov, p. 17.

93. Ibid., p. 34.

94. *Voprosy istorii*, no. 3, 1965, p. 20.

95. See M.A. Vyltsan, N.I. Ivnitsky, Yu.A. Polyakov, 'Nekotorie problemy istorii kollektivizatsii v SSSR', *Voprosy istorii*, no. 3; 1965, N. Ivnitsky, 'O kriticheskom analize istochnikov po istorii sploshnoy kollektivizatsii', *Istorichesky Arkhiv*, no. 2, 1962.

96. R.A. Medvedev, *K sudu istorii*, p.218.

97. Quoted in *Novy Mir*, no. 1, 1968, p. 259.

98. Ibid.

99. *Istoricheskaya nauka i nekotorye problemy sovremennosti*, p. 6.

100. Maria Markus and Andras Hegedüs, 'Tendencies in Marxist Sociology in the Socialist Countries', in A. Hegedüs *et al.*, *The Humanization of Socialism: Writings of the Budapest School*, 1976, pp. 124–5.

101. Rakovski, p. 17.

102. Ibid.

103. I have attempted to draw some general conclusions from A. Gurevich's work in my *Dialectics of Hope.*

104. A.Ya. Gurevich, *Problemy genezisa feodalizma v Zapadnoy Evrope*, Moscow 1970, p. 184.

105. *Voprosy istorii*, no. 9, 1970, p. 154.

106. *Istoricheskaya nauka* ..., p. 10.

107. His lecture was delivered in 1966, but not published and made available to wide circles of the intelligentsia until 1969, in Gefter's symposium.

108. '"Thermidor?"', we read in some notes by Lenin. 'Soberly, *that could be*, yes? Will it? We'll see. Let us not boast as we go into battle' (*Polnye sobranie sochineniya*, vol. 43, p. 403). But we must remember that he did not expect the danger of Thermidor from the quarter from which it did eventually come, but from the peasantry, seeing this foreboded in the Kronstadt mutiny. See above, Chapter 2.

109. *Istoricheskaya nauka* ..., p. 236.

110. Ibid., p. 248.

111. Ibid., pp. 248–9.

112. Ibid., p. 279.

113. *Voprosy istorii kapitalisticheskoy Rossii: Problema mnogoukladnost'*, Sverdlovsk 1972, p. 99.

114. *Problemy istorii dokapitalisticheskikh obshchestv*, Moscow 1968, p. 456.

115. Ibid., p. 478.

116. Ibid., pp. 535, 537.

117. Ibid., p. 435.

118. Ibid., p. 454.

119. Ibid., p. 635.

120. Ibid., p. 483.

121. Another aspect of this matter must be mentioned. In 1969–72 the most important centres for research in the social sciences were given a battering. The Institute of History and the Institute for Concrete Social Research suffered severely. V.P. Danilov

and the prominent sociologist Yu.A. Levada were subjected to official criticism. Work on Soviet material became extremely difficult. At the same time, Tvardovsky's *Novy Mir* was bashed. As a result, the leading figures in the social sciences moved to such other research centres as the Institute of World Economy and International Relations, the Institute of Oriental Studies and the Institute for the Study of the USA and Canada.

122. Proof of this may be found in the way the researchers became immersed in their material. Vasil'ev himself has become so 'Sinified' that, for example, he considers that the Yin dynasty 'was not fated to last long. Already in 1027 B.C., after existing for five centuries, it fell. ...' (*Problemy istorii dokapitalisticheskikh obshchestv*, p. 460). Here the categories are obviously Confucian.

123. Ibid., p. 509.
124. Ibid., p. 511.
125. *Voprosy filosofii*, no. 6, 1969, p. 39.
126. M.A. Cheshkov, *Ocherki istorii feodal' nogo V' etnama*, Moscow 1967, pp. 21–2.
127. Ibid., p. 135.
128. Ibid., p. 137.
129. Ibid., pp. 245–6.
130. V. Gel'bras, *Sotsial' no-politicheskaya struktura KNR 50-60-e gody*, Moscow 1980, p. 5.
131. *Problemy sovetskogo kitaevedeniya*, Moscow 1973, p. 31.
132. Ibid., p. 187.
133. *Voprosy filosofii*, no. 2, 1980, p. 116.
134. Ibid., p. 117.
135. F. Burlatsky, *Lenin, gosudarstvo, politika*, p. 464.
136. *Voprosy filosofii*, no. 2, 1980, p. 119.
137. Ibid.
138. Ibid., p. 124.
139. Ibid., p. 123.
140. Ibid.
141. *Voprosy filosofii*, no. 6, 1969, p. 42.
142. S. Vodolazov, p. 79.
143. Tsipko, *Optimizm istorii*, pp. 123–4.
144. Ibid., p. 125.
145. *Anti-Dühring*, 1936, p. 129.

Conclusion

'Artistic production (and intellectual production in general) cannot be *normalized*, but one might well wonder whether any creative project isn't necessarily but unwittingly *normative*.'[1] So wrote Régis Debray in his book on cultural problems in France. In short, his view is that although creative work cannot endure external control, it is itself fraught with the danger of authoritarianism: the creative personality who possesses new ideas is inclined to impose them on others. Debray's ideas, often formulated in the style of Pascal's aphorisms, must bewilder anyone brought up in the traditions of Russian culture. A genuine 'creative project' *cannot* be authoritarian because the artist or the scholar, unlike the engineer, does not carry out a project conceived in advance, but pursues a quest. The creative personality does not know exactly, beforehand, what it is he or she will create. What Debray calls a 'project' is merely the direction or the object of the quest. The 'project' acquires some definite outlines in the process of creation. Neither Tolstoy nor Dostoevsky, nor Lenin, nor Solzhenitsyn carried out a 'realized project'. In the creative process project and realization are not 'two' stages, they are one. Moreover, the 'realized project' does not precede creation, it can be seen clearly only *ex post facto*, so that it is not so much the departure point of the creative process as its culmination. After he had written *Anna Karenina*, Tolstoy understood what he had wanted to write this novel about. It may be that in the creative consciousness of a rational Frenchman everything happens somewhat otherwise than in our Russian heads, but there can be no doubt that any 'normative' project finds itself overtaken by the spontaneity, unpredictability and dialogicality of the creative process.

These thoughts about Debray are brought in here not so as to mention yet another foreign name, but in order to emphasize that art, science – everything that we mean by 'culture' and 'creativity' – are indissolubly connected with freedom. Nowhere and never have such efforts been made by a government to create an unfree culture as in Russia, but our country's experience has proved that this is impossible. In the course of cultural history any normative restrictions, internal and external alike, are overcome by the development of creative thought.

The history of the cultural-political struggle in our country, the history of the Soviet intelligentsia's cognition of its society and its role therein, has not yet been written. These essays cannot give a complete idea of the full richness of this many-sided and complex process. Outside the limits of my work lie a great deal of illegal literature, the problems of the non-Russian national cultures, and much else.

Nevertheless, some conclusions can be drawn. Despite all the negative consequences of the breakdown of the united cultural front of the sixties, the delimitation between different tendencies and schools can be seen as extremely positive and valuable. It was in the seventies, which seemed to be a period of spiritual crisis and stagnation of thought, that the cultural and political pluralism necessary for any progress towards a democratic society came about. In comparison even with Khrushchev's time, that was a big step forward.

Undoubtedly much, also, was lost, but one ought not to exaggerate the importance of those losses. Many liberals of the sixties became officials in the cultural sphere, but that should not surprise us. What is very much more important is that a significant section of those who came to the forefront during the 'thaw' remained loyal to their ideals. The epoch which began after 1968 was for our intelligentsia, on the whole, a time of disenchantment with socialism, like that which came upon the contributors to *Vekhi* after the defeat of the 1905 Revolution. But it became apparent that the ideology of disenchantment was unproductive – or, more precisely, that it could not provide concrete answers to the burning questions of social development. At the same time, a demand for practical conclusions and realistic solutions increased, along with the deepening of the statocracy's crisis.

People have grown disenchanted with disenchantment. Interest in democratic socialism has begun to grow again, aroused by events in Eastern and Western Europe and penetrations of the idea of neo-Marxism from the West. An opponent of socialism, K. Burzhuademov, wrote in 1974: 'Unfortunately, socialist-democratic ideas are widespread today, and not bourgeois-democratic ideas, as ought to be the case.'[2] Actually, it was in the seventies that the prestige of socialism declined in our country to a lower level than ever before. Yet Burzhuademov's admission shows that disenchantment with progressive ideas was not so profound as it sometimes seemed. His statement about socialist ideas being 'widespread' ought not to make us complacent. They are still far from being spread as widely as Burzhuademov apparently supposed. But what is much more important is that they *are* widespread and, we may hope, the day is not far off when they will become the real banner of our time. It is not a matter of returning to Marx or to the hopes of the sixties, but of carrying forward the struggle to renew the socialist idea.

In statocratic countries, wrote A. Michnik, one of the leaders of the democratic opposition in Poland, the Lefts

> find themselves in an exceptionally difficult position. They have to defend their socialist ideas against an antipopular totalitarian government which manipulates socialist phrases in demagogic fashion. But just because of that fact, this defence has to be firm, consistent and uncompromising, free from sectarianism, dogmatism and outworn schemas. Left thinking must be open to all ideas of independence and anti-totalitarianism – and, therefore, also to Christianity and all the richness of the Christian religion.[3]

Soviet society has changed since the seventies. Those were years of political equilibrium at the top, but the country's economic and social development did not mark time. The numbers of the engineering intelligentsia increased markedly:

> In the structure of personnel employed in productive industry [engineers] will be two or three times more numerous in the eighties than in 1960. On the average, there will be one engineer or technician for every six or seven manual workers.[4]

Sociological research reveals a higher cultural level in the working class, a *rapprochement* between this class and the intelligentsia and – most importantly – that it is no longer diluted by incomers from the countryside. The flight from the village to the town still goes on, but the multimillioned working class easily assimilates the thinned-out 'reinforcements'. The number of hereditary workers has greatly increased, while at the same time disbelief in official propaganda has become universal. The most important development of all is that the workers of today are keenly aware of the social antagonism between them and the statocracy, and draw a sharp line between 'us' and 'them'. From this differentiation between 'us' (the working masses, the people, the workers) and 'them' (the bureaucracy, the government, the exploiters) a class-consciousness is beginning to emerge, and the statocracy possesses no means of halting that process.

The remarkable economic and social stability of the system created by Stalin has deluded many, both supporters and opponents of the regime, and especially 'calm' observers. In the postwar period the system revealed its economic inefficiency, yet this society continued to exist and even to increase its well-being. The cessation of mass terror did not reduce but rather increased the stability of the system, for both the statocracy and the lower orders felt safer. However, there is no mystery in this.

It is not accidental that societies of the Soviet type *outside* the USSR proved much less stable. The point is not that the statocracy has ruled in Eastern Europe for a shorter time than in Russia and has been unable to educate the masses properly. The rulers of Eastern Europe made up, between the fifties and the seventies, for the short time they had been in power by means of greater economic efficiency than existed in the USSR. The explanation is simple. The Soviet statocratic system proved extremely stable owing to the abundance of resources in Russia. Until the eighties we had plenty of everything – sources of power, raw materials, land, manpower, and so on. These resources could be so squandered that no economic inefficiency, no bad management would hinder further growth. In Eastern Europe the Stalin-type system started to crack as early as the fifties, immediately after the cessation of mass terror. Only cheap Soviet power resources made possible the maintenance of a more or less high standard of living and comparative social stability in these countries during the sixties and seventies, although they did not prevent the acute crises in Czechoslovakia in 1968 and in Poland in 1968, 1970, 1976 and, finally, in 1980–81. However, Eastern Europe is not able to decide its future destiny on its own.

A qualitatively new stage began in the eighties when, for the first time in its thousand years of history, Russia came up against the problem of insufficient resources. The results of bad management came home to roost. 'The Brezhnev period of "historic compromise"', writes the Russian *émigré* sociologist V. Zaslavsky,

> is at an end. In fact we are on the eve of a conflict between the political rulers and wide sections of the working class, even if this conflict does not develop into open and organized struggle.[5]

The working class will remind the rulers of its existence through strikes breaking out now here, now there. Fresh forces will enter the historical arena. The workers experienced neither great expectations after the Twentieth Congress nor disenchantment after the invasion of Czechoslovakia. The independent spiritual development of our working class is only beginning, and the intelligentsia must help them from its own rich historical experience. This does not mean 'going to the people' and instilling the workers with new ideas: the masses will pick those ideas up in their own time, if the intelligentsia develops them and makes them widely known. What is wanted above all is not to form a 'Union for Emancipation' but to emancipate ourselves spiritually.

The French right-wing socialist J.-Ph. Revel wrote in his book *Ni Marx, ni Jésus* that democratic socialism cannot be realized first in the 'Third World' or in Western Europe. One can agree with many of his arguments, but this sober appreciation of the situation in the countries of the Old World has led the writer to the strange conclusion that the world revolution will begin in the USA. It may be, of course, that there is something here that we in Russia do not understand, but this prospect does seem, at the very least, unlikely. The complex processes going on in American society suggest anything but revolution. Revel does not even try to estimate the possibility of changes in Eastern Europe, yet Russia is becoming ripe for change.

In *The Dialectics of Hope* (my previous book), I tried to substantiate the proposition that the Soviet Union stands on the threshold of democratic socialism. How true that is we shall see in the coming decades. In any case, the second half of the eighties will greatly clarify the social situation in our country. Whereas in the sixties and seventies the democratic intelligentsia, despite its immense moral superiority over the bureaucracy, was like Pascal's thinking reed, lacking real power to resist the bureaucrats' policy, in the eighties it can already rely on the movement of wide sections of the working people and become part of that movement. The Polish experience has once again confirmed what Marxists have always said: social transformations are impossible unless the working class participates. The experience of summer 1980 in the Soviet Union showed that our working class, too, is able to come forward as an independent active force. The strikes of that time were only the first test, the first step.

> Only thus: to wager on the intellectuals alone in the Soviet Union would be as stupid as to count, in the West, on the students alone. Only when the majority of the working people really try to change something – not just protest in words or in intellectually refined manifestos, but when they go on strike, when they launch a general strike and street demonstrations, when all that becomes possible, then the way things are will be changed.[6]

One cannot disagree with Ernst Bloch. It is all just as Jerzy Lec said: 'It's not the same with freedom as with other goods. ... Freedom is the only thing that costs less the more it's in demand.'[7] From what has been said one should not conclude that the cultural struggle of past years was meaningless or useless. On the contrary, it prepared the social consciousness for the next steps, created the foundations for public opinion. And even if it began to seem, to participants in the events of the sixties and seventies, that everything they had done had been wasted, that deep process which they, consciously or unconsciously, had promoted was still going on. Although the results were not always visible, they were real. Forces had not been expended in vain. History will show what fruits will spring from the work done over many years.

Notes

1. Régis Debray, *Teachers, Writers, Celebrities: The Intellectuals of Modern France*, 1981, p. 238.
2. K. Burdzhuademov, p. 6.
3. A. Michnik, *Letters from Prison*, Berkeley 1985, p. 188.
4. *Voprosy filosofii*, no. 5, 1980, p. 93 (the figures relate to Azerbaijan).
5. *Mondo operaio*, no. 7–8, 1981, p. 10.
6. *Gespräche mit Ernst Bloch*, Frankfurt-am-Main 1975, p. 152.
7. *Der Spiegel*, no. 48, 22 November 1976, p. 46.

PART TWO

The Intelligentsia and *Glasnost'*

1

The New Cultural Context[1]

When, in the spring of 1985, the third ceremonial funeral in three years took place in Moscow, most of the intelligentsia were in a state of apathy and pessimism. This was due, not to regret for the passing of the CPSU general secretary, Konstantin Chernenko, but to quite different causes. The Brezhnev epoch of Soviet history was described by the ideologists of that time as 'an era of stability'. Later they took to calling it 'a time of stagnation'. There is an element of truth in both appraisals, but the main problem in the early eighties consisted not in knowing whether Brezhnevism had been good or bad, intrinsically, but in the fact that this policy had now exhausted itself. The country's economic situation was steadily worsening. Cultural life, based on the ideas and controversies inherited from the sixties, was in profound crisis. Brezhnev's passing had clearly 'come too late', and with it also the change of course. The accession to power of Yuri Andropov in November 1982 aroused in many the hope of seeing radical changes, but unfortunately he was to outlive Brezhnev by no more than fifteen months. In that space of time not only was he unable to carry out any serious changes in the economy and the political sphere, he could not even exert any influence on the general psychological climate. When Andropov was succeeded by Chernenko, whom Brezhnev himself had regarded as his successor, it became obvious that the hopes were not to be realized.

At the beginning of 1985 the most widespread view among the liberal and left-wing intelligentsia was that 'Brezhnevism without Brezhnev' would be the country's fate for ages to come. Some of the traditional spiritual leaders of the intelligentsia had died (Vysotsky, Trifonov), while others had emigrated (Lyubimov, Tarkovsky). Those who were left were sunk in deep pessimism. However, the times did change. Mikhail Gorbachev came to power with the firm intention of implementing the changes that Andropov had not lived to accomplish. The balance of forces in the Party leadership altered to the advantage of the reforming and technocratic tendencies, which dissociated themselves from Brezhnevism. The restructuring that now began was bound to affect all spheres of life in Soviet society.

In their profoundity and scale the changes can be compared only to the policy of de-Stalinization pursued by Nikita Khrushchev in the 1950s. Such a comparison, however, reveals both similarities and differences. When in 1956 Khrushchev came out with his exposure of Stalin at the Twentieth Party Congress, most of the population suffered shock. Among the intelligentsia the turmoil soon gave way to a reformist euphoria. Left-wing intellectual tendencies were formed and became active very quickly, even though they often based themselves upon rather naïve notions. Thirty years later the Twenty-Seventh Congress, under Gorbachev's leadership, featured no sensational revelations. The changes in the country were not at first so abrupt, although they went considerably deeper. Unlike in Khrushchev's time, it was now not a matter of 'correcting mistakes' in the political sphere but of an extensive 'restructuring' that affected economics, politics and culture.

The intelligentsia, in its turn, took some time to overcome its apathy. Just as before, everything began with a re-examination of history. Even before the Party Congress Moscow's theatres had presented Mikhail Shatrov's play *The Dictatorship of Conscience* and A. Buravsky's *Speak* ... The former, by an author who had been popular in the sixties, was dedicated to Lenin, and its main purpose was to revive the liberal ideas of Khrushchev's time. The latter came from the pen of a young writer who subjected these ideas to ruthless criticism from the left. In *Speak* ... the action takes place in the provinces in the early fifties. Stalin dies and Khrushchev comes to power. The local leaders are also replaced. The new ones sincerely want to improve the situation, to better people's lives. But until the masses take their fate into their own hands there can be no real changes. And when rank-and-file working people begin talking openly about their rights, putting forward their own demands and electing their own leaders, the progressive officials take fright no less than the conservatives. The initiative assumed by the lower orders appears as 'insubordination' and 'mutiny'.

There is no place in the eighties for the illusions of the fifties. This is a sign that society has matured, but a sober awareness of the difficulties standing in the way of change holds many people back. It is now harder to decide on serious actions and to work out a line of conduct than it was in the earlier period. Yet, after the Twenty-Seventh Party Congress, changes really did take place. Television became considerably more interesting, the powers of the censorship were sharply restricted, the influence of the Ministry of Culture on artistic creativity declined to a marked degree, and books began to be published which had previously been banned.

Reading the newspapers became a fascinating occupation. In *Sovetskaya Kultura* a column headed 'Direct Speech' allowed well-known artists and writers to talk frankly about problems that worried them – about censorship and freedom to create, about the demo-cratization of society, and about social injustice. Similar contributions also became a feature of *Literaturnaya Gazeta,* even though that paper's editor-in-chief, A. Chakovsky, was himself in no way a supporter of the changes. It emerged that Gorbachev and those around him not only read these articles but also paid them quite a lot of attention. For example, an article by the playwright Aleksandr Gel'man about conservative resistance to the reforms (the writer aptly called the opponents of the new course 'the new dissidents') was mentioned by the General Secretary in one of his speeches. There was also a big change in television. Whereas in Brezhnev's time they had taken care to pre-record and transcribe every programme, so that the authorities could check for anything seditious, more and more live broadcasts began to take place in 1986. Although this has mainly applied in the less controversial areas, it is now becoming difficult to define which programme deals with political problems and which does not. Even in the variety programme *Morning Post* the compère now and then allows himself to crack a joke about bureaucratic control of the media.

The most interesting innovation in television is probably the monthly programme for young people entitled *Twelfth Floor.* Its millions of viewers have had shown to them many of the acute social and psychological conflicts in our society, the processes at work among our young people, the changes in mass consciousness and behaviour which had come about by the beginning of the eighties. Those taking part in the programme – both experts invited to the studio and young people from the streets – converse honestly and sharply about the inefficiency of the state apparatus, about people's need for freedom, and about the spiritual crisis and conflict between generations. Important officials are obliged to answer irritated and sometimes abusive questions put by young people who are evidently trying to vent the social protest which has built up.

The editors of *Twelfth Floor* do, of course, try to soften the overall effect by resorting to all manner of technical and editorial devices and cutting some of the more barbed comments. But on the whole the picture is objective enough, and what ultimately matters for the viewer is not particular utterances by particular individuals but the general impression that is left. It is especially important that, through *Twelfth Floor*, the general public has got to know the leaders and ideas of the new movement among young people. Bit by bit, much of what is talked about on *Twelfth Floor* is taken up by the press, and serious discussions are started on problems which, until recently, people preferred to keep silent about.

A situation has arisen in which a newspaper is sometimes more interesting to read than a novel, and a TV discussion evokes more interest than an artistic film. This is giving rise to a sort of crisis in art. But it should be said that the responsibility is borne not only by the journalists or sociologists who have begun to write more honestly – which is not true of them all, incidentally – but also by the creative intelligentsia itself. It is significant that what most excited the public in the mid eighties were not new works but old ones that had been suppressed in an earlier period. As those bans were lifted, the aesthetic that had been held back was at last given satisfaction. New works conspicuously failed to compete with films or novels inherited from past years. The satirist Mikhail Mishin asked maliciously in the autumn of 1986: 'What shall we do when everything that used to be forbidden is permitted?'

The most popular films of 1985–87 – German's *Road Test*, Panfilov's *Topic* and Abuladze's *Repentance* – were all 'taken down from the shelf': *Road Test* had lain there for fifteen years until the ban was lifted under Chernenko. The publishing of works by Nabokov, Gumilev and other twentieth-century writers – which for political reasons had been struck out of the official history of literature – met with particular interest among readers, as did the appearance of unpublished writings by the recently deceased Trifonov and Vysotsky, or materials concerning them.

Not always, of course, was the screening of a film banned in Brezhnev's time a genuine cultural event. A long film by Shatrov, made in 1969 and shown for the first time in 1987, signally failed to move the audience. Formerly, one of the main reasons for banning it had been that its makers depicted Bukharin in a sympathetic light, whereas today talk about Bukharin is quite widespread. What is really important, however, is that Shatrov's oversimplified view of the events of the Revolution – Lenin always right, and those who disagreed with him (Mensheviks, Left Socialist-Revolutionaries, Left Communists, etc.) not villains but sincerely deluded people – is nowadays without much appeal to many. For some the history of the Revolution is no longer interesting and they have no time for the niceties of Shatrov's polemic with official party historiography. Others, who were pondering the lessons of 1917 all through the Brezhnev years, have come to the more profound conclusion that the grandeur of the Revolution does not exclude a tragic element, and that none of its leaders was 'a machine for taking infallible decisions' (an expression of Trotsky's). Incidentally, the absence of Trotsky from the screen also seriously undermined public confidence in Shatrov's film.

On the other hand, Anatoly Rybakov's novel *Children of the Arbat*, which is also devoted to a historical problem – Stalin's terror and the life of Soviet society in the thirties – was at the centre of the battle of ideas even before the Twenty-Seventh Party Congress. Bound up with it were hopes for renewed criticism of Stalinism and a fresh surge in social progress. For this very reason conservative circles did all they could to prevent the novel from being published. Yet *Children of the Arbat* was begun by the author as far back as the sixties and is principally an item in literary history.

The main body of the intelligentsia proved to be unprepared for change, and incapable of providing either new ideas or new forms. The 'revival of spiritual life' – of which the leaders of the liberal wing in the official writers' and artists' unions spoke so gaily – turned out in practice to be no more than the recovery of positions that had been lost in the seventies. Besides, many cultural personages were gravely compromised. Some who, not long before, had been full-throatedly glorifying Brezhnev now went all out to show themselves in the van of the supporters of change. As though in response to a word of command, they all set about denouncing 'shortcomings' of every kind. Criticism of social practices sometimes seemed to have become a kind of conformism, and discourses on freedom in the Gorbachev era called to mind the panegyrics to stability we had heard in Brezhnev's time. As a typical example one can take the poet Rozhdestvensky, who censured Abuladze in *Literaturnaya Gazeta* on the grounds that his film *Repentance* did not expose Stalinism thoroughly but preferred to use the language of allegory and mythological imagery. A rather serious charge, especially if one considers that the Georgian director made the film at a time when Rozhdestvensky was penning eulogistic odes to Stalin's heirs. However, Rozhdestvensky does not lay claim to the role of spiritual teacher to the intelligentsia. He is simply endeavouring 'not to be left behind by progress'. The position is a great deal more complicated in the case of persons who do claim to be leaders, or at least patriarchs, of the forward movement of society.

The well-known actor Mikhail Ul'yanov, who in 1986 became a leading figure in the Russian theatrical union even before the Twenty-Seventh Party Congress, appeared before Western journalists to attack Yuri Lyubimov and Andrei Tarkovsky, who had left the USSR. He said repeatedly that none of the productions put on by Lyubimov had ever been banned. Yet Ul'yanov himself knew very well indeed what had really happened. The reason why Lyubimov departed for the West was that, over a period of several years, the Ministry had refused to authorize *a single one* of his productions. Not only is Ul'yanov not ashamed of his lie, he is calling for a moral clean-up and talking of 'a harsh and unconcealed struggle' against conservative forces. True, he does at the same time stress that 'the crisis phenomena have not been created by the system itself', that particular individuals are responsible for them.[2] In the last analysis such calls for struggle turn into efforts to redistribute power 'upstairs' between different organizations and individuals.

Someone who compromised himself even more gravely was the playwright V. Rozov, who openly declared against democratizing the theatre. In his time Rozov had brought about a revolution in Soviet drama, by refusing to write plays in accordance with formulas left over from Stalin's time. Rozov's works in the sixties were models of truthfulness: he took as his subject not the grandeur of the state but the experiences of the individual. In the eighties, however, Rozov proved to be one of yesterday's men.

The opportunity for his declaration was provided by the death of the director A. Efros and the conflict in the Moscow Art Theatre. Efros had come to the theatre on the Taganka after the Ministry of Culture forced Lyubimov to quit the USSR. Efros's company did not accept him, and the productions he put on at the Taganka were pretentious and feeble. An outstanding director, Efros was stricken, so to speak, by creative impotence as the price for his moral surrender. But when Efros died suddenly in early 1987, the tragedy was used by Rozov as an illustration of how fatal it is for actors not to submit to their director. It was all clear to him. Efros was a victim: the company, which had been unwilling to accept the man assigned by the Ministry, was the villain. The conflict between the majority of the Moscow Art Theatre company and chief director Efremov produced the result that when, for the first time in our history, an elected council was formed to lead the collective. Efremov failed to get elected. Rozov understood: the time had come to put a stop to 'the saturnalia of the contemporary mob'.[3] His position was quite simple. There is 'good' democracy, which consists in unrestricted freedom, not bound by the will of the majority, for the creative personality to impose their correct decisions upon the 'mob'. And there is 'bad' democracy, when everyone is free to say what they think and decisions are taken on the basis of the views of the majority. In the latter case, democracy is carried to its 'most repugnant extremes' and the Ministry of Culture has to intervene so that 'a catastrophe does not occur'. It is typical that, despite such absolutely anti-democratic opinions, Rozov and his like still regard themselves as patriarchs of the spiritual renewal and – what is most lamentable – to some extent do play that role.

When everyone is hailing liberalization, it is hard to make out who is sincere and who is not. The sportsman and writer Yu. Vlasov maliciously remarked on television that there is nothing more repulsive than 'collective recovery of sight'. In his view, what the country needs is not general talk about freedom, but Marxist analysis of the social causes of lack of freedom, a struggle to change social conditions and not just the political conjuncture. Vlasov's address, which was shown twice on television, became one of the most important events in our spiritual and social life towards the end of 1986. The TV station received a tremendous flood of letters. Essentially it was a question of finding a radical cultural alternative, a fresh, more sober way of seeing society. However, a different mood prevailed among prominent members of the creative intelligentsia. While Rozov stood on the extreme right flank of the renewal movement and Vlasov demonstrated the vitality and necessity of the ideas of its left wing, the majority of the 'renewal' intellectuals preferred to remain somewhere in the middle, more or less faithful to the traditions of the Khrushchev period. This enabled them to preserve an appearance of unity. Rozov's statement evoked no serious protest, apart from an article in *Moskovskie Novosti,* which had become, under its new editor-in-chief Yakovlev, the mouthpiece of the radicals. As a rule, people wished to enjoy the new freedoms without effort, instead of thinking about far-reaching reforms. But the actual course of events was placing such reforms on the order of the day.

As Gorbachev himself has acknowledged, the economic reforms came up against vigorous and successful resistance from the bureaucracy, who were defending their privileges and power. The traditional measures for influencing the apparatus did not yield results. Orders were not carried out: on the one hand, many decisions taken in the localities were concealed from higher instances, while on the other hand resolutions adopted under the influence of Gorbachev and his supporters were hedged round with so many instructions and explanatory documents that their original significance was obliterated. Without some freedom of criticism it was proving impossible not just to smash but even to expose such 'bureaucratic sabotage'. Hence the logic of the economic reforms insistently called for intensified liberalization. The new leadership showed interest in, and began to encourage, certain manifestations of freedom of thought. In this situation what was needed was not only a relaxation of the censorship but also more serious transformations.

The film people were the first to appreciate this fact. At the Fifth

Congress of their union, in May 1986, they threw out their old leaders and elected a new set who, in most cases, had been put forward as candidates without prior 'agreement' with the Party organs. Many participants in the congress spoke of what happened as a 'revolution', and in fact nothing like it had been seen before in the entire history of the cultural unions in the USSR. In Khrushchev's time speeches no less radical had sometimes been made, but it had never been possible to oust the bureaucracy from the leadership of an organization. The new ruling body of the union, headed by Elem Klimov, undertook to prepare a fundamental structural reform of the whole system of film production. Klimov set new tasks before the union: not just to defend film-makers against the censorship, but to fight for decentralization of the industry's administration.

The debates at the writers' congress, in June 1986, were even fiercer. Liberal and left-wing authors criticized the censorship, corruption in the union leadership, and incompetent interference by state officials in cultural matters. However, thanks to the votes of provincial delegates, the conservatives managed to hang on to the key union posts. To ensure that provincial writers voted 'the right way', Party functionaries had been brought up to Moscow from certain towns to keep an eye on 'their' delegates, and although the presence of these outsiders was noticed at the congress nothing could be done about it. The progressive tendency later got its own back at the Russian theatrical union's congress in December, when the old bureaucracy and persons connected with the Ministry were excluded from the key posts in the union that was formed at the congress itself to replace the All-Russia Theatrical Society.

Thus, the left and liberal intelligentsia not only became politically active but won control of two of the three leading cultural unions. This achievement soon had its effect on the general course of events. Tarkovsky and Lyubimov were invited to return to the USSR. The invitation, to be sure, came too late: Tarkovsky died in Paris while pondering whether to go back; and Lyubimov, who had established himself rather well in the West, said that he had already signed contracts for several years ahead and, in any case, would not be able to work in Moscow in the immediate future. (It is quite possible that what lay behind his reply was also a wish to wait and see how the situation developed in the USSR.) At the same time there was a marked change in film-hire policy. Tarkovsky's films again appeared on our screens, and works by outstanding Western masters which had been considered 'too complicated' for the Soviet cinemagoer (such as Fellini's *8½*) were shown to a wide audience.

In these changes a very great role was played by the secretary of the

Central Committee, Aleksandr Yakovlev, whom Brezhnev had appointed to take charge of culture and propaganda. Yakovlev had subsequently fallen into disgrace when he spoke out against Russian nationalism and upheld the traditions of the Khrushchev period – actions which led to his removal from the Central Committee apparatus and a posting as ambassador to Canada. But Yakovlev returned to Moscow under Andropov and emerged as one of the most energetic and consistent leaders of the reform movement. Such successes as progressive groups in the intelligentsia achieved were due in no small part to the fact that Yakovlev gave most resolute support to their demands.

In February 1987 the Central Committee of the CPSU and the USSR Council of Ministers adopted a joint resolution enlarging the rights of the cultural unions. This document was drawn up by the Party and Government apparatus together with the leaders of the relevant unions and on the basis of their expressed wishes. Some questions, however, were not dealt with at all – for example, the organization of a publishing house for the film-makers' union. It was regrettable, too, that intervention by higher authority was requested to secure an increase in the number of pages in the newspaper *Sovetskaya Kultura*. Such matters can and should be decided by the editorial board itself. Structural reform of the cultural organizations was not obtained, because their leaders, with the exception of Klimov, had no clear-cut programme for change. Most members of the governing body of the Writers' Union simply feared change, and activists in the theatre union concentrated most of their efforts on getting jobs for themselves in the Ministry of Culture. Thus, despite the exceptionally favourable circumstances, supporters of the liberal tendencies among the intelligentsia achieved relatively little.

Meanwhile, the 'new dissidents' were not wasting any time. As early as autumn 1986 a number of conservative activists began openly to criticize the changes that had been made. Chakovsky, editor-in-chief of *Literaturnaya Gazeta*, speaking at a session of the secretariat of the Writers' Union, accused the supporters of change of 'surrendering ideological positions'. Before Abuladze's film *Repentance* was shown, several attempts were made to have it banned or cut. Rybakov's novel *Children of the Arbat* was the focus of acute political conflict over a long period. One moment they decided to publish it, the next they demanded that it be rewritten. 'How do things stand with Rybakov's novel?' became almost a ritual question in intellectual circles, a barometer of the political weather.

The process of cultural renewal proved to be far more complex and contradictory than it might have appeared to be at first sight. The principal problem, however, from the very outset, lay not in the stubborn resistance of conservative forces (nothing else was to be expected) but in the weakness of the positive programme put forward by the liberals.

The chief banner of the 'children of the Twentieth Party Congress' remains the criticism of Stalin. Abuladze's *Repentance*, which was shown in all the major cinemas in the capital, ought, so to speak, to have given the signal for a new wave of anti-Stalin publications in the press, compelling the public to face up to the problems which had concerned the generation of the sixties. Unfortunately Abuladze's film, for all its good qualities, was poorly suited for this role. The director had created neither a denunciatory pamphlet nor a realistic narrative of the terror, but instead a film-parable about the heirs of the murderers. The main theme is not the story of Varlam (a double of Beria) but the fate of those whose prosperity was based on the results of the terror. Varlam and his circle are murderers and executioners. His son and the children of his associates are transformed into complacent and almost respectable bourgeois. His grandson revolts not so much against Varlam's evil deeds as against the hypocrisy and dissimulation of his father, who has built his bourgeois prosperity upon contempt for the victims of the terror and defence of the practices established by Varlam. In short, what we see is the revolt of the young generation, directed against the present rather than the past.

Most of the critics concentrated solely on the image of Varlam, seeing in the film no more than an allegorical account of the terror of the thirties in Georgia. It became quite impossible to criticize Abuladze's work, which was far from being irreproachable in all respects. Since any reference to its weaker parts was taken by Moscow's liberal circles as an attempt to rehabilitate Stalin, there could be no discussion of the film from either the creative or the political angle. Abuladze had every reason to be proud of its success. But many liberals had hoped for more when they had sought to ensure that *Repentance* was seen by the largest possible number of people. The revolution in public consciousness failed to occur – nor could it have done so.

Liberalization of culture proves most effective when the public is presented with works on subjects which, generally speaking, have not been openly discussed before. Such works invariably arouse great interest, regardless of their degree of merit. In society everything is less and less subject to taboos. Previously, for example, it was unthinkable to write a satirical play about the morals of the ruling upper crust. In the late seventies, when Rozov tried to do something of this sort in *A Nest of Woodgrouse*, the result of censorship and self-censorship was a failure from which the public simply stayed away. However, in the 1986–87 season two plays on this subject were put on at the same time in Moscow. Zorin's *The Quotation* was a frank imitation of Griboedov's comedy *Woe from Wit,* which all of us remember by heart from our schooldays. In this play the places of the serf-owning landlords of old Moscow are taken by high-ranking officials. All the characters speak in verse, combining traditional high-flown style with bureaucratic jargon. At the end some images from the Bible suddenly appear. The high-ranking official Baltazarov is quite unable to grasp the meaning of a quotation which he has himself hung up in his office, and is still less able to discover who wrote it. At last light dawns: he has unintentionally put up a text from the Bible distorted by bureaucratic slang – 'The dead seize hold of the living.' The ancient saying proves to be absolutely to the point. The whole story of the quest for the author of the quotation assumes new meaning. The incomprehensible slogan on the wall is a reminder of the letters which appeared before King Belshazzar, presaging his doom.

Another play about bureaucratic morality was Radzinsky's *Sporting Scenes of 1981,* which shows the corruption, alienation and lack of spirituality prevailing 'among the elite', the degeneration of the grandchildren of the powerful leading figures of Stalin's time. In the form it takes, *Sporting Scenes* frankly recalls the plays of Edward Albee. Radzinsky does not hide this. Everything that happens in the play is quite absurd. Unfortunately, though, all the absurd situations are taken from life and the spectators recognize them. Many people are shocked by the cynical conversations about sex, the purchasing of articles in foreign-exchange shops and all sorts of intrigues. For the first time the unattractive aspects of the life led by the upper circles have been depicted on the stage, and this even in disgusting detail.

Both plays, *The Quotation* and *Sporting Scenes,* are brilliantly written, but neither opens up a new prospect. Instead, they sum up the lessons of the past, talking about things one wanted to discuss many years ago but was never allowed to. The appearance of several more works on the same theme might have undermined people's interest in it. What is much more important for people today is how relations are developing between the opposing social forces in the process of change – the anatomy of new political conflicts, so strange after eighteen years of Brezhnevite stability. The political scientist Burlatsky has made an attempt to answer these questions, choosing, for the sake of clarity, the unexpected form of a dramatic dialogue. Burlatsky's *Two Views from One Office* was first published in *Literaturnaya Gazeta* and then shown on television, the collocutors being played by the excellent actors Boltnev and Vel'yaminov. If we are to judge Burlatsky's success by the number of people who watched his work, his triumph is beyond any doubt. The production aroused enormous interest. But has the author answered the questions he posed?

By resorting to the dialogue form, Burlatsky remained true to himself. Previously he had written a book about Macchiavelli in which the attentive reader could easily note the resemblance between hero and author. Now, imitating his hero, Burlatsky chose a typically Renaissance form to set out his views. The trouble is that by doing so he merely demonstrated the unsuitability of the tradition of the sixteenth-century 'treatise in dialogue form' for an exposition of present-day problems. In Burlatsky's book the Florence of Macchiavelli bears a suspicious resemblance to Moscow in the early seventies, but one obviously needs to converse with today's Soviet reader otherwise than with the readers to whom Macchiavelli, Bruno or Campanella addressed themselves.

The participants in Burlatsky's dialogue are the progressive First Secretary of a regional Party committee and its conservative Second Secretary. The author obviously set out to refute the arguments used by opponents of change in their debate behind the scenes. In the upshot, however, it is Burlatsky's positive hero who proves the clear loser in the contest. The conservative speaks frankly about the dangers to the system with which the changes are fraught, about the destruction of established and more or less viable bonds and ties on which a great deal depends, and about the contradiction between the new slogans and the old ideological dogmas with which the people's heads have been stuffed for decades. In reply all the progressive can do is repeat general statements about the splendid future, the necessity of progress and the need for changes. Over many years most of our people have formed the habit of distrusting general talk and promises about the future.

The crisis of traditional concepts and of the old liberal-intelligentsia culture has found expression in prose literature no less than in drama. The fashionable books published in 1986 (Rasputin's *Fire*, Astaf'ev's *The Doleful Detective*, Aitmatov's *The Executioner's Block*) bear witness not only to the disappearance of many censorship restrictions but also to the decline of analytic thought. None of these writers is sparing with dark colours in their description of numerous outrages and injustices, acts of cruelty and social defects of all kinds. When we come to the question of who is guilty, the answers are most unexpected. Rasputin blames everything on European civilization and urbanization; Astaf'ev sees the root of evil in the Jews; and Aitmatov seeks to show the devil's hand behind it all. Each of these writers is convinced that men are bad because they have lost God. But where, then, is he to be found?

The anti-semitic pronouncements of Astaf'ev in *The Doleful Detective* could not have failed to provoke protests from many cultural figures. Eidelman, a historian fashionable among the Moscow intelligentsia, sent a letter to Astaf'ev in which he exhorted him to renounce his views. But the author of *The Doleful Detective* wrote back that we need to put an end to the activity of the Jews in Russian culture, to 'the seething pus of Jewish super-intellectual arrogance', and so on. The Jews must pay for having killed 'our last Tsar'. A position at which *The Doleful Detective* only hinted was thus given its ultimate development. Lamentations over the woes of the Russian people turned into a call for pogroms. Eidelman began to justify himself: it was not we who killed the Tsar, 'most of those who did it were Ekaterinburg workers.' Astaf'ev's letter, which had been sent as a private communication and not intended for publication, was duplicated by the historian and circulated by hand. Although, of course, one cannot put the two participants on the same level, it is plain that Eidelman did not come off the better. A critique which repeated general truths to the effect that it is bad to be a racist and an anti-Semite could hardly change Astaf'ev's position, while the unprejudiced reader would simply find nothing new in it. The misfortune of the liberal intelligentsia of the eighties lies in their lack of fresh, original ideas and their unwillingness to proceed from mere declarations to more profound analysis of the historical situation that has come about. Persons who claim the role of spiritually leading the renewal – Aitmatov, Eidelman, Shatrov – offer each their own recipe, but all their ideas are alike in being directed towards the past. Some talk of a return to Christian values (Aitmatov), others of the traditions of nineteenth-century liberalism (Eidelman), yet others of a rebirth of true Leninism and the heritage of the Twentieth Party Congress (Shatrov and the group around the paper *Moskovskie Novosti*); and sometimes these ideas are quaintly interwoven. The future turns out to be the hostage of the past.

Yet the young generation's frame of mind is, as a rule, much more radical. In the last days of 1986 the television showed an encounter between Leningrad youngsters and some singers known as 'the bards'. In the sixties the 'bard', the man with the guitar, was the symbol of spiritual independence, freethinking opposition to the Establishment. The leader of the 'bard' movement, Vladimir Vysotsky, actually became a national hero. Vysotsky died, however, and the movement has evidently lost its original radicalism. Those present at the meeting reproached the 'bards' for having stopped singing about social problems, about freedom, about how the masses live today. What we need now, they argued, are 'songs of protest', 'songs that lift people above themselves'. The popularity of some rock groups is to be explained precisely by the fact that, in one way or another, they have managed to strike a note that accords with this mood.

The 'Aquarium' group, led by B. Grebenshchikov, has had enormous success in seeking to assert new positive values. Towards the end of the Brezhnev era Grebenshchikov was expelled from the Komsomol and sacked from his job on account of his songs. Only in 1986 did it become possible for 'Aquarium' to appear on television, and its first record went on sale still later. Nevertheless, Grebenshchikov conquered his audience: they learnt his songs by heart and put them on cassette. To the surprise, it may be, of his enemies and of Grebenshchikov himself, he became one of the leaders of the new youth culture which slowly took shape underground in the late seventies and early eighties, and then burst vigorously on to the surface of social life.

Crowds queued to buy tickets for the Latvian film *Is It Easy To Be Young?* It is very unusual for a documentary to enjoy such sensational success in our country. The explanation, in this case, is to be found mainly in the subject of the film – young people talking openly about their problems, admitting that they need a lot of money, questioning the values of society, protesting against official requirements or simply asserting their right to be unlike other people. Among those who appeared on the screen were punks and adherents of the Hare Krishna sect, as well as men who had fought in Afghanistan. The film is very beautifully made, and even the scene where a morgue orderly is cutting up corpses is shown in a highly refined way: the cameraman obviously spent a long time selecting the best angles and compositions. One cannot help thinking that the makers of this fashionable film would have photographed a murder no less professionally.

In themselves, the interviews with young people are rather monotonous, and there is no attempt at analysis. *Twelfth Floor* offers a much fuller presentation of the views of the new generation. But it is the beautiful, professional images of the Latvian film that stay in one's memory. Its picture of the youth culture comes over in an indistinct way that fails to excite the spectator. The interview with Afghanistan veterans is used to show that war in general, regardless of its purpose, is a dirty business – but one in which somebody has to engage all the same. Somebody has to do 'the dirty work' – cut up corpses, shoot Afghan rebels. (It is interesting that people who fought against the Germans for the liberation of our country during the Second World War reasoned quite differently.) The film's objectivity is based on cynical indifference. With such an approach one inevitably ends by putting on the same level truth and lies, criminals and their victims. And yet the culture of youthful radicalism is a protest against just such a view of the world. There are, of course, cynical and indifferent people in every generation, but they are not the ones who create cultures.

In the opinion of youth movement activists, rock groups are persecuted first and foremost not for their music but for their 'striving to get away from ordinary forms of life, their fear of sinking into philistinism', their 'rebellious tendency', their protest against social injustice.[4] A movement of 'metallists' has been formed around the 'heavy metal' rock groups, with its own symbols, structure and leaders. At first the official organizations reacted with bans, and a list was compiled of 73 Western and 37 Soviet groups whose records were not to be played at discotheques or any other institutions for young people under Komsomol control. But after Gorbachev came in, this list, whilst not cancelled, simply ceased to be operative. It was just ignored. The 'banned' groups 'Mosaic' and 'Aquarium' were allowed to appear on television, and songs of the 'Kino' group began to be quoted in newspapers. It had been admitted by official personages that the movement of the 'metallists' and other informal youth groups constitutes 'a challenge to the Komsomol'.[5] To suppress them or drive them underground is simply not considered possible in the new conditions, even though many Komsomol officials would prefer just such a course. The changed relation of forces at the top and the new social situation have forced the legalization of informal youth groups. In 1987 in the Sevastopol district of Moscow a club of 'metallists' was registered for the first time. The rebels were permitted to speak openly about their feelings and their views.

What do the new radicals want? Up to now they have not formulated their ideas quite clearly. What is predominant is just moods, and they obviously lack a clear-cut platform. However, their moods are eloquent enough in themselves. For example, many people criticize Grebenshchikov because his lyrics are too abstract and his work too replete with mythological and even heraldic imagery. All the same, the singer's main idea reaches his audience all right: it is a call to emancipate human feelings, to unite with nature, to protest against alienation and cynicism. The name of the 'Aquarium' group harks back to the Beatles' famous song about people looking out from inside a glass onion, and Grebenshchikov is constantly stressing the link between his group and the traditions of the Liverpool quartet.[6] The lyrics, the music and the style of performance of 'Aquarium' remind many of Latin-American song culture, and even more of the best examples of Western youth counter-culture in the sixties, with its close connections to the 'New Left'. Paradoxically, despite the similarities in fashion and their interest in American music and the latest Western films, young Soviet people today are more reminiscent of the Western generation of the sixties than of their contemporaries in Italy or the United States.

This is quite natural. The well-known sociologists Nazimova and Gordon have pointed to the structural similarity, in a number of parameters, between social development in the West in the sixties and in the USSR in the eighties. Such a coincidence explains a great deal and opens some ground for optimism. The country which Gorbachev has inherited is already not the same as the one that came into Khrushchev's hands. It is an urbanized society with a large number of hereditary townspeople and skilled workers. A whole number of 'intellectual' processes have acquired a mass character and have simultaneously become devalued. Young people have no memory of the poverty of the forties, but react acutely to any threat to lower their present standard of living. Problems of personal freedom and responsibility have come to the fore. People are tired of Brezhnevite 'stability'. Protest against corruption and alienation of the personality calls forth a keen demand for new, democratic forms of collectivism.

> 'Change!' our hearts demand.
> 'Change!' our eyes demand.
> 'Change!' We want change.

So sing the 'Kino' group, and such songs are encouraged under the conditions of Gorbachev's *perestroika*. But the crux of the matter is that many young rock groups, including some in the provinces, had begun to sing about the need for freedom and renewal even before Gorbachev came to power. Their initiative was not a response to any appeal from above. Independently of the will of the leadership, a new cultural milieu began to be formed already in the first half of the eighties. A group of young admirers of Marx gathered around a rock ensemble – that would have been hard to imagine ten years ago. This actual case illustrates very well the processes which have taken place. As in the West in the sixties, interest has increased sharply in both Marxism and utopian socialism. Some are interested in Kropotkin, others in Narodnik ideas about the free commune, others still in the theory of alienation.

The cultural mosaic of the 'new protest' is a great deal richer than anything the ageing 'children of the Twentieth Congress' can offer. It is clear that without Khrushchev there would have been no Gorbachev, and without the intellectual movement of the sixties the current changes would not have been possible. But every epoch has to find its own means of self-expression. Renewal of the 'high culture' of the professional intelligentsia will depend on its ability to comprehend the impulses coming from the spontaneously formed counter-culture of those down below. Historical continuity is inconceivable without the reinterpretation of accumulated experience.

Interest in the past is no less characteristic of the eighties generation than it was of those who participated in Khrushchev's thaw. 'In order to stand I must stick to my roots', sings Grebenshchikov. The point, however, is that the new historical awareness that has spread so quickly among our young people has little in common with the ordinary ideas of cultural liberalism. The editor-in-chief of *Moskovskie Novosti*, Yegor Yakovlev, considers that the most important task of the day is criticism of Stalinism and, possibly, the rehabilitation of Bukharin. Yet an ever larger number of people are inclining to think that, instead of exposures and rehabilitations, what we need is a full, many-sided and objective interpretation of our historical past in all its contradictoriness. Society must find its memory again: not a selective but a complete memory.

In a programmatic article entitled 'Freedom to Remember' the left journalist Gleb Pavlovsky sharply criticized the liberal idea of selective rehabilitation: 'Today people are talking so much about the truth. But strange as it may seem, there is more selectiveness as well. Old names are being pulled out like rabbits from a hat. I suspect that under the banner of "the restoration of truth" publicists are preparing for a mass exhumation, but it will be selective like their own memories. In this gigantic literary morgue the remains will be laid out in rows, and the publicist-generals, orders in hand, will start marching along them. Yes, now is the time to get ready, so as not to miss the opportunity to engage in that traditional Russian "business" – turning repentance into gain . . .. And when the truth becomes a form of career, then again, as a classic writer predicted, "the boot will come down on the face of humanity".'[7] In Pavlovsky's view, any selectiveness with historical facts is impermissible. By eliminating references to Stalin from historical publications, Khrushchev was paving the way for his own defeat. He himself was forgotten 'on command' in just the same way that Stalin had been forgotten on Khrushchev's orders. And today the question arises: is the partial rehabilitation of Bukharin enough in order to understand the deepest roots of Stalinism? In truth, turning 'evil renegades' into 'true Leninists' with a stroke of the pen will hardly allow us to grasp the real tragedy of those people, their services and their responsibility before the nation, as well as the inseparable link between the two. Rybakov's *Children of the Arbat* has appeared. Gumilev is being published in the mass-circulation magazine *Ogonyok*. The appearance of Pasternak's *Doctor Zhivago* is due. But not a word has been said about Vasili Grossman's great novel *Life and Fate*, which came out in the West after the author's death and is to this day unknown to the Soviet public.[8]

There is a close link between freedom and memory that is well understood by representatives of the youth movement. In 1986, when it was decided in Moscow to demolish the seventeenth-century Shcherbakov Palaces, a group of students and schoolchildren, led by Kirill Parfenov, occupied the building and held it for two months. As a result, not only were the Shcherbakov Palaces saved but they remained in the hands of the 'invaders'. Parfenov himself appeared on the TV programme *Twelfth Floor* and spoke of the need to carry on the struggle to preserve the capital's historical aspect. The official society for the protection of historical and cultural monuments (VOOPIK) itself came under critical fire. The point was that, at the end of the Brezhnev era, right-wing Russian nationalists and anti-Semites secured complete control of this society, and the defenders of the monuments had shown that the leaders of VOOPIK were more interested in combating Jews and freemasons than in preserving and restoring the heritage. The spontaneous movement for the defence of monuments which arose in the eighties found that it had to confront not only the bureaucratic and technocratic groups responsible for destroying the city's environment but also, to a significant extent, VOOPIK as well. Despite the difficulties (perhaps even because of them), the activists of the spontaneous movement chalked up some real successes, in Moscow at least, and have become a real alternative to the official body.

The fight to preserve the historical aspect of our towns is closely associated with the movement to defend the environment generally. In 1986 the ecological lobby, which included the literary critic Academician Likhachev and the prominent writers Zalygin and Rasputin, secured the cancellation of the project to divert our northern rivers southward. This was a major event in social life, a proof of the power of the ecological movement. But the position was much worse where positive ideas and constructive proposals were concerned. The youth groups, unlike the eco-lobbyists of the older generation, were oriented towards a new conception of social development. Young architects set up a public laboratory, 'The Town of the Future', trying to combine ecologism with a new historical awareness in their practical work. When, in 1987, there was talk of the Government allowing free cooperatives to be established, the question also came up of alternative ways of organizing production and 'clean' technology. The Moscow Club and the Club for Social Initiatives (KSI), as well as some other clubs, which stepped up their activity after Gorbachev came to power, forged close links with the new social movements and informal youth groups, helping them to go over from protest to the elaboration of their own plan for society.

The changes are gradually ceasing to be the concern only of leading figures and veterans of the Khrushchev period. Thanks to *Twelfth Floor*, Parfenov has become known throughout the country. The talented publicist G. Pavlovsky has at last gained access to a wide readership. It was he who, at the end of the Brezhnev period, edited the *samizdat* periodical *Poiski* [Quests]. In those days the appearance of *Poiski* was an important event in the life of the opposition, its pages containing not only criticism of official practices but sober considerations on the defects and weaknesses of the dissident movement. *Poiski* showed how left-wing tendencies had grown stronger in the ranks of the opposition. One of the most determined spokespersons for these new moods was Pavlovsky himself. In 1982 he was arrested and sentenced for 'slandering the Soviet power'. When he returned from imprisonment, after Gorbachev's accession to power, he was given permission to live in the capital and later allowed to take up a job as a journalist – this time on the official periodical *Vek XX i mir.*

In Pavlovsky's view the movement for change stands in acute need of a renewed socialist strategy – not one artificially constructed by theoreticians but one that has grown out of our history, out of the everyday experience of the masses (just as in the first Russian Revolution). Socialism, wrote Pavlovsky, is

> a simple, industrious word, whose definition excites passions today. The workers in overalls and the artisans of the 1920s like my grandfather knew what it meant: after cleaning their machines they wiped their hands on a greasy cloth and went home, stopping by at a shop on the way for bread and kerosene. Yet hardly any of them would have passed an exam in scientific communism. So were they socialists? ... They were simply the Russian people. And from this arose their need for socialism. What kind? Today we can only guess. At that time there emerged a workers' definition of socialism, its basic features blending with popular speech and with the Revolution. We remember how it was distorted and lost and wish to believe that that is what surfaces in our memory, returns to the past, with a peculiar freedom, a peculiar love, a peculiar unwillingness to condemn.[9]

One must not suppose, of course, that it is only the progressive forces that are becoming active. Liberalization created new legal opportunities not only for left-wingers but also for the extreme right. For the latter the centre of attraction became the *Pamyat'* [Memory] and *Rodina* [Homeland] clubs which established branches in Novosibirsk, Moscow and Leningrad, together with VOOPIK as mentioned above. Their leaders do not hide their anti-semitic and anti-democratic views: they dream of a strong state and the revival of the true spirit of the old Empire. They have taken root in a number of the temperance clubs formed in the course of the campaign against drunkenness that was launched by the authorities in 1981–86. In the area around Moscow a semi-spontaneous movement has arisen called 'the Lyubers' (from the Lyubertsy suburb). Their programme is simple in the extreme: to beat up Muscovites, everybody who wears foreign clothes, to drive out the 'metallists' and to cut the hippies' hair. The 'Lyubers' belong to the same age-group as the admirers of 'heavy metal', but they represent, so to speak, two different epochs. The psychological basis for the Lyubers' activity is nostalgia for Stalinism. As the editor-in-chief of the youth magazine *Smena*, A. Likhanov, put it, they 'want to model their "behaviour" on the most distressing period of our history.'[10]

At the end of 1986 the Public Prosecutor's office began to investigate the doings of the Lyubers, since what was involved was a systematic and malevolent violation of public order. However, the investigation was not completed. After a demonstration in Moscow on 22 February 1987 by two thousand supporters of the youth movement, to demand that the activity of the Lyubers be stopped, some newspapers suddenly declared that Lyubers do not exist, any more than the Abominable Snowman. *Literaturnaya Gazeta* informed its readers of the demonstration, while stressing that there were no grounds for it since rumours about the Lyubers had been exaggerated by irresponsible journalists. The paradoxical feature was that this article was written by the well-known reporter Shchekochikhin, who had been the first to write about the Lyubers. Quite obviously, certain forces were not at all interested in mobilizing public opinion against this threat. Something else was obvious too – that the anonymous influential protectors of the Lyubers were one and the same with those opponents of Gorbachev's liberalization who were keeping quiet for the time being.

The strategy of the new right is to use the expanded legal opportunities so as to combat liberalization itself (just as the 'Black Hundreds' did in the period of the 1905 Revolution). The inevitable difficulties and contradictions of the process of change, the unsuccessful economic experiments, the costs of reform – all can be exploited by the reactionary groups in the hope that the course of events will inexorably bring the country to a 'critical point', when the 'restoration of order' and 'normalization' will become the slogans of the day. The economic strategy of the reactionaries presupposes a sharp reduction in demand, to provide the means for renewing productive equipment, introducing new technology and so on. The well-known economists Selyunin and Khanin aptly described this plan as a 'second edition' of Stalin's industrialization in the thirties.[11] Their problem is to find an ideological and cultural–psychological justification for such a policy in present-day conditions. Soviet society in the late twentieth century is different from what it was in the thirties, when Stalin carried through his 'revolution from above'. The way of life has changed, and so too have the social structures. Nevertheless, there does exist a certain nostalgia for the past, for 'totalitarian' order, and not just among people of the older generation. Erich Fromm once wrote of the 'flight from freedom': certain social groups in Western society saw in the development of democracy a threat to their firm traditions, way of life and security, and these were not only the privileged strata but also a section of the lower orders. After the January 1987 Plenum of the Central Committee of the CPSU, which proclaimed the need for more thoroughgoing liberalization, the editors of Soviet newspapers began to receive letters from readers who doubted the need for changes. Sometimes these letters also contained open threats to the journalists.[12] The disposition to flight from freedom is evidently characteristic of a certain section of the population; although, we must suppose, the strength of such feelings is not as great as the reactionaries imagine. In any case, the Lyubers' actions are not mere hooliganism, but constitute an alarming cultural–psychological symptom.

One should not think that the new Right are like the orthodox, bureaucratic, conservative admirers of Brezhnev. Their ideal is a strong master, such as Brezhnev never was, and their ideology is in the nature of a synthesis of patriarchal nationalism with the traditions of totalitarianism. Such a synthesis is quite feasible, since Stalin, in the last years of his life, was clearly gravitating towards Russian nationalism. In the present context Astaf'ev's ideas assume rather obvious significance. Hatred of Jews, Muscovites, Western influence, spiritual freedom, the intelligentsia and the Left unite this well-known writer with the Lyuber hooligans. Astaf'ev quickly became an ideal hero for the supporters of reaction. Whether Eidelman wished it or not, his correspondence with Astaf'ev helped the new right to consolidate, whereas traditional liberalism increasingly lost influence.

An effective alternative to Russian nationalism (and to the anti-Russian nationalism of the minorities which has arisen parallel with and in reply to it) is offered not by the heritage of the sixties but by the new culture which has sprung up or emerged from clandestinity. In essence the activity of the young rock groups, or the discussions organized by rebel architects protesting against the destruction of our old towns, may prove to be more important cultural events than the publication of *The Executioner's Block* and *The Doleful Detective*.

The new Left looks on the liberalism of the sixties as a heritage from the past. In their opinion, many 'children of the Twentieth Congress', who have now attained a respectable age, have failed to draw the lessons from their mistakes. Sixties liberalism was indifferent to social problems and, as a rule, felt no particular interest in the masses. There were, of course, exceptions to this rule (for example, Ovechkin's sketches, published in Khrushchev's time, provided material for Buravsky's play). In the last analysis, however, the masses were not affected all that much by the ideas of the Twentieth Congress, and the intelligentsia did not take much trouble to change this attitude. In the eighties, on the contrary, the changes that are being made affect directly the lives of the majority of the Soviet people, and it is on the activity of the lower orders that the fate of the new political course will ultimately depend. Objectively, the process of change has already gone much further than under Khrushchev. This provides grounds for optimism.

The chief weakness of the new Left is the persistent gap between 'high' culture and the 'low' culture of the youth. Among the representatives of 'high' culture the ideas and the people of the sixties predominate. So long as there is no synthesis, or at least dialogue, between the two cultures, liberalism will inevitably retain hegemony. Radical moods by no means always engender constructive programmes. From protest to alternative ideas the road is long and complicated, especially when what is involved is not the settling of some partial question but the transformation of a culture. The new Left has no press organs of its own, whereas the 'children of the Twentieth Congress' were able to group themselves around the journal *Novy Mir*, which became in the sixties a real headquarters for the radical movement. The radicals and youth leaders who are outside the bounds of that milieu do not enjoy the same authority as was possessed by the *Novy Mir* group.

Lakshin, who once directed the literary criticism section in *Novy Mir* and figured as one of the ideologists of the Left in the sixties, has acknowledged that many members of his generation have failed to appreciate the true dynamic of the process that has been taking place, and that they display a characteristic 'lack of feeling for their times'.[13] It seems to the 'children of the Twentieth Congress' that their hour has come at last. The new Left fear that people who already missed their chance twenty years ago are liable to repeat that unfortunate experience. Everyone argues about how long the present 'thaw' will last, and echoes of these debates have already been heard on television. On 16 March 1987, for example, viewers were able to see how the political columnist Pozner – who made his name in discussions with his American colleague Donoghue – was obliged to defend himself in the face of aggressive questioning from young people who were not very confident of the effectiveness and durability of *glasnost''*. But only a few are giving thought to the question of what can be done to provide structural consolidation for the changes that have begun, how to make firmer the ground under their feet.

'How much time is left?' people ask each other. Hypnotized by their own question, they fail to realize how much depends on society itself, on themselves. Writers hasten to 'force' into print their old novels which could not previously pass the censor. But this vanity of theirs merely destabilizes the situation. One wants to shout: 'Stop! Think of the present, try to understand the tasks of today!' Up to now, however, the heritage of the past has had priority over ideas addressed to the future. This is why, already in its first stages, the social movement bears within itself elements of internal crisis. And this crisis can be overcome only when the new Left formulates its positions more precisely and constructively and wins the influence among the intelligentsia that it still does not have.

On 1 March 1987 *Moskovskie Novosti* published an article by L. Karpinsky, 'It Is Silly To Hesitate Before An Open Door', which dealt with the dissidents, or, more exactly, with those among them who hold left-wing views. The writer was himself once expelled from the Party for propagating the ideas of the 'Prague spring', so he is able to speak from knowledge in this matter. Karpinsky stressed the similarity between the way Brezhnevism was criticized from the Left in the seventies and the conclusions drawn officially by the Twenty-Seventh Party Congress and the January 1987 Plenum of the Central Committee. According to Karpinsky, most dissidents hold progressive views, and the socialist opposition ought now to take an active part 'in the practical work of building a new reality'. Criticism of the past must be combined with work for the future, on the basis of the revolutionary formula: 'More socialism, and therefore more democracy'.

When Karpinsky's article appeared, the release of Academician Sakharov from exile was still being discussed: Sakharov had been for many years the actual leader and symbol of the dissident movement. Political prisoners were returning home one after another. Activists of the socialist youth groups remained in the camps, as before, but their release in the near future was also expected. True, Karpinsky was dissembling a little when he wrote that the dissidents adhered to the ideals of the left-wing movement. Most of the well-known dissidents of the seventies were either indifferent to the question of social organization, being concerned exclusively with the provision of guaranteed civil rights, or else were supporters of free enterprise. But the *Moskovskie Novosti* article had to provide an ideological basis for the liberal decisions of the reforming leadership, to show that in freeing Sakharov and other dissidents the country's leaders were acting not only wisely but in accordance with principle.

The real problem, however, lay elsewhere. For the representatives of the Left opposition, there could be no question of whether or not to participate in the changes. Every one of them who was at liberty was already doing all they could, without Karpinsky's advice. The problem was, *how* to participate. If Karpinsky's logic meant simply that one should support the liberal initiatives from above, there could be no particular significance in such support. The trouble with the liberal intelligentsia was that it showed itself quite incapable of any constructive initiative of its own, preferring just to applaud Gorbachev's decisions. The louder the applause, the more energetic the support. However, an acute need for new ideas, a new culture, had arisen in society; what was wanted was criticism not so much of the past as of the present, not so much of others as of ourselves, and a rejection of liberal dogmas no less resolute than our rejection of any others. The events which have taken place in our country are important not only for us. The wave of conservatism which swept over the world in the early eighties is beginning to subside. The need for radical reforms is beginning to be realized by ever wider circles in countries of every type. Socialist ideas may once more become attractive to public opinion in the West. How well the progressive forces in the USSR cope with their new role will determine more than their own future. The present state of things is not as wonderful as one might have wished, and events are developing less smoothly than some journalists make out. Yet there are no grounds for pessimism. We shall hope for the best.

Notes

1. First published as 'The Intelligentsia and the Changes' in *New Left Review* 164, July–August 1987.
2. See *Sovetskaya Kultura*, 7 February 1987.
3. *Literaturnaya Gazeta*, 18 February 1987.
4. *Knizhnoe Obozrenie*, no. 7, 1987, *Yunost'*, 1987, no. 2.
5. *Knizhnoe Obozrenie*, No. 9, 1987.
6. A typical statement is that it is necessary 'to create something like that, but our own, Russian thing.' *Sovetskaya Kultura*, 24 January 1987.
7. *Twentieth Century and Peace*, English-language journal, Moscow, no. 4, 1987, p. 46.
8. See 'War and Peace in Stalin's Russia', a review of *Life and Fate* by Tamara Deutscher, in *New Left Review* 163, May–June 1987 [*Ed. note*].
9. *Twentieth Century and Peace*, no. 4, 1987, p. 48.
10. *Knizhnoe Obozrenie, 1987*, no. 9.
11. See *Novy Mir*, no. 2, 1987, pp. 196–7.
12. One such missive was published in *Moskovskie Novosti*, with a commentary by Yegor Yakovlev.
13. *Izvestiya*, 3 December 1986.

2

Glasnost', the Soviet Press and Red Greens[1]

One of the most dramatic consequences so far of *perestroika* [reconstruction] in the Soviet Union is the rapid growth of interest in newspapers and magazines. In the final years of the Brezhnev era the circulation of many publications fell steadily; newspapers and magazines lost subscribers and often contributors. As for *samizdat*, it too was in a crisis – all the most interesting unofficial journals had ceased to exist, either under pressure from the authorities or because editors no longer saw any particular sense in continuing. Moreover, *samizdat* was not able to compete with Russian-language publications based abroad (*tamizdat*), and surreptitiously brought into the country in ever-increasing quantities. Many people complained that *tamizdat* had gobbled up *samizdat*, but without itself becoming a force in the internal literary life of the country. Thus there was no one and nothing to fill the cultural vacuum created by the crisis in the official press under Brezhnev.

Perestroika has changed the situation radically. The circulations of newspapers and magazines have started to rise despite the paper shortage. Since interesting material can now be found everywhere, subscribers have started forming consumers' cooperatives, through which a number of families divide the cost of subscriptions and then share the periodicals. Otherwise the attempt to 'keep pace with *glasnost'*' would be a very heavy drain on the average Russian family's budget.

A.N. Yakovlev, who in 1985 was head of the propaganda section of the Central Committee of the Communist Party of the Soviet Union, made energetic efforts to enliven public life. The editors of many magazines and newspapers were replaced, censorship was relaxed. As commercial success began to be valued at least as much as ideological steadfastness, relatively sharp competiton broke out among publications which strove to attract readers' attention with sensational material. Some newspapers and magazines which had previously eked out a pretty miserable existence suddenly achieved mass popularity. The most famous of these is *Moskovskie Novosti* [Moscow News]. This weekly newspaper, published in five languages, was for several years a symbol of inefficient propaganda. Its readers were predominantly students who aimed to extend their vocabulary from English, French or Spanish newspapers, but were not allowed to study real Western publications for that purpose. Very few people even knew that a Russian-language edition of the paper existed.

Within a few months of Yegor Yakovlev's editorship, the paper became the flagship of *glasnost'*. The circulation of the Russian edition is still limited, in part because of the paper shortage and various bureaucratic obstacles, and perhaps in part because of political considerations. Nevertheless, long queues form in front of the state newspaper kiosk on the day the paper comes out, and by nine o'clock in the morning no copy of the paper can be bought anywhere in Moscow. Readers pass round some issues as they once did *samizdat.*

Yegor Yakovlev's paper is far from being the only one to experience a heady upsurge in vitality. After Vitaly Korotich was made editor-in-chief of the illustrated weekly magazine *Ogonyok* [Light], what had once been the mouthpiece of extreme Stalinists rapidly became popular among an intellectual readership when it published a series of pieces devoted to the victims of Stalinist terror. The literary sections of the magazine also improved noticeably. The bulletin of the Soviet committee for the defence of peace, *Vek XX i mir* [The Twentieth Century and Peace], which had never managed to achieve the slightest popularity among readers, suddenly became fashionable. A significant role in this change of fortunes was played by Gleb Pavlovsky, who had once been among the founders of the left-wing *samizdat* journal *Poiski* [Searches], and who had returned to Moscow from internal exile. Thanks to Pavlovsky, *Vek XX i mir*, which, like *Moscow News*, appears in several languages, has become an important source of information on the activities of left-wing 'unofficial groups'. The magazine has also run interviews with the independent Marxists, Pinsky and Gefter, who until recently were considered dissidents. The readers' letters section has become especially interesting, since it is an indication of how people react to the new political opportunities, and evidence that they are gradually becoming used to sharp political discussion. *Moskovskii Komsomolets* [Moscow Young Communist] publishes reports on concerts by popular rock groups. *Izvestiya* organizes discussions which consider the shortcomings of economic policy, not only in the past but also in the present, with startling frankness. Sometimes provincial newspapers publish material which has seemed too daring to Muscovite editorial boards. As new facts and new ideas are aired in the press, they naturally attract the interest not only of the intelligentsia but also of wider social strata. Readers are becoming better informed, and more demanding towards the press in general.

These changes have naturally also had an effect upon literary journals. Sergey Zalygin, who was put in charge of *Novy Mir* in 1986, immediately made it clear that he would strive to re-establish the reputation of the journal, which in the 1960s was the voice of the progressive anti-Stalinist intelligentsia. Alexander Tvardovsky's achievements as editor in that period are well known. All the best journalists, poets and prose writers were published in the magazine at that time, including Alexander Solzhenitsyn and Vasily Aksyonov. For a whole generation of Soviet citizens, *Novy Mir* became a symbol of independence. But the journal's new editorial board has to face stiff competition from other publications. Grigory Baklanov, the new editor of the journal *Znamya* [Banner], has brought on to his editorial board Vladimir Lakshin, who in Tvardovsky's day was the chief ideologist of *Novy Mir*. The journal *Druzhba Narodov* [Friendship of the Peoples] was for several months indisputably in the forefront of developments owing to its publication of Anatoly Rybakov's novel *Deti Arbata* [Children of the Arbat]. Each issue of the magazine was passed from hand to hand and read until it fell apart. Some people secretly made copies of the text using photocopiers at their place of work (private citizens are not allowed to have photocopying machines in the Soviet Union).

Rybakov's novel can hardly be called a masterpiece. The chapters in which he tries to explain the Stalinist terror are very superficial and the portrayal of historical figures is unconvincing. Historians have pointed out a large number of factual errors: Rybakov's attempts to depict the terror of the 1930s as the result of the personal psychological peculiarities of the 'great leader' are to say the least naive. In his portrayal of Stalin as some sort of 'evil genius' of the terror, Rybakov remains trapped in the traditional formulations of the propaganda of the 1930s about the 'leader's omniscient genius'.

Nevertheless, the impact on the majority of readers was one of shock. For the first time in an official journal people could find a description of Stalinist prisons, of interrogations, of the mechanics of the fabrication of false accusations. Some material of this nature appeared in the 1960s (such as Solzhenitsyn's *One Day in the Life of Ivan Denisovich*), but this is the first systematic account of the prosaic side of the terror, of the everyday concerns of executioners and victims.

Until now, pages like this could be found only in *samizdat* or in Western publications. The autobiographical parts of the novel, which describe the experience of a man who fell into the mincing-machine of the 'great terror', are written with powerful simplicity and authenticity.

Rybakov's novel has become accessible to the public thanks to the politics of *glasnost'*, but he started writing it in the time of the Khrushchev reforms. This is not an isolated case. The relaxation of censorship has brought about the mass publication of many works which have been banned until now. The editorial boards of literary journals are striving to outdo each other by announcing their intention to publish more and more 'rehabilitated books'. The battles that were waged over the publication of Pasternak's *Doctor Zhivago* and Akhmatova's poem *Requiem* are already well known in the West. Such a masterpiece of post-revolutionary prose as Andrei Platonov's novel *Kotlovan* [The Foundation Pit] has become accessible to Soviet readers. There are constant discussions about a Russian translation of George Orwell. A full list of 'rehabilitated books' would stretch over several pages, but some concrete examples are amusing in their way. For example, it has emerged that permission was long withheld for the publication of books by the Argentinian writer Ernesto Sabato only because he had allowed himself some critical remarks about Fidel Castro.

The most important of these rehabilitations so far seems to be the decision of the journal *Oktyabr'* [October] to publish Vasily Grossman's novel *Life and Fate*, during 1988. The book stands out for the extraordinary depth of its comparative psychological analysis of Stalinism and Fascism. Ironically, *Oktyabr'* was the chief stronghold of diehard Stalinists during Grossman's lifetime (indeed, denunciations from these circles played an important role in the banning of the novel). But today *Oktyabr'*'s new editorial board is eager to be among the leaders of *glasnost'*, and as the Grossman case shows, is doing so quite successfully.

Unexpectedly, all this growth of interest has in no way subverted the position of *samizdat*. In fact the opposite has happened: as official publications have become freer, the number and the circulation of unofficial publications have grown as well. Undoubtedly the most important of these is the Leningrad publication *Merkur* [Mercury]. The city's authorities cannot afford to ignore it. The Moscow newspaper *Sovetskaya Rossiya* (Soviet Russia) has referred to it as a reliable source of information. The journal's editor, Yelena Zelinskaya, has great authority both in unofficial and official journalistic circles. The quarterly journal is disseminated in more than a thousand copies – a remarkable circulation for a typewritten publication.

The *samizdat* journals of the Gorbachev period can be divided into various categories. First of all, the literary journals and almanacs, many of which have existed since the Brezhnev period, continue to appear. They include *Chasy* [Hours], *Obvodny Kanal* [The Obvodny Canal] and *Mitin zhurnal* [Mitya's journal] in Leningrad, *Tret'ya modernizatsiya* [Third Modernization] in Riga, and so on. In most cases these publications bring together poets and prose writers from various avant-garde groups who, while not very interested in politics, have long been in conflict with the official Union of Writers. The relatively apolitical nature of such journals helped them to survive even through the period when the *samizdat* press was being most vigorously suppressed. Alongside the literary magazines, rock music journals such as *Roxy* in Leningrad and *Ukho* [The Ear] in Moscow have sprung up. In the opinion of Il'ya Smirnov, who is one of the ideologists of, and a regular contributor to, these magazines, what we are seeing here is no longer just an artistic phenomenon: it has taken on a social dimension, since rock music is linked to the growing movement of the 'Soviet new Left'.

It is this movement which is providing the basic stimulus for the development of 'new *samizdat*'. Its success is due above all to the close link between the journal and a Leningrad Left informal group called Epicentre. The activities of Epicentre and its rival organization, the Council for the Ecology of Culture (SEK), have become widely known beyond Leningrad. Despite tactical differences between them, these two groups constitute a kind of bloc of ecologists and neo-Marxists which is a little like the West German Green Party. They organize discussions and wage a campaign against the demolition of old buildings and against economic plans which will destroy the ecological balance. Many leftist clubs and groups are growing up not only in Leningrad but throughout the country. They either attempt to issue their own typescript bulletins, or exchange information through the most popular *samizdat* journals. The Leningrad *perestroika* club publishes a bulletin called *Perekryostok mneniy* [Crossroads of opinions], and in the same city a club of 'revolutionary Marxists' with the peaceful name *Adelaida* [Adelaide] disseminates its journal *Voves' rost* [Standing Upright]. In Moscow the *Obshchina* [Commune] socialist club is publishing an information bulletin once a fortnight called *Den' za dnyom* [Day by Day].

The most serious publications are all linked in one way or another with associations of clubs. The first meeting of unofficial leftist groups from all over the country took place in Moscow in August 1987. It decided to create a 'Circle of Social Initiative' and a Federation of Socialist Social Clubs (FSOK). The 'Circle', conceived by its founders as a wide association of cultural, ecological and political clubs without a single ideology or platform, has not really developed substantially, although its prospects remain good. The FSOK, on the other hand, has, in the few months since the August meeting, become a competent and united organization, in no small measure thanks to the appearance of its own *samizdat* journal, first called by the neutral title of *Svidetel'* [Witness], but in November renamed *Levy povorot* [Left Turn].

Of course this 'new samizdat' co-exists with other publications whose stance is based on the traditions of 1970s dissidence. The magazine *Glasnost'*, edited by Sergei Grigoryants, is well known in the West. In Moscow and Leningrad, however, this journal is constantly subjected to harsh criticism, and not just from the authorities. Grigoryants is accused of thinking more about reception abroad than about his readers within the country. It is also contended that the magazine's published material is often of doubtful accuracy. Greater authority is enjoyed by *Express-Chronicle*, another publication which attempts to continue the traditions of 'classical *samizdat*' of the 1970s, though it too is accused of aiming at 'export only'.

The main problem for the *samizdat* press, whatever its political or cultural orientation, is how to forge a relationship with official publications in a period of liberalization. If traditional *samizdat* (the heirs of which are *Glasnost'* and *Express-Chronicle*) tried to become an alternative to the official press, then the new *samizdat* is striving to co-exist and cooperate with it. Copies of *Mercury* and other leftist publications can be found in the editorial offices of 'real' papers. And when Yelena Zelinskaya organized a meeting in Leningrad of the editors of *samizdat* magazines, it received official sanction. Representatives of practically all the unofficial publications except *Glasnost'* were invited to the meeting, and correspondents from *Literaturnaya Gazeta* and *Izvestiya*, the Novosti Press Agency and other organs of the state press were also present. Not a single one of these official organs ran a report on the meeting, but the very fact of the presence in Leningrad of representatives of the 'mainstream Soviet press' is very significant.

What also became clear at the Leningrad meeting was that there are not one but three different *samizdats* in the country. But the literary avant-garde, the traditional dissidents and the 'new Left' hardly argued – they could not find any common subjects for discussion. Some were discussing 'freedom from the government and the nation', others were talking about 'the unreformability of Communism', while others were trying to work out a concept of a 'social movement for structural reforms'.

It seems that the change in the political situation has created no fewer (though possibly more) problems for *samizdat* than for the official press. Attempts by certain *samizdat* publications to compete with official newspapers in the area of 'the criticism of individual shortcomings' will get nowhere. More and more subjects are being opened up for discussion, and it is very much easier for the correspondents of state newspapers to gather information than it is for the editors of *samizdat* bulletins.

It is clear, however, that even with liberalization the independent small-circulation publications cannot be squeezed out by the state. This is not just a question of degrees of radicalism and sharpness of criticism. The very same writers (myself included) sometimes consider the same questions in both *samizdat* and official publications.

Soviet society's real need for *samizdat* does not arise only because of the continuing 'shortage of *glasnost*'' in various areas. Thanks to their independence, *samizdat* journals can follow a consistent editorial line without glancing over their shoulders at the establishment's view. The movement of the Soviet new Left could not have developed without the existence of its own information and discussion bulletins. In short, *samizdat* is beginning to function in the same way as small-scale radical publications in the West. In addition, for writers and poets the existence of *samizdat* (and the relatively tolerant attitude of the authorities) gives increased freedom of choice. Things which cannot get into the mainstream press can be disseminated by the independent publications.

Both the revived state press and *samizdat* are contributing to the creation of a civil society in the Soviet Union. The question is how stable and long-term these tendencies will be, and to what extent the growing social movement will be able to exert real influence on how the situation develops. This depends not only on the stance taken by the authorities, but also on the degree in which progressive elements – in journals and in the clubs – take advantage of the opportunities which *glasnost'* has opened up to them.

Note

1. From *Times Literary Supplement*, 25–31 December 1987.

3

The Soviet New Left: Robin Blackburn Interviews Boris Kagarlitsky

R.B. *You were imprisoned in the Brezhnev period because of your oppositionist ideas. What was prison like?*

B.K. The really difficult thing was that you were forced to stay with the same person for months on end. A manager who had been arrested for taking bribes taught me a lot about the functioning of the Soviet management structure and the way the economy worked, but even so you cannot spend day after day with the same person: it becomes psychologically destructive. You may not hate each other, but you do get very irritated. There was a good library in the prison but it had no works by Marx. Marx's writings were reserved for the prison officers! So I wrote to the Governor asking for books by Marx. I did this after I found out that a right-wing dissident of monarchist inclinations had asked for the Bible and had been allowed it.

R.B. *Why were you released?*

B.K. There were a lot of protests from the Western Left but this was not sufficient. There was a change of administration in the Soviet Union: Brezhnev died and Andropov succeeded him. We started to get more information, some detailed allegations, and we thought that a show-trial might be in the making. But Andropov evidently didn't want to start his rule with a show-trial and the preparations ceased.

R.B. *When did you become a critically-aware Soviet citizen?*

B.K. You see those houses? They are part of the housing co-operative of the Writers' Union. All those who live here are writers. So at the very beginning of my life, in my childhood, I lived in a world where all the problems of the Khrushchev period and the post-Khrushchev period, and all the discussions of the dissidents, could be followed. These things were discussed daily, and one could get hold of writings that were not yet published or had been suppressed.

R.B. *You were only ten years old at the time of the Prague Spring?*

B.K. It was my first political experience. The people around me, including my parents, were very excited about what was happening in Czechoslovakia: 'socialism with a human face' corresponded to their hopes for the Soviet Union. Much later, I discovered that people were also discussing the trial of Daniel and Sinyavsky. In fact, I can remember the events of August 1968 almost day by day. It was an awful shock for me: I kept seeing older people who were quite destroyed by what had happened.

R.B. *What course of studies did you take?*

B.K. I wanted to do a general course in the humanities. Everybody at school did some social studies: a bit of Marxism and a bit of Soviet history, all in the official version – but something comes through nevertheless. I was very impressed by Lenin just as I was finishing school. First, because he was very logical, everything was spelled out very clearly. And secondly because much that he said was evidently at odds with what we saw around us – for example, that officials should live no better than ordinary workers or that they should be recallable by vote. You began reading and you could see the discrepancies appearing on page after page. This made me wish to pursue political and social studies, but my father advised me to study drama and criticism at the Theatre Institute. He said I'd get a good course in the humanities at the Institute, including history and world culture, and I could study politics and society on my own account. So I followed his advice and eventually became a specialist in the sociology of the theatre.

R.B. *What does that involve?*

B.K. Studying the response of the audience to different acting and directing strategies and to different types of drama. We have many sociologists in the Soviet Union, perhaps thirty thousand, who are assigned to gather information on every aspect of life and to see how our institutions are working. Many of the ideas of *glasnost'* and *perestroika* have come from these people. I myself became very conscious of the need for economic and political change as a student but I was not attracted to the dissidents. I respect Sakharov, for example, very much, but he made declarations in the seventies that seemed to justify the United States' policy in Vietnam and this made me very angry. Solzhenitsyn began to express his reactionary views and this also disgusted the younger generation; there was a contempt for democracy and enlightenment in his ideas that was reminiscent of the Party ideologists.

R.B. *How did you know of his writing?*

B.K. From the radio. His letter to the Party leaders was broadcast by the BBC – generally, intellectuals listened to the BBC while the workers listened to the Voice of America.

R.B. *They liked the American music better?*

B.K. Yes. Some of the skilled workers performed technical miracles constructing receivers that could pick up the signal whatever the jamming. We could learn about the world from the different radio stations, which is not to say that we believed everything we heard, but you can put together a picture for yourself. I also did a lot of reading. I was quite sure there needed to be a big change. Finally I managed to make contact with a group who put out a *samizdat* journal called *Varianti*. This group, centred on people at the Institute of World Economy, was opposed both to the existing system and to the dissidents. Strongly anti-Stalinist, they were also critical of the half-hearted reforms of the Khrushchev period. Around this time I began to read Gramsci. I managed to pay a visit to East Berlin to study in the libraries there. Their rules were somewhat more liberal than those in Moscow, but I still came across a section of political and historical books to which the ordinary citizen was denied access.* I showed the people there my Soviet passport and asked to see books from the reserved section. They immediately gave me access to them. Curious! I read the first two volumes of Isaac Deutscher's *Trotsky*, but my visa expired after one month and I was not able to read the third. I also read some Eurocommunist writings, books by Roger Garaudy, Cohen's biography of Bukharin and some copies of *New Left Review*.

---

*It was announced in August 1988 that the closed sections of Soviet libraries would be opened to the general public.

R.B. *Why do these questions of Soviet history loom so large in contemporary life?*

B.K. In the West things happen very quickly. Before Thatcher or Reagan seems a long time ago. Brezhnev still seems like yesterday and we are still concerned about what happened in the twenties and thirties. In Russia, if you want to understand anything, you have to start with 1917 and even that is not really good enough; you have to go right back to Ivan the Terrible and Vladimir, the first Christian king of Russia. I don't think British or American intellectuals discuss 1688 or 1776 in the kitchen. In the seventies we would have heated discussions about Bukharin and Trotsky after dinner – we still do! My wife said the other day that we talk about them as if they'd just left the room. One of the books I read in East Germany – I think it was Cohen's biography of Bukharin – had a picture of the Politburo just after Lenin's death. There were seven members and I was astonished to see who they were: according to our official history, every one of them, Stalin included, was a traitor or political criminal. And they were in charge of the country! Of course I didn't myself believe that Trotsky, Bukharin, Kamenev and the others were traitors. At first, I was sympathetic to Bukharin, as portrayed by Cohen, but I did not like his dogmatism or his collaboration with Stalin. It seems that he accepted the bureaucratic rules of the game, which helped him to beat the Trotskyist Left but without realizing that the same would happen to him. I was impressed by Trotsky but I could not understand why he came to see Bukharin as more of an enemy than Stalin in the late twenties.

R.B. *The first part of* The Thinking Reed *was written in 1981–2. The fact that you were sent to prison shortly afterwards was not connected?*

B.K. I was arrested just a few days after completing it, but there was no connection. They did seize the manuscript and later, during the time I was in prison, they told me that they considered parts of the book anti-Soviet. In fact, I was obliged to discuss it with the prosecutor, but this was not the reason for my original arrest. At the time I was arrested I had been helping to produce a *samizdat* journal called *Left Turn*. The journal had an audience and the audience was growing. This created a problem for the authorities, who had almost destroyed the traditional dissident movement only to have a 'New Left' emerge. In addition, everyone thought Brezhnev was dying; and the view in official circles was that political stability had to be safeguarded by arresting trouble-makers.

R.B. *Presumably the book reflects the political discussions you were having at the time in the* Left Turn *group?*

B.K. Naturally. It was a very interesting period at the end of the seventies. It was clear that the traditional dissident movement had run out of steam. Many had gone abroad and even those who hadn't seemed to write mainly 'for export'. They seemed to think their only possible course of action was to hold press conferences with Western journalists: that was self-destructive and I think it was linked to the fact that they had right-wing and pro-capitalist positions. Young people simply stopped joining the dissidents and began to look for different solutions. We had discussion groups and studied left-wing Western journals. In those days we used to read each issue of *New Left Review* from cover to cover; today we don't always have time for that. At that time young Soviet left-wing intellectuals knew more about the Western Left than they did about the way things worked in their own country. To read Alec Nove's criticism of the centrally planned socialist economy was very interesting for us.

R.B. *I gather that the Russian critic Mikhail Bakhtin had an influence on you?*

B.K. Yes, he did. He died in the seventies and no sooner was he dead than everybody began to study his writings and to appreciate his theses on the necessity for a dialogic structure in true art – that is to say, for a pluralism of voice, of point of view, within the work of art itself. This is sometimes called heteroglossia. Bakhtin was very old by this time, and it's a pity he had to die for people to take account of his views. Just after his death he became very fashionable – this often happens in Russia. For a time, if you hadn't read Bakhtin in Moscow you weren't treated as a human being. I see his argument on dialogic structure, which I use in my book, as very useful for Marxist critical theory and for enriching our conception of culture. But Bakhtin himself was not a Marxist. That should be stated quite clearly. He was a very open person, who had participated in the classic debates with the Formalists in the twenties and who lived long enough to pass on the spirit of these debates to a younger generation.

R.B. *Were the people in the club movement the same as those who participated with you in these discussions of the late seventies and early eighties?*

B.K. Many of them were, but there was also a younger generation.

We again had a magazine called *Left Turn* as a mark of continuity, but there were many younger people who helped to form clubs in the period after 1985. So there were two age-groups in the movement. One was from teenagers up to the age of about twenty-five and this comprised the majority of activists. The second was from thirty-five to fifty or even sixty, and most of these people had had some involvement in independent activity in the seventies and before. Such people tended to be less active but they did take part in our discussions. Then there were a few like myself between these groups, who were involved in *Left Turn* and other *samizdat* journals. We are the link between the new 'Gorbachev levy' and those who remember the Khrushchev thaw.

R.B. *Did the emergence of independent clubs, debating and campaigning on public issues, mark a new stage?*

B.K. The clubs represented the first, tentative signs of a rebirth of civil society in a country where bureaucratic stagnation was threatening to smother all life. We had already thought about the need for a radical initiative 'from below' in our country, but we didn't expect it to take the form of the club movement. The first informal clubs began to form in 1985. In Moscow we persuaded the authorities to accept the existence of a club that met to discuss the country's future but was not controlled by the Party, though some Party members might be involved. Gorbachev's talk of the need for restructuring and openness seemed to invite independent initiatives; the Chernobyl disaster underlined the message. Boris Yeltsin allowed the clubs to make use of official premises in Moscow, and we held a national meeting in June 1987. By this time there were scores of clubs with a combined membership of several thousand. Some were principally student groups, others mainly economists and technicians, others were organized around ecological and conservationist issues. Workers were in a minority, though they were to be found in some clubs. Where industrial sociologists were involved in the club movement they had sometimes been able to draw workers in; and sometimes when workers had had problems with management, the clubs were able to play a role in putting their case. We didn't all have the same understanding of *perestroika*. Some of the students were attracted by anarchist ideas. Not all the groups had a clearly socialist objective, though we did manage to found a federation of all those which had an explicitly socialist orientation. The dismissal of Yeltsin in November last year made our work more difficult, but it also provided a rallying-point for protests here in Moscow. We were very alarmed by the way he was sacked and denounced; his re-emergence as a public figure is a good sign.

R.B. *What proportion of those who participated in the clubs were women?*

B.K. It varied, but about 15 per cent. An Italian comrade said to me: 'You have all the trends that we had in the West from the late sixties, but no women's movement.' I think that's right.

R.B. *In your book you say that one of the achievements of the seventies and early eighties was the development of the theory of the 'planned market', which could help to galvanize the Soviet economy. Do you continue this work in the clubs?*

B.K. Some people in our government advocate the market in an almost Friedmanite sense; others see the market as a supplement to bureaucratic centralized planning. The problem for us is not to find ways to combine the plan with the market, but rather to democratize the planning system. We must make democracy the first priority and then we'll see. This also means self-management within the factories. In some cases, members of our clubs, again usually industrial sociologists, have been invited to help set up councils of labour collectives to represent people as producers. We also need to find ways to represent them and organize them as consumers, in order to make the whole system more responsive to consumer needs. But we have to be careful that we don't just cater to the interests of a privileged minority.

R.B. *In* The Thinking Reed, *why did you use the problems of intellectuals as the vantage-point from which to examine Soviet society?*

B.K. The book is part of a project to discuss what is left of the Revolution and its traditions for us. The Russian Revolution was made by the people, but the thinking of the Bolshevik intelligentsia played a large part in determining its outcome. When the Revolution reached its peak it was a popular revolution, but at its low points, after the Civil War, the influence of intellectuals, Bolshevik or not, increased. I have tried to establish the links between the traditional Russian intelligentsia and its Soviet successor, and to show the fate of the intelligentsia in Stalin's and Brezhnev's time. As I show, our rulers have always had to contend with the independent traditions of the intelligentsia, which have time and again stubbornly asserted themselves as, in a way, they are doing now. Stalin sought to control all intellectual life but he never completely succeeded. Intellectuals were accomplices as well as victims, but at a deep level their traditions retained a critical potential.

R.B. *You write that Stalin, representing a new social force – the 'statocracy' – cut short the debate between different Bolshevik currents and imposed a solution that was neither of the Right nor of the Left.*

B.K. Stalin's project was to exploit the post-war exhaustion of social energy in order to adapt society to the bureaucracy, making everything governable. That involved the elimination of most elements of civil society which existed after the Revolution. It meant attacking the NEP, the farmers, the intellectuals and, eventually, the party cadres themselves. Stalin eliminated the NEP, not because he favoured the workers, but because doing it made the country easier to adminster. In the same way, he asserted state control of the rural co-operatives, and created one big union of writers, one big union of film-makers, and so on. In the twenties there was a variety of institutes and publishing houses, of tendencies and factions in our cultural life: Stalin found it easier to control a big all-embracing organization. Stalin needed terror to reshape society after the Revolution, because during the Revolution people had learnt to defend themselves, had learnt that the common people had rights and a role in society. All this had to be eradicated. I don't want to talk about exactly how much terror was 'needed', but the extent of the terror does give us some idea of the strength of the revolutionary forces that had to be overcome.

R.B. *You write that the official doctrine of Socialist Realism helped to steamroller the cultural pluralism of the twenties.*

B.K. The Stalinist tutelage of art was not established until the early thirties. The Commissar for Education and Culture, Lunacharsky, supported Stalin in politics, but kept his own Commissariat as a personal fief in which he tolerated considerable experiment and diversity. But in the early thirties there was a striking change. After I had finished my book a friend showed me runs of the covers of early Soviet artistic and literary magazines: before 1932, the covers were colourful, different and exciting; after 1932 all the covers are the same – the same lettering, the same grey colour, the same designs.

R.B. *In your book you concentrate on literature. In the cinema, however, Eisenstein and Pudovkin, for example, had their problems with Stalin, but nonetheless produced some remarkable work.*

B.K. When we discuss the problems of our culture, we tend to take the main evidence from literature. The written word is considered the most important thing. Cinema demands more resources and thus the freedom of the producer raises more questions. In the Soviet cinema there was also a great falling-off in the early thirties, but the change is complicated by technical factors – films began to speak, a transformation that reinforced the official demand for propaganda.

R.B. *Didn't Soviet art have a need to keep the attention of the audience? Would this not allow the artist some leeway?*

B.K. In cinema this was not a problem. There was a film called *The Kuban Cossacks*. For a long time after Stalin's death it was considered a symbol of official lies and prettification. When the country was almost starving after the war, it showed happy people, eating a lot – always eating, singing and being so happy! Recently a critic has argued in *Soviet Culture* that this film should be seen as an 'idealization' rather than a 'falsification' of reality. It was a great success with audiences because people wanted life to be like that. Certainly a lot of people went to see the film, sometimes more than once. But we should remember that only a few films were made in Stalin's time – perhaps eight a year – and almost no foreign films were seen, so there wasn't much choice. In literature we had a long cultural and critical tradition; the classics are always in print.

R.B. *I have the impression that the horrors of the Nazi invasion made the bureaucracy more acceptable to the mass of Soviet people.*

B.K. The war once again did the work of destroying links and making the people dependent on the political and military bureaucracy. On the other hand, the conditions and needs of the military struggle gave scope for a lot of grass-roots initiatives among the people, and in that sense, the war produced dangers for the Stalinist model of government. You can see it in Grossman's novel *Life and Fate*, where he writes of two possibilities: either the people will win the war or the system will win the war. Because if the people win the war, the system will lose, and vice versa. Grossman's book has now been published in *Oktyabr'* magazine, and this view of his is echoed by commentators in the media. During the war, the Soviet people learned a lot about personal initiative and dignity. They thought that after the war there would be more freedom, but just the opposite happened. The beginning of the war had been a disaster for the bureaucracy, but by the end it had regained control and credibility. People still say: 'Maybe Stalin was not so good, but at least he helped us win the war.'

R.B. *It seems to me that* Life and Fate *excellently illustrates Bakhtin's* *theses about the dialogic structure and heteroglossia. It has an enormous cast of characters and a genuine diversity of voices which shows up the limitations of much Western literature today.*

B.K. It's interesting that Soviet writers of the modern period can still make use of nineteenth-century models. This is what I like in the novel; probably Westerners find it rather strange to come across a culture where nineteenth-century forms still have validity. We live in this culture and feel comfortable in it. Though, of course, there is modernization as well. Rock music flourishes and helps independent and radical ideas to find a wider audience just as it did in the West in the sixties. And with *glasnost'*, television has become far more interesting and independent. People can come and discuss their problems in a quite uninhibited way. Literature, however, remains relatively free from Modernist concerns. I would say that the Russians are still keeping up the old-fashioned traditions. Maybe someone has to.

R.D. *In the West, Bakhtin's exploration of carnival is seen as valorizing popular revolt, the turning of the world upside down.*

B.K. For us, the significance of the idea of carnival was not the act of revolt but rather the essential value of a dualistic culture. The unofficial popular culture comes to the surface during carnival, but it is always there even when its presence is concealed by high culture. The Western idea of Bakhtin as a theorist of cultural transgression only seizes on one aspect of his thought. I should add that the informal movements here are nourished by the most various radical currents; so that for members of, for example, the student group Obschina, Bakunin would be more significant than Bakhtin.

R.B. *In Soviet literature the writer is often concerned about the fate of society as a whole. While there is plurality, there isn't fragmentation.*

B.K. I have just now been writing about these matters. If experience is fragmented and an attempt is made to generalize this, as in some avant-garde work, the results can be dangerous. Bakhtin's critical aesthetics helps to bridge the gap between the fragmented analysis and a fragmented reality. It supplies a generalizing moment which is all the more necessary when reality itself is fragmented.

R.B. *At some points in your book you talk of the heavy weight of what you term 'Asiatic' backwardness and despotism in your country. This theory of 'Asiatic despotism' has been quite widely criticized by* *historians and is in any case problematic because it's* . . .

B.K. A bit racist?

R.B. *Well, at least ethnocentric.*

B.K. I should make it clear that I didn't mean to impose a stereotype on the East. In fact, my interest in this problem has brought it home to me that some Asiatic societies have developed quite resilient forms of democracy. Tariq Ali and Achin Vanaik have been right to focus on the problem of why bourgeois democracy survives in India; and because India is a large multi-national state like the Soviet Union, this is a very interesting case for us.

R.B. *You mentioned just now the new openness of the Soviet media. Does this mean that members of the unofficial clubs could present their views on television?*

B.K. There is a programme called *Vzgliad,* or *Look,* which has done this. It is supposed to be a youth programme but it doesn't only discuss the problems of the young. It showed one of our activists talking of the need for international solidarity and criticizing reactionary dissident ideas. I think reform-minded officials were glad to be able to show their conservative opponents inside the Party that these people are not pro-capitalist, or pro-dissident, as Stalinists would like them to be. Stalinists were very unhappy that the opposition represented by the clubs expressed real socialist ideals. They would have been far more comfortable with a right-wing liberal or pro-Western opposition.

R.B. *Could you tell me about the libel action you won in 1988?*

B.K. At first the growth of the informal left-wing groups aroused most apprehension in the Komsomol leadership, because the bulk of the activists were young people. Moreover, in the autumn of 1987, some official youth papers began to publish reports on the activity of the 'New Left'. Naturally, the Komsomol bureaucracy felt obliged to defend itself, and found no other way of doing this than to publish a whole series of articles aimed at discrediting the socialist movement. The biggest article – you might say, the 'programmatic' one – appeared in *Komsomolskaya Pravda* of 31 January 1988. I figured as the principal villain. They depicted me as a scoundrel who dreamed of undermining the Soviet economy and had gathered round him a set of 'trouble-makers, layabouts and spoilers'; they said that I had assumed without authority the title of 'sociologist', and so on. This article was subsequently quoted and re-quoted in a number of provincial youth papers, undoubtedly on the instructions of the Komsomol Central Committee. Mironenko, the Committee's First Secretary, himself admitted, in an interview with the *New York Times*, that the article expressed the view of the Komsomol's leadership. The effect was exactly the opposite of what had been expected. Out of the blue we had been given publicity. Many readers of the papers concerned learnt for the first time about the activities of the socialist groups through what they published about us. All the same, I had to react. The article contained an outright libel on the movement and on me personally. I brought an action against the authors. They refused to appear in court. The representatives of *Komsomolskaya Pravda* said that the article had been handed to them 'from on high' and they could not be held responsible for it. Sometimes all this bore a marked resemblance to a comedy. Eventually the case ended in victory for me, and *Komsomolskaya Pravda* published a retraction. For the first time, a Soviet citizen had shown that the official press cannot with impunity stick labels on persons who think differently about politics and slander those whom it finds objectionable. Nevertheless, the importance of my success must not be exaggerated. The press continues to be used to vilify individuals and groups that the authorities dislike, and this kind of material often gets published in papers which enjoy a reputation for being 'liberal'. The latest example is the tendentious article by Gleb Pavlovsky in *Moscow News*, in which the Left is accused, without any proof, of having 'totalitarian ways'. It is interesting that Pavlovsky has learnt from the example of his predecessors on *Komsomolskaya Pravda* and doesn't give any names or concrete facts in his article, so that he cannot be sued.

R.B. *In July 1988 the Popular Front for Perestroika was formed. Could you tell me what forces are involved in this new grouping?*

B.K. The 'club phase' of the socialist movement ended in summer 1988. The clubs were in crisis. Inter-club associations like the Federation of Socialist Clubs had broken up. Paradoxical as it may seem, this crisis was due to our successes. The spring saw the rise of a mass movement in our country which could not be, and did not wish to be, confined within the narrow limits of political youth clubs. The rise of this movement was connected with general discontent at the undemocratic way in which the election of delegates to the Party Conference was conducted. In reality, not only the non-Party masses but even the rank-and-file Communists were kept out of the taking of decisions. As a result, a wave of demonstrations swept the country – in some cases, there were even strikes. A people's front was now being called for, a new form of democratic self-organization on the part of the masses. In certain towns powerful organizing committees arose, which can still bring thousands of people out on demonstrations. In Moscow, where sectarian traditions had already established themselves in every group, it proved difficult to unite the forces of the Left. Nevertheless, even there the majority of the Left did unite under the banner of the People's Front. The number of workers in the movement has increased, though not very steeply, and persons neither young nor old (around thirty years of age) have joined – who we hardly ever saw in the first phase. It has to be said that the rise of the People's Front has clearly evoked displeasure, not only among the conservatives in the Party apparatus, but also in liberal circles. The example of Gleb Pavlovsky is significant. He came forward at the beginning of *perestroika* as one of the ideologists of the Left, attacking the liberal conception of history (selective rehabilitations) and pointing to the need for 'free civic initiatives'. No sooner, however, had an actual mass movement begun than he not only stood aside from it but even started, in concert with the *apparatchiki*, to denounce 'the social danger'. In some cases Stalinists and liberals actually form a united front against the Left.

R.B. *What is your assessment of the overall situation in the wake of the Party Conference in June 1988 and the more recent reshuffle of the Politburo?*

B.K. The preparations for the Party Conference gave rise to stormy debates all over the country and, as I have mentioned, to the rise of a mass movement, but the Conference itself produced no great result. It failed to make a decisive move in the direction of reform, even though the reformers themselves did not suffer defeat. Many people were simply disappointed. The prestige of Boris Yeltsin, who had boldly criticized the Party leadership, increased sharply, while that of Gorbachev declined somewhat. On the whole, however, everything remained as it was. Even the changes in the Politburo didn't alter the situation to any great extent. People were already tired of following the endless permutations among the cadres. It will be much more important to see how free the elections are in 1989. The Supreme Soviet is this time to be constituted through indirect rather than direct elections, which is obviously due to fear of the electors on the part of the Apparatus. Nevertheless, the People's Front means to participate actively in these elections. A great deal will depend on whether or not the forces of the Left manage to achieve real success in this struggle.

Index